W9-CZM-381

FUNDAMENTALS
OF
MODERN
MARKETING

THIRD EDITION

FUNDAMENTALS

OF

MODERN

MARKETING

Edward W. Cundiff
Emory University

Richard R. Still
University of Georgia

Norman A. P. Govoni
Babson College

60586

prentice-hall, inc. englewood cliffs, new jersey 07632

Library of Congress Cataloging in Publication Data

CUNDIFF, EDWARD W.
    Fundamentals of modern marketing.

    Includes bibliographical references and indexes.
    I. Marketing.   I. Still, Richard Ralph, (date)
joint author.   II. Govoni, Norman A. P., joint author.
III. Title.
HF5415.C793 1979   658.8   79-19314
ISBN 0-13-341388-8

Editorial/production supervision by *Linda Stewart*
Interior and cover design by *Linda Conway*
Cover illustration by *Maria Termini*
Manufacturing buyer: *John Hall*

Printed in the United States of America
10 9 8 7 6 5 4 3 2 1

Prentice-Hall International, Inc., *London*
Prentice-Hall of Australia Pty. Limited, *Sydney*
Prentice-Hall of Canada, Ltd., *Toronto*
Prentice-Hall of India Private Limited, *New Delhi*
Prentice-Hall of Japan, Inc., *Tokyo*
Prentice-Hall of Southeast Asia Pte. Ltd., *Singapore*
Whitehall Books Limited, *Wellington, New Zealand*

CONTENTS

preface
xiii

PART ONE

PREPARING FOR THE
MARKETING
CONCEPT
1

the emerging role of marketing
3

What Does Marketing Do? 4
Definition of Marketing 5
Organizational Conditions Preceding Adoption of the Marketing Concept 9
Environmental Factors Influencing Adoption of the Marketing Concept 11
The Marketing Concept—A Preliminary View 17
Planning and Operating Under the Marketing Concept 18
Implementing the Marketing Concept 19

v

organizing for marketing

25

Company Goals and the Marketing Organization 26
Marketing Organization and Transition to the Marketing Concept 27
Organization of Marketing Responsibilities in the Manufacturing Firm 31
Organization of Marketing Responsibilities in Business Engaged
Mainly in Marketing-Type Activities 35
Organization of Marketing Responsibilities in a Service Business 38
Organization of Marketing Responsibilities in a Nonprofit Organization 40

the marketing process

45

Identification of Marketing Activities 46
A Classification of Marketing Activities 47
Variations in Classification of Marketing Activities 57
Performance of Marketing Activities and Marketing Efficiency 57

PART TWO
FINDING THE MARKET
61

marketing information systems

63

Marketing Information and Marketing Decisions 64
Marketing Information Systems 65
Operating Data as an Internal Source of Marketing Information 69
Analysis of Sales Records 76
Marketing Information from External Sources 78
Simulation of Marketing Decisions in Information Systems 80

marketing research

87

Marketing Research and the Marketing Information System 88
Scope of Marketing Research 91
Marketing Research Procedure 93
Costs of Marketing Research 102

markets and market segmentation

109

Market Segmentation—A Definition 111
The Why of Market Segmentation 113
The Who of Market Segmentation 113

buyer behavior

127

Buyer Behavior—External Influences 129
Buyer Behavior—Insights from Psychology 141
Buyer Behavior—Life-Style 147
Buyer Behavior—Industrial Users 148

PART THREE
PRODUCTS
153

products: marketing characteristics life cycles, and innovation

155

What Is a Product? 156
Consumers' Goods 157
Industrial Goods 160
Product Life Cycles 162
Product Innovation and Product Line Policy 166

product-market strategies

173

No Product Change—No Market Change *175*
No Product Change—Improved Market *177*
No Product Change—New Market *183*
Product Change—No Market Change *184*
Product Change—Improved Market *186*
Product Change—New Market *187*
New Product—No Market Change *188*
New Product—Improved Market *188*
New Product—New Market *189*

PART FOUR
DISTRIBUTION
195

the field of distribution

197

Some Basic Definitions in Distribution *198*
The Process of Distribution and Its Elements *200*
Physical Distribution *202*

distribution: roles of producers and wholesalers

213

Producers *214*
Wholesaling *218*
Merchant Wholesalers *219*
Agent Middlemen *225*

distribution: retailing

235

The Retail Field: Size and Importance 236
House-to-House Selling 238
Independent Stores 240
Large-Scale Integrated Retailers 242
Retailer Cooperatives 250
Wholesaler-Sponsored Groups 250
Consumer Cooperatives 251
Supermarkets 251
Discount Houses 252
Automatic Selling 254
Franchising 255
Shopping Centers 257
The Wheel of Retailing Hypothesis and Trends of Future Growth 260

marketing channels

267

Types of Marketing Channels 268
Factors Influencing Channel Usage 272
Producers' Problems in Channel Determination and Usage 274

PART FIVE
PRICING
285

pricing management

287

Factors Influencing Pricing 288
Pricing Objectives 293
Price Policies 295

15

pricing strategy

307

Influence of Marketing Controllables on Price *308*
Pricing Strategy and the Competitive Situation *312*
Pricing Strategy for Products of Lasting Distinctiveness *313*
Pricing Strategy During Market Pioneering *314*
Pricing Strategy During Market Growth *316*
Pricing Strategy During Market Maturity *317*
Pricing Strategy During Market Decline *319*
Price-Setting Procedures *319*

PART SIX
PROMOTION
327

16

promotional strategy

329

Overall Marketing Strategy and Marketing Communication *330*
Communications and Promotion *331*
Forms of Promotion *334*
Promotional Mixes and Strategies *338*
The Promotional Appropriation *344*
Promotion and Demand Stimulation *345*

17

personal selling

349

Planning the Personal Selling Operation *351*
Managing the Sales Force *357*

advertising
365

Planning the Advertising Effort 366
Advertising Objectives 367
Advertising Policies 368
Advertising Organization 369
Advertising Strategy 372
The Advertising Appropriation 376
Managing the Advertising Effort 380

PART SEVEN
MARKETING
STRATEGY
389

marketing and society
391

How Marketing Influences Society—The Economic Aspects 392
How Marketing Influences Society—Buyer Behavior 396
How Marketing Influences Society—The Environment 398
How Society Influences Marketing—Public Opinion and Political Pressure 399
How Society Influences Marketing—Legislative Action 401

overall marketing strategy
413

Competitive Settings 416
Marketing Decisions in a Competitive Setting 419
Formulating Overall Marketing Strategy 424
Factors in Selecting Marketing Inputs 425
Optimum Combination of Marketing Inputs 426
Implementation of Marketing Strategy 427
Evaluating Overall Marketing Strategy 428

contents

glossary

437

index

449

PREFACE

This is the third edition of *Fundamentals of Modern Marketing,* an introductory marketing text emphasizing key concepts and issues underlying the modern practice of marketing. Although the basic format of the first two editions has been retained, in this edition certain changes have been made in keeping with the dynamic character of modern marketing. Statistical data have been updated wherever possible, additional figures and tables have been added, and new materials, such as the inclusion of more examples from international marketing, have been added.

The text is designed to meet the needs both of students taking only the introductory marketing course and of those planning to take more advanced courses in the field. We hope that both groups will find that this book provides a clear understanding of marketing's role in modern organizations (business and nonprofit) and in society. Even more fundamentally, we hope, too, that readers will conclude that marketing is a highly interesting subject extremely important, not only in the world of affairs but also to each individual as a consumer and citizen.

The plan of presentation is straightforward. Part One, the general introduction, is a survey of the general nature of marketing, marketing organization, and the marketing process. Part Two is an overview of marketing information systems and marketing research, markets, and buyer behavior. Parts Three through Six are descriptions and analyses of the four main decision areas in marketing—products, distribution, pricing, and promotion. Part Seven, the conclusion, gives special emphasis to the interactions of marketing and society and provides an integrated view of overall marketing strategy.

Each chapter's content has been planned to constitute a unit of understanding. Each opens with a statement of learning objectives, proceeds with
descriptions and analyses of key concepts and issues, and closes with a high-
light of the chapter's coverage. We have sought, in other words, to adhere
closely to the time-tested pedagogical formula of "telling them what you're
going to tell them, telling them, and telling them what you've told them." In
addition, being strong believers in the discussion method, we have included
for each chapter a wide variety of questions, problems, and short cases
aimed at provoking interesting and meaningful discussion.

For successful completion of this book, we owe a great deal to a great
many people. For providing us with rather definite notions on what should
and should *not* be included in an introductory marketing text, our greatest
debt is to our present and former students. For candid appraisals and helpful suggestions made at various stages in the development of the manuscript,
we are indebted to numerous reviewers and users of the earlier editions. For
contributing frank criticism and advice—most of it informally—we owe considerable thanks to numerous present and former members of the marketing
staffs at Emory University, the University of Georgia, and Babson College,
as well as to our ex-colleagues at The University of Texas at Austin, Syracuse University, Cornell University, The University of Missouri at Colum-
bia, and Bowling Green State University. For providing continual help and
encouragement we are deeply indebted to the following Prentice-Hall personnel: John Connolly, Editor-Marketing; Linda Stewart, College Book
Editorial-Production Department; Linda Conway, College Design Department; and Ernest Hursh, Marketing Manager College Division. Last, but by
no means least, for consistently aiding us through their sympathetic understanding, we are indebted to our wives and families. For all of this assistance—both that acknowledged here and throughout the book, as well as
that received from business executives and others—we express our sincere
thanks. However, as usual, we accept full responsibility for any and all
deficiencies.

EDWARD W. CUNDIFF
RICHARD R. STILL
NORMAN A. P. GOVONI

FUNDAMENTALS
OF
MODERN
MARKETING

PART ONE

PREPARING FOR
THE MARKETING CONCEPT

When you have mastered the contents of this chapter, you should be able to:

1 Explain the basic role of marketing in different kinds of profit-seeking and nonprofit organizations.

2 Define marketing in terms of product–market interrelationships and ownership transfers.

3 Identify the different environmental factors influencing marketing decisions and activities.

4 Explain the marketing concept in terms of its essential features.

5 Identify the key environmental factors that influence companies in their decisions to adopt the marketing concept.

6 Identify the organizational conditions that generally precede management's recognition of the necessity for adopting the marketing concept.

7 Illustrate how a company should view its planning and operating activities under the marketing concept.

8 Explain how management should go about implementing the marketing concept.

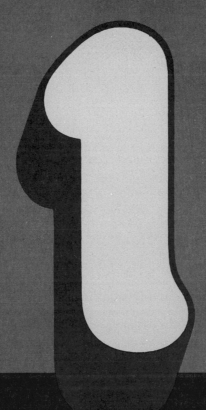

the emerging role
of marketing

This opening chapter is designed to provide you with an understanding of marketing and its role in different organizations and in the societies of which it is a part. Discussion focuses first on the various kinds of marketing activities performed by each organization. Then marketing is formally defined and analyzed with respect to its relationship to production and to the environment. Finally, the *marketing concept,* a philosophy of management that strongly influences the management of marketing effort, is examined. Recent significant changes in markets, in technology, and in the ways available for reaching and communicating with markets have intensified competition. These changes, coupled with the growth in size and complexity of business and nonprofit organizations, have made it increasingly important for companies to move toward adoption of the marketing concept.

WHAT DOES MARKETING DO?

Marketing basically involves relating the needs and desires of people with the producer's products or services in order to achieve transfer of ownership of the product or enjoyment of the service. A shoe manufacturer, for example, expects its marketing experts to provide information on consumer preferences in shoe styles, materials, and colors and on the location of these prospective buyers, also on the relative strengths and weaknesses of competitors' products; tell prospective consumers about its products and where to find them; make the shoes available where consumers can buy them conveniently; and provide recommendations on prices that will sell the product and yield a profit. Marketing plays the same basic role for all producers of goods, whether they produce steel for industry buyers, pencils for schoolchildren, or fresh fruits and vegetables for household consumption.

Marketing is not concerned solely with tangible goods, it also plays a similar role in connection with the distribution of services. A life insurance company (which basically sells the service of protection) expects its marketing staff to provide information about potential buyers and the kinds of insurance service they need and want, provide channels through which these services are made available to prospective buyers, make potential buyers aware of the types and nature of services offered, and participate in the determination of prices that will both be acceptable to potential buyers and yield profits to the company. Whether the service is dancing instruction, travel advice, or hair styling, marketing is responsible for the ultimate delivery of the service to buyers and for the inward flow of income to the organization.[1]

Marketing is a vital function in both profit-seeking and not-for-profit organizations. Marketing has traditionally been studied only from the viewpoint of profit-seeking institutions; only recently have the marketing-type problems of not-for-profit institutions been given more than scant attention.[2] Perhaps because marketing is so essential to the production of income (and profit) in the profit-seeking organization, nonprofit types of institutions (such as community chests and charitable foundations) are reluctant to identify their own marketing activities as marketing. For example, the marketing executive of a nonprofit institution may be called the director of public relations or business manager. Nevertheless, the top management of a symphony orchestra needs very nearly the same kind of help as a profit-making record company with respect to identifying its market and its preferences in music, providing ways to make the music available to prospective patrons, informing them about and stimulating an interest in the music offered, and establishing a price that optimizes customer patronage and income to defray expenses. Similar marketing activities are essential, whether the nonprofit institution is a hospital, a university or school, or an art museum. Unfortunately, in the past, this reluctance to recognize marketing as a necessary and integral part of the nonprofit institution's total function has resulted in marketing ineptitude and operating inefficiency.

DEFINITION OF MARKETING

Marketing activities are those most directly concerned with the demand-stimulating and demand-fulfilling efforts of the enterprise. These activities interlock and interact with one another as components of the total system—by which a company develops and makes its products available, distributes them through marketing channels, promotes them, and prices them. Specifically, then, we define mar-

---

[1] A notable description and analysis of service marketing may be seen in John M. Rathmell, *Marketing in the Service Sector* (Cambridge, Mass.: Winthrop Publishers, Inc., 1974).

[2] See, for example, Frederick E. Webster, Jr., *Social Aspects of Marketing* (Englewood Cliffs, N.J.: Prentice-Hall, Inc., 1974), pp. 73-92; and Philip Kotler, *Marketing for Nonprofit Organizations* (Englewood Cliffs, N.J.: Prentice-Hall, Inc., 1975).

keting as the managerial process by which products are matched with markets and through which the consumer is enabled to use or enjoy the product.[3]

It should be noted that **product** as used in the above definition is an all-inclusive term which includes services as well as physical goods. In this sense, piano lessons are just as much a product as the piano itself. The matching of services with markets to effect consumption is also marketing.

product–market interrelationship   Our definition states, in part, that "marketing is the managerial process by which products are matched with markets." Marketing and production activities are interlocked—we can only market products that can be produced, and we should only produce those that can be marketed. Thus, it is logical to think of marketing as the business process by which specific products are matched up with specific markets and to think of production as the business process concerned with manufacturing these products.

Matching products with markets is both a marketing and a production problem. It involves selecting, manufacturing, and marketing products that possess as many as possible of the characteristics desired by those who make up the markets while at the same time attempting to achieve maximum progress in reaching the company's overall goals. While top management bears the ultimate responsibility for satisfactorily solving these problems, marketing management plays a highly important role.

Consider, for instance, how products are matched with markets. In some cases, marketing research first uncovers the product characteristics wanted by final buyers, then top management (working with both production and marketing executives) translates these wants into product specifications. In other cases, the products are initiated through technical research carried on within the company, and marketing research focuses on finding out if there are potential users, and measuring their numbers. In all cases, if management decides to go ahead and market the product, marketing management is responsible for making decisions on such matters as personal selling, advertising, other promotion, distribution policy, and price to gain and hold market favor (these decision areas are described jointly as **marketing controllables**). In addition, marketing management is responsible for the continual adjustment of marketing controllables with respect to the company's existing products, while production management, of course, is responsible for manufacturing them. Thus, modern management regards market-

[3] The American Marketing Association defines marketing as consisting "of the performance of business activities that direct the flow of goods and services from producer to consumer or user." See Committee on Definitions, *Marketing Definitions* (Chicago: American Marketing Association, 1960), p. 15. There are two main reasons why we have chosen to use our own definition rather than the "official AMA" definition: (1) we believe that the interrelatedness of *product* and *marketing* is an essential idea and should be explicitly included in a definition of marketing, and (2) since there can be no marketing unless the user acquires access to the product, we believe also that this point should be explicitly included in a definition of marketing.

ing and production as interdependent subsystems—marketing as the subsystem by which specific products are matched up with specific markets and production as the subsystem charged with manufacturing these products. This combination of marketing controllables used to market a product or service is often described as the marketing mix or strategy.

ownership transfers and consumption activities

Ownership transfers occur repeatedly as physical products flow from producers to final buyers. For instance, a manufacturer may sell its output to wholesalers who, in turn, resell it to retailers who, again in turn, resell it to consumers. In this instance, every unit of the manufacturer's product that is finally purchased by a consumer has had its ownership transferred three times (from manufacturer to wholesaler, from wholesaler to retailer, and from retailer to consumer). Of course, for an ownership transfer to take place, buying as well as selling is necessary and, in moving a product to market, the producer only sells. The resellers (wholesalers and retailers) both buy and sell, and the consumer only buys.

As services are provided by the producer to consumers, these consumers acquire the right to enjoy these services. Thus, the purchaser of a theater ticket is permitted access to the performance. Owners of television sets are given access to shows by turning the knob, but they pay for service (at least in one sense) by listening to advertising messages. A person who is ill seeks the services of a physician, and the physician (the producer of the service) may be reimbursed directly by the consumer or by society.

Consumers or users are the "targets" of marketing activities. The whole movement of products from producers to users anticipates a final buying action by the users, and the whole distribution of services anticipates consumption on the part of these buyers. There can be no marketing, then, unless ownership transfers or consumption are effected. Marketing decisions and activities are strongly influenced by environmental factors beyond the control of the producer or the consumer alone. Figure 1-1 illustrates this relationship of internal and external factors affecting marketing. Within the circle are the decisions areas controlled by marketing management, each of which is discussed in detail in later chapters. Around the rim of the figure are the various factors which clearly affect marketing decisions and strategy but which marketing management cannot control directly. Thus, management in making decisions and taking action on the controllables must necessarily take these environmental (uncontrollable) factors into account.

One of these factors—availability of resources (financial, physical, and human)—clearly limits the range and variety of decisions marketing management can make. Resources may be available to the company but not available to marketing management, for example, when top management assigns higher priorities to nonmarketing activities in allocating resources.

Three types of external factors—competition, political and legal, and science and technology—directly restrain management's freedom to make

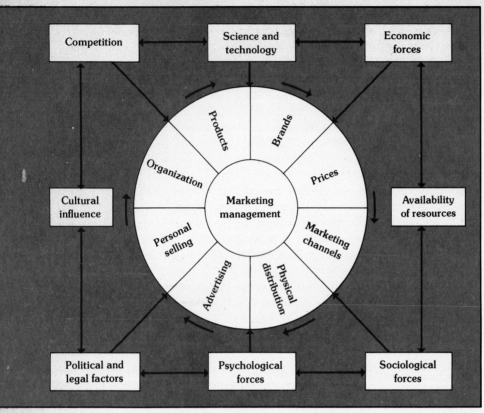

Figure 1-1 Marketing and its environment

marketing decisions and to formulate marketing strategy. No marketing decision of major importance should be made without giving consideration to competition. When contemplating any marketing action, management must be ever aware that there is some chance that competitors will react in ways that may have adverse effects on the company; similarly, each company's management must be prepared to evaluate and possibly to counteract the marketing moves of competitors. Likewise, both existing legislation (and its interpretation) and the political climate limit management's freedom to make marketing decisions; for example, even though there are not many laws prohibiting environmental pollution through packaging (as through using "throwaway" packages), the climate of public opinion is such that management must examine all proposed marketing changes carefully to determine whether or not they might produce adverse ecological effects. Similarly, the current state of science and technology has limiting effects on the range of possible marketing moves; for instance, science and technology have not yet progressed to the point where it is possible to make a self-loading automatic dishwasher that will also clear dishes from the table. But there would probably be a market for such a product, if developed.

The other four types of external factors—psychological, cultural, sociological, and economic—indirectly restrain management's freedom to make marketing decisions through the influences they exert on buying behavior. Psychological forces internal to the individual, such as physiological needs and the needs for self-esteem and the esteem of others, influence all human behavior, including buying behavior. Cultural factors help explain why U.S. consumers eat very little rice and Japanese consumers use rice as a main staple in their diet—thus, the problem of increasing rice consumption is different in the United States than it is in Japan. Sociological factors, such as the preferences of an individual's close friends and associates as well as the influences they exert on him or her, strongly affect the individual's behavior in buying clothes, automobiles, houses, and numerous other products. Diverse economic forces, such as the present size of a consumer's income and his or her future income expectations, are basic to his or her decision to buy or not to buy many products. Because these four types of external factors influence the behavior of potential buyers, they limit management's range of appropriate marketing decisions (appropriate in the sense that possible decisions will produce desired results).

ORGANIZATIONAL CONDITIONS PRECEDING THE ADOPTION OF A CUSTOMER OR MARKETING ORIENTATION

Historically, three organizational conditions generally precede management's change from a production to a marketing orientation concept.[4] The most prevalent of these is product orientation.

product orientation

The traditional orientation of top management in many companies, particularly those emphasizing mass production, focuses mainly on the product. Such product orientation involves falling in love with the company's own products: concentrating on making them better (technically, mechanically, and aesthetically), improving the production process, bringing down product costs, and the like, while simultaneously neglecting to consider changes in the market and competitive situation.

A product-oriented company expects marketing to serve the seller's interests alone and not those of buyers. Focusing on ever-more-efficient manufacturing, top management assigns marketing the task of selling increased outputs—literally, if necessary, of "forcing it down customers'

[4] Many of the ideas in this section trace to ones first put in writing by Theodore Levitt. See his article, "Marketing Myopia," *Harvard Business Review,* July-August 1960, pp. 45-56. This article was reprinted along with further comments by the author in *Harvard Business Review,* September-October 1975, pp. 26ff.

throats." If the world does not see the company's product as a "better mousetrap" and does not "beat a path to the company's door," the marketing department is expected to go out and sell the output any way it can.

In the product-oriented company the great danger is that top management will not realize what business the company is really in: that is, to serve a market and not simply to dispose of a product. There is always the risk that this market will find some more satisfactory way of meeting its needs. Eventually, the owners of horse-drawn buggies decided that automobiles better serve their needs. Where did that leave the makers of buggies? As a pure matter of survival, companies with product orientations must sooner or later change them in order to stay in business at all.

communications problems and uncoordinated proliferation of specialists

As a company grows, various functions (such as marketing, finance, and production) are split into smaller and smaller parts, each in charge of a specialist. Complexities of administering the growing number of people in the organization also bring into existence a wide range of bureaucratic positions. Thus, with organizational growth, departmental walls tend to rise ever higher, causing some tasks to be duplicated, as department heads and other bureaucrats seek to build their own little empires.

As the number of specialists grows, they tend to lose effectiveness in communicating with others not sharing their specialties. As various technical languages for communicating with others sharing the same specialties develop, overall communications deteriorate because things and events take on a variety of special meanings for different specialists. Additionally, certain specialists feel the need for justifying their own positions, and may seek to legitimatize their positions by transforming everyday speech into technical jargon. Management tends to fail to coordinate the proliferation of specialists; so they are inclined to work at cross purposes, and frictions and inefficiencies as well as communications problems permeate the entire organization. As management becomes preoccupied with internal operations, it exhibits a growing inability and unwillingness to see opportunities on the outside caused by market shifts, technological changes, and the like.

conflicts among departmental goals

Also, there is often a natural conflict among departmental goals. In the production department, costs are uppermost in importance. Thus, emphasis is placed on minimizing the number of products, standardizing product variety, lengthening the interval between model changes, and maximizing the length of production runs. In the marketing department, everything tends to revolve around sales volume. Hence, to increase sales, pressures are exerted to offer the widest variety of products, to change models at short intervals, to get the products into every conceivable outlet, to promote them continuously and heavily, and to price them at or below competitive levels. Finance specialists also are involved in the effort to justify their own positions—often seeking to maximize short-run returns to stockholders to the neglect of customers' wants and desires, opposing research and development projects needed to keep the firm competitive, frustrating the efforts of both production and marketing to install innovations that cost money now but pay off in the long run, and generally trying to minimize costs and maximize short-run revenues at the same time. As each department emphasizes attainment of its own goals, the total enterprise's future potential for serving its markets profitably is reduced. With each department trying to optimize its own performance, the company's overall performance is suboptimized.

ENVIRONMENTAL FACTORS INFLUENCING THE ADOPTION OF A CUSTOMER ORIENTATION

Certain key environmental factors provide the setting within which companies tend to change their orientation toward marketing and the consumer. Consider the consumer market: long-term population and income trends have caused large potential markets to exist for the continual stream of product improvements and new products that have been made possible through advances in technology. These market and product factors have produced a rising crescendo of competitive activity, as more and more marketers vie for shares of consumers' buying power. Competitive activity has been further heightened by evolution and change in marketing channels and by development and growth of successive new waves of mass communications media, which make it possible to adjust marketing controllables in new ways.

The environmental changes are causing marketers of consumer products to alter both their marketing philosophy and organization. They are becoming less product-oriented and more market-oriented, gearing their operations primarily to customers' needs, wants, and desires and only secondarily to particular products. Promotional emphasis, at the same time, is shifting away from selling the product per se to selling the function that the product can perform for customers; for example, rather than promoting the technical features of a self-cleaning oven, one marketer now advertises "this oven will clean itself, permitting the user to avoid a dirty and time-consuming job."

Marketers of industrial products have been slower in adopting a marketing orientation. Nevertheless, developments in the consumer market have "spilled over," and industrial marketers are also adjusting their operations according to the needs of their customers. Each of the key environmental factors influencing this change of orientation, first among consumer goods marketers and then as a spillover among industrial goods marketers, is examined more closely in the following discussion.

changes in markets POPULATION GROWTH Consumer markets are made up of people with money, and the American market has been growing both in population and income. Total U.S. population has grown from fewer than 100 million people in 1910 to around 217 million in 1978, and the projection for the year 2000 is that population will then exceed 248 million. The American population is growing at a net rate of between

1.5 and 2 million persons a year.[5] Thus, large and growing potential markets exist for the widening stream of new consumer products being introduced to the market. However, not all parts of this market have been growing at the same rate. Figure 1-2 shows that the age groups of between 6 and 25 years have been decreasing since the mid-1960s, while the over-65 group has been increasing.

GROWING NUMBER OF HOUSEHOLDS   For some products (e.g., household appliances, automobiles, and other consumer durables) market growth is related more closely to the total number of households than to the total population. In 1978 the number of households approximated 75.5 million, and even though total population growth is slowing, an average of over 2 million new households is being added each year. A total of more than 87 million households is predicted by 1985.[6] The number of households is increasing at a faster rate than the total population, and marketers of many consumer durables can look forward to potential markets that grow faster than the consumer market as a whole.

GROWTH IN DISPOSABLE PERSONAL INCOME   Total disposable personal income (what people have left to spend or save after paying taxes) rose from a little over $83 billion in 1929 to almost $686 billion in 1970 and was running at an annual rate of over $801 billion in 1975 (in terms of current dollars). In terms of purchasing power (i.e., real income), the growth has not been so great, but it is still striking. Stated in constant (1972) dollars, the increase

[5] U.S. Department of Commerce, Bureau of the Census, *Statistical Abstract of the United States,* 1977.
[6] *1978 Commercial Atlas and Marketing Guide* (Chicago: Rand McNally & Co.).

Figure 1-2   The changing population age mix

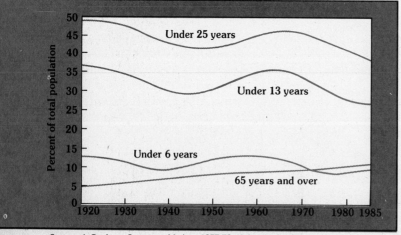

Source: A Guide to Consumer Markets 1977-78, Helen Axel, ed. (New York: The Conference Board, 1977).

was from $384.4 billion in 1950 to $883.2 billion in 1976, a net gain of about 130 percent.[7]

In current dollars, *per capita* disposable income increased from $705 in 1929 to $5,493 in 1976 and is expected to reach $6,869 in 1980. Thus, from 1929 to 1976 the increase was nearly 680 percent. What has been the impact of rises in price level on real purchasing power? In terms of constant 1972 dollars, the change in real purchasing power is reflected in the fact that per capita disposable income rose from under $2,386 in 1950 to about $4,140 in 1972, roughly a 73 percent increase. The American market has grown increasingly affluent and, in spite of rising prices, American consumers have enjoyed continuing increases in purchasing power.

INCREASES IN DISCRETIONARY INCOME   There is also a trend for households to have increasing amounts of **discretionary income**, which is money left over after buying essential food, clothing, shelter, transportation, and other items a household regards as necessities. Such income may be spent, saved, used for buying nonnecessities, or for a combination of these. Experience indicates, however, that a rise in discretionary income usually results in more spending for nonnecessities (discretionary spending). Discretionary spending grew from about $106 billion in 1955 to about $407 billion in 1967.[8] Another measure of consumer affluence is **supernumerary income,** all income in excess of $20,000 a year flowing to each family unit. Figure 1-3 shows the

[7] *Statistical Abstract of the United States,* 1977.
[8] *A Guide to Consumer Markets 1977-78,* Helen Axel, ed. (New York: The Conference Board, 1977).

Figure 1-3   Supernumerary income

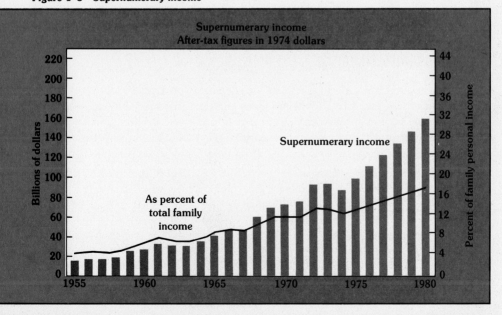

increase in supernumerary income from 1955 projected to 1980, when it is expected to be 17 percent of total family income.

Continuing increases in discretionary purchasing power in consumers' hands have resulted in dramatic expansions in the market potentials for such items as automatic dishwashers, color television sets, and home swimming pools. Moreover, with consumers becoming more affluent, they are also becoming more particular about what they buy and more choosy about what they will accept. Increasing consumer sophistication has led more manufacturers to research consumers' wants and desires more thoroughly and to develop and market products more in line with these findings. Simultaneously, growth in market potentials for nonnecessities has encouraged other firms to enter such markets, thus adding to the incentive all competitors have for adjusting their products more closely to what consumers demand.

THE GIANT NEW MIDDLE CLASS   There is also a trend toward a leveling off of the extreme ranges of income among consumers, a trend that is contributing importantly to growth of mass markets for such luxury items as motorboats, which until recently only a few could afford. A few generations back, income distribution resembled a pyramid with the vast bulk of the incomes (the low incomes) at the pyramid base. Today this distribution more closely approximates a diamond shape, with a large middle-income group positioned between a rich minority above and a poor minority below. Median family income reached $14,958 in 1976, with 44.1 percent of all U.S. families in the middle income group ($12,000 to $25,000), 38.1 percent in the rich minority (over $25,000), and 17.8 percent in the poor minority (under $12,000).

Although the rate of rise in discretionary income slowed markedly in 1974, still more people tend to have more income, and this is causing new mass markets to develop. More and more products once regarded as luxuries have become necessities. Washing machines, radios, television, telephones, and automobiles all have, for ever-increasing segments of the market, moved from the luxury class to the necessity class.

NEW ATTITUDE TOWARD DEBT   Ever since the Great Depression of the 1930s, less and less stigma has been attached to credit buying, and fewer people save in order to pay cash for such products as automobiles, television sets, furniture, and major household appliances. Each year, for instance, more than six in ten new car buyers borrow from banks, finance companies, and other lenders, so, in effect, they also buy on credit but make their payments to lenders rather than directly to sellers. Credit buying has become a way of life for millions, including many who could pay cash but prefer not to.

The amount of credit a consumer can obtain is related to the size of his or her present income. Marketers of such products as mobile homes, boats, and camping trailers have adopted credit plans to accelerate expansion of their markets; and "Go now—pay later" plans have made international air travel possible for the average person. In addition, the spread of bank-sponsored credit card plans has made it progressively easier to buy on credit even from those retailers who formerly sold for cash only. The changing attitude toward debt and the increasing ability of consumers to obtain credit has added to the intensity of competition for the consumer's dollar.

product changes resulting from new technology

No company has a guarantee that its product will not be made obsolete by some technological advance. Time and again, and with increasing frequency in recent years, technological change has brought overnight obsolescence to products, whole product lines, and even entire industries. The fountain pen was replaced by the ballpoint, which was, in turn, reduced in importance by subsequent newer innovations is writing instruments; the movie industry was diminished in strength by television; the market for natural fibers has been greatly diminished by synthetics. At the same time, technology has just as suddenly created vast new markets for other products and industries. For example, electronic calculators have created an entire new market for computing equipment.

Total expenditures for research and development (R&D) soared from under $2 billion in 1945 to over $34 billion in 1977 in the United States alone. Research in other nations has also contributed heavily to the pace of technological change. In just one industry, the auto industry, foreign research has produced two important new power plants, the diesel and rotary engines. One important result of increased R&D spending has been the shortening of product life cycles—time spans from market introductions to market discontinuances—as new products account for an increasing proportion of sales. Another has been that technological developments in one industry often create products sold to markets traditionally supplied by a different industry.

Technological change, then, is a key element in the competitive struggle among companies. An ever-growing number of new products is being introduced to the market each year. Thus, the list of products from which consumers may choose also grows longer.

changes in marketing channels and physical distribution

Changes in marketing channels have occurred at an ever-increasing rate during the past 50 years. The evolution of sophisticated new types of retailing institutions has tended to shorten many marketing channels and to reduce the manufacturer's control over the channel. At the same time, older institutions have adjusted their operating methods to compete, and they, too, have added to the distributive problems and challenges of the marketer.

General merchandise chains, such as Sears and J. C. Penney, have broadened their merchandise lines and deepened their market impact. Discount houses have carved out an important share of the retail market. In the food line, convenience stores are replacing the disappearing "Mom and Pop" stores. In Europe, the hypermarkets (a kind of super discount store) have revolutionized retailing. In many foreign markets the rate of change in recent years has been much greater than in the United States. Thus, the range of distributive options available to manufacturers has considerably broadened, making their task of marketing channel selection more complex. At the same time, the development of stronger types of middlemen has frequently reduced the manufacturer's ability to control the channel.

Noteworthy improvements in physical distribution also have been occurring, making it possible to distribute products faster, more economically, more efficiently, and more widely than ever before. Transportation improvements include jet air freight, containerized shipping, piggyback, fishyback, and unitized train. Materials handling and storage improvements include palletization, resulting in reduction of manhandling. Computerization has made possible better inventory control, optimal size and location of inventories, and reduced delivery time to the customer. Technological improvements in physical distribution yet to come will make possible still further gains in the ease with which manufacturers may distribute their products. And, this will be of special significance in foreign markets, where physical distribution frequently looms as the most difficult and costly marketing input to manage.

growth of mass communications media

With the appearance and growth of successive new waves of mass communications media—newspapers, magazines, AM and FM radio, black-and-white and color television—it has become possible to "spread the word" about new product developments faster, more widely and, for the most part, more effectively than before. They have also made it possible for advertising to play a large role in marketing. Furthermore, the growth of mass communications media has been further stimulated by increasing pressures for rapid development of mass markets brought on by the ever-accelerating rate of technological change and by businessmen's efforts to secure the economic advantages of large-scale production.

At the same time, communications effectiveness has tended to increase. Development and growth of different kinds of mass media have made it possible for marketers to deliver advertising messages in more ways, each medium reinforcing messages delivered by other media and each boosting the combined impact on potential buyers.

summary of environmental factors influencing adoption of a customer orientation

We can sum up the four main environmental factors helping bring about adoption of a customer orientation as follows:

1. More people have more money although the rate of growth in discretionary income varies from nation to nation.
2. More things are being made—more types of products, more versions of particular products, and closer adaptations of individual product characteristics to the wants and desires of specific market segments.

3. There are more ways to move products to markets, institutionally and physically—nationally and internationally.
4. Prospective buyers can learn about the products available for sale through more communications media and learn about them more effectively.

Every reason exists for predicting that these trends will continue in the near future. Consumers have an increasing number of ways to spend the incomes they receive. As the growth in incomes slows down, the tempo of competitive activity for the consumer dollar will intensify. Under these environmental conditions, the company following policies consistent with the marketing concept is helping to ensure its own survival. It is also in a good position to capitalize on marketing opportunities as they develop. Figure 1-4 illustrates a framework for assessing these opportunities.

Figure 1-4   A framework for assessing marketing opportunities

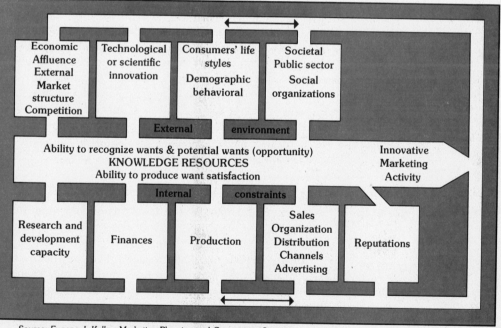

Source: Eugene J. Kelley, Marketing Planning and Competitive Strategy
(Englewood Cliffs, New Jersey: Prentice-Hall, Inc., 1972), p. 36.

THE MARKETING CONCEPT

The result of the growing customer orientation upon the part of business was the development of the marketing concept. Figure 1-5 portrays the essential features of the **marketing concept**. A company operating under this concept takes its principal direc-

Figure 1-5   The marketing concept

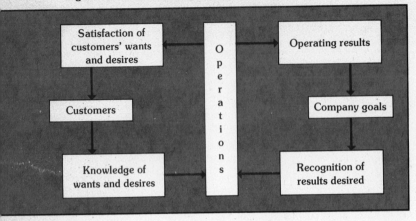

tion from the marketplace; that is, from its knowledge and understanding of its customers' needs, wants, and desires. This becomes, then, the main basis for organizing operations; not only marketing, but production, financial, and other organizational units are geared toward satisfying customers' needs, wants, and desires. However, the organization of operations also is influenced importantly by the company's overall goals; department heads must recognize what results top management is looking for if they are to manage their departments in ways that not only satisfy customers' needs, wants, and desires but also facilitate achievement of company goals. Thus, the marketing concept has three main features: (1) a market or customer orientation, (2) a subordination of departmental aspirations to company-wide goals, and (3) a unification of company operations.

PLANNING AND OPERATING UNDER THE MARKETING CONCEPT

Figure 1-6 shows how a company should view its planning and operating activities under the marketing concept. Research and analysis is needed both to identify market needs and to clarify company goals as well as to provide relevant information on both for decision making. Then, management formulates an overall company operating plan—integrating marketing, production, financial, and other plans into a unified whole. After this extensive planning, management initiates the actions needed (i.e., it puts into effect the various actions required to make the plan work). The anticipated results—in the ideal situation—would be both the fulfillment of market needs and the attainment of company goals. Note carefully, however, that should the ideal situation not occur, then the entire process recycles—as indicated by the closure arrows (i.e., those running back from attainment to company goals and from fulfillment to market needs).

Figure 1-6 Planning and operating under the marketing concept

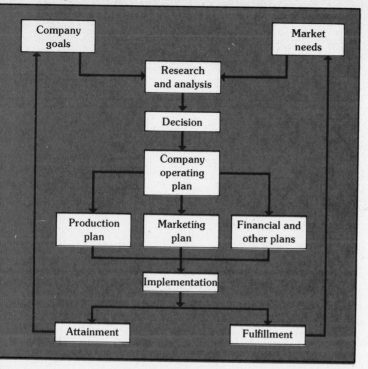

IMPLEMENTING THE
MARKETING CONCEPT

Three main features distinguish the company managed according to the marketing concept: (1) adoption of a predominantly market or customer orientation, (2) subordination of departmental goals to a set of company goals, and (3) unification of company operations, both to serve markets effectively and to meet company goals.

market orientation

In adopting a **market orientation**, management focuses on the customers' wants and desires primarily and on the product only incidentally. Thus, emphasis is put on using marketing research to keep abreast of market trends and developments and on doing research and development work (even if it results in making present products obsolete). Specifically, management exerts every effort to keep up to date on the changing answers to five important questions:

1. What business are we really in?
2. Who are our customers?
3. What do they want and desire?
4. How can we best distribute our products to them?
5. How can we communicate most effectively with them?

formulation of company goals   Top management formulates a set of company goals to which individual departmental goals are subordinated, thus giving tangible recognition to the fact that the company exists to achieve something as a company rather than as a collection of uncoordinated individual departments. Such total company goals as achieving a given profit level or a certain return on investment become of prime importance. Therefore, in working toward achievement of a given profit level, for instance, the production department is made aware that obtaining low manufacturing costs is not enough. The marketing department is guided toward placing less emphasis on high sales volume and more on making profitable sales. The financial department is alerted to top management's desire not only to provide a satisfactory short-run return for the stockholders but to serve the company's markets profitably over the long run. In other words, a coordinated effort is made to optimize the company's total performance, recognizing that this undoubtedly means suboptimizing the performance of individual departments.

unification of company operations   In seeking to achieve company goals by effectively serving chosen markets, management works continuously to weld the different parts of the organization into an efficient operating system. An orchestration of effort is required to correct such organizational deficiencies as the communications problems among the specialists and the parallel tendency for their proliferation to go uncoordinated. Management strives to secure a **synergistic effect**—to achieve greater total results than could be obtained by the individual departments working separately and not coordinated with each other. Therefore, a company managed under the marketing concept plans, organizes, coordinates, and controls its entire operation as *one system directed toward achieving a single set of goals applicable to the total organization.*

SUMMARY   Marketing is the managerial process by which products and services are matched with markets and ownership transfers or consumption is effected. Marketing takes place in an environment that affects the manner in which marketing operations can be and are performed. This environment includes not only the availability of resources but competition, political and legal factors, science and technology, and cultural, sociological, psychological, and economic forces affecting consumer behavior.

This chapter has also focused upon what is perhaps the single most important idea in modern marketing—the marketing concept. You should now thoroughly understand both the meaning of this concept and its significance for the management of marketing efforts. You should know how the critical changes that have been—and are—occurring in markets, in technology, and in the ways available for reaching and communicating with markets have exerted—individually and collectively—increasing pressures on managements to adopt the marketing concept. You now should know and understand how the growth in size and complexity of business organizations has made it increasingly important for their managements to adopt the marketing concept. Recognition of these changes and conditions by management leads ultimately to adoption of the marketing concept which requires management to view its planning and operating activities in a new light. In implementing the marketing concept, management must adopt a market orientation, formulate company goals, and unify company operations.

REVIEW
AND
DISCUSSION
QUESTIONS

1 "He who builds a better mousetrap will find the world beating a path to his door." How much truth is there in this age-old saying? Has it ever been true?

2 Someone has said that "marketing both begins and ends with the consumer." Explain.

3 Explain why marketing is important in nonprofit institutions as well as in profit-seeking institutions.

4 How does marketing add value to goods? Give a few examples.

5 "Marketing and production activities are interlocked." Discuss.

6 Figure 1–1 illustrates the relationship between internal and external factors affecting marketing. Explain this relationship.

7 Why do marketing changes generally seem to appear first in consumer goods markets rather than in industrial goods markets?

8 Explain how technological change contributes to the tempo of competition.

9 Outline the main environmental factors that have helped bring about adoption of the marketing concept. Do you anticipate that these factors will continue to play an influential role in shaping the nature of marketing in the future? Why or why not?

10 Explain the differences between a company with a product orientation and one with a market orientation.

11 How can less-than-optimal overall performance occur in a company when each of its departments emphasizes attainment of its own goals?

12 Explain fully what the marketing concept is all about. How would you convince a skeptical business person of its value?

13 Many marketers contend that the solution to every marketing problem lies with the consumer. Do you agree with this? Why or why not?

14 What reasons are there for believing that marketing will be of increasing importance in the future?

15 As an enterprise grows, there is a tendency for communications to lose effectiveness. Why? What can be done to improve this condition?

16 Marketing has been described as a process of adjusting controllable factors to uncontrollable factors. Comment.

CASE PROBLEM

The Tri-City Taxi Company had been operating for 10 years offering transportation services in three adjacent small cities in the Midwest. The taxi company had managed a modest profit every year in spite of two major competitors, both larger than Tri-City. The current year's record, however, showed not only a 10 percent decline in passenger fares, but also increasing complaints by customers, upset by unreliable service.

Last year, Dan Littleton, President of Tri-City, hired an energetic young marketing manager, Ruth DuBois, who launched an advertising campaign for "Plan-a-Ride" designed to increase ridership. The Plan-a-Ride theme promised fast dependable service at a 10 percent discount if the cab company received at least one hour's notice of a person's need for a ride. The idea caught on and, in the first two months of the campaign, many new customers called Tri-City for service. Management was pleased with initial results. But, because of the sudden strain on a barely adequate fleet of cabs, service proved quite unreliable. Half of Tri-City's cabs were over five years old and subject to frequent breakdowns. The company simply did not have enough cabs in operation to meet the sudden demand while maintaining good service to old customers and on-demand service at public transportation facilities such as the airport and railroad stations.

Littleton had approved the Plan-a-Ride campaign concept and the funds requested by the marketing manager for use on radio and newspaper advertising. It was by far the largest advertising expenditure ever undertaken by Tri-City Taxi, although the company had rarely advertised in the past. Little thought, however, had been given to anticipating the effects of a successful advertising campaign.

The garage manager had not been consulted or advised of a possible increase in maintenance work and was short two mechanics during the first month of the new service. The operations department had hired only one new driver for the campaign. The resulting service to customers was poor. More often than not, cabs were at least 15 minutes late, resulting in a flood of complaints and loss of many old customers. With the increased mileage per day, there were more cars in for repair than the mechanics could handle and breakdowns while a cab was in service were increasing.

Littleton was puzzled by the fact that an advertising campaign with such great initial response had fizzled into a loss as year's end approached. After ridership increased 20 percent during the first three months of the campaign, it declined 10 percent the last three months of the year. Littleton was also besieged by more problems and bickering from his various departments than he had ever experienced in his 10 years of running the taxi company. Life had become one crisis after another, with constant breakdowns resulting in disgruntled drivers and angry customers. In the past, his management philosophy had been characterized by delegating most of the operating decisions to the department heads. "I don't tell DuBois about marketing, Williams about operations and repair, or Kelly about accounting and purchasing. My role is to formulate policy and handle problems as they arise."

Chaos had developed from what had first appeared to be a highly effective advertising campaign that seemed sure to elevate Tri-City Taxi Company's position in the local taxi industry. Littleton knew things just could not be allowed to continue this way. Something had to be done.

1. What problems face the Tri-City Taxi Company?
2. Identify and evaluate the alternatives.
3. Recommend an appropriate course of action for Littleton.

When you have mastered the contents of this chapter, you should be able to:

1   Explain the relationship of company goals and the marketing organization.
2   Analyze the impact of the marketing concept on the marketing organization *and* the company organization.
3   Explain why nonmarketing executives should help formulate certain marketing policies and why marketing executives should help formulate certain policies in other functional areas.
4   Outline the conditions under which each of the various bases for dividing marketing line authority is appropriate.
5   Describe the reasons for the creation of product manager positions and the general nature of the product manager's job.
6   Contrast and compare the formal marketing organizational plans of manufacturers, retailers and wholesalers, service businesses, and nonprofit organizations.

organizing
for marketing

People, as individuals and as members of groups, do the actual work of marketing. In order to understand how marketing work gets done, then, you must know a good deal about both organization in general and marketing organization in particular.

An **organization** is the mechanism through which a managerial philosophy is translated into action. As this philosophy changes, organizational goals are revised and basic changes are made in the organization itself. In moving toward the marketing concept, especially significant changes occur in the marketing organization, which is the company's main link with the market. The **marketing organization** provides the vehicle for making decisions on products, marketing channels, physical distribution, promotion, and prices. It is also the vehicle through which these decisions are implemented.

COMPANY GOALS AND THE MARKETING ORGANIZATION

The modern view of an organization is that it is a group of people brought together to participate in a common effort to accomplish certain goals. The basic goals of a company, then, indicate, to a large extent, what the company wants to be, since they tend to override and to permeate the rest of its administration. Certain goals have particularly important implications for the marketing organization.

1. *Desired Financial Results.* Traditionally, businesses are intended to be economic institutions. Generally, the organizers anticipate that a company's operations will generate profits. Once operations are under way, profits must be forthcoming on a sufficiently regular basis to permit the company's continued survival. The company's profit goal is of great importance to the marketing organization. It affects both the amount of sales volume that is sought and the level of costs allowed. Also important is the time allowed for reaching a target profit goal, as this

affects management's willingness or unwillingness to trade current profits for potentially greater future profits.

2. *Desired Place in the Industry.* A company defines its desired place in the industry in terms of such variables as size of operation, major function (manufacturing, wholesaling, retailing, etc.), quality and price levels for its products, and specialization or diversification of its activities. Different decisions on these variables result in different marketing organizations. For instance, a company that strives to have the largest market share in the industry requires a different marketing organization than one that wants to have the highest quality products.

3. *Disposition Toward Change.* A company's attitude toward change largely determines the types of employees who are attracted to it and the scheme by which they are welded into an organizational framework. Clearly, firms operating under the marketing concept have opted in favor of emphasizing change rather than stability. They recognize the need for making continual adjustments in operations and organizational structure in the process of adapting to changing market requirements and competitive conditions.

4. *Social Philosophy.* The basic goals controlling a company's relationship with the community and governmental units affect the operations of all departments and, most certainly, the marketing department.

5. *Competitive Posture.* A company's posture with respect to its competition has direct implications for the marketing organization, such as whether or not it will incorporate features permitting aggressive selling and advertising.

6. *Desired Customer Service Image.* There is a world of difference between a company seeking long-run customer satisfaction and one emphasizing quick "one-time" sales. This facet of the company image is important to all company departments producing, selling, and servicing the product line.

7. *Relationships with Suppliers.* The nature of a company's desired relationships with suppliers has indirect but important implications for marketing organization, since such relationships affect product quality, availability of repair and replacement parts, pricing practices, and the like.

MARKETING ORGANIZATION AND TRANSITION TO THE MARKETING CONCEPT

Top management determines how far a company moves toward adopting the marketing concept. Such factors as executives' personalities and experience influence this decision, but perhaps the most critical is top management's appraisal of the current state and probable future intensity of competition. The more directly such environmental trends as those discussed in Chapters 6 and 7 impinge upon a company's operations, the more severe is its competition and the more crucial is adoption of the marketing concept to its survival, especially during periods of shortages, recession, and inflation.

historical shifts in top management's business philosophy

PRODUCTION EMPHASIS   In the nineteenth and early twentieth centuries, when production problems were of prime importance, top management generally visualized a need for only a skeletal marketing organization. A slow rate of technological change made product changes infrequent; marketing channels were well defined and adhered closely to traditional patterns; little promotion was required due to the absence of strong competition; and pricing was mainly based upon cost plus a desired profit margin. Under these conditions, the marketing organization was little more than an adjunct to the factory—charged with physically distributing its output.

PERSONAL SELLING EMPHASIS   As early as the 1920s in the United States, as introduction and refinement of mass production techniques caused greatly increased factory outputs, the key problem became that of selling at the highest possible price what the factory was capable of producing. Advertising and other marketing activities were cast in supporting roles, being viewed mainly as the means for making personal selling more effective. Products and quantities manufactured were determined according to what the factory could produce, and the sales force was charged with selling that output. The sales organization often constituted the entire marketing organization or, at least, dominated other marketing activities.

MARKET EMPHASIS   Many industries in developing nations are still operating under the production or personal selling stages. However, in many nations top management in a growing number of concerns has recognized that focusing solely on what the factory can produce makes far less sense than determining what consumers want and then designing, manufacturing, and marketing products capable of satisfying those wants. With this shift in orientation, sweeping organizational changes occur. Marketing information becomes an important input of marketing organizations, and it sees increasing use in improving market knowledge and understanding. Product research and development gain in organizational stature as consumers become steadily more sophisticated in what they will buy. At the same time, advancing technology makes it possible to tailor product specifications ever more closely to what consumers want. Even though personal selling—and the sales department—continues as the backbone of most marketing organizations, advertising's organizational stature is elevated, as evolution and expansion of mass media help make it a more powerful element in marketing strategy. Recently, advertising has focused more on "reason why" advertising, with emphasis placed upon the information value of advertising. This change in emphasis has been in response to the fact that buyers, more than ever before, because of inflation, are looking for wise ways to stretch their dollars. Changes in marketing channels, in operating methods of distributive institutions, and in physical distribution facilities have made channel and distribution decisions more important and have earned a place in many marketing organizations for specialized units dealing with these areas. Finally, in industry after industry, the competitive tempo has risen, making pricing decisions more important and sometimes causing reallocations of decision-making authority. Summing up, all types of marketing decisions are rising in importance, resulting in changed organizational structures as companies move toward adoption of the marketing concept.

SOCIETAL EMPHASIS During the latter third of the twentieth century, in many nations throughout the world substantial segments of society have become concerned about the strong consumption orientation that characterizes the market-emphasis stage. Until fairly recently, almost everyone viewed consumption as the route to prosperity and increased standards of living. Today, growing concerns about shortages of energy and other critical products and pollution of the environment have focused attention more on conservation and less on consumption.

In a conserving society, marketing's objectives change considerably. It must increase the durability of products and reduce the wastage of raw materials. It must improve the effectiveness and efficiency of distribution channels. It must reduce wasteful and/or throwaway packaging, and improve promotional communication in order to provide clearer information for consumers. These changes are reflecting and will continue to reflect a more "socially responsible" role for marketing in the organization.

institutional organization and the marketing concept

Probably the most noteworthy characteristic of modern thought on organizations is that it is based upon a study of the organization as an integrated whole, that is, a "system." Proper organization under the marketing concept must result in a total integration and coordination of all organizational units (marketing, research and development, manufacturing, financial, etc.) into a single operating system directed toward achieving institutional goals and, at the same time, toward effectively serving the market and its changing wants and desires. Neither marketing nor any other organizational unit should dominate. All should be welded into an operating system whose components are so orchestrated that the market is served effectively while company goals are being reached.

The organizational structure of a company operating under the marketing concept is subject to frequent, sometimes drastic, modifications. Shifts in environmental factors, such as technological breakthroughs by competitors or changes in distributive institutions, may require changes in operating strategies that can only be effectuated by changing the organizational structure. Ideally, the organization should have built-in flexibility, enabling it to adapt readily to unstable conditions; the hierarchy itself should change with changing conditions, each member performing his or her speciality according to a common understanding of the company's goals.

The marketing concept is equally appropriate for profit-seeking and nonprofit organizations. Nonprofit organizations have frequently been as slow in recognizing and accepting the concept as have many profit-seeking organizations. But the marketing concept implies that museums should tailor their offerings to the public's interests rather than the curators' interests, that hospitals should adjust their services to patients' needs rather than the staff's needs, and that symphony orchestras should adjust their offerings to the public's interests rather than those of conductors and musicians. Implementing the marketing concept in these institutions generally requires extensive organizational restructuring.

organizational responsibility for marketing policy formulation

As a company reorganizes in line with the marketing concept, a hard look should be taken at the ways in which responsibility is assigned for formulating marketing policies. Traditionally, sales force management, advertising, marketing research, and the management of marketing channels have been recognized as marketing activities. Traditionally, too, marketing executives have been responsible for policy formulation in these areas. But certainly other departments, such as production and finance, have strong interests in how salespeople are trained and operate, in the messages advertising conveys, and in the data the marketing information system gathers. Therefore, in the modern organization, good reasons exist for nonmarketing executives to participate in making policies for these areas of marketing.

Similarly, marketing executives should help make policies in organizational areas where there are important marketing implications. One such area is pricing, which often is the responsibility of the treasurer, controller, or production manager, or the combined responsibility of several people. Another is the product line, traditionally the province of production, research and development, or both. Still another is physical distribution, often under the production department but also run as a separate department. Policies on pricing, products, and physical distribution all have important implications for marketing; by their very nature, these are interfunctional activities and, as such, marketing executives should share the responsibility for policy formulation. When a company is in the process of changing to the marketing concept, every effort must be made to pull down the walls between departments. The main way to do this is to discard traditional authority and job-task relationships wherever they prevent or act as deterrents to effective coordination of the organization as an operating system.[1]

integration of marketing activities

As marketing receives recognition as a major business function, one requiring coordination of numerous activities, top executives reexamine the ways in which these activities are incorporated in the formal organizational structure. Sales force management, advertising, and marketing research, for instance, have traditionally operated as separate departments reporting directly to top management. Integration or centralization of these activities under a single high-ranking marketing executive, because it improves coordination, generally increases

---

[1] Hollester Spencer, "On the Essential Vitality of Organization," *The Conference Board Record,* May 1975, pp. 60-62.

marketing effectiveness. There has been a strong trend in this direction during the past 25 years. Top executives of nonprofit organizations should also reexamine the place of marketing, but too frequently they have never considered its role in their organizations.

ORGANIZATION OF MARKETING RESPONSIBILITIES IN THE MANUFACTURING FIRM

Executives in small marketing departments must handle all types of problems, but in large departments dividing the work is not only desirable but critical. In a large marketing organization, numerous executives are specialists, with technical knowledge of activities such as advertising, marketing information, and physical distribution. The chief marketing executive is responsible for dividing the work among these specialists and other subordinates.

the chief marketing executive

Increasing centralization of marketing responsibilities and growing complexity of the marketing function have led large companies to search for a new "breed" of **chief marketing executive,** whose time is devoted primarily to planning and coordinating all marketing activities. The traditional line marketing responsibility—management of the sales force—is delegated to a subordinate, the general sales manager. Other marketing staff responsibilities—such as advertising, marketing information, and credit management—are moved from various other organizational slots and now come under the direction of the chief marketing executive, enabling him or her to exert a greater total impact on marketing strategy and tactics. Similarly, newly created staff divisions, such as product management and physical distribution, are organizationally located in ways that facilitate their coordination—by the chief marketing executive—with other marketing activities.

dividing marketing line authority

Line executives are those in the direct chain of command whose jobs consist mainly of managing subordinates who directly accomplish the company's goals of selling the product or service. In a marketing organization, the chief marketing executive is also its top line executive, and the direct chain of command runs from him or her down through the sales organization (since it is the sales force that ultimately and directly performs the work leading to company goals). Generally, however, he or she assigns the major responsibility for sales force management to a subordinate—the sales vice-president or general manager—who is then regarded as the marketing organization's principal line executive. When the sales force is small, the principal line executive manages it directly. But as the sales force expands, line authority is divided among subordinate sales executives.

GEOGRAPHIC DIVISION When a sales force is deployed over a wide area, line authority is often divided geographically: with an Eastern sales manager, a Southern sales manager, and so on. Geographic division of authority is especially appropriate when the market or buyers or both vary in character from region to region. Each sales region can adapt its selling methods more closely to the needs and customs of local markets. However, the underlying reason for dividing line authority geographically is to improve the sales force's effectiveness by increasing the frequency of executive contacts with sales personnel and by simplifying and strengthening their supervision. Subordinate sales managers devote their main efforts to improving the performances of the sales personnel under them.

PRODUCT DIVISION   Sometimes a company's products dictate the organization of its sales force. When variations among products requires that sales personnel apply considerably different selling methods and possess a wide range of technical know-how, line authority may be divided by products and separate sales forces set up for each product or product group. General Electric requires different kinds of sales personnel to sell large electrical generators and small household appliances. Generator salespeople need technical training and sometimes must be prepared to wait years for their first order from a utility company; small appliance salespeople need little technical training and perform routine selling work. It would be wasteful to use the more technically trained personnel to sell both types of products, so separate selling groups are maintained, each qualified to sell its particular products and each reporting to its own sales executive.

Maintaining separate sales forces for different products is expensive because it frequently results in more than one salesperson covering the same geographical areas. Thus, the benefits should clearly outweigh the extra cost. These benefits are greatest for companies selling broadly diversified product lines (such as IBM's computer and typewriter divisions), for companies reaching different markets with different products (such as GM's autos and refrigerators), and for companies having individual products with unique selling problems (such as Dupont with industrial chemicals and nylon fiber).

CUSTOMER OR MARKETING CHANNEL DIVISION   When customers or marketing channels for a product or group of products vary substantially, it may be appropriate to divide line authority on a customer or market basis. A power-saw manufacturer, for example, sells identical products to two very different markets: the lumber industry and the construction industry. These two markets have both different geographical characteristics (lumbering is heavily concentrated in the Northwest and Southeast, whereas construction is broadly distributed relative to population and industrial concentration) and different buying practices. Under these market conditions, separate sales forces are justified.

Many marketers sell the same consumer products through multiple marketing channels. Part of the factory's output may reach consumers through wholesale distributor and independent retailer channels, another part through chain stores buying directly from the factory, and still another part through export middlemen selling to overseas markets. The type of selling required in each case is quite different, and the number and kinds of buyers vary greatly. (It takes, for example, only a few salespeople to reach all chain-store buying offices in the United States, but it takes dozens or hundreds to reach all wholesalers.) Marketers using multiple channels often find it advantageous to organize separate sales forces for each channel.

DIVISION ON SEVERAL BASES   Many companies use more than one basis for dividing line authority. Large sales organizations require several levels of management, and different bases of division may be used at different levels. When product differences require division of authority along product lines, the sales force may be organized accordingly, but if further subdivision is needed, it may be on a geographic basis. Thus, the resulting organization provides sales specialization in terms of both different product lines and geographical market differences.

division of marketing staff authority   Theoretically, staff people have purely advisory roles, with no place in the command structure and without the right to give orders, but this does not exist in practice. The nature of each staff executive's work gives him or her an intimate and broad view of line executives' problems that almost inevitably gives him or her formal authority. Furthermore, with higher management relying increasingly on processed information, the staff authority to advise becomes the authority to screen and, thus, to make decisions. Generally, divisions and allocations of staff authority are decided according to areas of special competence.

the product manager   The product manager does not fit neatly into either the line or staff categories. In large multiproduct companies, product managers are becoming increasingly common and more important. In such companies chief marketing executives are responsible for all products but neither they nor their staff subordinates give equal attention to all products in the line. Thus, there is no individual who is specifically responsible for the success or failure of a particular product. It is possible for some products to receive too little or too much promotion, for advertising programs for particular products not to be coordinated properly with sales activities, and for changes in consumer wants and competitors' actions with respect to individual products to go unheeded. The product manager's position was created in an attempt to fill such vacuums—in effect, the product manager serves as a deputy marketing director for a particular product or product group.[2] Normally, product managers concern themselves with all phases of the planning, execution, and control of marketing activities for their assigned products. They are deeply involved with the buying public, distributors, sales force, advertising agencies, product development, market-

[2] Victor P. Buell, "The Changing Role of the Product Manager in Consumer Goods Companies," *Journal of Marketing*, July 1975, pp. 3-11.

ing research, and other marketing and corporate personnel. Thus, the broad scope of their duties make product managers combination line and staff executives with respect to the products for which they are responsible.

Another way to view the organizational status of product managers is that they operate on a horizontal plane, in sharp contrast to most marketing personnel, who operate primarily on a vertical plane. Since the product manager's specialization is cross-functional, with a central focus on a specific product line or brand, his or her position is somewhat of a major departure that is not easily inserted into and absorbed by the existing organization. As a result, the position of "product manager" is difficult to define, staff, and implement for action. Yet, many companies credit a large measure of their success to the product manager concept.[3]

*organization under
the marketing concept*
Figure 2-1 shows a typical formal marketing organization for a large manufacturer operating under the marketing concept. The organization is divided into three main parts; marketing services (mainly staff responsibilities), management of personal selling (including the line organization and staff activities closely related to sales force operations), and product management. The subdivisions on the marketing services side illustrate the broad range of

[3] Ibid., pp. 6-8.

Figure 2-1   Organization under the marketing concept

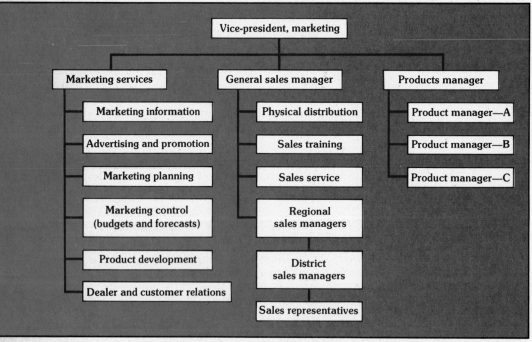

staff-type responsibilities. Those under the general sales manager, who here serves as the principal line executive, are: field sales (made up of line executives managing the sales force); sales training (a staff activity concerned with increasing selling efficiency); sales service (a staff activity involving installation, maintenance, and repair services); and physical distribution (concerned with transportation, storage, materials handling, inventory management, and movement of customers' orders). Those under the products manager are in charge of product groups A, B, and C, each product manager being responsible for coordinating all marketing activities (staff as well as line) exerted in behalf of the group's products.

Staff personnel are generally concentrated at the central office because many of their activities are similar for all products, marketing channels, and geographic regions. Centralization allows coordination of efforts and a pooling of financial resources so that the best available personnel and equipment can be brought together. Without good staff liaison at headquarters, some divisions might make decisions for their own good rather than for the good of the entire company; for example, long-range research projects might be omitted because of their immediate adverse effect on a division's profits. A strong central staff keeps division executives aware of broad company goals.

In large marketing organizations, it may still be necessary to provide staff assistance in field sales offices. In such instances, it must be decided whether (organizationally) to place these staff field executives under the authority of central office staff executives or under local line sales executives. As in other organizational decisions, the solution rests in compromise among the authority, communication, coordination, and human relations needs of the individuals and groups involved.

ORGANIZATION OF MARKETING RESPONSIBILITIES IN BUSINESS ENGAGED MAINLY IN MARKETING-TYPE ACTIVITIES

Retailers and wholesalers are specialists in marketing. They are not involved in making products, only in their distribution. They serve as stepping stones in the channels that move goods from producers to the final buyers. While to most manufacturers and other producers the marketing concept is a relatively new idea, most successful retailers and wholesalers have long had strong orientations toward their customers. Marshall Field and Company, a Chicago department store organization, for example, has promoted its slogan "The customer is always right" for nearly a century.

Marketing businesses are organized with merchandising as the primary or line function. Merchandising is defined as knowing what the customer wants and making it available at the right time and place for him or her to buy. The senior officer, or president, of most retail or wholesale establishments is generally a merchandiser, one who has moved up through various merchandising positions in the organization.

Figures 2-2 and 2-3 illustrate the organizational structures of two retailers—a large department store and a retail chain. In each of these insti-

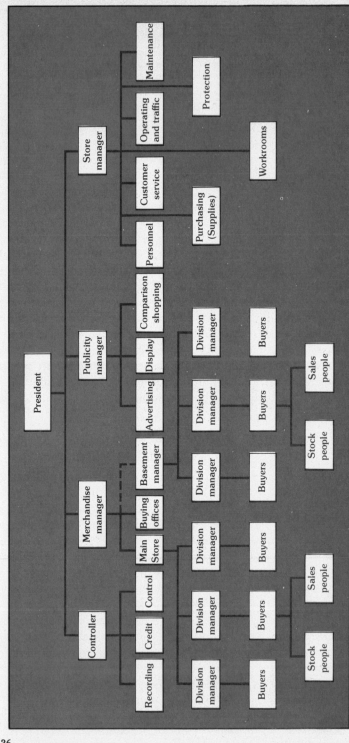

Figure 2-2   General organization chart of a department store

Figure 2-3 Organization chart for a retail chain

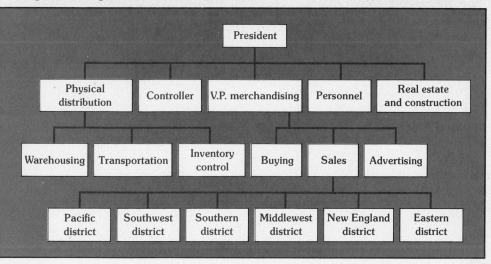

tutions merchandising responsibility is assigned to an executive who reports directly to the president. This executive, then, has primary responsibility for the buying of all merchandise for resale. Generally, too, he or she is responsible for the preparation and administration of the merchandise budget, which determines the amount of merchandise that should be bought and on hand. Yet another of his or her primary responsibilities is often that of selling the merchandise bought, through personal selling, advertising, and point-of-purchase and window display.

merchandising Department stores and independent specialty stores organize the merchandising responsibility in much the same way. Buying responsibility is divided by groupings of similar merchandise items and assigned to buying executives. In some instances, these buyers are also assigned supervisory responsibility for the sales personnel; in other cases, specialized sales executives supervise the sales personnel.

Wholesalers and chain organizations normally separate the buying and selling activities and assign responsibility for their performance to different executives. In chain organizations, buying responsibilities are centralized at the home office, but selling responsibilities are necessarily decentralized to each of the chain's retail outlets.

nonmerchandising activities The supporting, or nonmerchandising, activities common to all marketing institutions are controlling, personnel, and management of the physical plant. Both the wholesaler and the large retailer tend to organize these activities along similar lines. Controlling includes record keeping, control over costs and profits, and credit management—which is very important to market success in many marketing institutions. Personnel activities include, among others, recruitment and selection, training, supervising, and motivating of both selling and nonselling personnel. Management of the physical plant includes receiving and processing merchandise, purchasing supplies, customer service, maintenance, and protection. A wholesale or retail organization operating only a single establishment generally assigns the responsibility for traffic management and storage to the physical plant manager; but those operating multiple establishments generally have a manager of physical distribution responsible for storage, transportation, and inventory control activities. Normally, retail outlets combine promotional activities—advertising, display, and publicity—and assign the responsibility for their performance to a specialized executive.

ORGANIZATION OF MARKETING RESPONSIBILITIES IN A SERVICE BUSINESS

Businesses that market services rather than products have been slow, generally speaking, in recognizing marketing as a key element in their operations. The same has been true of nonprofit institutions, most of which continue to operate without personnel designated as marketing personnel.[4] The general tendency among service businesses has been to fragment the responsibility for performing various marketing activities; most, for instance, have no single high-ranking executive who has total responsibility for the marketing function. This is in spite of the fact that the typical service business performs marketing activities very similar to those performed by manufacturers. The failure to recognize marketing as a separate and important function and to organize personnel accordingly often results in ineffective performance of marketing activities.

In some service businesses, however—especially in those primarily engaged in providing advisory services for other businesses—the failure to recognize marketing as a separate and important function is not particularly serious. This category of service businesses includes, among others, advertising agencies, marketing research firms, and management consultants. In this type of service business, generally the head of the organization—the chief executive—personally directs and coordinates the organization's marketing activities, and, in addition, he or she is generally a marketing professional. Responsibility for performance of specific marketing activities, of course, is divided among various groups in the service organization. In the advertising agency, for example, typically the major responsibilities are divided among three groups: (1) the creative people, who develop campaign ideas and themes, write copy, do art work, and design advertising layouts; (2) the account executives, who provide liaison and continuing sales contact with the customers; and (3) the media buyers, who are responsible for determining which advertisements should appear in which media at what times.

[4] Philip Kotler, *Marketing for Nonprofit Organizations* (Englewood Cliffs, N.J.: Prentice-Hall, Inc., 1975), p. 229.

commercial banks   Although a few commercial banks have well-organized and effective marketing operations, the typical
bank gives marketing only slight organizational recognition. The typical,
traditional type of bank has an executive, often with the title of vice-president for public relations or vice-president for business development and
advertising, who is responsible for selling various banking services such as
loans, saving accounts, charge cards, and safety deposit boxes. Generally,
this executive is not at the senior vice-presidential level but, rather, reports
to an executive on that level, as illustrated in Figure 2–4. Essentially, his or
her job is that of a "sales manager" and, as such, he or she rarely plays direct
roles in such important marketing activities as market evaluation and measurement, designing service innovations and modifications, or formulating
pricing strategy. Thus, in the typical bank, responsibility for performing the
marketing function is diffused throughout the organization, with no one
executive responsible for overall marketing performance. The lack of coordination frequently results in overemphasizing some marketing activities, such
as advertising, at the expense of others, such as providing adequate customer
service at tellers' windows.

insurance companies   Again, although there are notable exceptions, the
                               typical insurance company, like the typical bank, lags
behind most manufacturers in recognizing the marketing concept in their
organizations. Insurance companies tend toward a strong sales orientation,

Figure 2–4   Organization of a typical traditional commercial bank

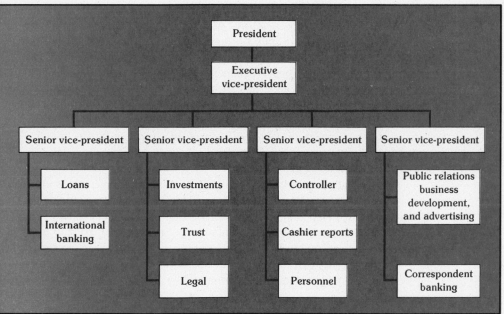

since the services they sell, although certainly necessary ones, rarely sell themselves. Potential policyholders are reluctant to think about disaster and death, so they postpone planning for these possibilities until they are contacted and influenced by insurance agents. Thus, the insurance company's natural orientation is toward sales, not marketing. Typically, its organization chart shows a sales executive on the same level as others responsible for selection of risks (product planning), policy writing (customer service), rating or actuarial (pricing), and agency management (distribution)—all marketing activities. As is true of most banks, then, no insurance company executive has responsibility for or control over the whole group of marketing activities that make up an integrated marketing strategy.

ORGANIZATION OF MARKETING RESPONSIBILITIES IN A NONPROFIT ORGANIZATION

Until recently marketing has been viewed as of concern only to profit-seeking organizations. This reflected the narrow concept that marketing is nothing more than demand creation. With a broadening in the concept of what marketing is, many scholars have pointed to the opportunities nonprofit organizations have to benefit from marketing.[5] Nonprofit organizations generally recognize the need for promotional inputs (advertising, special promotions, and even personal selling), but they tend to ignore other marketing inputs. For example, they give little consideration to consumer desires or needs in product planning. For example, hospitals could serve patients much more effectively by setting up a separate *nonemergency* facility to serve such patients who now have no choice but to go to the emergency room along with the more critical cases. Symphonies could serve their constituencies much more effectively by measuring listeners' preferences in music. Although conductors may feel a responsibility to educate the public through exposure to new and innovative music, they can also balance their programs with present favorites. Other marketing inputs can also prove beneficial to nonprofit institutions. A museum could enormously increase its exposure and impact by providing traveling exhibits in semitrailers scheduled for visits to schools or shopping centers. A careful look at pricing and price elasticity by concert givers might result in increased usage of existing facilities. A symphony could offer vacant seats to high school students at drastically reduced rates, thus developing a group of future regular patrons.

Figure 2-5 illustrates the present lack of marketing expertise input in most nonprofit organizations. In this case, product decisions are made by the music director, with no organized input from patrons and customers. The organization is clearly production- (production of music) oriented, and marketing decisions are divided among a number of people, mostly unpaid board members. Pricing decisions are based on cost (not on market) factors, and promotion is minimal and unimaginative.

[5] Philip Kotler and Sidney J. Levy, "Broadening the Concept of Marketing," *Journal of Marketing*, January 1969, pp. 3–9.

Figure 2-5   Organization of a typical symphony orchestra

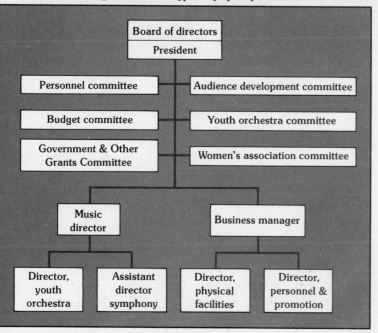

SUMMARY   You should now have a good understanding of how businesses organize the complex relationships among both people and activities to achieve their various goals. Developing an effective marketing organization begins with the identification of overall company goals and determination of their implications for marketing. As the necessity for making the transition to the marketing concept becomes increasingly clear, management looks more and more to its target markets for guidance and seeks to structure the organization so that both the market is served effectively and overall organizational goals are reached. Managerial attitudes toward the marketing concept show up in the ways in which marketing activities are organized in various kinds of enterprises.

Management's approach to total company organization, as well as to marketing organization, should be dynamic. An organization that is satisfactory today may prove inadequate tomorrow. Markets themselves change because of changes in income, shifts in population, changes in tastes and life-styles, and the like. Market changes, coupled with technological advances, result in a flow of new products and the continual modification of old products. Furthermore, important developments in mass communications media and in marketing channels have been occurring and more such changes should be expected. A significant change in any market factor can reduce the effectiveness of an organizational structure not only for serving the market's needs but as a vehicle for achieving the company's goals. Since market factors are forever in a state of change, continual monitoring and regular reappraisal of organizational effectiveness are imperative.

41

1. "Management of an organization largely involves the solution of problems in communication." How does this generalization apply to the management of a marketing organization? Give some examples.

2. Company A wants to have the largest sales volume in its industry. Company B wants to be the first to introduce product innovations in the industry. Assuming that both A and B compete in the same industry, how would these differences in goals likely result in rather different types of marketing organizations? What impact do company objectives have on a company's marketing organization?

3. Who is responsible for bringing the need for adopting the marketing concept to top management's attention? Why?

4. As more and more "market emphasis" permeates top management's business philosophy, what changes come about in marketing organization?

5. Should the marketing function dominate the organization in a company operating under the marketing concept? Why or why not?

6. Which type of responsibility, staff (e.g., marketing research manager) or line (e.g., sales manager), is likely to give the best preparation for the job of chief marketing executive?

7. "Staff executives represent the thinking arm of the organization, and line executives tend to react more automatically on the basis of experience." Evaluate this statement.

8. Why are product managers so common today? Why is it that the product manager does not fit neatly into either the line or staff category? Do problems arise because of this? Explain.

9. Under what circumstances should a marketing organization divide line authority geographically? By products? By marketing channels? On more than one basis?

10. The almost continuous change in the structure of many marketing organizations has been explained as resulting from the dynamic character of marketing. Do you agree? Why or why not?

11. Why have most service businesses been slow in recognizing marketing as a key element in their operations? Discuss.

12. Are the principles of sound marketing organization as applicable to nonprofit organizations as they are to profit-seeking institutions? As applicable to service businesses as in companies marketing a product? Why or why not?

13. It has been said that use of product managers results in excessive intracompany competition. Comment.

14. Are manufacturers more likely or less likely than retailers to exhibit a commitment to the marketing concept? Explain your choice. Is one in a more advantageous position than the other when it comes to a consumer orientation?

15. Describe the historical shifts in top management's business philosophy.

16. What are the implications of the company's profit objective for the marketing organization?

CASE PROBLEM

Quality Foods was a large food products company with manufacturing and distribution centers throughout the country. The company had four major divisions: food products, beverages, coffee, and pet foods. For the individual divisions, the product management system was used to direct the development of each specific product group. Each division had a marketing manager responsible for guiding its overall marketing program. The marketing manager supervised the product managers. Official company policies stated that the product manager's role was to create strategies and plans for a group of products, to see that these plans were implemented through the production, distribution, and promotion functions, and to evaluate results and take corrective action where needed.

A particular problem had arisen in the pet foods division. In the past year, sales of the Top Pride line of canned and dry dog food had not grown nearly as fast as anticipated. Elizabeth Bynam, product manager for the Top Pride line, thought that a good part of the problem stemmed from poor shelf position in three of the major supermarket chains carrying the line. Her appraisal was based on several reports by field salespeople who complained that competitors were gaining advantageous shelf positions, and they were not sure why. Subsequently, Bynam offered a package of special incentives, such as a consumer coupon campaign, a discount for utilizing an elaborate end-of-aisle display she had developed personally, and a series of advertising specialties (calendars, pens, and key chains). Believing that better rapport between the company and its dealers was the key, she also launched a campaign to improve cooperation from these major distributors. To lend authenticity to the company's desire to improve distributor relations, Bynam felt that she had to maximize her own personal contact with the distributors. Over the past two months, while Bynam spent most of her time in the field working on her distribution strategy, other aspects of her job received less than normal attention. She delegated responsibility for coordinating the advertising campaign to her new assistant, who had difficulty establishing rapport with the advertising agency. The marketing research department hounded the assistant for some major decisions concerning the study planned to estimate new market potential, a study that was supposed to get under way soon. Accounting sent memos concerning the poor profit picture during the last quarter. Bynam was aware of the buildup of problems back at headquarters, but she felt that her time was needed right now in the field ironing out the distribution network.

Mark Ganet, marketing manager for the Pet Foods Division, felt that Bynam should be spending the bulk of her time at headquarters managing the long-range planning and sales forecasting for the Top Pride dog food line. He felt that troubleshooting in a specific area should be delegated to Bynam's assistant. Furthermore, the sales force, he believed, should do much of what Bynam was doing. He was convinced that without coordinated long-range strategy, the product group would lose market position.

But, Bynam persisted in her belief that improved distributor relations were so important as to deserve nothing less than management attention.

questions:

1. Whose side of the argument do you favor?
2. Explain the role of the product manager in a situation such as that described here.
3. What should be done?

When you have mastered the contents of this chapter, you should be able to:

1   Identify examples of marketing activities, given descriptions of situations in which marketing activities are or are not being performed.

2   Name the nine activities generally classified as marketing activities.

3   Give examples of the different ways in which each of the four kinds of merchandising activities may be performed.

4   Explain why performance of the physical distribution activities (storage and transportation) is both necessary and important.

5   Explain why marketers perform (or do not perform) each of the three supporting activities.

6   Explain why no general scheme for classifying marketing activities is universally applicable.

7   Discuss the relationship of the performance of marketing activities to marketing efficiency.

the marketing process

Marketing, as defined earlier, is the managerial process by which products and services are matched with markets and through which ownership transfers are effected. Thus, the two general purposes (goals) of marketing are to obtain and to service demand, but each company also has additional and more specific marketing goals whose nature varies both with its own situation and its overall company goals. For example, a company that has a reputation for leadership in product innovation not only attempts to obtain and service demand but continues to work toward furthering its reputation as a leader in product innovation. Both the inputs (marketing activities) and the outputs (marketing goals), then, vary with the company and its overall goals. Specific companies perform and combine different marketing activities in highly individualized ways, not only to obtain and service demand but to work toward other more specific marketing goals. [1]

IDENTIFICATION OF MARKETING ACTIVITIES

Identifying marketing activities might seem simple because it would appear necessary only to itemize those steps required to move products and services from producers to final buyers. But the task is complicated by difficulties met in determining just where marketing begins and ends. It is oversimplifying to assume that marketing activities are concerned only with the flow of products and services. To achieve marketing efficiency, there must also be a reverse flow of information, from the market to the producer. To produce salable records a recording company must know what the buyer wants (what

[1] Our thinking on this subject has been strongly influenced by the perceptive article of R. J. Lewis and L. G. Erickson, "Marketing Functions and Marketing Systems: A Synthesis," *Journal of Marketing*, July 1969, pp. 10-14. See also T. L. Sporleder, "Marketing Functions and Marketing Systems: A Synthesis—A Comment," *Journal of Marketing*, July 1970, pp. 63-64.

is currently popular). Conceptually, then, the marketing process both begins and ends with the final buyer, with information flowing back to the producer and products flowing forward to the final buyer.

Those marketing activities most easily identified are ones concerned with bringing products into contact with markets. Selling is one of these. Buying, the other side of selling, is not so easy to identify as a marketing activity, the ease of identification varying with who is buying. For instance, the buying of merchandise for resale is one of the retailer's most important tasks, for, to achieve his goal of selling goods to consumers, he must buy those things consumers need and want. But is buying as clearly a marketing activity for the manufacturer? In some cases, the manufacturer's buying decision is influenced by the effect the purchase has on the product's market-ability; in other cases, it is influenced by the effect on product costs. The selection and purchase of materials for television cabinets mainly affects the finished product's marketability, but the selection and purchase of parts and materials for the receiving equipment itself is largely a production and cost problem. In most instances, both marketing and production needs influence buying decisions. So manufacturers properly look upon buying as a market-ing activity whose performance is frequently conditioned by production and cost considerations.

Activities not directly concerned with bringing products into contact with markets are more difficult to identify. For instance, although planning and designing the product may not seem like marketing activities, products must possess those characteristics that final buyers want and desire. In order to prevent market failure, these wants and desires should be discovered in an early stage of product development.

The final buyer often personally performs some marketing activities. Marketers strive to move products and services into the hands of final buy-ers, but it does not follow that all marketing then ceases. For example, storage is generally classified as a marketing activity. Potatoes, produced seasonally, are held and sold throughout the year by marketing institutions, but sometimes individual consumers take over part of the storage activity—they may buy potatoes by the bushel to store in their homes. The storage activity continues to be performed, but by consumers rather than marketing organizations.

A CLASSIFICATION OF MARKETING ACTIVITIES

Classification of marketing activities facilitates analy-sis of specific situations, but no general classification does or can apply to every marketing situation. Any classification scheme needs some modification to fit the particular analytical requirements imposed by an individual company's marketing circumstances. Keeping this restriction in mind, we classify marketing activities into three general categories, containing nine activities in all:

Merchandising Activities
  1. Product planning and development
  2. Standardizing and grading
  3. Buying and assembling
  4. Selling
Physical Distribution Activities
  5. Storage
  6. Transportation
Supporting Activities
  7. Marketing financing
  8. Marketing risk bearing
  9. Obtaining and analyzing marketing information

These activities are arranged in a logical sequence. Merchandising begins with an analysis of market needs and the development or procurement of products to meet these needs, and it ends with the activities involved in stimulating market demand most directly. Physical distribution makes the products available at the times and places desired by final buyers. Supporting activities, generally speaking, have the main purpose of improving the effectiveness with which merchandising and physical distribution activities are performed.

merchandising   Merchandising consists of activities necessary to determine and meet market needs with products or services and to stimulate market demand. Some marketing writers classify standardizing and grading as auxiliary or supportive activities. We include them as merchandising activities chiefly because they involve managing product uniformity and consistency.

PRODUCT PLANNING AND DEVELOPMENT   Most products, to be marketed successfully, must possess characteristics that conform rather closely to buyers' needs, wants, and desires, and this requires frequent product adaptation, or **product planning and development.** In most industries this process is endless—with product improvements flowing from changing technology, while shifts in buyer preferences simultaneously create continuing product obsolescence. In a rapidly changing industry such as pharmaceuticals, products developed within the last 20 years normally account for over half the sales and profits of the leading companies. In such industries, the noninnovating company almost certainly faces eventual elimination from the market. In other industries, where rates of product obsolescence are slower, the elimination process takes place over longer time spans. For example, in the writing-instrument industry, over a 20-year period of time the Parker Pen Company slipped from a position of dominance to only a small market share because their very successful fountain pen was made obsolete by ballpoint pens.

Growing recognition of the importance of satisfying buyers' changing product preferences is evidenced by the trend among manufacturers toward making the marketing department increasingly responsible for product planning and development. Middlemen have always regarded product planning and development, which for them usually takes the form of changes in products handled or services offered, as crucial to their success.

A hardware wholesaler who adds a line of lawn seed and fertilizer is engaging in product planning. A men's clothing store that adds a selection of women's clothing or abandons delivery service is also doing product planning. Both retailers and wholesalers call such changes merchandising, but what they are actually doing is comparable to what manufacturers do under the name of product planning and development.

STANDARDIZING AND GRADING These activities involve establishment of basic measures or limits to which articles must consistantly conform. A standard specifies what basic qualities a product must have to be designated consistent with established characteristics. Standards should be based on the qualities desired by buyers or on the use to which the article is to be put. For example, in clothing manufacturing, it is useful to establish standards of size so that all size 12 dresses will fit the same people. Grading is the act of separating or inspecting nonmanufactured goods according to established specifications. The specifications are set by the standards established and may include size, weight, or quality.

Standardizing and grading are important to efficient marketing. Both make it possible for customers to purchase by description instead of by inspection: for example, to order a ton of steel or coal of a specified grade by mail or by telephone. Both make it possible to merchandise products closer to what customers want. A mixed lot of ungraded fruits is less attractive to prospective customers and commands a lower total price than the same lot after it has been graded into lots of equal size and appearance and priced by grade.

Grading also helps in streamlining the physical handling of many farm crops because it makes possible the mixing of lots belonging to different owners for storage and transportation. This permits the grain elevator operator to store the crops of different farmers in a single elevator. It also allows the transportation company to mix the same crops in shipment.

Standardization, the application of standards, relates mainly to manufactured products. Its first step involves establishing physical standards to which the product should conform. After an industry has selected standards, each manufacturer should assess its own place in the market. Thus, a men's suit manufacturer can measure the potential market for each suit size and either produce each size in proportion to the probable demand or produce only certain more popular sizes.

Grading refers to the application of basic descriptive standards—such as size, color, or weight—to the products of nature where growers or producers have very limited control over their products' physical specifications. Since the U.S. Department of Agriculture has set standards for the sizes and grades of oranges, for example, growers sort their crops according to these sizes and end up with oranges in each of several sizes or grades, each of which commands a higher price than ungraded fruit. For grading to be used, all properties to be graded must be measurable. Thus, canned peaches can be graded in terms of properties such as sugar content, color, and size, but they cannot be graded in terms of taste, since there is no objective way to measure differences in individual tastes.

Standardizing is most effective when adopted on an industry-wide basis. Otherwise, a consumer may not confidently expect a size 9 to be the same regardless of the maker. Standardization in each industry is normally voluntary.

BUYING AND ASSEMBLING   **Buying**, as a marketing activity, is the procurement of items for eventual resale to ultimate consumers or industrial users. Most of the items purchased by producers are used in the manufacturing process and generally reach final buyers in a different form as part of finished products. By contrast, the products middlemen buy are resold by them in essentially the same form to other middlemen or to final buyers.

Assembling is closely related to buying. It involves bringing together either (1) different quantities of a wide variety of items for resale by a single establishment or (2) a large quantity of similar items for resale in a particular region. The first type of assembling is performed by retailers, such as department stores and supermarkets, who bring together products from many diverse sources, making it possible for consumers to satisfy a variety of wants on a one-stop shopping trip. The second type is illustrated by the operations of centrally located wholesalers of agricultural produce, who buy from numerous growers throughout the country and distribute the assembled produce to local wholesalers for eventual resale by retailers. Although the manufacturer also engages in assembling when it procures materials, and the like, most assembling is performed by middlemen.

Successful buying requires the ability to estimate customer's needs weeks and even months in advance. When ordering merchandise that will be delivered and placed on sale two or three months later, retailers, for example, try to anticipate what consumers will do in the future, even though consumers are not sure themselves. The successful fashion goods buyer, for example, must guess in January which styles, colors, and skirt lengths will satisfy customers buying dresses in June. It is important to know customers' needs and buying habits to predict their buying actions. A retail store must know the consumers who comprise its market, their income levels, their product preferences, their shopping habits, and so forth. A wholesaler must have just as complete an understanding of its customers—the retailers—and at least a general knowledge about their customers. Similarly, the manufacturer must be familiar with the buying habits, financial capabilities, promotional policies, and other characteristics of its immediate customers and must also be acquainted with the needs and buying patterns of other marketing intermediaries and of final buyers.

SELLING **Selling,** in its broad sense, has the purpose not only of making sales (i.e., effecting ownership transfers) but of identifying prospective customers, stimulating demand, and providing information and service to buyers. In working toward these goals, the marketer must combine such activities as personal selling, advertising, sales promotion, packaging, and customer service. Management does not usually rely on any one selling activity but tries, through continuous experimentation, to find an effective combination. (A blend of selling activities coordinated into a sales program is called a **promotional mix.**) Skill is needed not only in planning an optimum promotional mix, but in coordinating the different selling activities.

1. *Personal Selling.* **Personal selling** is the chief means through which marketing programs are implemented. The unique strength of personal selling lies in its ability to personalize sales messages for individual customers. Capitalizing fully on this strength, however, requires trained and competent sales personnel. Substantial investments must be made in recruiting, training, paying, and supervising the sales force—thus, personal selling appears to be a relatively high cost selling method.

The cost of each advertising message per prospect reached is much lower than the cost of each personal sales contact. But since it often takes many advertising messages to move a prospect to buying action, personal selling is not necessarily most costly. Generally, management seeks to minimize selling costs through the use of some combination of personal selling and other sales activities. In theory, all selling activities—personal selling, advertising, and so on—should be used up to the point where their marginal efficiencies are equated.

2. *Advertising.* Because **advertising** generally is a relatively low-cost way to convey selling messages to numerous prospects, it is important in most marketing programs. It is used not only to stimulate demand but for many other purposes. It can secure leads for salespersons and middlemen by convincing readers, listeners, and viewers to request more information and by identifying outlets handling the product. It can force middlemen to stock the product by building consumer interest. It can help train dealers' salespeople in product use and applications. And it can build dealer and consumer confidence in the company and its products by building familiarity.

Marketing management's most frequent assignment to advertising is to stimulate market demand. By using advertising to presell customers—that is, to arouse and intensify their buying interest in advance—management hopes to facilitate the sales force's selling task. Although advertising alone may sometimes succeed in achieving buyer acceptance, preference, or even demand for the product, it is usually most efficiently used with at least one other sales method, such as personal selling or point-of-purchase display. These are generally more effective in directly moving customers to buying action. Effective advertising by a manufacturer, for instance, often arouses consumers' interest, but it will rarely send them to retail stores actively seeking the product. However, when they are in a store, and alert clerks or attractive displays call their attention to the manufacturer's product, the impact of previous advertising often helps in persuading them to buy.

3. *Point-of-Purchase Display.* **Point-of-purchase display** supplements and coordinates personal selling and advertising, helping to make them more effective. Its main purpose is to impel on-the-spot buying action by prospects. An attractive display of fresh strawberries can attract many shoppers who had not planned to buy them at all. It is used much more extensively in marketing consumer products than in industrial marketing, chiefly because ultimate consumers are more susceptible to making impulse purchases. Furthermore, with the spread of self-service retailing, consumers seeking product information have come to depend less on salesclerks and more on such sales promotional devices.

4. *Packaging.* Marketing management expects the package to attract consumers' attention at the point of purchase, furnish them with needed information about the product, and provide the extra push so often required to propel them into buying. With the spread of self-service retailing, **packaging**—like point-of-purchase display—has risen in importance as a marketing activity. Traditionally, the package was regarded solely as a container for the product, and production departments had exclusive responsibility for packaging.

The package's basic role is still that of a container, but today it is also expected to play important marketing roles. In most consumer product marketing programs, for example, the package is designed to relate the product to the manufacturer's advertising, thus improving the chances that consumers will recognize it in retail outlets. In selling through self-service retail outlets, the manufacturer's sales personnel are responsible for persuading retailers to stock the product; advertising is responsible for making consumers aware of the product, its uses, and its advantages; and packaging is responsible for tying in the sales force's efforts and advertising's impact.

5. *Customer Service.* As a selling activity, **customer service** provides assistance and advice on such things as product installation, operation, maintenance, and repair. For many prospective buyers, availability and adequacy of customer service are major factors in the choice among competing sellers. Thus, consumers may prefer Dodge cars because they like the local dealer's repair service. By providing superior customer service, a seller may obtain the patronage of certain buyers even in the face of strong price competition. As more technical features are added to a product and it becomes more complicated to install, operate, and maintain, customer service gains in importance as an instrument of competition.

physical distribution   Storage and transportation are the activities necessary to move products from their times and places of production to their times and places of consumption. In a highly developed and complex economy, such as that in the United States, most of each producer's customers are located hundreds and even thousands of miles away, and products must be transported to and stored at points more accessible to them. Furthermore, in developed countries, such as those in Western Europe and North America, most manufacturers produce in anticipation of market demand and hold inventories until orders are received and filled. In developing countries, by contrast, many manufacturers wait for orders before they begin manufacturing and have minimum stocks of finished products. As countries develop and as multinational trade increases, both storage and transportation, as well as inventory management and the processing and handling of customers' orders, increase in importance.

STORAGE Products are held in **storage** for either or both of two reasons, to ensure their availability to customers when they want them, or to meet the needs of the marketer.

1. *Ensuring Availability to Customers.* In our complex economic system products are generally produced in anticipation of market demand so that they can be delivered to customers without undue delays. Stocks may be maintained at all levels of distribution, and when a purchase is made at one level, these stocks fluctuate all along the line. When the family lawn mower breaks down, a new one is purchased from the hardware dealer, who then replaces the mower from the wholesaler, who, in turn, buys more mowers from the manufacturer. Each distribution level maintains an inventory of mowers so as to provide instant service to customers on the next level.

2. *Needs of the Marketer.* Marketers have three important reasons for holding products in storage. One is to even out the seasonal factor in production or in sales. A manufacturer of Christmas ornaments, for example, has a market for its products only during the immediate pre-Christmas period, but its costs are lower if production is carried on throughout the year; so it stores its output from one selling season to the next. Similarly, many farm products are harvested in one season but are bought and consumed throughout the year, so growers and middlemen store them from one harvesting season to the next. A second reason for storage is to obtain economies in other business operations: for instance, manufacturers who make products in a large number of sizes, such as nuts and bolts, use the same machines to produce different sizes. It is often more economical to schedule long production runs of several weeks' supply of particular sizes rather than making the total needs of each size weekly. A third reason for storing products is to improve their quality and value—products such as cheese, whisky, and tobacco must be aged or conditioned to improve their flavor and, hence, to increase their value.

TRANSPORTATION Because most markets are geographically separated from production areas, **transportation** is a necessary and important marketing activity. Many factories are located away from urban areas to avoid population and traffic congestion and high land costs, with the expectation that the lower costs incurred in a nonurban location will more than offset the costs of moving finished products to urban markets. Other factories are separated from their largest markets through historical accident. For instance, many businesses start up in the founder's hometown, and as they prosper and grow, the founder seeks ever-farther-removed markets for the expanding production. Eventually, strong reasons develop for building additional plants nearer the larger and more distant markets, but many manufacturers conclude that lower production costs in a single large plant more than offset transportation costs to distant markets. Or, as in the situation of Coors beer, a desire for better quality control in a single brewery results in high transportation cost. In some industries, such as lumber and steel, where transportation costs for raw materials are higher than for the finished products, manufacturing facilities are located near raw material sources with little regard for market location. Regardless of the location of production facilities, transporting products to markets is an important distributive activity.

supporting activities   The supporting activities do not relate directly to ownership transfers but support or contribute to other marketing activities. Supporting activities include marketing financing, marketing risk bearing, and obtaining and analyzing marketing information. Because of the relationships these activities bear to the formulation of marketing and other basic business policies, top management often seems to pay closer attention to them than it does to others.

MARKETING FINANCING   Marketers, both as receivers and sources of credit, are concerned with financing. As receivers, they sometimes use short-term financing to tide their operations over seasonal peaks that require additional inventory investments and higher promotional expenses. Many retailers, for instance, increase their inventories 50 percent or more during the months just before Christmas and increase their salesforces and advertising outlays accordingly; if permanent capital investments were kept at a level high enough to meet these seasonal needs, much money would lie unproductive the rest of the year. Consequently, most enterprises finance seasonal variations in marketing expenses through credit.

Marketing organizations have two main sources of credit: trade credit and banks. **Trade credit,** highly important in short-term financing, is extended by suppliers. Manufacturers and middlemen offer their customers credit terms allowing them from as few as 10 to as many as 120 or more days in which to pay. Trade sources are usually willing to assume greater credit risks than are banks, but trade credit can also be more expensive, especially when interest is charged on overdue balances.

Providing credit to customers is essential to the success of most marketers. Most "big ticket" consumer durables, such as automobiles and furniture, are sold on the installment plan; surprisingly few consumers are both able and willing to pay cash for such items, and there is no doubt that **installment credit** has contributed significantly to the development of mass markets for many consumer durables. Many retailers use credit (in the form of charge accounts or through honoring various credit cards) as one means of attracting patronage. At the wholesale level, most transactions are on a credit basis. **Mercantile credit,** which is granted by manufacturers and wholesalers, not only assists in but simplifies ownership transfers. By extending credit to buyers, the seller avoids the undesirable alternatives of having transportation companies make collections on delivery or asking customers to pay at the time of order placement.

MARKETING RISK BEARING Marketing risks arise from both supply and demand changes and natural hazards; one such risk is **inventory risk.** Any institution that carries an inventory takes the risk that supply and demand conditions may change, that buyers will no longer want the product, or that prices will fall. Thus, marketers who perform the storage activity also perform not only financing (by taking ownership) but risk bearing. Most marketing institutions have the problem of deciding on the proper size of inventories. There is always risk that an inventory will not be sold if it proves too large relative to market demand. But there is also risk that if it proves too small, orders will be lost because they cannot be filled.

Risk transfer occurs when a marketer transfers part of its risk burden, eliminating some risks entirely and converting others from unpredictable amounts of potential loss to known items of expense. For example, when a seller agrees to reimburse a buyer for any drop in a product's price within a given period, the buyer succeeds in transferring the entire risk of a price decline during the period to the seller. **Hedging** provides another way to transfer the risks of price changes in a limited number of items traded on organized commodity exchanges. [2]

Risks attached to such natural hazards as fire and floods, deterioration of products in storage, and damage in transit can often be transferred to institutions that specialize in assuming such risks. Insurance companies cover all these risks in return for premium payments. When risks are transferred in this way, unpredictable amounts of potential loss become known amounts of expense.

Because many marketing risks cannot be transferred, marketers concentrate on trying to reduce them, which is known as **risk reduction.** Risks of changes in market demand are reduced through accurate sales forecasting and marketing research. For example, while available techniques for market measurement are by no means foolproof, a well-considered sales forecast can help reduce the margin of error in deciding on inventory size. Also, risk of a change in market demand is reducible through aggressive programs of advertising, personal selling, and the like. Reasonably accurate sales fore-

[2] *Hedging* is a procedure involving simultaneous sales in the futures market when purchases are made in the current (spot) market, and simultaneous purchases in the futures market when sales are made in the current market, so that gains or losses on current transactions are approximately balanced off against the opposite experience in the futures market.

casting should also help in reducing the supply risk of being out of stock and unable to fill customers' orders.

Other risks involved in changing supply conditions, such as the risk that an oversupply will cause competitors to cut prices, may be partially offset by differentiating products with the aim of making customers reluctant to accept substitutes. To the extent that **product differentiation** succeeds in building customer loyalty, a marketer gains a degree of monopoly control over the product's supply. However, product differentiation only reduces the risk of price competition; it does not eliminate it. Few marketers ever succeed in completely differentiating their products.

OBTAINING AND ANALYZING MARKETING INFORMATION   Both for the sound formulation of marketing programs and for the intelligent direction of marketing activities, management needs to obtain and analyze a great deal of **marketing information.** The success of a company's marketing operations depends largely upon management's knowledge and appraisal of such important information as the size, location, and characteristics of different markets for the products; the nature of present and prospective customers making up various market segments, their needs and wants, and their buying habits and preferences; competitors' strengths, weaknesses, activities, and plans; and trends in market supply and demand. Management secures these types of marketing information, appraises the significance, and adjusts company operations accordingly.

Besides the general types of information mentioned above, particular items of market information are often important. For example, the fact that a market glut for lettuce exists in Chicago is important to a Texas lettuce grower planning shipments to that area. Similarly, knowing the extent to which Pacific Coast steel users are buying Japanese-made steel is important information to a domestic steel producer. Likewise, it is important for an upstate New York manufacturer of room air conditioners to learn as soon as possible of a run on its product in Washington, D.C. Such items—which have immediate, though often fleeting, implications—are called **market news,** to distinguish them from other pieces of marketing information that generally have longer range and continuing significance.

Marketing information is gathered in diverse ways. Executives obtain much market news rather informally through casual conversation; from reading business and trade publications, syndicated market newsletters, and daily newspapers; from newscasts; and from reports submitted by field sales executives and sales personnel. More formal information-gathering methods are used to obtain marketing information of long-range significance. Sales analysis techniques are applied in combing company records for information about customers and markets. Marketing research methods are used in tapping information sources outside the company. Economic and business forecasting techniques are used to secure important information on future market conditions.

VARIATIONS IN CLASSIFICATION OF MARKETING ACTIVITIES

Although availability of a systemized classification of marketing activities assists in studying marketing and its problems, no such classification scheme is universally applicable in analyzing the activities of particular companies or industries. For a cosmetics manufacturer, packaging and advertising may be so important that they deserve classification as separate marketing activities; while storage may be so unimportant as not to deserve separate classification. Each marketer should set up its own classification of marketing activities, emphasizing those important to the operation's success, deemphasizing others. Each company has its own individualized set of company and marketing goals, and the list of marketing activities is simply a compilation of those necessary to achieve these goals.

The numbers and kinds of marketing activities required vary with the marketer, the product, and the distribution method, and we may reasonably ask whether it is meaningful to classify activities performed under diverse circumstances into general groups. Certainly, for example, farmers, unlike manufacturers, cannot change the design of their products. Melon growers know that consumers would prefer seedless watermelons, but they cannot develop them personally. They can only hope that plant scientists will eventually succeed in doing so. Hence, farmers appear naturally to have little practical interest in product design. Despite such variances, different marketers still share enough common goals and activities to justify generalizations about the marketing activities they perform.

PERFORMANCE OF MARKETING ACTIVITIES AND MARKETING EFFICIENCY

Some marketing critics assert that repetition in performance of marketing activities is a sure sign of inefficiency. In evaluating this criticism, we must admit that some activities are performed at each distribution level—buying and selling, for example, may be performed several times, since each middleman, interposed between producer and final buyer, customarily both buys and sells. But, seeing this as further evidence of inefficiency, the critics suggest that marketing costs could be reduced through eliminating certain middlemen. Following this line of reasoning to its logical end, the most efficient marketing system would stress direct sales by producers to final users. In some instances, of course, as in marketing certain industrial products, direct sale is the most efficient marketing system; but, in most situations, direct sale is not very efficient, and in marketing many consumer products it is impractical. Agricultural marketing provides numerous examples—direct distribution of potatoes or oranges by thousands of growers would not only be prohibitively expensive but highly inconvenient for consumers, most of whom prefer to buy several food items at once and at a time of their own choosing.

Even with such manufactured products as soap and flour, produced mainly by a few large companies, direct sale is impractical because consumers buy these products frequently and in small quantities so that the amount of money realized from each transaction would be insufficient to cover the costs of reaching the customer. Marketing channels for such products are necessarily complex and long, and individual marketing activities must be performed repeatedly as products move from producers to final buyers. At each distribution level, these activities are performed in specialized ways; under these conditions, shortening the marketing channel often results in increased costs and reduced efficiency.

The question is not which activities have to be performed but rather which combination of marketing institutions can perform them most efficiently. Ultimately, marketing efficiency results from finding the optimum division of responsibility among the institutions performing the activities at different distribution levels.

SUMMARY   Discussion in this chapter has focused on the marketing process and the activities performed during its various phases. While the marketing process, conceptually speaking, both begins and ends with the product's final buyer, specific companies combine and perform different marketing activities (making up the process) in highly individualized ways, not only to obtain and service demand but to achieve other, more specific goals. Thus, no general classification of marketing activities does or can apply to every marketing situation, but individually designed classification schemes do facilitate analysis of specific situations. Consequently, each company needs its own classification scheme, detailing those activities necessary to achieve its own unique set of company and marketing goals. Such goals determine which marketing activities are necessary, and marketing efficiency results ultimately from finding the optimum division of responsibilty among different institutions performing them.

REVIEW AND DISCUSSION QUESTIONS

1 | Identification of marketing activities is sometimes a complicated matter. Explain.
2 | What department in a company do you feel should be responsible for product planning and development? Why?
3 | Discuss the reasons why standardizing and grading are important to efficient marketing.
4 | In what way is assembling related to buying? Discuss.
5 | Selling is the most important marketing activity. Agree or disagree? Justify your position.
6 | Explain the importance of storage.
7 | The only reason transportation is an important activity is that markets and production sites are geographically separated. Discuss.
8 | Assess the role of marketing financing.
9 | Marketers attempt to reduce marketing risks that cannot be transferred by a variety of means. Explain.
10 | A company's marketing success is directly related to its ability to obtain and analyze marketing information. Explain.
11 | Explain why it is impossible to have a single classification of marketing activities which is universally applicable.

12 "More efficient marketing would result if more marketers viewed marketing as a 'system' of interrelated activities that have to be coordinated toward common goals." Comment on this statement.

CASE PROBLEM

Jerry Seager and Chris Whichard, next-door neighbors in a Pittsburgh suburb, were discussing marketing's role in a free enterprise economy. In particular, they were discussing whether or not marketing activities were justified.

Jerry, a computer programmer for a large company, complained loudly about prices. "My feeling," said Jerry, "is that if you eliminated the middleman, we'd get lower prices and we'd all be better off. In fact, the entire marketing system would function more smoothly and we would all benefit from the increased efficiency by being able to get the same goods at much lower prices which we all could afford."

He went on to cite a recent purchase of a refrigerator that cost him $650. He estimated the cost of manufacturing the refrigerator at approximately $400 and suggested that he failed to see how $250 worth of value was added to the product as it passed through a "totally unnecessary" channel of distribution. "So," Jerry said, "I'm forced to pay $250 for the mere existence of a bunch of middlemen who don't do anything to the refrigerator except pass it on to the next guy. It just doesn't seem right."

Chris, a local men's clothing store operator, took the position that greater efficiency, not less, resulted from the activities performed by middlemen. "Take my case, for example," said Chris. "Eliminate me. Where does that leave you? I'll tell you—when you want a suit of clothes, rather than hopping into your car and driving the few miles to my store and making your selection from among a wide assortment of brands, you'd have to deal directly with the manufacturer. You might save a few dollars on the price of the suit, but I don't think you'd find it a very desirable situation." Chris said further: "And I'm talking only about a suit of clothes. How about the shirts, ties, socks, belts, and other things that go along with it, all of which you can get under my store roof? Do you think you'd like to have to maybe deal with a different manufacturer for all of your clothing needs? And, one other thing—think about it for *all* the products you, your wife, and your kids buy. You're asked to pay for the activities performed by various middlemen, sure, but you never get something of value for nothing, do you? You're able to enjoy your standard of living because of marketing, not despite it. So, be thankful for the middleman—he helps to make it possible for you to live the kind of life you like."

questions:

1. Evaluate the arguments of Jerry Seager and Chris Whichard.
2. What are the justifications for the various activities of marketing?

When you have mastered the contents of this chapter, you should be able to:

1   Identify the appropriateness of intuition-based decisions or the need for information-based decisions, given descriptions of different marketing problem situations.
2   Explain the nature and purpose of a marketing information system (MIS).
3   Describe how an MIS should be designed.
4   Calculate four different types of operating ratios (gross margins, expense, sales returns and allowances, and net profit), given the data required.
5   Compute three other analytical ratios (markup, markdown, and stockturn rate), given the data required.
6   Explain the nature of sales records and describe how they can be used in making effective marketing decisions.
7   Describe the probable direction of future development of MISs.

marketing information

systems

Even though management must resolve the vast bulk of day-to-day marketing problems on the basis of inadequate information or intuition, really important marketing problem situations should be resolved—to the extent possible—through analysis of factual information. The marketing information system provides the facts for decision making. In this chapter analysis focuses on (1) the relationship of marketing information to marketing decisions, (2) marketing information systems, and (3) sources of marketing information. Internal sources, marketing intelligence, and forecasting are discussed in this chapter. The remaining external source, marketing research, is discussed in Chapter 5.

MARKETING INFORMATION AND MARKETING DECISIONS

In guiding an organization's activities toward the achievement of marketing goals, management must (1) recognize problem situations, (2) determine alternative courses of action, (3) appraise the alternatives, and (4) decide on a particular course of action. The heart of decision making, therefore, relates to the choosing of courses of action aimed toward achieving desired outcomes. From management's standpoint, however, different problem situations require that it devote varying amounts of attention to the four decision-making steps. So management makes some decisions with minimal forethought, others only after a great deal of deliberation. Generally, decisions made quickly are intuition-based, while those made after considerable analysis are information-based.

intuition-based decision making

Not every problem situation in marketing is sufficiently important to justify decisions based on rigorous and time-consuming factual analysis. A supermarket manager, for example, cannot afford to spend much time deciding whether to stock one or two dozen crates of tomatoes for the weekend trade. And some problems are so serious as to require immediate decisions—before the situations worsen. Even if a marketing executive could consider all problems before they became serious, their sheer number would still force him or her to make most decisions intuitively.

In making intuitive decisions, however, executives generally draw on more than just their intuition. Usually, they draw on their previous experience and their knowledge of similar problem situations, combining common sense and judgment. Only when they have no information whatever are their decisions wholly intuitive.

While time and expense considerations force marketing managers to make most decisions intuitively, they should confine intuitive decisions to relatively minor problems. Such problem situations are alike in that their possible consequences, financial and otherwise, are not particularly serious, and decisions on them are relatively easy to change if necessary. Therefore, the marketing manager requires skill in discriminating between major and minor problem situations. Such skill involves the development of mental processes calling for considerable judgment and keen insight.

information-based decision making

Major marketing problems deserve information-based decision making. Major marketing problems have two characteristics: (1) they arise at irregular intervals, so decisions on them are not made frequently; and (2) they have important consequences which must be lived with for a long time, as it is extremely difficult to change such decisions once they are made. Examples of major marketing problems include those involving the introduction of new products, opening up new markets, changing the basic structure of sales organizations, choosing marketing channels, or determining the types and the amount of personal selling and advertising and other elements in promotional mixes. Decisions on such matters are critical to marketing success, so they should be reached only after thorough analyses of relevant information. Their possible consequences are of such far-reaching importance that a marketing executive should not risk making them intuitively. He or she should take whatever steps are necessary to assure the availability of sufficient marketing information to permit information-based decisions on all major marketing problems.

MARKETING INFORMATION SYSTEMS

For the company operating under the marketing concept, a clear need exists for coordinated, systematic, and continuous information gathering. Meeting this need is the main purpose of a **marketing information system** (MIS), which is an organized set of procedures, information-handling routines, and reporting techniques designed to provide the information required for making marketing decisions. An effective MIS makes it possible to reduce the volume of intuition-based decisions, since it makes available to decision makers relevant and usable information from both internal and external sources. Another important, although secondary, purpose of an effective MIS should be mentioned—it provides a mechanism for reducing the often overwhelming flood of available marketing information to pertinent, usable amounts.

Ultimate responsibility for the effectiveness of a company's MIS rests with the top marketing executive. He or she, along with subordinates, must provide the MIS's designers with clear-cut statements of their needs with respect to the supply and flow of marketing information. The design and operation of the actual MIS is delegated to specialists (systems analysts) thoroughly acquainted with the MIS's various objectives (provided by the marketing executives) and highly skilled in information-gathering and information-handling techniques capable of meeting these objectives. Generally, the systems analysts are assisted by an advisory group made up of representatives from marketing, finance and accounting, operations research, data processing, and other organizational units. The advisory group helps not only in the initial design but later on, as the MIS becomes a functioning reality. The group then maintains continual surveillance over the MIS, suggesting modifications to meet the company's evolving marketing information needs.

components of the information system

The job of a marketing information system is to process large quantities of marketing data—every bit of pertinent data that can be gathered—and to present it to management in the most usable form for decision making. The handling of vast quantities of data requires a sophisticated processor computer, which is necessarily the heart of the information system. The processor is controlled by a data bank, a statistical bank, and a model bank.[1]

THE DATA BANK   The **data bank** provides an orderly basis for storing the myriad bits of information that flow into a marketing information system. This information is stored in as disaggregated a form as possible. For example, if a company records daily sales merely as a total for each day, it is not subsequently possible to analyze this information by class or size of customer or by geographical region. If each bit of information is entered into the data bank separately, it is subsequently possible to evaluate performance in many ways.

THE STATISTICAL BANK   The **statistical bank** is a set of instructions that automatically analyzes all incoming data to provide regular standardized reports to managers who need them. Thus, the sales supervisors might receive weekly analyses of the performance of each of their sales personnel; the sales manager might receive monthly statistics on company sales by

---

[1] Lawrence D. Gibson, Charles G. Mayes, Christopher Nugent, and Thomas Vollman, "An Evolutionary Approach to Marketing Information Systems," *Journal of Marketing,* April 1973, pp. 2-6.

product, district, or consumer type; and the marketing manager might receive monthly or quarterly market share data, an analysis of sales by foreign markets, or an evaluation of the performance of a new product.

THE MODEL BANK   The **model bank** is designed to provide management with suggested courses of action or answers to problems. Through the use of predictive models, the bank provides recommended solutions for routine recurring problems. Only the most sophisticated marketing information systems have evolved to the point of using a model bank. And even in these systems the more important and complex problems must still be decided by management.

desired information outputs   Identifying the desired information outputs is the most critical aspect of MIS design. Since the basic purpose is to implement more and better information-based decisions, system designers should focus their efforts on the decisions each executive in the marketing organization must make to perform his or her job effectively, so as to clarify the marketing information requirements that the MIS should provide. The composite of the marketing information requirements for the entire organization thus identifies the variety and nature of specific information outputs that the MIS should provide. While differences among organizations cause them to have varying information requirements, one expert says that "whether the products involved are building materials, breadsticks, or bonds," marketing managers want the kinds of information required to answer questions such as those in Figure 4-1.

Another important aspect of MIS design relates to tailoring information outputs to fit each executive's individual information needs. Each executive wants complete and accurate information received on a timely basis, yet not provided (routinely) in overwhelmingly and confusingly large quantities. It is ironic that while organizations generate increasingly massive volumes of data, many executives continue to voice complaints that available information is too incomplete and not sufficiently relevant or timely to use as a basis for marketing decisions. The MIS should have the built-in capability of extracting from the data bank timely items of information relevant for each executive's use in decision making.

Some executives need certain kinds of information only when a given situation shifts outside a range of acceptable normalcy. In one company, for example, the general sales manager is not concerned with individual salesperson's day-to-day performances, leaving that responsibility to subordinate executives. This general sales manager does, however, want to know whenever any salesperson's performance increases or decreases by as much as 25 percent in a month's time. Effective MISs are capable of providing such **exception reports** to those executives who want them.

The real challenge in designing a MIS lies in determining what kind and how much information is required how often by each executive in the

Figure 4-1 Examples of questions most marketing managers want answered

CUSTOMER INFORMATION
—Where is volume concentrated?
—Who are specific major customers, both present and potential?
—What are their needs for products?
—What are their needs for sales coverage and service?
—What order activity and volume are expected?
—What are the differences in profitability between types and classes of customers?
—Where is performance significantly short of expectations?

PRODUCT INFORMATION
—What are the relative profitabilities of products at the gross margin level? After direct marketing expenses?
—Which elements of variable product cost are influenced by marketing decisions? What is the current cost structure?
—Which products tend to respond most favorably to sales promotion at the wholesale, retail, and consumer levels?
—What are the major advantages and disadvantages of current products in the eyes of consumers, relative to competitive products?
—What factors have the greatest influence on sales volume?
—What is the status of volume and profitability relative to objectives?

SALES FORCE INFORMATION
—What area and which customers are assigned?
—What call activity is required, both for protection of present volume and development of new business?
—Do current compensation systems motivate the desired mix of salesmen's activity?
—What is current performance relative to objectives?

Source: N. Doppeit, "Down-to-Earth Marketing Information Systems," Management Adviser, September–October, 1971, pp. 19–26.

marketing organization. Modern data-processing equipment and techniques make it possible to provide total information daily on certain facets of the marketing operation, but executives can neither cope with nor digest and use total information. An MIS makes its most significant contributions through evaluating information needs and uses and through providing information output accordingly.

information sources   The MIS's information inputs come from diverse sources, both within and outside the organization. Internal sources provide the major information flows of a routine and continuous nature. Such information sources include the controller, research and development department, long-range corporate planning unit, the legal department, economic research groups, and, of course, the sales department. These internal sources produce two broad categories of data: (1) operating data and (2) sales analysis data. Three types of information are obtained from external sources: marketing research, marketing intelligence, and forecasts.

OPERATING DATA AS AN
INTERNAL SOURCE OF
MARKETING INFORMATION

No other type of marketing information sees more frequent or varied use in marketing decision making than operating data. Almost daily, the marketing executive uses such data to help him or her throughout

the entire range of decision-making steps: recognizing problems, developing alternative solutions, appraising them, and deciding courses of action. The company's own financial, accounting, sales and production records are the sources of operating data. The marketing executive needs to know not only the types of operating data that are or can be made available but also how to use them in decision making.

the operating statement

The operating, or **profit-and-loss**, **statement** is the most used internal source of marketing information.

By definition, it is a financial summary of operating results for some period—usually a month, a quarter, or a year. It shows whether the firm operated at a profit or a loss and explains how that profit or loss resulted from the quantitative relationships that existed between sales and cost of goods sold and expenses. **Cost of goods sold** represents the total cost value of the goods actually sold during the period and not the value of the goods on hand at any particular time. **Expenses** are the total of the marketing, general, and administrative costs incurred during the operating period. If sales income exceeds the total cost of goods sold plus expenses, then the statement shows a net profit. If sales income is smaller than the total of cost of goods sold plus expenses, the statement shows a net loss. These relationships, then, are:

Item	Sales
Minus:	Cost of Goods Sold
Equals:	Gross Margin (or Gross Profit)
Minus:	Expenses
Equals:	Net Profit (or Net Loss)

This skeleton operating statement portrays only the relationships among the major operating items—sales, cost of goods sold, and expenses. Each major item is, in its turn, the result of a set of relationships existing among more detailed items of financial operating data. Figure 4-2, an operating statement shown in considerable detail, illustrates these several sets of relationships as well as the interrelationships among the major operating items.

The "Cost of Goods Sold" section in the operating statement in Figure 4-2 illustrates the way a retailer or wholesaler would determine this amount. Such middlemen are buy-and-sell businesses. By contrast, manufacturers are make-and-sell businesses; hence, their operating statements substitute a "Cost of Goods Manufactured" subsection for the "Purchases" subsection used by retailers and wholesalers.

operating ratios   The "Percentages" column in Figure 4-2 expresses the relationships between net sales and several important items in the operating statement. These ratios are expressed as a percentage of net sales with net sales equal to 100 percent. Thus, when a businessperson says that net profit is 5 percent, this means 5 percent of net sales. Similarly, when gross margin is 39 percent, this means 39 percent of net sales.

GROSS MARGIN RATIO **Gross margin** is the difference between sales and cost of goods sold. Expressing this amount as a percentage of net sales, the **gross margin ratio,** allows comparison with previous operating periods or with competitors' figures. The ratio may be increased or decreased in two ways—by changing the selling price per unit or by changing the cost per unit. When marketing executives believe the gross margin ratio is high or

Figure 4-2 Operating statement for the year ending December 31, 198–

				Percent
Gross sales			$1,050,000	105.0
Less: returns and allowances			50,000	5.0
Net sales			$1,000,000	100.0
Cost of goods sold:				
Opening inventory at cost		$100,000		
Purchases at billed cost	$650,000			
Less: purchase discounts	15,000			
Net cost of purchases	$635,000			
Plus: freight-in	40,000			
Net cost of purchases delivered		675,000		
Cost of goods handled		$775,000		
Less: closing inventory at cost		165,000		
Cost of goods sold			610,000	61.0
Gross margin (or gross profit)			$ 390,000	39.0
Expenses:				
Advertising	$ 40,000			
Sales salaries and Commissions	105,000			
Warehousing and delivery	90,000			
Administrative	40,000			
General and other	60,000			
Total expenses			335,000	33.5
Net profit on operations (before income taxes)			$ 55,000	5.5

low relative either to past performance or to competitors' experience, they may try to change prices, reduce costs, or both. Thus, a retailer alerted by an abnormally low gross margin ratio might reevaluate the buying procedure to find more economical sources of supply, improve the working capital position to take advantage of cash discounts, improve traffic control to decrease freight costs, or improve merchandise selection to command higher markups. In the same manner, a manufacturer might be alerted to reduce its production costs or improve its product to command a higher markup. Without this analytical tool, such inefficiency might go unnoticed.

EXPENSE RATIO   The **expense ratio** provides the basis for evaluation of the relationship among sales, gross margin, expenses, and profit. It is not concerned with a breakdown analysis of individual expense categories but with a comparison of total expenses with other figures on the operating statement. The ratio of expense to sales may vary considerably between companies, even in the same industry. A company that attracts its customers mainly on the basis of low prices will naturally spend less on selling and will, thus, have a low expense ratio. Another that emphasizes promotion rather than prices to attract patronage will have a high expense ratio. For this reason, expense comparisons between companies must be made with caution.

SALES RETURNS AND ALLOWANCES RATIO   The **sales return and allowances ratio,** like other operating ratios, is expressed as a percent of net sales, even though sales returns and allowances are subtracted from gross sales to arrive at net sales. Analysis of sales returns and allowances ratios helps management to determine whether these figures represent normal or abnormal experience. A certain number of returns and allowances is to be expected because of human error and product failings, but excessive returns and allowances may reflect bad merchandise or overselling.

NET PROFIT RATIO   The **net profit ratio** relates most directly to the profit objective but, used alone, it has limited value. A profit decline may alert management to possible trouble, but since profit results from a combination of sales, gross margin, and expense, evaluations of all three ratios are necessary to pinpoint the problems. Likewise, if management wishes to increase profits, proposed operational changes should be considered in light of other operating ratios. For example, a retailer may want to estimate the effects on net profit of an anticipated increase in "store traffic." "Supposing," he says, "that increased store traffic causes a 60 percent rise in sales but requires the hiring of two additional clerks, thus raising weekly expenses by $188." "I would expect," he continues, "that the percentage relationship of cost of goods sold to sales would be unchanged." The weekly operating statement of the retailer's store, together with the expected operating statment for the next week based on his assumption, are as follows:

	Present Situation		Contemplated Situation	
		Percent		*Percent*
Sales	$1,000	100	$1,600	100
Cost of goods sold	670	67	1,072	67
Gross margin	$ 330	33	$ 528	33
Expenses	300	30	488	30.5
Net profit	$ 30	3	$ 40	2.5

This analysis indicates that the retailer's dollar profits will rise from $30 to $40 a week, but the net profit percentage (profit as a percent of sales) will fall from 3 to 2.5 percent. It is quite possible, then, for a change in operations to produce more net profit dollars but a smaller net profit percentage. This, of course, does not always happen, but it does happen often enough that management should be aware of the possibility. Marketing executives agree that the dollar payoff is the most important item to consider, but they also agree that percentage relationships are helpful in making comparisons.

other analytical ratios and their uses in decision making
Certain analytical ratios serve as everyday aids in decision making. Included are the markup, the markdown, and the rate of stockturn. One preliminary word of caution: the following discussion uses retailing-type situations to illustrate the ratios and their uses. Wholesalers use the same ratios, the methods of calculation are identical, and there is no need for duplicate illustrations. These particular ratios do not apply directly to the operations of manufacturing firms but apply instead to the operations of middlemen handling the products of manufacturers. Marketing executives in manufacturing firms not only should know how middlemen use these ratios but also should use them themselves in planning marketing and promotional programs.

MARKUP   The amount by which an item's intended selling price exceeds its cost to the seller is known as the **markup**. When a discount house pays $15 for a transistor radio and prices it at $20, the $5 difference is the markup. Out of the total of all such markups placed on all the items it sells, the discount house seeks to cover its expenses and earn a net profit.

A retailer thinks of a markup not only as so many dollars and cents but also as some percentage, either of original selling price or of cost. The retailer often uses the markup concept, in other words, as an analytical ratio to express the relation between dollar markup and original dollar selling

Figure 4-3

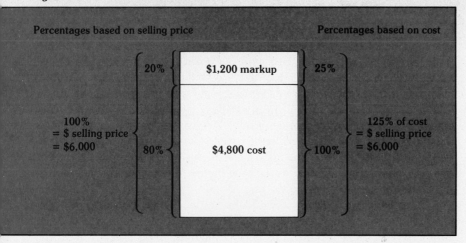

price or dollar cost. If an automobile dealer pays the manufacturer $4,800 for a vehicle and prices it at $6,000, the markup percentage is 20 percent (i.e., $1200/$6000) on the selling price.

Most sellers use selling price rather than cost as the base, and whenever we speak of markup as a percentage we will mean markup as a percentage of original selling price. Keep in mind, however, that under either system of computing markup percentages, you are dealing with the same dollar markup, as illustrated in Figure 4-3.

MARKDOWN   Merchandise does not always sell at the original selling price placed on it and a seller may, in an effort to make it move, mark down, or reduce, the price. When a giftshop proprietor, for example, concludes that a fancy ashtray is not going to sell at the $10.00 price she put on it in the beginning, she may mark it down to $7.50, at which price a customer finally buys it. The difference between the original selling price and the actual selling price is called the **markdown**. The dollar markdown, then, is $2.50 in the ashtray example. Customarily, retailers compute markdown percentages using actual selling price as the base.[2] So when an item is marked down from $10.00 to $7.50, the $2.50 price reduction is a 33⅓ percent markdown (i.e., $2.50/$7.50). The foregoing type of markdown does not appear on the operating statement, since the first item on the statement is gross sales, and markdowns occur before sales are made.

[2] The opposite seems to be the widespread practice in Puerto Rico and Latin America. Retailers there claim that by computing markdown percentages from original selling price they can recognize more readily the actual price markdown that was required in order to make the actual sale.

However, "Allowances to Customers" does appear on the operating statement, and such allowances are also properly viewed as markdowns. Most markdowns occur before sales are made, but some keep sales from becoming unmade! To illustrate this point, say the ashtray sold at the $10.00 price but that the customer became dissatisfied with the purchase and brought it back to the store. The proprietor, seeking not only to keep the sale from coming undone but wanting to keep the customer's goodwill, might say, "Keep the ashtray and I'll grant you a $2.50 allowance." If the customer agrees, the accounting system will show $10.00 as the original sale, $2.50 as the allowance to the customer, and $7.50 as the net amount of the transaction. Because markdowns and allowances to customers are both downward adjustments in price, merchants ordinarily lump both together in calculating the markdown ratio for the operating period.

Merchants recognize that every item in their stocks carries some possibility of having to be marked down. Such markdowns can occur either before or after sales are made. Both types should be considered in setting original selling prices, for the total of original markups should be sufficiently high that subsequent markdowns will not reduce sales below the total of cost of goods sold and expenses. The formula, then, for computing the markdown ratio is

$$\text{Markdown \%} = \frac{\text{\$ Allowances to Customers} + \text{\$ Markdowns}}{\text{\$ Net Sales}}$$

The markdown ratio provides information needed in planning original markups. Its existence serves as a reminder to price setters that prices have to be set (sooner or later) at levels customers are able and willing to pay. If the original markup is too high to satisfy the market, markdowns are inevitable.

The markdown ratio is used, too, as a measure of the efficiency of store buyers and retail sales personnel. Reasonably low markdowns are an indication of effective buying, realistic pricing, and good selling. When using the markdown ratio as a performance measure, management should define what it considers a desirable markdown ratio. Such standard markdown ratios are derived either through studies of store markdown ratios over past periods or from trade associations' reports on competitors.

STOCKTURN RATE The **stockturn rate** is an analytical tool used for measuring operating efficiency. It indicates the speed at which the inventory "turns over"—the number of times the average inventory is sold during an operating period. If a retailer, for instance, starts the year with an inventory costing $20,000 and ends the year with a $30,000 inventory at cost, the average inventory at cost has been $25,000. If the cost of goods sold during the year amounted to $100,000, the business has a stockturn rate of four, calculated as follows:

$$\text{Stockturn Rate} = \frac{\text{Cost of Goods Sold}}{\text{Average Inventory at Cost}}$$

$$= \frac{\$100,000}{\frac{1}{2}(\$20,000 + \$30,000)} = 4$$

This retailer, in other words, sold the average inventory four times during the year, or once every three months. If the store makes a net profit of 3 cents every time it sells something costing a dollar, we can say the store had an annual return of 12 cents (3 cents $\times$ 4) on each dollar invested in inventory.

We computed the stockturn rate above by the method most commonly used. Both the numerator and denominator in the formula were cost figures, readily available from accounting records. There are, however, some businesses that value their inventories in terms of selling prices rather than in terms of costs, and they are said to use the retail method of inventory valuation. In such businesses, the following formula is used for computing stockturn rate:

$$\text{Stockturn Rate} = \frac{\text{Net Sales (\$)}}{\text{Average Inventory at Selling Price}}$$

Thus, a department store using the retail method of inventory valuation might start the year with a $100,000 inventory at retail and end it with an inventory of $80,000 at retail, or an average of $90,000. If net sales during the year were $720,000, the stockturn rate would be eight (i.e., $720,000/$90,000). Notice that the only real difference between this formula and the earlier one is that here we express the numerator and denominator in terms of selling price rather than of cost.

The stockturn rate provides a yardstick for measuring operating efficiency. An increase in the rate of turnover of capital invested in inventory will normally increase total profits, unless the net profit ratio is decreased proportionally. Thus, a higher stockturn is a much-sought-after goal.

The stockturn rate is also used as a basis for comparing the effectiveness of branches or different outlets. The unit with the highest stockturn rate may be the most efficiently managed, but not always. Where, for instance, are the two units located? The store with the fastest turnover rate might be across the street from the factory with the opportunity to replenish inventory daily, while the other might be 3,000 air miles away with the necessity of maintaining a large reserve inventory. Also, one store may cater to only a small market segment—for example, men only—while the other may serve the whole family, necessitating a much larger basic stock. Or, perhaps, the store with the high turnover handles only low-priced, low-margin lines. Of course, such considerations are less likely to be important when the stockturn rate is used for comparing the same store's operating efficiency during two different periods.

ANALYSIS OF SALES RECORDS   An important problem in MIS design involves **infor-mation retrieval,** making internally generated information easily retrievable for use by marketing executives. Sales invoices, for example, have historically flowed into the accounting department and, after providing needed data for accounting purposes, have been buried in that department's files. But sales invoices constitute a valuable source of such kinds of marketing information as sales performance by product line, by type of customer, or by market area. Even some companies with highly developed data-processing systems are guilty of storing information from sales invoices so that it is either impossible or prohibitively expensive (in terms of computer time) to retrieve for nonaccounting uses. Consequently, all data that might provide useful input for marketing decisions should be stored in as disaggregated (i.e., broken down) a form as possible, making it easy and economical to retrieve for diverse uses.

Analysis of a company's sales records, generally with the aid of a computer, makes it possible to detect various marketing strengths and weaknesses. Although sales records are regularly summarized in the "sales" section of the operating statement, such summaries reveal little about strong or weak features of the company's marketing efforts. Periodic computer-assisted **sales analysis** is used to uncover significant details which otherwise lie hidden in the sales records. It provides information that management needs to allocate future marketing efforts more effectively.

misdirected marketing effort   In most businesses, a large percentage of the customers, territories, orders, or products bring in only a small percentage of the sales. One sales executive, using a diagram (Figure 4-4) to illustrate this, said, "The column on the left represents our total number of dealers, and the column on the right our total dollar sales volume. The diagonal indicates that 80 percent of our customers give us only 20 percent of our volume." Similar situations exist in most companies, a large percentage of the customers accounting for a small percentage of the total sales and, conversely, a small percentage of customers accounting for a high percentage of total sales. And comparable situations are found where a large percentage of the sales territories, products, and orders bring in only a small percentage of total sales. Sometimes such situations are referred to as examples of the **80-20 principle.**

Such sales patterns do not always result in a loss, but operations are often less profitable than they should be. Why is this so? Simply because marketing efforts all too frequently are divided on the basis of customers, territories, products, orders, and so forth, rather than on a basis of actual or potential dollar sales. It usually costs, for example, just as much to maintain a salesperson in a bad territory as in a good one, almost as much to promote

76

Figure 4-4

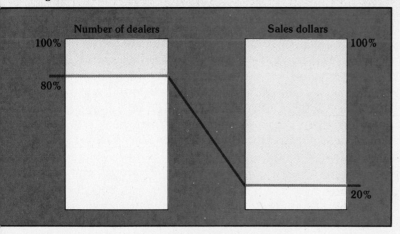

a product that sells slowly or not at all as one that sells in large volume, and as much to have a salesperson service a customer who orders in small quantities as another who gives the company large orders. It is not uncommon for a large proportion of the total marketing efforts to produce only a very small proportion of the total sales and profits. Detecting such situations—identifying customers, products, or territories that are actually unprofitable—is the important task of sales analysis. Abandonment of these losers would reduce expenses more than it reduced sales and would increase total profit.

nature of sales records   Companies vary greatly in the type and form of information they have available on sales. At one extreme, some have none, other than accountants' records of sales and carbons of customers' sales invoices. At the opposite extreme, some firms, when extracting necessary accounting information from sales invoices, also record highly detailed marketing information on computer tapes so that it is readily available in usable form for analyzing sales by individual salespeople, types of products, classes of customers, sizes of orders, and other pertinent breakdowns.

Generally, the most important sources of data useful in sales analysis are customers' sales invoices, which contain two types of information, both essential for sales analysis. One identifies and describes the customer (e.g., the name and geographical location), and one contains data on the specific transaction (e.g., the date of the order, the products sold and the quantities, the price per unit, total dollar sales per product, and total amount of the order). Companies with highly developed systems of sales analysis organize these basic items of sales information systematically—that is, in ways which facilitate analysis.

specific purposes of main types of sales analyses — The purpose of sales analysis is to detect marketing strengths and weaknesses. Each main type of sales analysis sheds light on a different aspect of these strengths and weaknesses. Analysis of sales by territories answers the question of how much is being sold *where*. Analysis of sales by products answers how much of *what* is being sold. Analysis of sales by customers answers the question of *who* is buying how much. All types of sales analyses relate to the question of *how much* is being sold, but each answers it in a different way. Although sales analyses can identify marketing strengths and weaknesses, they cannot explain *why* they exist. Answering the "why" question is management's task.

MARKETING INFORMATION FROM EXTERNAL SOURCES

Three forms of marketing information are obtained from external sources: marketing intelligence, forecasts, and marketing research. Intelligence and forecasts are discussed briefly below. Marketing research is discussed in more detail in Chapter 5.

marketing intelligence — The term "intelligence" means the same in marketing as it does in a military context. It involves an organized procedure to collect regularly from diverse sources information of potential usefulness for the making of marketing decisions. It includes raw data, summary statistics, qualitative inferences, expert and lay opinions, impressions, and even rumors. The majority of items of intelligence are available from public sources. A trade journal publishes an article about a competitor's new product. A news broadcast mentions an F.T.C. action against a competitor for its pricing policies. The newspapers report that a competitor is being sued by one of its distributors for collusive action. It is the role of the intelligence system to see that such information is gathered, fed into the data bank, and brought to the attention of concerned executives. Some firms subscribe to news clipping services that search current media for such information and supply it to their clients. Since the marketing plans and strategies of competitors have obvious intelligence value, some firms turn to nonpublic sources for such information. Trade associations often provide competitive information in anonymous form to their members. Clandestine means are also available, and business espionage, using the same sophisticated tools as military espionage, is an important activity in some industries. In general, however, the public and legal sources of information are by far the most important intelligence input into the marketing information system.

sales forecasting — The starting point for any marketing plan is a forecast of sales for the planning period. For this reason a sales forecast and a continuous procedure for updating it is a necessary input for the marketing information system. The sales forecast is an estimate of sales tied to a particular marketing program and assuming a particular set of economic and other forces outside the forecasting unit. There are two main classes of forecasts, sophisticated and unsophisticated.

The unsophisticated methods are jury of executive opinion, poll of sales force opinion, and projection of past sales. The first two methods rely upon the accumulated experience of people working every day with the market. The senior executives of a firm often know more about its market than any other source and can frequently produce accurate forecasts. Particularly in those situations where the market fluctuates widely, the salesperson who is in day-to-day contact with the customers is by far the most reliable source of future market information. On the other hand, in markets that are very stable, a simple projection of past sales trends can provide a good forecast.

Companies desiring greater accuracy in their forecasts use techniques that are more sophisticated. [3] The sophisticated methods of forecasting ordinarily start with a forecast of the economy and move on to a forecast of industry and company sales. The two most widely used of these methods are regression analysis and econometric model building. In regression analysis, leading indices, such as gross national product and housing starts, which correlate highly with company sales, are identified and used to forecast sales. In econometric model building, complex models of a whole economy or an industry are built to provide accurate forecasts; the level of sophistication is still rather low, but this forecasting method has great future potential. A third sophisticated method, the survey of consumers' buying power, uses marketing research techniques to measure future buying plans; it is a costly but useful forecasting method. Since forecasting deals with the future, even the most sophisticated methods are no better than educated guesses.

marketing research   Other information from external sources is gathered through marketing research on both a routine and a nonroutine basis. Routine information, for example, might be a monthly report on sales of competitive products in selected retail outlets. On a nonroutine basis, management, for instance, may want to learn more about its customers: Who buys the products? How do buyers differ from nonbuyers? What do buyers like and dislike about the products? Or management may desire to test the market for a new product and to determine and measure the reactions of final buyers and middlemen. Information from marketing research studies provides important inputs to an MIS, but usually a separate organization unit, the marketing research department, or, in some cases, an independent marketing research firm, is responsible for its generation. The main reason for this arrangement is that marketing research requires specialized skills and rather unique methodologies. While the marketing research

---

[3] Judy Pan, Donald Nichols, and O. Maurice Joy, "Sales Forecasting Methods of Large U.S. Firms," *Financial Management,* Fall 1977, p. 77.

director may report directly to the MIS director, more usually he or she reports to the top marketing executive. This topic is discussed in detail in the next chapter.

SIMULATION OF MARKETING DECISIONS IN INFORMATION SYSTEMS

Marketing information systems are made up of several subsystems, each providing information for a particular problem or, ideally, providing an automatic decision. If the system analysts who design the system are to prepare a system to aid in decision making, they must start with theoretical foundations. Consequently, decision makers must tell the systems analyst the kind and amount of data that constitute the theory or model on which they base their decisions and the structural relationship of the variables—how they are interrelated and fit together. This forces the decision maker to think through the decision process in great detail. This may be the first time he or she has ever tried to analyze his or her own process of decision making, and that step alone may improve future decisions.

The ultimate goal in developing each subsystem is a situation in which the computer is fed current information, and it selects from the model bank a course of action, informing the decision maker only when the predetermined alternatives do not provide an adequate solution to the problem. It is rarely possible to develop such an ideal, automatically functioning subsystem on anything but the simplest kinds of decisions, either because the decision maker is unable to reduce the decision process to a formal model, or because it is not possible to obtain all the necessary information in a sufficiently accurate form. Nevertheless, the long-term goal of the designers of marketing information systems is to simulate reality to the extent of providing automated responses in as many subsystems as possible. Until such a goal is reached, the information system will serve the narrower function of providing the optimum amount of information useful to management in making each decision as it arises.

SUMMARY

You should now have a good understanding of the role of marketing information in the making of marketing decisions and the systems necessary for accumulating and processing such information. Many routine or unimportant decisions are necessarily made upon an intuitive basis, relying upon past experience and accumulated information. However, important decisions should be supported by information in as much detail as can be made available, and the marketing information system is designed to provide such data. Marketing information comes from both internal and external sources. Internal sources are more readily available and more accurate, and they provide financial statements and ratios, other analytical ratios, data from analysis of sales records, and simulations developed from historical data. External sources include marketing intelligence, sales forecasting, and marketing research (which is discussed in Chapter 5). Finally, you should now have a good idea how the marketing executive uses operating data as an important internal source of information.

REVIEW AND DISCUSSION QUESTIONS

1 Clearly distinguish between intuition-based decision making and information-based decision making.

2 What is the importance of marketing information systems? Discuss.

3 Who should be responsible for initiating development of a marketing information system? Explain.

4 What are the characteristics of a good marketing information system? Discuss.

5 What is marketing intelligence?

6 Distinguish between:
   a. Gross margin ratio and net profit ratio.
   b. Markup and markdown.
   c. Markup on selling price and markup on cost.

7 Define the following terms:
   a. Operating statement.
   b. Stockturn rate.
   c. Sales analysis.
   d. Misdirected marketing effort.

8 What reasoning lies behind the fact that operating ratios are usually expressed as percentages of net sales?

9 How would you account for a situation in which two companies, both in the same industry and with comparable products, have different expense ratios?

10 What are the main causes of markdowns? Why is it that all markdowns do not appear on the operating statement? Should retailers strive to eliminate markdowns completely? Why? What corrective measures would you suggest to a retailer who says that his markdowns are too high?

11 Under what conditions are stockturn rates appropriate as measure of operating efficiency? What are the reasons why different businesses have different stockturn rates?

12 Summarize the various ways a marketing manager might use sales analysis.

13 "The starting point for any marketing plan is a forecast of sales for the planning period." Explain in detail.

14 Find the missing figures in the following table:

Cost	Markup percent on cost	Markup	Markup percent on selling price	Selling price
$12.00		$3.00		
2.75			35	
	67	4.00		
			15	$18.00
0.65	40			
		8.00		32.50

15 | Find the missing figures in the following table:

Markup percent on cost	Markup percent on selling price
35	
	40
64	
	19
250	
	26
150	
	70

16 | A retailer purchased an item for $1.70, originally priced it at $2.29, and finally sold it at $1.99. What was the markdown percentage?

17 | On the basis of the following operating data, calculate the opening inventory at cost:

Cost of goods sold	$170,000
Stockturn rate	4
Closing inventory at cost	12,000

18 | Last month, Retailer A had gross sales of $14,000, sales returns and allowances of $800, opening inventory at cost of $2,500, purchases at cost of $4,500, closing inventory at cost of $1,900, and expenses of $2,600. What was A's net profit? Gross margin?

19 | Last month, Retailer B had cost of goods sold of $4,000, expenses of $3,000, and a gross margin of $3,500. What was B's net profit? Net sales?

20 | Last month, Retailer C had an opening inventory at a cost of $3,600, closing inventory at cost of $4,100, and cost of goods sold of $11,000. Find C's purchases at cost.

21 | A wholesaler is planning his operations for the coming year. After analyzing company records, he estimates that during the coming year expenses will amount to $29,900 and gross margin will be $35,000. The wholesaler says that he will be satisfied with a net profit of 4.5 percent on sales. What sales volume goal should he set for the coming year?

22 | On the basis of the following operating data, compute stockturn rates (a) using cost figures, and (b) using selling price figures:

Net sales	$21,500
Markdowns	400

Allowances to customers	375
Cost of goods sold	11,850
Opening inventory at cost	3,200
Opening inventory at selling price	6,100
Closing inventory at cost	2,050
Closing inventory at selling price	4,350

How do you explain the difference between the two stockturn rates?

23 A retailer currently has monthly sales of $150,000 and an average inventory of $40,000 at selling price. He wants to increase the stockturn rate from four to four and a half. Explain at least two different alternatives he might consider in working toward this target stockturn rate of four and a half.

24 In analyzing the operations of a supermarket, an investigator obtained the following data:

Department	Percent of Store Sales	Percent of Store Gross Margin	Sales Per Square Foot	Gross Margin Per Square Foot
Grocery	39.65	32.04	$1.76	$0.34
Meat	34.39	39.49	3.10	0.11
Produce	12.71	15.78	1.80	0.46
Dairy	8.75	4.92	4.57	0.62
Bakery	2.37	5.47	1.33	0.37
Frozen food	2.13	2.30	1.20	0.33
	100.00	100.00		

a. Suppose that you are the owner of this supermarket. How might you go about analyzing the foregoing data?

b. How might various suppliers of supermarkets make use of this information?

c. What is the significance of the sales per square foot figure? The gross margin per square foot figure?

Kruger Building Products enjoyed steadily expanding sales since its founding in the early 1950s by brothers Ed and Harry Kruger. The company was among the first major suppliers of plaster wallboard and later expanded into the paneling market. It benefited directly and heavily from the suburban building boom. The company had expanded every year, adding related interior building products as market demand arose. Harry managed the operations division, which included the three manufacturing plants. Ed, who had a background in accounting, managed the business and planning end of the company. Ed handled much of the sales forecasting on the basis of his observation of building trends and economic conditions, his study of trade magazines, and occasional conversations with key customers. For years, Ed Kruger's one-man estimates were adequate for approximating production estimates and territorial sales quotas. In the past three years, however, increasingly large discrepancies developed between sales forecasts and actual results. While the forecasts were revised monthly, the discrepancies tended to be disruptive of normal operations. It seemed that Ed was spending an unusually large amount of time revising the sales forecast.

Kruger Products were distributed nationwide by a field sales force of 56 representatives operating out of nine district offices. The sales force was paid on a salary plus commission and bonus arrangement. The products were sold in three markets: contractors, including residential, industrial and commercial contractors; industrial; and retail, made up of hardware and building supply operations.

Last year, a new sales manager, Joe Pernaw, had been hired to improve the coordination of the sales efforts. He had previously been sales manager for a leading building supply retail chain. He had some experience in retail sales forecasting but had never interacted with large contractors or industrial accounts.

After three years of progressively more inaccurate sales forecasts, Ed Kruger decided to assign to Joe Pernaw the major responsibility for sales forecasting. Based on his previous experience, Joe believed that the sales force should be involved in a sales forecasting procedure which started at the district level and was then combined into territory and national forecasts. He felt that a number of benefits would be gained. First, company sources closest to the market would be tapped. Second, if sales personnel participated, they would likely have greater confidence in sales quotas and would, more likely than not, work harder to achieve them.

Ed Kruger admitted that Joe had some strong points concerning the use of the sales force but felt that these advantages would not outweigh the fact that sales personnel were trained to sell not to forecast sales. Salespeople, Ed argued, would be biased in their estimates and would often be unaware of economic developments and of company marketing plans that could influence future sales in each territory. Furthermore, Mr. Kruger was also concerned that salespeople would have neither the time nor the concern to prepare careful estimates. Besides, salespeople are born optimists, contended Kruger.

Joe Pernaw argued that training procedures and company guidelines could aid the sales force to gain skill in estimating market demand. Joe did not feel that he could generate accurate forecasts without involving the sales force. Ed Kruger insisted that use of the sales force would require too much training and organizational expense and would likely produce questionable results.

questions:

1. Should salespeople have been involved in the sales forecasting process?
2. How should the sales manager proceed?

When you have mastered the contents of this chapter, you should be able to:

1   Explain the relationship of marketing research to the various stages of the decision-making process.

2   Describe the nature and purposes of market measurement studies, studies of influences of the controllables, studies of the competitive situation, and studies of influences of the uncontrollables.

3   Explain the general nature of marketing research procedure.

4   Identify and illustrate the key decisions involved in planning a marketing research project.

5   Compare the different research methods used in marketing research.

6   Define the following terms: probability sample, nonprobability sample, sampling error, nonsampling error.

7   Discuss the problem of balancing the value of having information against the costs of obtaining it.

marketing research

Marketing research, broadly defined, is the systematic gathering, recording, and analyzing of data about marketing problems to facilitate decision making. The information inputs for a marketing information system, as brought out in the previous chapter, come from diverse sources, both from within and outside the organization. Marketing research studies are an important source of external information. They focus on the relationship of the firm to its environment and particularly to its markets.

MARKETING RESEARCH AND THE MARKETING INFORMATION SYSTEM

Marketing research is a vital component in the marketing mix, providing a foundation for the planning and execution of marketing programs. The importance of marketing research is borne out in a study of over 1,100 companies conducted by the American Marketing Association.[1] The results showed a steady growth in the total number of marketing research departments in both industrial goods and consumer goods companies and an increase in the number of marketing research directors reporting to top management. Marketing research, as an integral part of a marketing information system, should provide a flow of information inputs, mainly from external sources, useful in marketing decision making. (See Figure 5-1.) A logical place to start, then, in understanding research's role is with the decision-making process itself. Figure 5-2 shows how marketing research, through systematic gathering and analysis of information, should assist in answering questions that management must resolve at each stage in the decision-making process.

Starting with the problem identification stage, for example, suppose that a sales analysis reveals that sales have fallen off by 10% in the western

[1] Dik W. Twedt, *A Survey of Marketing Research* (Chicago: American Marketing Association, 1974).

Figure 5-1 Marketing research within the company's total
marketing system

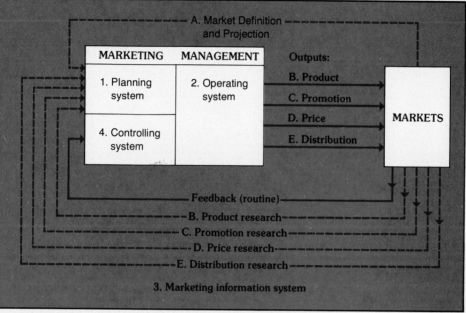

Source: David J. Luck, Hugh G. Wales, and Donald A. Taylor, Marketing Research
(Englewood Cliffs, New Jersey: Prentice-Hall, Inc., 1974), p. 28.

region, and marketing research is asked to determine why. Any of several explanations might be uncovered. Perhaps, a local competitor introduced a superior new product. Perhaps, the closing of a major area industry (an uncontrollable) created a local recession. Perhaps, the local distributor adopted a new credit policy (a controllable factor) that antagonized the retailers. Such a preliminary exploration assists marketing management in recognizing the problem.

Marketing management at the next stage seeks to answer the question "What can be done about the problem?" As Figure 5-2 indicates, this is a question that ultimately management must answer, but even here marketing research makes a contribution. It can help in the creative thinking involved in developing alternative solutions to the problem. Thus, it can suggest that to compete against the competitor's new product management should cut the price, increase promotional effort, modify the product, or apply some combination of these inputs. Before marketing research can make this contribution, however, marketing management must clarify what it wants to accomplish. Formulating the statement of goals is management's responsibility.

Next comes the evaluation of alternative solutions and the prediction of their consequences. Answering management's question "What results can

Figure 5-2 The decision-making process

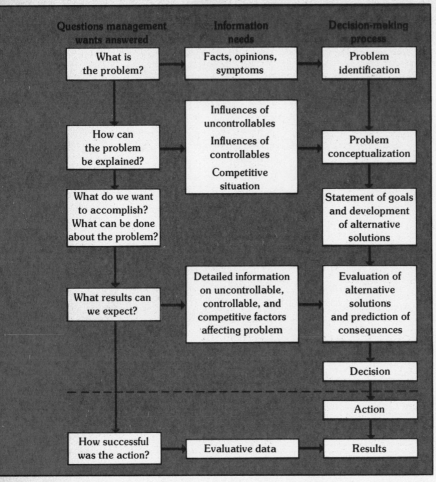

Questions management wants answered	Information needs	Decision-making process
What is the problem?	Facts, opinions, symptoms	Problem identification
How can the problem be explained?	Influences of uncontrollables / Influences of controllables / Competitive situation	Problem conceptualization
What do we want to accomplish? What can be done about the problem?		Statement of goals and development of alternative solutions
What results can we expect?	Detailed information on uncontrollable, controllable, and competitive factors affecting problem	Evaluation of alternative solutions and prediction of consequences
		Decision
		Action
How successful was the action?	Evaluative data	Results

we expect?" often requires that marketing research gather and analyze additional and detailed information on the factors affecting the problem—the uncontrollables, controllables, and the competitive situation. This added information may be gathered through various research methods and techniques—for example, consumer surveys, test market studies, and motivation research.

After considering all this information (tempering it with previous experience, judgment, and imagination), marketing management reaches its decision and takes whatever actions are required to carry out the decision. Later, as management wonders how successful was the action, marketing research may be called upon to provide the necessary evaluative data.

90

SCOPE OF MARKETING RESEARCH

Marketing research has a broad scope, embracing numerous types of studies, tapping diverse information sources. For purposes of the following discussion, marketing research studies are divided into four major categories: (1) market measurement studies, (2) studies of influences of controllables, (3) studies of the competitive situation, and (4) studies of uncontrollables.

market measurement studies

Market measurement studies are aimed toward obtaining quantitative data on potential demand—how much of a particular product can be sold to individual market segments over a future period, assuming the application of appropriate marketing methods. These data relate to market potential, sales potential, or both. Market potential is the maximum possible sales opportunities open to all sellers of a good or service during a stated future period or particular market segments. Sales potential is the maximum possible sales opportunities open to a specified company selling a good or service during a stated future period for particular market segments. To illustrate, consider the sales opportunities for 19-inch portable color television sets in Dade County, Florida, during the coming year—the *market* potential for the television set industry is a somewhat higher figure than the *sales* potential available to a particular manufacturer, such as to the Zenith Radio Corporation.

Market measurement data are particularly helpful in planning overall marketing strategy. In evaluating a proposed new product, for example, management must estimate its probable marketing success. Analysis of market measurement data provides insights as to whether a potential market exists and, if so, its likely size. If management decides to add the new product, market measurement data are again helpful in determining the geographical sequence of market introduction. In addition, breakdowns of potentials by types of customers make it possible to ascertain which groups should be the targets for promotional efforts of varying amounts, and in what order. Management makes similar use of market measurement data in resolving questions regarding dropping certain products from the line, or deemphasizing their promotion to particular market segments.

studies of influences of controllables

The widest variety of marketing research studies focus on the influences of controllables—products, distribution, promotion, and price. Management uses studies of controllables to appraise the effectiveness of current product, distribution, promotion, and pricing policies and practices and to plan future policies and practices. For example, many companies make frequent studies of the effectiveness of advertising and other promotional devices, individual salespeople, existing sales methods, and sales compensation plans. Management can manipulate controllables without such formal studies, but manipulation is more effective with the added insight gained from special studies.

91

studies of the competitive situation
Many companies emphasize studies of the competitive position of their own products more than they do studies of the nature and impact of their competitors' activities. Specifically, a study measuring the share of the market owned by a company's product is much more common than one appraising the marketing strengths and weaknesses of a competitor's products, evaluating the marketing effects of a competitor's product improvement, measuring the impact of a competitor's price change, or appraising the effects of a competitor's change in advertising approach. The most likely reason is that share-of-the-market information is often obtainable through outside research organizations, generally on a subscription basis.[2] Companies also find it easy to estimate share-of-the market percentages for their own products, especially if industry sales figures are gathered and distributed by trade associations.

Most companies could benefit significantly if they would do more intelligence type studies—studies specifically designed to delve into competitors' marketing practices and policies. Management needs this information to understand how competitors' actions affect the company's marketing situation. Only if management has such intelligence can it do a really effective job in plotting marketing strategy and counterstrategy.

studies of influences of uncontrollables
Relatively few marketing research studies focus directly on the influences of uncontrollables. This is probably because most executives feel that they can obtain the needed information from their regular business reading. Published information is readily available on such uncontrollables as the level of consumer credit, business expansion plans, age- and income-distribution trends, and consumer buying intentions. Federal government publications such as the *Statistical Abstract of the United States,* the *County and City Data Book,* the *Survey of Current Business,* and the *Federal Reserve Bulletin* are rich sources of quantitative data on the uncontrollables and, in addition, provide analyses of trends in income distribution, population growth and shifts, and consumer installment credit. The U.S. Department of Commerce's Office of Business Economics gathers and publishes data on the national economic situation and outlook and the balance of international payments. The Department of Commerce also maintains field offices to help business managers looking for specific types of information. Considerable information on the uncontrollables also appears in such publications as *Business Week, Forbes, Dun's Review, Advertising Age, The Wall Street Journal, Nation's Business,* and *Sales and Marketing Management.*

[2] The A. C. Nielsen Company, for example, provides a number of information services widely used by manufacturers. One of these services—the Nielsen Retail Index—provides continuous factual marketing data on foods, drugs, pharmaceuticals, toiletries, cosmetics, confectionery, tobacco, photographic, and other products. For the food industry, for instance, Nielsen provides its subscribers with reports on sales to consumers measured at the point of sale, sales of competitors' products made to consumers, and breakdowns of sales figures to consumers nationally or by the manufacturer's sales territories and by size and/or type of stores.

Even though executives obtain information on the uncontrollables from their regular business reading, they seldom have the time required to organize and to analyze data gathered from numerous sources in terms of their own company's marketing problems. Marketing researchers, however, when assigned the task of studying the uncontrollables, assemble and analyze data, putting it into a perspective more useful to decision makers.

The motivation research studies, which probe psychological and sociological variables affecting buying behavior, are in a class by themselves. Relatively few companies conduct this type of study. Why do many companies not do motivation research? Part of the answer is that doing and interpreting motivation research requires trained specialists—psychologists and sociologists skilled in the research methods of their own fields. Few companies employ such people, and most motivation research is handled by outside consultants. Then, too, since motivation research is highly subjective, many executives not only doubt its value but are also suspicious of its findings.

MARKETING RESEARCH PROCEDURE

While the marketing manager need not be a qualified researcher, he or she should understand general marketing research procedure. The marketing manager, in other words, is primarily a user of marketing research, not a researcher. Whether a company does its own research or uses an outside agency, the marketing manager must know enough about procedure to be able to evaluate research findings. Table 5-1 shows the largest marketing research companies in the United States, by estimated research volume in dollars.

The marketing manager, as well as the researcher, must bear in mind the current business environment, because the effectiveness of marketing research, in part, depends upon responsiveness to trends in the economy.[3] For example, one basic change in the business environment has been the shift from a concept of virtually unlimited growth to a more deliberate, planned growth in light of shortages of materials and the resulting limited product availability. Marketing research procedure, therefore, should reflect a consideration of such trends.

problem identification and marketing research

Even though marketing management may have already identified the problem to be investigated, it must make certain that the researcher understands its precise nature. The marketing researcher, like the marketing decision maker, looks upon **problem identification** as a basic first step in designing a research project that will provide the needed information. Only if he or she has the problem clearly in mind can he or she be expected to direct the resulting

[3] David K. Hardin, "Lower Profits Put Pinch on Researcher," *Advertising Age,* July 15, 1974, p. 26.

TABLE 5-1   TOP 20 MARKETING RESEARCH
ORGANIZATIONS (Based on 1977 Marketing and
Advertising Volume Only)

Firm by Rank	1977 Research Revenue (in Millions)	Gain Over 1976 (%)	Research Outside United States
1. A. C. Nielsen Co.	$205.3	18	45
2. I.M.S. International	61.9	17	60
3. Selling Areas—Marketing	40.8	20	—
4. Arbitron Co.	29.0	16	—
5. Burke Int'l Research	23.1	24	33
6. Booz, Allen & Hamilton	17.5	47	—
7. Market Facts	17.1	19	—
8. Audits & Surveys	12.2	20	—
9. ASI Marketing Research	10.2	(5)	29
10. Marketing & Research Counselors	10.0	33	—
11. Westat Inc.	8.4	29	—
12. National Family Opinion	7.9	27	—
13. Ehrhart-Babic Associates	7.9	13	2
14. Data Development Corp.	7.7	10	—
15. NPD Research	7.3	27	—
16. Tankelovitch, Skelly & White	6.9	15	—
17. Louis Harris & Associates	5.8	18	28
18. Walker Research	5.2	26	—
19. Chilton Research Services	5.1	19	—
20. U.S. Testing Co.	5.0	14	—
	$494.3	19%	

Source: Advertising Age, *April, 1978*

project intelligently. A competent marketing researcher, therefore, does not undertake any study until he or she is certain that the executive making the request has some problem already "pinned down" and until that executive has communicated the problem's nature clearly. All too frequently, executives originate requests for studies that subsequently prove of little value simply because they had not probed deeply enough to identify the basic problem. In one such case—where management asked for a study of advertising effectiveness—further probing (by an alert researcher) revealed that a sales decline was not a result of ineffective advertising, but traced it directly to the effects of a newly inaugurated distribution policy that was slowing up deliveries to retail outlets, thus causing them to be out of stock frequently.

preliminary exploration and the "situation analysis"   In the course of identifying the problem, marketing researchers begin **preliminary exploration** of data sources which, they hope, will help them gain insights into the problem's nature. Because the specific problem is not yet identified, they are required to do a certain amount of groping around for information.

Therefore, the preliminary exploration is an informal and, to a large extent, unplanned investigation.

In doing a preliminary exploration, researchers tap as many sources of readily available data as time permits. They examine company records (sales, financial, production, and others) that might shed some light on the problem. They skim trade and professional publications for reports on similar situations encountered and/or researched by others. And they study their own company's reports of previous investigations of similar and related situations. Thus, they build background for their own thinking. Marketing researchers refer to this phase of preliminary exploration as the **situation analysis**.

project planning for marketing research Basically, a marketing research project is a planned search for information. Time spent in project planning should not only reduce the time required to conduct the project but also ultimately produce more reliable and meaningful information. The earmarks of **project planning** in marketing research, as elsewhere, are well-defined goals, an organized effort, and a step-by-step schedule—all aimed at uncovering, reporting, and analyzing as reliable and meaningful information as it is possible to obtain in the available time.

Planning a marketing research project involves making decisions on (1) research objectives, (2) specific information needed to achieve these objectives, (3) sources to tap in seeking the information, and (4) research designs to employ, (5) sampling procedures, and (6) methods of data analysis.

DECIDING ON RESEARCH OBJECTIVES After the marketing problem has been identified and the preliminary exploration finished, the first key project-planning decision is to set the research objectives. In studying how the company spends its advertising appropriation, for instance, the researcher may have concluded tentatively that less money should be devoted to newspaper advertisements and more to radio. Thus, the purpose of formal research might be to test two hypotheses:

1. The company should spend less on newspaper advertising.
2. The company should spend more on radio commercials.

The statement of research objectives should, whenever possible, be limited to a small number of hypotheses to test or questions to answer. The number must be small because no project can produce timely and reliable information for managerial decision if it is directed toward obtaining too many facts. In pruning the list of objectives, the researchers should consider two questions about each tentative objective:

1. If we succeed in obtaining this information, of what value will it be to the decision maker?
2. If this information is of possible value, is it valuable enough to justify the cost of obtaining it?

DECIDING ON INFORMATION NEEDED   The second key project-planning decision is to determine the specific information needed to achieve the research objectives. The researcher considers the different types of information that seem pertinent to achieving the objectives and ascertains that each bit of specific information finally decided upon is relevant to achieving them. Suppose, for example, that the project being planned has the objective of answering a business executive's question, "Should I open a self-service shoe-store in Middletown, Pennsylvania?" What kinds of information are necessary to answer this question? The researcher should search out, as a minimum, the following:

1. Number of Middletown residents who are potential customers for this type of store.
2. Probable frequency and intensity of patronage. (How often and how much will members of different market segments patronize this store?)
3. Competing stores, their relative advantages, and their comparative costs.
4. Amount, kinds, and costs of persuasion (advertising and so forth) needed to move Middletown residents to patronize the store.

DECIDING ON INFORMATION SOURCES   The third key decision is to identify the sources for the different items of information. Information can be obtained both from within the firm and from the outside; it may be existing information or new information.

1. *Secondary Information.* The data sources for **secondary information** are mostly externally published materials, such as government census publications and *Sales Management's Survey of Buying Power* or internal information from company records, invoices, and so forth. Such material was not gathered for the specific research purpose in mind, but it may be useful. The researcher should always look to the secondary sources first to save the time and expense of regathering the same data from primary sources. In the Middletown study on opening a self-service shoe store, for example, census publications (a secondary source) should reveal the number of residents who are potential users, and city directories (another secondary source) could be consulted to identify competitors selling shoes in the trading area. But to obtain other desired items of information, primary sources (namely, the potential consumers) would have to be tapped.

2. *The Survey Method.* In the **survey method**, information is obtained directly from individual respondents either through personal interviews, mail questionnaires, consumer panels, or telephone interviews. Questionnaires are used either to obtain specific responses to direct questions or to secure more general responses to open-ended questions. A direct type of question is designed to force the respondent to choose among a limited number of answers as, for example, in the question: "How do you feel about the styling of this new cordless electric shaver? Do you rate it as EXCELLENT _____, GOOD _____, FAIR _____, or POOR _____?"

This question contrasts sharply with the open-ended question: "What do you think about the styling of this new cordless electric shaver?" The open-ended question permits respondents to formulate their own answers.

The survey method has three main uses: (1) to gather facts from respondents, (2) to report their opinions, or (3) to probe the interpretations they give to various matters. The survey method's accuracy and reliability varies in each application. Generally, it is most accurate and reliable when used to gather factual data, less so when used to record opinions, and least so when used to gain insight into respondents' interpretations.

In the factual survey, respondents are asked to report actual facts, as exemplified by questions such as: "What brand of cigarettes do you smoke?" "Where do you do most of your shopping for groceries?" "How many persons live at this address?" Even the answers to factual questions are subject to error because some respondents have faulty memories, are unable to generalize about personal experiences, or may give answers they believe interviewers want to obtain.

The opinion survey is designed to gather expressions of personal opinions, to record evaluations of different things, or to report thinking on particular matters. Opinion surveys share the potential errors of factual surveys and, in addition, by forcing immediate answers to questions on subjects that the respondents have not thought about lately, may produce answers not accurately reflecting real opinions.

In the interpretive survey, the respondent acts as an interpreter as well as a reporter. Interpretative data are gathered by using such questions as "Why do you use Brand X spray deodorant?" and "What feature of the new Thunderbird appeals to you most?" A limitation of the interpretive survey is that respondents' answers often reflect an inability to consciously interpret personal feelings, motives, and attitudes.

3. Indirect Interviews. Psychologists have long known that direct questioning is often ineffective in eliciting information on motivation. Indirect or projective techniques are used to gather such information. The focus group is perhaps the best known and most widely used of these methods. In this method a group of from 8 to 12 people participate jointly in an unstructured interview. The resulting spontaneous discussion often discloses attitudes and opinions about a situation which would not result from direct questioning. In this manner the Borden Company conducted a series of focus group interviews to learn housewives' real feelings about instant dried milk.

4. The Observational Method. Here, marketing research data are gathered not through direct questioning of respondents, but by observing and recording consumers' actions in a marketing situation. One example is the store audit, which records the movement of products through a store or sample of stores to measure competitive sales performance. So, for example, in studying the impact of a department store's mass display of shelving paper, observers, stationed unobtrusively, record the total number of people passing by a display, the number stopping, the number picking up and

examining the product, and the number making purchases. In another study, whose purpose was to determine which types of consumers bought what brands of home remedies, researchers made inventories of the contents of household medicine cabinets. In a third study, researchers used concealed tape recorders and posed as customers as part of a project to evaluate selling techniques used in florist shops.

The main advantage of the observational method is that it records respondents' expressed actions and behavior patterns. Its principal shortcoming is that its design does not provide for detection of buying motives and other psychological factors since, in its pure form, at least, this method involves simply watching or listening or both, with no attempt being made to probe the reasons lying behind actions and behavior patterns.

RESEARCH DESIGNS TO EMPLOY   Often the marketing researcher wants to do more than merely measure what is happening in the market—how many people are buying, where they are, and so forth. The researcher may want to learn what will happen if new conditions are introduced—a new product, a change in price, a new promotional program, a new method of distribution. Under these circumstances the researcher must select the research design that will best provide answers.

One of the most useful research designs is the **experimental method**. Patterned after the procedure used in scientific research, the experimental method as used in marketing research involves carrying out of a small-scale trial solution to a problem while simultaneously attempting to control all relevant factors except the one being studied. An advertiser, for example, may run two versions of a proposed advertisement (ad A and ad B) in a city newspaper, with half of the copies of the issue carrying ad A and the other half ad B. This experiment, called a **split-run test,** might be used to determine the most effective advertisement in one or more market areas, which might then be placed in newspapers in other markets or in national media.

The main assumption in the experimental method is that the test conditions are essentially the same as those that will be encountered when conclusions derived from the experiment are applied to a broader marketing area. Of course, test conditions are never quite the same as parallel conditions in the broader market. But, a well-designed experiment, even though it cannot replicate total market conditions, provides guidance and information for decision making.

Test marketing is another useful research design. The proposed new strategy is tested under real market conditions in one or more selected markets. Thus, to test customer reaction to a new larger package, the package is actually placed on sale in regular retail outlets in selected cities.

Another research design is the use of **simulation**. A simulated market environment is set up in a laboratory under the assumption that with a carefully designed simulation, the actions and reactions of buyers will predict what will happen in real market conditions.

An adaptation of the Delphi technique is sometimes used. A group of expert or knowledgeable individuals is polled under the assumption that their reactions will be predictive of the broader market.

GATHERING PRIMARY DATA THROUGH SAMPLING   In gathering data from primary sources, most marketing research projects make use of sampling. A sample is, by definition, only a portion of the "universe" from which it is drawn; therefore, studying the characteristics and attitudes of the members of a sample, rather than of all members of the relevant universe, not only makes possible completion of a study in less time but also results in lower research costs.

Data obtained through sampling may contain fewer errors than data gathered through a complete census. For instance, when the universe size is very large and scientific sample selection methods are used, there is a strong possibility that sampling will result in fewer errors. The possibility is even stronger when, as often happens in marketing research, limited funds are available for the study. With limited funds, making a census requires that expenditures be spread thin; by contrast, restricting the size of the field operation (through sampling) makes relatively larger amounts available, both for better control of data collection processes and for using higher caliber interviewing and other research personnel.

However, a word of caution is necessary. Even though management wants to avoid basing decisions on erroneous data, it also wants to avoid demanding such error-free data that inordinate amounts of time and money are spent on the study. Greater expense and longer periods of investigation, in other words, are the price of reductions in marketing research errors. If, for management's purpose, accuracy within 10 percent of the true picture is sufficient, aiming for accuracy within 5 percent wastes both research time and money.

1. *Classes of Samples.* All marketing research samples fall into one of two classes: probability and nonprobability. The fundamental distinction between these two classes lies in the way items are selected for inclusion in the resulting samples. Probability samples result from a process of random selection whereby each member of a universe has a known chance of being selected for the sample. Nonprobability samples result from a process in which judgment (and, therefore, bias) enters into the selection of the members of a sample. Judgment is also involved in using probability samples (in deciding, for instance, on a particular sample design), but the actual selection of the individual items for inclusion is made solely through a probability mechanism as, for example, a table of random numbers (eliminating the human bias otherwise entering into the selection).

This difference as to the extent to which judgment enters into selection of the sample may be illustrated as follows: In a "quota" sample, one type of nonprobability sample, interviewers may be given quotas specifying that they are to select for interviewing a certain number of people who possess given characteristics; one such quota might specify, "Interview 20 women in the 35 to 45 age bracket, half of whom have full- or part-time jobs and half of whom are not employed outside the home." If the same study were to be made using a probability sample, the probability mechanism itself would be relied on to select representative proportions of people with the given characteristics, and the interviewer would play no part whatever in the actual selection of respondents.

2. *Errors.* There are two kinds of errors in samples: nonsampling and sampling. Samples contain both kinds of errors, whereas complete censuses contain only nonsampling errors. This does not mean, however, that census results are necessarily any more error-free than sample results. It means only that there is one kind of error in a census and two kinds in a sample.[4]

Nonsampling errors are the accidental (or deliberate) mistakes or errors that can happen during any of the stages of data collection, recording, and enumeration. Here are some examples: a field worker checks off a wrong answer; a respondent misinterprets a question; an interviewer misinterprets an answer; a field worker selects a wrong respondent; a field worker falsifies an interview; a clerk tabulates some data incorrectly; an interviewer biases respondents' answers by the way he or she asks questions; a poorly designed question elicits erroneous responses. Nonsampling errors, in other words, are blunders, and they occur both in complete censuses and in samples. Nonsampling errors cannot be measured (as can sampling errors) and taken into account in evaluating study results. Thoroughness in project planning and careful control over all phases of the subsequent study are the only ways to minimize these errors.

Sampling errors trace to the sample itself, causing it not to be completely representative of the universe from which it is drawn. The measurements produced by samples are really estimates of the true parameters. Statisticians, in evaluating a sample, use the term **accuracy** to refer to the difference between a sample result and the real statistic, and the term **precision** to refer to the difference between a sample result and the result of a complete count (parameter). Although it is virtually impossible to measure the accuracy of sample results, precision is statistically measurable but only for probability samples.[5] Measures of sampling error (i.e., standard error measures)[6] can be computed for such values as arithmetic means and percentages pertaining to probability sample results. Because it is not essential to our discussion to go into the calculation methods, and because marketing research texts explain these calculations in detail, we need not go into them

---

[4] Martin R. Frankel and Lester R. Frankel, "Some Recent Developments in Sample Survey Design," *Journal of Marketing Research,* August 1977, pp. 281-282.

[5] The statistical sampling error of probability sample results is a measure of precision and not of accuracy.

[6] The measure of sampling error is known technically as the "standard error of the sampling estimate," and is defined as "a measure of the variability inherent in a sample value, due only to the sampling process (sampling error); (it) may be computed for almost any mathematically determined value obtained from a probability sample." See K. P. Uhl and B. Schoner, *Marketing Research: Information Systems, and Decision Making* (New York: John Wiley & Sons, Inc., 1969), p. 121.

here.[7] It is sufficient to keep in mind the fact that it is possible to calculate the sampling error present in probability samples.

3. *Sample Size.* Common sense tells us that the larger a sample, the greater are the chances that research results will be reliable. Sampling errors are the only errors that can be reduced by increasing sample size. And, because the statistical formulas for computing sampling errors apply solely to probability samples, only in their case can we obtain measures of the adequacy of sample size. The amount of sampling error considered acceptable in each situation (and, hence, the acceptable sample size) depends mainly on management's willingness to assume risk (i.e., to risk making a bad decision because of erroneous data) and on the amount of money available for the project. In other words, "once the sample attains a certain size," as two statistics experts say, "additional observations will not reduce the *sampling error,* that is, the allowance for sampling variability in the conclusions, enough to be worth the additional cost."[8]

METHODS OF DATA ANALYSIS The first steps in analysis of data drawn from marketing research are simple tabulation and cross tabulation. The researcher learns, for example, that 90, or 41 percent of the total, people interviewed preferred a larger package. Cross tabulation reveals that 63 percent of the families in the stage of the life cycle with children under 12 preferred a larger package. Such data can be further refined by applying statistical methods.

Measures of central tendency and dispersion provide a picture of the distribution of the respondents. The mean or median clarifies the nature of the average respondent, and the standard deviation shows how far respondents are dispersed around the average. Another useful statistical tool is the **confidence interval.** Instead of stating the probable accuracy of a single statistic, a range is used. Thus, in the previous example there is 95 percent certainty that 41 percent plus or minus 2 percent (39 to 43 percent) of the families prefer a larger package.

Tests of significance are useful in measuring whether two occurrences are related to each other. It is important, for example, to know whether a price decrease caused an increase in sales, or whether the two events just happened to occur simultaneously. The *t*-test, the chi-square test, and analysis of variance (ANOVA) are all usable tests of significance. Each is better for certain uses.

Correlation and association provide a more sophisticated method of making the same kind of analysis made in cross tabulation. One of the most useful of these is regression analysis, which allows the researcher to estimate the relationship between a dependent variable and one or more independent variables and to determine whether or not one variable causes another.

[7] See P. E. Green and D. S. Tull, *Research for Marketing Decisions,* 4th ed. (Englewood Cliffs, N.J.: Prentice-Hall, Inc., 1978), pp. 204ff.

[8] John E. Freund and B. M. Perles, *Business Statistics* (Englewood Cliffs, N.J.: Prentice-Hall, Inc., 1974), pp. 204ff.

TABLE 5-2 USE AND RANK OF DATA ANALYSIS TECHNIQUES BY COMPANY SALES VOLUME

Data Analysis	Under $20 Million		$20 to $200 Million		Over $200 Million	
	% Use	Rank	% Use	Rank	% Use	Rank
Measures of dispersion	27	1	56	2	79	1
Regression/correlation analysis	24	4	59	1	75	2
Confidence intervals	27	1	49	4	75	3
Time series analysis	25	3	53	3	65	4
Statistical test of significance	24	4	39	5	63	5
Analysis of variance	15	7	20	6	35	6
Factor analysis	18	6	15	7	31	7
Cluster analysis	7	8	11	8	22	10
Multidimensional scaling	5	9	4	10	25	8
Discriminant analysis	5	9	4	10	24	9
Bayesian analysis	4	11	8	9	17	11
Canonical analysis	0	12	0	12	5	12

When more than two variables change together, it is necessary to use multivariate analysis to determine the degree of association involved. A description of these highly sophisticated techniques is not appropriate here, but they are discussed in detail in marketing research and statistics texts under such titles as factor analysis, cluster analysis, multidimensional scaling, discriminant analysis, canonical analysis, and Bayesian analysis, to name a few of the widely used techniques.[9]

Table 5-2 shows the level of usage of these data analysis techniques among 262 companies surveyed. Both the large and small companies place greatest emphasis on the simpler techniques, and only the larger firms are likely to make much use of the more complex techniques.

COSTS OF MARKETING RESEARCH
While most companies engage in some type of marketing research, few spend as much on it as they should. One study of annual expenditures on marketing research by nearly 250 firms revealed that 90 percent of them spend less than 1 percent of their annual sales on marketing research.[10] This contrasts sharply with expenditures on product research and development (R&D), where budgets often amount to 10 percent of sales or more. Although there is wide variation among companies with respect to how much is spent on marketing research, three factors appear to influence budget size: the com-

[9] See D. N. Bellenger and B. A. Greenberg, *Marketing Research: A Management Information Approach* (Homewood, Ill.: Richard D. Irwin, Inc., 1978).

[10] W. Forman and E. L. Bailey, *The Role and Organization of Marketing Research,* Experiences in Marketing Management No. 20 (New York: National Industrial Conference Board, 1969), p. 8.

pany's size, nature of operations, and aspirations for market leadership. Generally, the bigger the company, the more complex, widespread, and intricate its operations; and the higher its aims for a market leadership position, the greater the size of its marketing research budget.

value and cost of having information

To the question of "how much should a particular marketing research project cost?" the theoretical answer is, "Something less than the value the decision maker places on the information produced by the research." Both amounts—the "should cost" and the value of having the information—are difficult to estimate. Not only is it hard to put a dollar tag on the worth of specific items of information, it is at least as hard to say how much should be spent on obtaining that information.

But, in spite of these difficulties, we can say a few things about the costs of individual marketing research projects. For one thing, it is never worthwhile to launch an investigation seeking all the possible items of information about a particular decision situation; we can never get all the information anyway because decisions are made for the future and there are always some uncertainties about the future. Research information can help reduce these uncertainties, but it cannot eliminate them entirely.

We can also say that the cost of a project is related to the degree of precision management expects the research results to have—increased precision is bought at the price of higher project costs and greater amounts of time spent in processing the results. Another way of making the same point: the more confidence management wants to be able to put in the results, the larger and more expensive the sample and the more costly the research techniques that are needed to obtain data with the desired level of precision.

SUMMARY

You should now understand marketing research's relationship to marketing decision making. Marketing research, through systematic gathering and analysis of information, should assist management in answering questions that must be resolved at each state in the decision-making process. Marketing research has potentials for furnishing data on diverse factors affecting marketing decisions—market measurement data, influences of controllables, the competitive situation, and influences of uncontrollables. The starting point of any marketing research project should be mutual agreement on the identity of the problem (by management and the researcher), because both research time and money are wasted if the problem is not clearly defined. Each project should be truly a planned search for information, directed toward obtaining as reliable information as is possible to obtain within the limits of time and money available. Both with respect to total marketing research expenditures and the costs of individual projects, management must try to balance the costs of obtaining information against its value for decision-making purposes.

1 Discuss the contributions marketing research can make during each of the several stages in the decision-making process. Analyze the relationship of internal and external studies to marketing decision making.

2 Comment on the following statements:
   a. "To manage a business well is to manage its future; and to manage the future is to manage information."
   b. "It is equally important for management to know when not to use research as to know when to use it."

3 Who should identify the problems to be studied—the marketing researcher or the marketing decision maker? Justify the position you take.

4 Why should a marketing research project be a planned search for information? In planning a marketing research project, what types of decisions are required? Who should make them? Why?

5 Discuss the various criteria for choosing the research method(s) to be used in carrying out particular marketing research projects.

6 How do you explain the fact that the size of the marketing research budget varies greatly from company to company and from industry to industry?

7 How should the decision be made on the amount of money to invest in a particular marketing research project? Who should make this decision? Why?

8 What is your opinion of the value of test marketing for determining the likelihood of success for a product? Explain. Do you think all products should be test marketed? Why or why not? Under what circumstances should new products be test marketed?

9 How does marketing research relate to the marketing concept?

10 Is marketing research an "invasion of privacy?" Why or why not?

11 Can marketing success be attainable without a continuing program of marketing research? Explain your answer.

12 You have just been hired by a medium-size manufacturer of dog food to set up and manage a marketing research department. You are to report directly to the vice-president in charge of marketing but, since the company has not previously had a formally organized marketing research department, there is no clear-cut statement of departmental objectives and you have no job description as yet. Formulate a statement of department objectives and write a job description for your position as department head.

13 Why is it that the widest variety of marketing research studies focus on the influences of controllables?

14 Explain why it is important to view marketing research as a process involving several interrelated activities.

15 Distinguish between probability and nonprobability samples.

16 What is meant when it is said that the cost of a research project is related to the degree of precision management expects the research results to have?

17 In your own words, answer the following question: Why engage in marketing research?

Jonathan Lynch Company, a well-known furniture manufacturer located in the southeastern United States, was a family-run company that had successfully produced lines of traditionally styled furniture for over 50 years. Included were both upholstered and hardwood pieces in colonial, federal, and contemporary styles. Jonathan Lynch furniture was distributed nationally by 158 salespersons, who sold to the finest retail stores. After years of steady growth, sales had leveled off in the past three years. The marketing manager, Dorothy Kellar, felt that the best way to increase sales would be to expand the present lines of furniture styles or to introduce a new line under a different brand name (company products were marketed under four distinct brand names). Based on some reading she had done on home furnishings trends, Kellar believed that the best market potential lay in a moderately priced line of contemporary modular furniture geared to the need for flexible, multiuse furniture pieces in today's compact living quarters. Before committing the company to a substantial investment in a new line, however, Kellar saw a need for a marketing research study on potential market demand for possible items in the line, such as types of shelving, storage units, tables, and desks and on competitor's offerings and market position in the contemporary furniture industry.

Thomas Lynch, Jr., company president and general manager, did not think formal research was necessary. The company had no full-time marketing research staff and had but a few years previously engaged an outside research firm to do a few preliminary market studies before expanding its distribution network. Lynch observed that the company had done well in the past without relying on marketing research every step of the way. He pointed to several key new product decisions made in the past, ones based on executive judgment. He also was convinced that normal communications between field salespersons, district managers, and the home office were sufficient to keep pace with new marketing developments. He acknowledged that communications were often distorted or lost in the feedback process, but he could not see how formal research could provide perfectly accurate information.

During a recent marketing strategy meeting, Kellar made a forceful presentation, contending that the features of a potential new product line could not be determined in the absence of formal marketing research. She stated that the competitive conditions in which the Lynch Company was operating dictated that a continuing marketing research program was absolutely necessary to keep abreast of new developments. The fact that the company had been successful for years without marketing research, she said, was a matter of good luck that should not be pressed any longer. Kellar believed that, in the furniture industry, frequent reevaluation would be needed in coming years to keep up with changing life-styles. Every major competitor had a marketing research staff and used the services of outside firms. Kellar advocated establishment of a "Director of Marketing Research" position, and she suggested that the sooner the search for a person to fill the role was begun the better. Her opinion was that outside research firms should be used only to supplement a continuous in-house research program.

Jonathan Lynch then restated his faith in the soundness of the company's present marketing approach, which had been so successful for so many years. He saw no reason to change it in view of "costly expenditures for returns of questionable value." In addition, he felt that for any needed formal marketing research could be done more economically by an outside research firm.

questions:

1. Should the Jonathan Lynch Company do marketing research for the proposed new line of furniture?
2. Should the company establish a marketing research department?
3. Can a company get along without a continuing program of marketing research?
4. What are the advantages and disadvantages of an in-house marketing research department versus an outside firm?

When you have mastered the contents of this chapter, you should be able to:

1   Define the concept of a market.
2   Define market segmentation.
3   Explain the need for market segmentation.
4   Explain how the consumer market differs from the industrial market.
5   Explain why segmentation exists.
6   Name and illustrate the several bases used for segmenting consumer and industrial markets.

markets
and market
segmentation

The concept of a market is extremely important in marketing. The American Marketing Association defines a market as the aggregate demand of the potential buyers for a product.[1] An aggregate demand is a composite of the individual demands of all potential buyers of a product or service. Thus, the U.S. market for bicycles consists of the total of all the demands for bicycles by all those people in the United States who are potential buyers of bicycles. If a person is considered as a prospective bicycle buyer, he or she is included in the total that makes up the aggregate demand for bicycles.

But an aggregate demand, or total market, also consists of the sum of the demands of different market segments, each containing a group of buyers or buying units, who share qualities that render the segment distinct and make it of significance to marketing. For example, the total market for bicycles is made up of many market segments, one of which is children. Children constitute a distinct market segment for bicycles, with respect both to product preferences and buying patterns. Children have exhibited strong preferences for the "Sting Ray" or banana-seat type of bicycle. Bicycle purchases by children, in most cases, are influenced or made by parents, and they look for toughness and durability in their children's bicycles. Other bicycle market segments include: hobbyists, who prefer racing models; health faddists, who want bicycles for exercising; and adults, who want bicycles simply to use for transportation—a rapidly growing segment. Thus, a market is not only an aggregate demand for a product but the sum of the demands of different market segments.

[1] See Committee on Definitions, *Marketing Definitions* (Chicago: American Marketing Association, 1960), p. 15.

MARKET SEGMENTATION—
A DEFINITION

A **market segment**, then, is a group of buyers who share qualities that make the segment distinct and which has marketing significance. Existence of a group of individuals with common characteristics does not in itself constitute a market segment. Only when they have common characteristics as *buyers* do they form a market segment. For example, to the extent that teenagers as consumer-buyers behave differently than do other age groups, a teenage market segment exists. The distinctive marketing characteristics of each such market segment make it productive for the marketer to adapt its product and marketing program to meet the needs of each. Thus, modern marketers devote considerable attention to the identification and study of the various market segments for their products.

the need for market segmentation

Before the adoption of mass production, markets were automatically segmented. Each product or service was tailored to the needs of the buyer who had ordered it. The aim of mass production was to standardize products in order to achieve greater production efficiency and lower product cost; to enjoy the benefits of mass production costs savings, consumers were constrained to accept standardized products. One classic example of such a standardized product was Henry Ford's Model T. Beyond the three basic models (touring car, coupe, and sedan) the Ford buyer was offered essentially no opportunity for choice. Under the mass production orientation, each manufacturer treated the market as a single unit. Consumers could satisfy differences in preference only by buying competing brands which were sometimes somewhat different from competitors' brands.

Most major industries, as they shifted to mass production, also shifted to the notion of a single market. Each of the major manufacturers of soap and detergents produced a single laundry soap and a single face soap aimed to serve all users. Each major manufacturer of cigarettes produced a single brand. Each major brewer bottled one beer and/or ale. Not until the 1950s in the United States did manufacturers began to recognize the opportunities present for broadening their markets by designing different products targeted to serve different market segments.[2] The detergent manufacturers recognized that not all consumers were looking for the same qualities in a laundry detergent and that even the same customer might want "deep cleaning qualities" for some laundry loads and "gentleness on fragile fabrics" for other loads. Introduction of differentiated products to serve these different market segments by Procter & Gamble, for example, (Tide, Cheer, All, etc.), allowed this manufacturer to capture and serve a larger share of the total market.

Cigarette manufacturers recognized the advantages of segmentation at about the same time. Instead of allowing prospective customers with prefer-

[2] Contributing importantly to this new market segmentation approach was the article by Wendell Smith. See Wendell R. Smith, "Product Differentiation and Market Segmentation as Alternative Marketing Strategies," *Journal of Marketing,* July 1956, p. 308.

111

ences for filters or for mentholated cigarettes to buy competitors' brands, each major manufacturer introduced its own brands targeted to appeal to these particular market segments.

In the 1960s the national brewers recognized that they could compete directly for the patronage of those who consumed lower-priced local brands by introducing new lower-priced brands of their own. In the mid-1970s, national brewers identified another new market segment (made up of those preferring a light, lower-calorie beer) and introduced new brands to serve this segment. Miller with its Lite brand led the pack in discovering this new market, and gained a substantial market share before its competitors entered the market.

The decision to serve different market segments with different products goes contrary to the philosophy of mass production, which aims to reduce product variations in order to keep production costs low. Production and marketing executives have had to reach a compromise. The major segments in the market may still be large enough to make possible achievement of optimal production efficiency, particularly when the marketer serves large national, or even international, markets. The decision as to how small a segment can be and still be served at a profit involves a balancing of production and marketing costs and price.

the consumer market and the industrial market

The broadest basis for market segmentation is that separating the consumer from the industrial market. This division, so broad that each part is too extensive to consider as a single market segment, separates potential buyers into two categories: ultimate consumers and industrial users. **Ultimate consumers** buy either for their own or for their families' personal consumption. **Industrial users** buy to further the operation of businesses or other institutions.

There are striking differences between ultimate consumers and industrial users, because their ways and means of purchasing differ considerably. Obviously, ultimate consumers buy in much smaller quantities and generally for consumption over much shorter periods than do industrial buyers. More important, ultimate consumers are not usually so systematic in their buying as are industrial users. Some industrial users are business enterprises that exist to make profits, which encourages them to adopt systematic purchasing procedures. Other industrial users are nonprofit institutions (such as governmental agencies, schools, and hospitals) whose operations are audited and reviewed by outside authorities, which also encourages systematic purchasing procedures.

Another important difference is that ultimate consumers spend only part of their time buying, whereas the industrial user employs professionals who devote all their time and effort to purchasing. Furthermore, the ultimate consumer spreads all his or her buying skill over a wide range of goods and services, whereas the professional tends to specialize and, therefore, has more opportunity to perfect purchasing skills. These are only a few of the many differences between ultimate consumers and industrial users, but they indicate that marketers must use significantly different approaches in marketing to the two broad types of markets.

THE WHY OF MARKET SEGMENTATION

Market segmentation has existed since the beginning of marketing. The concept of **market segmentation** is based on the fact that markets, rather than being homogeneous, are really heterogeneous. No two buyers or potential buyers of a product, in other words, are ever identical in all respects. However, large groups of potential buyers share certain characteristics of distinctive significance to marketing, and each such group constitutes a market segment. When we consider the market for automobiles, for example, we think of a most heterogeneous group of buyers—buyers representing every income group, every age group, every section of the country, both sexes, married and single people, and so on. And of course industrial buyers, such as the business firm buying a fleet of automobiles for its sales force, increases further the heterogeneity. If we segment the automobile market by income groups—for example, into lower-, middle-, and high-income groups—we achieve some homogeneity. If, next, we segment each of these income groups into further subsegments—for example, into such subsegments as the Eastern urban, age 30-39, middle-income group—we gain still more homogeneity among buyers within each subsegment. Through the segmentation of markets, management improves its ability to tailor products and marketing programs uniquely fitted for each segment. Continual refinement and increased sophistication in market segmentation are required on the part of management.

Knowing the market, then, is important to a marketer's success. Knowing the market, however, means knowing the different market segments that make up the total market. Alternatively put, it is essential for the marketer not only to know "who buys the product" but to also recognize that not all buy for the same reasons. Only if they have this knowledge are marketers in a position to design optimal marketing strategies.[3]

THE WHO OF MARKET SEGMENTATION

Once management has recognized the need for and value of market segmentation it faces the dilemma of determining the most satisfactory basis or bases for segmentation. Since industrial and consumer markets are so very different, the bases for determining who falls into each segment are discussed separately.[4]

[3] An excellent overview of market segmentation is provided in J. F. Engle, H. F. Fiorillo, and M. A. Cayley, *Market Segmentation* (New York: Holt, Rinehart and Winston, Inc., 1972), pp. 1-19.

[4] Discussion of means of market segmentation can be found in Joseph T. Plummer, "The Concept and Application of Life Style Segmentation," *Journal of Marketing,* January 1974, pp. 33-37.

segmenting the consumer market   There are many different groupings that can be used for segmenting consumer markets. Most of these groupings can be classified under one of three main categories: geographic, demographic, and psychographic.

GEOGRAPHIC BASES   Management must usually segment markets along national lines. Although economic and political barriers have been removed between the nations in the European Economic Community (Common Market), in many instances each of the EEC countries must be treated as a separate market. In consumption patterns for food, for example, wide variations exist among these countries along national lines, and many a food manufacturer must treat each country as a separate market.

Within different parts of a nation, there are frequently sufficient variations in consumption patterns to justify geographical market segmentation. These variations may result from differing cultural heritage or topography and have significant implications for the marketer of some products. Furniture manufacturers, for example, find that consumer style preferences vary considerably among different geographic sections of the United States. The Southern consumer shows a much stronger preference for traditionally styled furniture than does the Midwesterner. Similarly, many a Far Western consumer has a noticeable strong preference for furniture styles incorporating oriental influences. Other examples of distinctive regional preference are found in food, clothing, floor coverings, paint, and housing. Climatic differences among regions can also have an important marketing impact. Manufacturers of outerware sell heavier coats in the Northeast and Midwest than in the Southeast and Southwest and more rainwear in the Pacific Northwest.

Segmentation by degree of urbanization—based on whether buyers live in urban, suburban, or rural areas—differentiates buying behavior for

TABLE 6-1   U.S. POPULATION BY LOCATION OF RESIDENCE, 1976

Location	1976 Population		Change Since 1970 (%)
	Number (Thousands)	% of Total	
Total	210,300	100.0	
Urban	142,500	67.8	+ 4.01
Central cities	60,700	28.9	− 3.5
Urban fringe	81,800	38.9	+10.2
Rural	67,800	32.2	+ 8.0

Source: U.S. Department of Commerce, Bureau of the Census, Statistical Abstract of the United States, 1977.

114

many products. Table 6-1 shows the distribution of population in the United States by location of residence. People in the urban fringe and outside urbanized areas (which together constitute *suburbia*) now comprise the largest population group, and they account for a disproportionally higher share of sales of products such as removable floor coverings, sporting goods, and lawn and garden equipment. Although suburbia is not as important in many nations as in the United States, the urban versus rural differentiation is an equally valuable segmentation base in most parts of the world.

City size is another useful segmentation base. For example, some very expensive luxury products serve such a limited share of the total market that only major population centers contain a sufficient number of potential buyers to justify distribution. Thus, Rolls-Royce is distributed in only a few major cities throughout the world. Still another geographic factor influencing use of this segmentation base is population density. Population in Japan is so dense in many areas that few people have gardens large enough to use mechanized garden equipment.

DEMOGRAPHIC BASES   Demographics are the most frequently used bases for market segmentation, both because they are easy to measure and because they are perceived as being particularly important in differentiating between markets. Demographics include: income, age, education, stage in the life cycle, social class, sex, occupation, religion, and race. Each can be of value in segmenting markets for particular products.

Because **income** is the main source of consumer purchasing power, market segmentation based solely on income is widely used. An individual's income, in most cases, limits not only how much he or she can buy but also what is bought. The person with low income, for example, is often so hard pressed to pay for such necessities as food, clothing, and shelter that he or she cannot afford to buy tickets for a football game and contents himself or herself with watching it on television at home. Table 6-2 shows the distribution of income among U.S. households in 1976: 46.2 percent of U.S. households earned between $10,000 and $24,999, while 60.8 percent of the households earned $10,000 or more. In 1960, only about 14 percent of the households earned $10,000 or more, and, in 1970, approximately 48 percent achieved incomes of $10,000 or more. In the 16-year period, there has been roughly a 334 percent increase in the number of households earning $10,000 or more.

Market segmentation on the basis of the *ages* of prospective buyers is important for many products, especially those designed specifically for certain market segments. For example, some brands of breakfast cereal are aimed to suit the tastes of children, while other brands are intended to be attractive to consumers within a broader range of ages. Clothing is another product that benefits from market segmentation by age, since different age groups have different clothing needs and preferences. Table 6-3 shows the age structure of the U.S. population in July 1976. Nearly three-fifths of the population was less than 35 years old.

TABLE 6-2 NUMBER AND PERCENT OF AMERICAN
HOUSEHOLDS, BY 1976 HOUSEHOLD INCOME

Household Income	Households	
	Number (thousands)	Percent
Total	74,166	100.0
Under $ 3,000	6,228	8.4
$ 3,000–$ 4,999	7,043	9.5
$ 5,000–$ 6,999	6,623	9.0
$ 7,000–$ 9,999	9,194	12.4
$10,000–$14,999	14,161	19.1
$15,000–$19,999	19,900	16.4
$20,000–$24,999	24,900	10.7
$25,000 and over	10,825	14.6

Source: U.S. Department of Commerce, Bureau of the Census, Statistical
Abstract of the United States, 1977.

Not all age groups are equally good markets for all goods. This is both because of a correlation between age and income and because of variations in needs at different ages. Table 6-4 shows, for example, that in households where the head is aged 35–44, total expenditures are $10,262, as compared with only $4,888 in households where the head is 65 or over. The purchase of individual items varies considerably with age; the under-25 household spends less on food and more on automobiles than the average.

TABLE 6-3 AGE STRUCTURE OF THE U.S.
POPULATION, JULY 1976

Age	Population	
	Number (thousands)	Percent
All ages	214,649	100.00
Under 5 years	15,339	7.1
5–13 years	32,955	15.4
14–17 years	16,896	7.9
18–24 years	27,922	13.0
25–34 years	31,891	14.9
35–44 years	23,012	10.7
45–54 years	23,636	11.0
55–64 years	20,064	9.3
65 years and over	22,934	10.7

Source: U.S. Department of Commerce, Bureau of the Census, Statistical
Abstract of the United States, 1977.

TABLE 6-4 LIFE CYCLE OF THE HOUSEHOLD BUDGET*

				Age of Household Head			
	Total	Under 25	25-34	35-44	45-54	55-64	65 and Over
Households (millions)							
Percent distribution of:	71.6	6.2	14.8	12.0	12.9	11.6	14.1
All households	100.0	8.6	22.6	16.7	18.1	16.3	19.7
All expenditures	100.0	6.3	21.9	21.2	22.7	15.9	11.9
Expenditures for current consumption	$8,080	$5,880	$8,596	$10,262	$10,148	$7,922	$4,888
Allocation of expenditures	100.0%	100.0%	100.0%	100.0%	100.0%	100.0%	100.0%
Food	19.4	11.5	15.9	21.6	20.5	20.3	22.8
Food at home	17.0	9.1	13.3	18.7	18.0	18.1	21.2
Food away from home	2.2	2.0	2.3	2.6	2.2	1.9	1.5
Alcoholic beverages and tobacco	2.6	2.8	2.8	2.5	2.6	2.7	1.9
Clothing and upkeep	8.3	8.3	8.6	9.2	8.6	7.7	6.4
Men's	2.8	2.6	3.0	3.3	3.0	2.4	1.5
Women's	4.0	3.4	3.8	4.5	4.3	3.9	3.6
Housing	30.5	36.8	35.2	29.5	26.6	27.1	32.7
Shelter	16.2	24.5	20.3	15.2	13.4	12.9	15.8
Operations and utilities	9.2	6.9	8.8	8.6	8.4	9.8	12.9
House furnishings and equipment	5.1	5.4	6.1	5.7	4.7	4.3	4.0
Automobiles	18.6	23.7	18.5	17.7	20.1	19.8	13.3
Purchases (net)	9.1	13.0	9.3	8.5	10.0	9.6	5.4
Operations	9.5	10.7	9.2	9.2	10.1	10.2	7.9
Health and personal care	7.4	4.4	5.9	6.3	7.1	8.8	11.9
Recreation	8.3	8.6	8.7	8.4	8.0	8.5	7.2
Vacation trips	3.1	2.1	2.7	2.7	3.1	3.8	4.0
Other	5.2	6.5	6.0	5.7	4.9	4.7	3.2

* Based on a U.S. government survey conducted in 1973. Sources: U.S. Department of Labor; The Conference Board.

Some markets can be effectively segmented upon the basis of level of education. Most magazines are targeted toward a consumer group with a specific level of general education. "True romance" and "movie" magazines are aimed at high school graduates and less; the *Saturday Review* and the *New Yorker* are directed at college graduates. "Cultural" types of entertainment, such as opera, legitimate theater, and ballet, appeal primarily to highly educated segments of the market in the United States. But, in Italy, opera appeals to almost the entire population. Wrestling matches, roller derbies, and carnivals appeal most strongly to the less-educated portion of the population.

Market segmentation by stage in the family life-cycle adds another dimension to age as a basis for segmentation. Expenditures on selected items vary with the life-cycle stage. For example, families with young children typically are very good customers for labor-saving appliances, and families with teenage daughters spend relatively more for women's and girls' clothing. The most commonly used scheme for market segmentation by family life-cycle stage has five major classes.[5]

First Stage:	Single or married head, under 40, no children
Second Stage:	Married head, under 40, young children, with or without older children
Third Stage:	Married head, under 40, older children, no young children
Fourth Stage:	Married head, 40 or older, no children under 20
Fifth Stage:	Head living alone, over 40, no children

Other demographic bases for market segmentation exist. Sex is obviously an important basis for segmenting certain markets. Physical differences require variations in the design and styling of clothing, but cultural differences have affected clothing styling, cosmetics, and many other products more than have physical differences. With the growing emancipation of women, however, the number of cultural bases for segmentation has been decreasing. Social class has been thought to be an important basis for market segmentation, but its use has been limited for two reasons—it is difficult to measure, and it frequently correlates very highly with income, which is easy to measure. Occupation is important for products consumed in job-related ways—purchase of tools or equipment for the job and uniforms or special clothing are cases in point. Religion is an important segmentation base in certain limited areas—specific food requirements, such as kosher foods for Jews, and prohibitions, such as liquor for Moslems, affect the structuring of a market. A few years ago, considerable interest developed in the potential of race (particularly blacks) as a basis for segmentation of markets; but research has shown that except for a few obvious physical differences reflected in product varieties found in cosmetics and hair-care items, there are few racially determined segments. Many differences are better explained by income, although a few cultural differences are reflected in food preferences.

PSYCHOGRAPHIC BASES It is often useful to segment markets upon the basis of how people act rather than where they are or what they are. These psychographic bases are often difficult to measure, but they offer potential rewards in terms of providing management with a more relevant basis for differentiating between segments of a market.

Personality affects the consumption of many goods, particularly those consumed publicly. An aggressive personality may be reflected in the choice of ostentatious clothing, furniture, and automobiles, for example. Preferences are frequently so different that it is impossible to serve all personality

[5] For an excellent discussion of the effects of the life cycle on needs and purchase behavior, see C. Glenn Walters, *Consumer Behavior* (Homewood, Ill.: Richard D. Irwin, Inc., 1974), pp. 249-250.

types with the same product or brand. A recognition of important personality types can help management "position" its product toward a profitable segment or segments.

Life-style is another important segmentation basis.[6] Swingers, home-family types, social or political activists, all have different life-styles. These life-styles influence the allocation of incomes across consumption categories, as well as among types and brands. The swinger wears different clothing,[7] buys different recreation equipment, even eats differently. The swinger buys a speedboat, while the home-family type buys a recreation camping vehicle instead.

It is often useful to categorize people as to their status as **users** of a product. Some people are **nonusers**; some are regular users; some are potential users. Maxwell House coffee, which already has a large share of the national market, may find it difficult to increase its share among those who are already users. Instead, the company might find more potential business by concentrating on young nonusers who have not previously consumed coffee. For some marketers the rate of usage is very important. In the beer industry, for example, a small group of heavy users (who will drink a six-pack or more at a sitting) account for a large portion of total industry sales. Shifting a heavy user to your brand may be equal to adding a dozen light users. A marketing campaign, then, can be most profitably directed toward this segment.

The stage of **readiness to buy** a particular product affects the design of many a marketing campaign. When electronic hand computers were first introduced on the market, very few consumers were at a stage of readiness to buy. First, they had to be educated to the advantages of carrying a computer in a pocket. Today a large segment of the market is sold on the basic product idea. Thus, if a significantly improved new product is introduced, the marketing campaign can be directed toward those in a high state of readiness to buy. If the product is essentially unchanged, the campaign must concentrate on increasing the readiness of market segments not now ready to buy.

Not all people seek the same benefits from a product. One person may buy an automobile for transportation to work, another for recreation, another for hauling loads, another for family driving, and another to impress the neighbors; others may seek a combination of benefits. Automobile manufacturers, by providing different products and different marketing campaigns, try to appeal to as many of these segments as possible.

SUMMARY ON SEGMENTING CONSUMER MARKETS   It is often good practice to break market segments down into subsegments by cross-classifying a grouping of market segments in terms of another grouping system. Table

[6] Joseph T. Plummer, "The Concept and Application of Life-Style Segmentation," *Journal of Marketing,* January 1974, pp. 33-37.
[7] Elizabeth A. Richard and Stephen Sturman, "Life-Style Segmentation in Apparel Marketing," *Journal of Marketing,* October 1977, pp. 89-91.

TABLE 6-5

Age Group	Income Group				
	Under $7,500	$7,500–$9,999	$10,000–$14,999	$15,000–$19,999	$20,000 & over
18-24			X		
25-34					
35-44					
45-54					
55 & over					

6-5, for instance, shows how an analyst might break down income market segments into subsegments according to the ages of income recipients, each box representing a subsegment. The box marked X, then, would represent those persons with incomes of $10,000-$14,999 who are in the 18-24 age group.

Table 6-6 and Figure 6-1 present a summary of the several bases used for segmenting consumer markets. Table 6-6 provides in addition an illustrative product that could benefit from each particular basis for segmentation.

segmenting the industrial market In terms of dollar value of the goods marketed, the industrial market is nearly as large as the consumer market. The industrial market, like the consumer market, is composed of different market segments. Thus, market segmentation is as appropriate for

Figure 6-1 A classification scheme of alternative bases for market segmentation

		Customer characteristics	
		General	Situation specific
M e a s u r e s	Objective	**(1)** Demographic factors (Age, stage in life cycle, sex, place of living, etc.) Socioeconomic factors	**(3)** Consumption patterns (Heavy, medium, light) Brand loyalty patterns (Brands, stores) Buying situations
	Inferred	**(2)** Personality traits Life style	**(4)** Attitudes Perceptions and preferences

Source: Ronald E. Frank, William F. Massy, and Yoram Wind, Market Segmentation (Englewood Cliffs, New Jersey: Prentice-Hall, Inc., 1972), p. 27.

TABLE 6-6 SUMMARY OF BASES FOR SEGMENTATION AND TYPICAL PRODUCTS THAT WOULD BENEFIT FROM EACH SEGMENTATION BASIS

Basis for Segmentation	Typical Product
Geographic Basis	
Region	Cowboy boots
Urban, suburban, rural	Tennis equipment
Climate	Ski clothes
City size	Rolls-Royce
Density	Riding lawnmowers
Demographic	
Income	Dishwashers
Age	Baby food
Education	Books
Stage in life cycle	Home furnishings
Social class	Wrestling matches
Sex	Clothing
Occupation	Job-oriented equipment
Religion	Food and drink
Race	Cosmetics
Psychographic	
Personality	Home furnishings
Life-style	Leisure clothing
Use of product	Coffee
Frequency of use	Beer
Readiness to purchase	Computers
Benefits desired	Automobiles

industrial as for consumer products. Separating industrial users into groups facilitates analysis of the industrial market. Many different bases are used for segmenting the industrial market, but the four most important and most used bases are kind of business or activity, geographical location of the user, usual purchasing procedure, and size of user.

KIND OF BUSINESS OR ACTIVITY Market segmentation by kind of business is usually approached through use of the U.S. federal government's Standard Industrial Classification System (known as the S.I.C. system), under which all places of business are classified into one of 10 divisions, covering the entire field of economic activity. Each of these divisions is, in turn, broken down into several "major groups," representing specific kinds of business and, again, are broken down further, to even more specific kinds of business. Thus, with the use of the S.I.C. system, the industrial market can be divided into relatively small, medium or large market segments—depending upon the degree of homogeneity desired in the analysis. For instance, manufacturers of furniture and fixtures are classified under S.I.C. No. 25. Further subclassification is effected through three- and four-digit numbers. Thus, manufacturers of household furniture come under S.I.C. No. 251, and those of metal household furniture come under S.I.C. No. 2514.

GEOGRAPHICAL LOCATION OF THE USER   Such factors as variations in topography, climate, and historical tradition cause considerable variations in the way industrial marketing is conducted in different areas. The topography of an area, for example, affects the types and costs of transportation available for shipping industrial goods. Thus, it often proves more expensive to ship bulky and heavy products across the Rocky Mountains than to ship it an equal distance over the Great Plains. Similarly, variations in climate affect the needs of industrial users for building materials and heating and cooling equipment. In addition, geographical segmentation of the industrial market may exist because some kinds of business and service organizations seem to settle in certain areas—for example, steel producers and auto makers in the Great Lakes region.

USUAL PURCHASING PROCEDURE   Industrial users are generally more systematic buyers than are ultimate consumers. But even among industrial users there is much variation in the amount of consideration given to buying different items. The decision to buy a major installation, such as a blast furnace or cement kiln, nearly always requires extensive market and other technical investigations, plus the approval of several high executives in the industrial user's organization. But the same firm may treat the purchase of supplies, such as office stationery or pencils, as a routine procedure of concern only to the purchasing agent. The industrial marketer must apply different selling tactics and strategies to each of these buying situations.

SIZE OF USER   The industrial market is characterized by wide variation in the sizes of customers, and sizes of industrial purchases also vary greatly. Since it is generally more economical to sell in large lots than in small ones, the industrial marketer often quotes lower prices to buyers of large orders. This is often the main reason why marketers use different methods for reaching different industrial users, who vary greatly in size.

SUMMARY   Among the most basic concepts in marketing are those of market and market segmentation. A market is the aggregate demand of the potential buyers of a product. Market segmentation refers to the analysis of a total market in terms of its component segments, each being made up of prospective purchasers who share common characteristics as buyers. Figure 6-2 summarizes the Market Segmentation Decision Process.

Figure 6-2   The market segmentation decision process

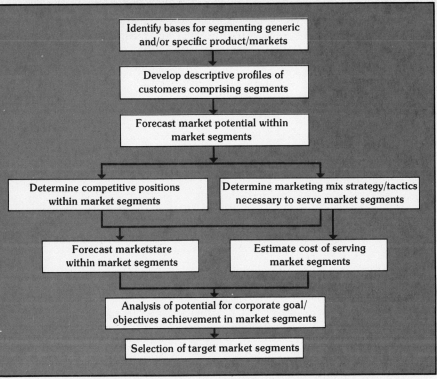

Source: David W. Cravens, Gerald E. Hills, and Robert B. Woodruff, Marketing Decision
Making (Homewood, Illinois: Richard D. Irwin, Inc., 1976), p. 246.

REVIEW AND DISCUSSION QUESTIONS		
	1	Why is there a need for market segmentation? Explain.
	2	The idea of market segmentation is based on the fact that markets are heterogeneous rather than homogeneous. Agree or disagree? Explain.
	3	"With products being differentiated more and more, markets are virtually certain to become increasingly segmented." Agree or disagree? Why?
	4	Is market segmentation a concept that is equally valuable to marketers of all kinds of products? Does it have much to offer a deodorant soap producer? An automobile manufacturer? A maker of refrigerators? A life insurance company? An airline? A producer of road-running shoes?
	5	Identify and fully discuss the various bases used for segmenting the consumer market.
	6	What is psychographic segmentation? Is it a meaningful way to differentiate among market segments? Why or why not? Give several examples.
	7	Explain the marketing significance of market segmentation by stage in the family life cycle.
	8	What are the differences between ultimate consumers and industrial users? Are there some similarities?

123

9	Is the concept of market segmentation equally applicable and important for both consumer markets and industrial markets? Why or why not?
10	What several bases are used for segmenting industrial markets?
11	In most marketing situations, several segmentation variables might be used. What factors are important in deciding upon which specific market segmentation base(s) to use in a given situation?
12	Does market segmentation increase the efficiency of marketing? Why or why not? Cite examples.
13	"The decision to serve different market segments with different products goes contrary to the philosophy of mass production." Explain this statement.
14	What does it mean to "know the market?"
15	Identify the advantages of market segmentation. Also, what are the potential dangers of market segmentation?

CASE PROBLEM

Midland State Bank was the oldest bank in Midland County and had an established reputation for dependable service. Roy Cranshaw, the main office's manager, and the three branch officers knew most customers by name and relied on personal contacts to maintain a steadily growing business. New housing and apartment developments led to a rapid expansion in population in the last five years and new businesses were moving into the growing market. Within the past six months, the First National Bank, headquartered in the state capital, had opened two branch offices in the county. For the first time, Midland State Bank found itself faced with a tough competitor for new accounts.

The First National Bank had a strong marketing campaign which offered multiservice accounts custom tailored to each customer's needs. These included NOW (negotiated orders of withdrawal) accounts, charge-free accounts, advance accounts, and automatic savings accounts, which reflected differences in customer needs for savings and credit combined with regular checking service. Cranshaw was convinced that Midland County Bank had to develop new services and then launch an advertising campaign to convince potential customers that his bank could meet their particular needs with a convenient package of services.

What little advertising the bank had done in the past had been a combined effort with the local radio station or newspaper. No advertising agency had been used, and no thought was being given to using one this time. Cranshaw decided on a campaign with the theme "Whatever Your Banking Goals—We'll Find You an Answer with a Midland Bank Custom Account." He thought the ads should feature brief descriptions of individuals with problems together with the bank's solutions. He believed that by treating each customer as an individual with an individualized banking need, he could attract new accounts on the basis of a more personal approach. It would be a way, he reasoned, of showing that Midland recognized that not all people use a bank for the same reasons.

questions:

1. Identify the different market segments that Midland might serve.
2. List several different types of individuals whose "banking problems" could be featured in the advertisements.
3. What appeals should be used?
4. Does it make sense to segment the market for banking services?

When you have mastered the contents of this chapter, you should be able to:

1 Explain the model of economic man and *evaluate* its usefulness in analyzing buying behavior.

2 Show how conglomerations are turned into assortments as indicated by sorting theory.

3 Identify the more important "uncontrollable" economic factors influencing personal consumption spending.

4 Name the basic factors influencing learning and *explain* how they provide marketers with several keys to understanding consumer behavior.

5 Identify the several contributions made by clinical psychologists to the explanation of buyer behavior.

6 Show how need satisfaction theory helps to explain buyer behavior.

7 Explain how the concepts of self-image and brand image and Festinger's theory of cognitive dissonance help to explain buyer behavior.

8 Explain the following as influences on human (and buying) behavior: reference groups, the individual's concept of social role, the diffusion process, social class, and culture.

9 Understand how life-style segmentation improves our understanding of buyer behavior.

buyer behavior

To understand marketing, you must also understand buyer behavior. Marketing success, or failure, depends importantly on target customers' individual and group reactions expressed in the form of buying patterns. Analysis in this chapter focuses on two main influences on buyer behavior: environmental, and individual or internal. As illustrated in Figure 7-1, the environmental influences include economic and business, cultural, and social. The individual influences include: learning and attitudes, motivation, needs, and perception—all concepts drawn from the field of psychology. Social scientists in each of these areas—economists, anthropologists, sociologists, and psychologists—attempt to explain why people behave as they do—most important to us are their explanations of why people behave as they do as buyers. Such relevance exists in economists' explanations of consumer motivation and the relationship of certain economic factors to buyers' behavior. Relevance is also found in psychologists' explanations of how people learn about products and services, the motivations that underlie buying behavior, the influences of individual needs and drives on buying behavior, and the perceptions individuals have of themselves and the products they buy. Similar relevance lies in the explanations advanced by sociologists and cultural anthropologists concerning: the influences of group behavior upon individual behavior, the diffusion of ideas (and new products) among various groups, and the impact of the culture on its members (e.g., consumers may act very differently in their purchases of goods and services, depending on the country in which they live). All these influences interact in highly complex ways, affecting the individual's total pattern of behavior as well as his or her buying behavior.

Buyer behavior may be viewed as *an orderly process whereby the individual interacts with his or her environment for the purpose of making marketplace decisions on products and services.* Every consumer goes through the same decision process, which consists of the following stages: problem recognition, search for information, evaluation of information, purchase decision,

Figure 7-1   Influences on the Buying Process

Source: Adapted from C. Glenn Walters, Consumer Behavior
(Homewood, Ill.: Richard D. Irwin, Inc., 1978), p. 1.

and postpurchase or postdecision evaluation. The individual's specific behavior in the marketplace is affected by internal factors such as needs, motives, perception, and attitudes, as well as by external or environmental influences such as the family, social groups, culture, economics, and business influences.[1] To achieve a better understanding of the consumer decision process and the factors influencing that process requires an in-depth search of those disciplines which can offer some explanation as to why people behave as they do.

BUYER BEHAVIOR— EXTERNAL INFLUENCES

insights from economics

Economists were the first to advance formal explanations of buyer behavior. In addition, their studies of income and personal consumption and the concept of discretionary income help us to understand buyer behavior.

[1] C. Glenn Walters, *Consumer Behavior* (Homewood, Ill.: Richard D. Irwin, Inc., 1978), pp. 7-17.

129

ECONOMIC THEORY   Generally, economists visualize the market as made up of homogeneous segments of supply and homogeneous segments of demand. Economic theory describes man as a rational buyer who has perfect information about the market and uses it to obtain optimum value for his buying effort and money. Price is regarded as his strongest motivation. He compares all competing sellers' offerings and, since all are alike in every respect, he buys the one with the lowest price. Above all, economic man's behavior is rational. Under these circumstances, his buying choices are predictable and yield maximum value.

In some situations the model of economic man helps us understand and even predict consumer buying behavior. It explains why a housewife may select the food store with the most or best "weekend specials" for her Friday shopping trip. It explains why a special price on Brand X may attract a customer who normally buys Brand Y. It also explains why a consumer, having decided to buy a new Ford station wagon, visits several Ford dealerships to get the best trade-in and price.

However, for the most part, decision making by individuals is far too complex to reduce to the simplistic model of economic man. Although this model may explain, for example, why a buyer chooses one Ford dealer over another, it does not explain why the decision was to buy a Ford instead of a Chevrolet, a station wagon instead of a sedan, or a V-8 instead of a six-cylinder model. This suggests, then, that in order to analyze buyer behavior, we must consider both economic and noneconomic factors.

MARKETS ARE HETEROGENEOUS   In striving for a realistic explanation of buyer behavior, we must discard one assumption that pervades the concept of economic man—that markets are homogeneous. **Heterogeneity**, not homogeneity, characterizes markets. The entire notion of market segmentation is based on the realization that not all buyers are alike—that they differ in numerous and distinctive ways. Furthermore, this heterogeneity is evident on both the supply (sellers') and demand (buyers') sides of every market. Essentially, then, the overall marketing problem of the total economy is to match heterogeneous segments of supply with heterogeneous segments of demand.

One way to explain buying behavior is in terms of what buyers are trying to do. **Sorting theory**, as shown in Figure 7-2, regards the entire economic process as starting with conglomerations, going through various types of sorting, and ending with assortments. Ultimate consumers, for example, are engaged in building assortments, in replenishing or extending inventories of goods for use by themselves and their families. This means that the consumer buyer enters the market as a problem solver.[2] Solving a problem, on behalf of either a household or a marketing organization, means reaching a decision in the face of uncertainty. In the **double search** that

[2] See W. Alderson, *Marketing Behavior and Executive Action* (Homewood, Ill.: Richard D. Irwin, 1957), pp. 164–184.

Figure 7-2 Sorting theory

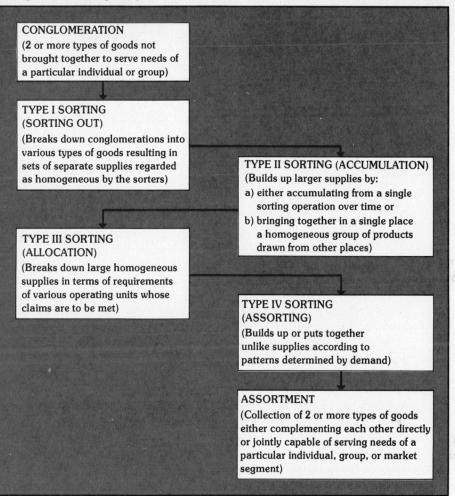

CONGLOMERATION
(2 or more types of goods not brought together to serve needs of a particular individual or group)

TYPE I SORTING (SORTING OUT)
(Breaks down conglomerations into various types of goods resulting in sets of separate supplies regarded as homogeneous by the sorters)

TYPE II SORTING (ACCUMULATION)
(Builds up larger supplies by:
a) either accumulating from a single sorting operation over time or
b) bringing together in a single place a homogeneous group of products drawn from other places)

TYPE III SORTING (ALLOCATION)
(Breaks down large homogeneous supplies in terms of requirements of various operating units whose claims are to be met)

TYPE IV SORTING (ASSORTING)
(Builds up or puts together unlike supplies according to patterns determined by demand)

ASSORTMENT
(Collection of 2 or more types of goods either complementing each other directly or jointly capable of serving needs of a particular individual, group, or market segment)

pervades marketing, the consumer buyer and the marketing executive are opposite numbers. The consumer buyer looks for products in order to complete an assortment, while the marketing executive looks for buyers who need the company's products.

This explanation is consistent with those economic theories that explain competition among sellers by emphasizing innovative competition, product differentiation, and differential advantage. The position occupied by every firm engaged in marketing is in some respects unique. Each is differentiated from all others by the characteristics of its products, its services, its geographic location, or its particular combination of these features. Therefore, each firm's survival requires that it present, to some group of buyers, a **differential advantage** over other suppliers. Any marketing organization

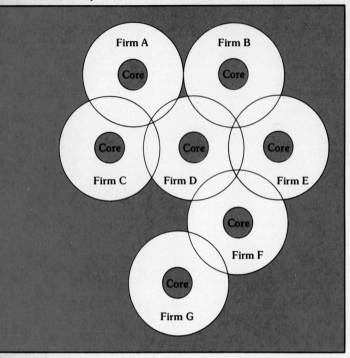

Figure 7-3 The core market concept for a specific industry

makes sales to a core market composed of buyers who prefer this source and to a **fringe market** made up of buyers who find the source acceptable, at least for occasional purchases.[3] A firm's **hard-core market** is that segment composed of brand-loyal buyers. The farther one goes from the core, out to the fringes, the less brand loyalty is shown by buyers, to the point where brand name is of little importance. The core market concept has special meaning for the firm that wants to increase its market share, since this normally means that it must concentrate its marketing efforts in areas where its fringe overlaps that of another firm's. Figure 7-3 shows the core market concept, with the overlapping fringe areas. Note that a given firm's fringe area overlaps with varying numbers of other firms' fringes. This connotes the idea that not all firms are in direct competition with one another, even though they are part of the same industry. The key point is that, for a firm to increase its market share, it must expand at the fringes.

INCOME AND PERSONAL CONSUMPTION SPENDING   Numerous economic factors influence consumers in the ways they spend their incomes for personal

[3] W. Alderson, "The Analytical Framework for Marketing," *Proceedings of the Conference of Marketing Teachers from Far Western States,* D. J. Duncan, ed. (Berkeley, Calif.: University of California, 1958), p. 18.

132

consumption. In this section we examine a few of the more important *uncontrollable economic factors,* that is, those that individual firms cannot influence to any significant extent.

1. *Disposable Personal Income.* Goods and services are produced for purposes of consumption; purchasing power is used to convert production into consumption and **disposable personal income** (i.e., what people have left to spend or save after they have paid their taxes) represents potential purchasing power in the hands of consumers. In most years, however, people do not spend *all* their income. Disposable personal income is used both for personal consumption spending and for saving.

Personal consumption spending tends both to rise and fall at a slower rate than does disposable personal income. But in inflationary periods, such as throughout most of the 1960s and 1970s, spending sometimes rises faster than income. Generally, however, in years of higher income a lower proportion is spent and a higher proportion is saved. In years of lower income, the proportion spent tends to increase while that saved declines.

2. *Size of Family and Family Income.* Size of family and size of family income affect spending and saving patterns but, unfortunately, little research has been reported on these relationships, and what studies have been done are relatively old. Two studies are cited here to illustrate the type of research that can provide useful information concerning spending behavior as it relates to size of family and family income.[4] The Wharton study disclosed that in urban families with lower incomes, average personal consumption spending exceeded income. It also showed that the average propensity to consume declined rather rapidly as income rose above the poverty level.

A second study provided insights on spending behavior relative to household gross income (i.e., income before taxes). It confirmed what business managers had long assumed: average annual household spending rises with increases in gross income per household; those with above-average incomes are above-average spenders, those with below-average incomes are below-average spenders. But, contrary to what is commonly assumed, this study found that the number of people in a household appears directly related to the size of its annual income. As the numbers of people in a household increase, annual household income rises—perhaps because more members have incomes and/or because people with larger incomes can afford larger families. This study also revealed that high-income households accounted for a disproportionately high share of total spending—53 percent of the households with above-average incomes accounted for 67 percent of total spending.[5]

Findings such as these are important to the marketing analyst. They imply that significant changes occur in a family's spending and saving pat-

[4] See *Study of Consumer Expenditures, Incomes, and Savings* (Philadelphia: Wharton School of Finance and Commerce, University of Pennsylvania, 1958), Vol. 18; and *Social Indicators,* U.S. Office of Management and Budget, Bureau of Research in Higher and Professional Education, 1973.

[5] *The Life Study of Consumer Expenditures,* Vol. 1, 1957, pp. 18-21.

tern as it moves from one income bracket to another. They also indicate that changes in the distribution of all the families in a population, relative to income brackets, may bring about significant changes in propensities to consume and to save.

3. *Consumers' Income Expectations.* The incomes that consumers expect to receive in the future have some bearing on their present spending patterns. In particular, spending for automobiles, furniture, major appliances, and other expensive items tends to be influenced by consumers' optimism or pessimism about future income. This tendency has been confirmed by the annual surveys of consumers' buying plans made by the University of Michigan's Survey Research Center. Consumers' expectations of higher or lower income have a direct effect on spending plans.

4. *Consumers' Liquid Assets.* Consumer buying plans are influenced, especially those for "big ticket" items, by the size of their holdings of liquid assets, that is, cash and other assets readily convertible into cash—for example, balances in checking and savings accounts, shares in savings and loan associations, deposits in credit unions, and holdings of government bonds and readily marketable stocks and bonds. Even though a consumer may buy with current income, the freedom with which he or she spends is influenced by his or her accumulation of liquid assets. Retired and unemployed individuals may use liquid assets to buy everyday necessities. Other consumers may use liquid assets to meet major medical bills and other emergencies.

5. *Consumer Credit.* Availability of consumer credit influences the pattern of consumer spending. Through credit, which allows one to buy now and pay later, a consumer commands more purchasing power than that represented by his or her current income. Availability of credit has been a key factor in the rapid growth of the markets for mobile homes, boats, camping trailers, and the like.

Personal debt includes all short- and intermediate-term consumer debt other than regular charge (i.e., nonrevolving) accounts, and excludes mortgage and business debt. Personal debt, thus defined, is equivalent to installment credit; that is, the consumer pays off the debt in a number of installments. Generally speaking, more than half of all spending units have such debt. The size of income is directly related to the amount of credit a consumer can obtain; lower income groups tend to have either no debt or smaller debts than higher income groups. Since 1975, the volume of installment consumer credit has been nearly five times that of noninstallment credit.[6]

DISCRETIONARY INCOME A family with money left over after buying such necessities as food, clothing, shelter, and transportation has discretionary income. During the 1970s, for example, families with disposable personal incomes under $10,000 generally had little or no discretionary income. But, as families moved above $10,000, there was extra income for other purposes.

[6] *Federal Reserve Bulletin,* April 1978, p. A42.

They could buy better food and drink, or better furniture, or they could take a small fling in the stock market, or they could spend it all on one big fling, such as a trip to Europe.

By the time families move above the $20,000 income level, about half of their income is discretionary, and the decisions are not between purchasing certain items or others but rather of choosing an entire life-style. The skilled laborer with a $20,000 income can choose to live in a working-class neighborhood and save a large portion of his income, or he can choose to live like a junior executive. It is estimated that in 1978 roughly half of all disposable income was discretionary.

Even small fluctuations in income cause sharp repercussions in consumers' purchases of durables. This traces partly to the fact that consumers can postpone or speed up their purchases of such durables as automobiles, furniture, and major appliances. If a family is temporarily short of income, it can use the old refrigerator for another year or so. Or, if it finds itself suddenly with more discretionary income, it may replace the refrigerator this year instead of next. The quick response of durable goods expenditures to income changes traces also to the wide use of installment credit in financing such purchases. Consumers are willing to increase installment debt when income is rising and are reluctant to incur additional indebtedness when income is declining. Lenders are also more agreeable to debt creation in prosperous times. Purchases of nondurables and services, which are much less postponable than purchases of durables, react less violently to changes in income.

sociological influences   Sociologists view marketing as involving the activities of groups of people motivated by group pressures as well as by individual desires. Their studies have emphasized the significance of reference groups, the individual's concept of social role, the diffusion process, and social class as influences on human behavior. These studies have demonstrated the importance of social factors in analyzing and influencing consumer behavior.

REFERENCE GROUPS   The people with whom an individual regularly associates exert strong influences on his or her behavior. He or she must conform at least partially to their standards of behavior to gain group acceptance. An individual's behavior is also influenced by groups with whom he or she has little regular contact but with whom he or she identifies closely. Both types of groups are called reference groups, which include family and peer groups, social groups, and others, such as religious or fraternal organizations.

1. *Primary Groups.* These groups, fundamental in determining the social nature of the individual, are groups of people engaged in intimate, face-to-face contact and cooperation. The most pervasive and traditionally the most influential primary group is the family, but, with the emergence of the modern small, two-generation family, much of this influence has passed to other primary groups, particularly peer groups. Peer groups are composed of

individuals who spend considerable time together and are of fairly common age and social background. Among children, these are often play groups; among adults, they include neighborhood and community groups. Other groups with varying degrees of socializing influence are religious, educational, and political institutions, and work groups.

Each individual may hold membership in several different primary groups. At work one may be a part of a close-knit, friendly group of coworkers. As a church member, one may or may not have close personal contacts with other members. As a member of social or fraternal organizations, one may be a part of still other primary groups. Any of these groups is classified as a peer group if it is sufficiently homogeneous. Purely social groups are most likely to qualify. Some peer groups transcend national boundaries; scientists and professional men often identify strongly with counterparts in other nations. The peer group has the greatest influence on the individual as a consumer because the group's general interests and mode of life are most nearly like his or her own.

2. *Significance of Reference Groups to Marketing.* Knowledge of reference groups and their influences makes it easier to explain why consumers behave in particular ways and—more important to marketers—to predict their behavior. It explains, for example, why two groups of young people in the same community—one, high school seniors, and the other, college freshmen—adopt different styles of dress or other behavior even though they are nearly the same age and come from similar family backgrounds. Even within a college freshman group, different reference groups dictate wide variations in dress and behavior. Even the same individual behaves differently at different times as he or she identifies with different reference groups. A young executive, for example, may dress and act conservatively when on the job and in other contact with his business associates, but off the job he may be a sportscar-racing buff and behave and dress very differently.

3. *Individual's Concept of Social Role in Groups.* The way a person sees his role in the social groups in which he holds membership is important in explaining his motivation. If he is a "rugged individualist," he may enjoy establishing a reputation as one who sets his own patterns of behavior—within existing group norms of acceptable conduct. Individualism was once a common mode of behavior in the United States and is still important in some nations. Group behavior has since evolved and become more important in the United States. The newer mode of behavior requires close conformity to group norms. The group-oriented individual is anxious to fit into the behavior patterns of his peers. What they do, he must do. This does not imply, however, that his pattern of behavior is rigidly frozen. Group norms may change, and he adjusts his behavior accordingly. The group-oriented individual is seldom motivated by the traditional appeals of "being an innovator" or "leading the pack." If he is to be motivated to action, he must first be persuaded that the suggested action is accepted by his peers as the proper thing to do.

4. *Influentials.* An influential is a person who serves as an opinion leader of a group. Such opinion leaders are not confined to a single social

class; they are found at all levels of society. Outwardly, influentials and those they influence (i.e., others in the same social groups) are very much alike—they have similar incomes, occupations, family backgrounds, and so on. Accordingly to one sociologist, an individual's influence is related to (1) who one is, (2) what one knows, and (3) whom one knows.[7] For example, an unmarried girl may be a fashion leader because of who she is; an older woman her group's cooking expert because of what she knows; and a man his group's political leader because of whom he knows, not only in the group but also outside it.

Influentials play key roles in marketing. If an influential tries or uses a product, his or her followers are prone to do the same. Marketers, therefore, often target their promotional efforts to reach influentials and, through them, reach their followers by word of mouth or other subtle influences exerted by the influentials.

THE DIFFUSION PROCESS   The social process of spreading information about new products or services to persuade consumers to accept them is known as **diffusion.** Studies of the diffusion process reveal that most users do not adopt an innovation simultaneously. The first group to adopt an innovation is made up of a small number of "innovators." They are soon copied by another group, who, although not venturesome enough to try first, want to be among the early users. Gradually, members of other groups adopt the innovation until it finally reaches market saturation. For a dramatically new product, such as television, the entire process may take 10 years or more.

A model of the diffusion process is shown in Figure 7-4. The diffusion process is visualized as a curve approaching a normal distribution, with 16

[7] E. Katz, "The Two-Step Flow of Communication: An Up-to-Date Report on an Hypothesis," *Public Opinion Quarterly,* Spring 1957, pp. 61-78.

Figure 7-4   Classification of adopter groups

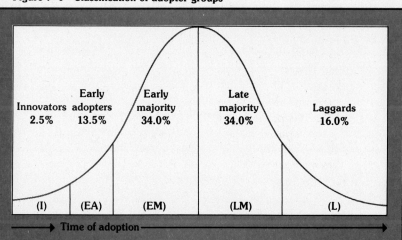

percent of the consumers in the combined innovator and early adopter groups, 34 percent each in the early and late majority groups, and 16 percent in the laggard group. It is important to identify target market segments at each stage in the diffusion process. In the initial phases of market introduction, for instance, effort and money may be wasted if the marketer tries to cultivate the entire market all at once.

The various adopter groups exhibit marked differences. The innovators are usually the youngest and have the highest social status and wealth; they are frequently cosmopolites and have professional, business, and personal contacts outside their own immediate social circles. Those in the early adopter group are generally influentials (i.e., opinion leaders), but their contacts are restricted largely to their own local group, they enjoy high status within their own social groups, and they are usually younger than those in the groups following. Those in the early majority group are the most deliberate; they will not consider buying a new product until a number of their peers (innovators and early adopters) have done so. Those in the late majority have below-average income and social prestige and are older than members of earlier groups. Laggards have still lower incomes and social status;[8] by the time they buy a new product, the earlier groups are often already trying something newer.

SOCIAL CLASSES Every society classifies its members according to some social hierarchy. All have people who occupy positions of relatively higher status and power. Most sociologists divide American society into three broad, roughly defined classes: the upper, middle, and lower classes. W. Lloyd Warner, on the basis of studies in three American towns, set up a hierarchy of six social classes: upper upper, lower upper, upper middle, lower middle, upper lower, and lower lower.[9] Under Warner's system the class status of each person is ascertained by asking his equals, his superiors, and his inferiors to rank him. This dependence on the ratings of others has been the main criticism of the Warner system. The ordinary citizen does not think in terms of this complex hierarchy and, when asked to classify his or her fellow citizens into the six groups, he or she shows little agreement with others who are asked to do the same thing.[10]

STATUS SYMBOLS Despite difficulties in classifying individuals by social class, most sociologists agree that the twin urges for self-expression and self-betterment take the form of aspiring to higher status. Sociologists explain the status symbol by holding that (1) people express their personalities not so much in words as in symbols (e.g., mannerisms, dress, ornaments, possessions), and (2) most people are increasingly concerned about their social

---

[8] E. M. Rogers, *The Diffusion of Innovations* (New York: The Free Press, 1962), p. 314.
[9] W. L. Warner and P. S. Lunt, *The Status System of a Modern Community* (New Haven, Conn.: Yale University Press, 1942), pp. 88-91.
[10] Arun K. Jain, "A Method for Investigating and Representing Implicit Social Class Theory," *Journal of Consumer Research,* June 1975, pp. 53-59.

status. Different products vary in their status symbol value, and these values may change. The automobile was once the major status symbol, but many now assert that it has been replaced by the house and its furnishings. The status symbol concept is a valuable one, for when the marketer recognizes that it is selling a symbol as well as a product, it views its product more completely. The marketer should understand not only how the product satisfies certain needs but how it fits into modern culture, because social classes exhibit differences in life-style. [11]

cultural anthropological influences   Every culture evolves unique patterns of social conduct. Analysis of these patterns helps in explaining the buying behavior of individuals. Thus, the Japanese culture provides for certain patterns of eating, of dress, and of social interaction; the Arabian culture provides for different patterns; and both are different from those prevalent in the United States. Many aspects of American culture and subcultures within the United States are unique, including the roles of ethnic groups, religion, women in society, leisure time, and fashion, as well as the population composition itself. [12]

ETHNIC GROUPS   The United States is a melting pot of cultures and peoples, but this blending has not been complete. An identifiable American national culture has emerged, but it has not equally permeated all portions of society or all geographic regions. There is, for example, an African influence not only in the Deep South but wherever black people have moved in large numbers, a Mexican influence in the Southwest, a Scandinavian influence in Minnesota and the Pacific Northwest, and a Cuban and Puerto Rican influence in many cities, including Miami, Chicago, Washington, New York, and Philadelphia. Although ethnic differences tend to decrease with each generation in the United States, their continuing existence helps explain differences in consumer motivation and behavior that would not exist in a country with a population of common cultural heritage. Yet, there are also nations which have multiple cultural heritages that remain distinct for generations, as for example, Switzerland. In such nations, marketing plans must take into account variations in the different cultures. [13]

RELIGIONS   Whereas the predominant religions in some nations stress passive acceptance of life and man's role, the Christian and Jewish religions, which comprise the basic religious heritage of American society, emphasize the perfectibility of man and his environment and, hence, encourage him to improve himself and his way of life. Therefore, the production and con-

[11] Thomas S. Robertson, *Consumer Behavior* (Glenview, Ill.: Scott, Foresman and Company, 1970), pp. 116-129.

[12] Walter A. Henry, "Cultural Values Do Correlate with Consumer Behavior," *Journal of Marketing Research,* May 1976, pp. 121-127.

[13] Ronald D. Michman, "Culture as a Marketing Tool," *Marquette Business Review,* Winter 1975, pp. 179-183.

sumption of goods are acceptable activities because they contribute to these goals. Within the American Judaeo-Christian religious pattern, however, there are many individual sects and creeds; and, although they share similar feelings about the overall social roles of production and consumption, consumption patterns of selected foods, beverages, and apparel vary considerably among them. In other nations, religion has a different impact. Hinduism, for example, with its passive acceptance of one's role, affects consumption patterns in India.

THE ROLE OF WOMEN   Roughly one-half of adult American women work and have incomes of their own; labor-saving appliances provide the other half with more time free of domestic responsibilities and, hence, more time for shopping. American women have either sole or major responsibility for making many kinds of purchases and exert increasing influence on all buying decisions. As the Women's Lib movement has gathered strength, increasing numbers of women take active rather than passive roles in society—this trend has great significance to marketing, especially in the choice of advertising themes. Throughout the world, women's role varies from a very small but growing place of women in Arab countries to the place of near equality in Scandinavia.

LEISURE TIME   Increasing numbers of people have greater amounts of leisure time, and this is reflected in changes in values and the way of life. Instead of buying an expensive car to impress friends, a consumer may buy an economy model in order to buy a boat, shop tools, or fishing equipment. New homes are planned to simplify participation in leisure-time activities. People have ceased being producers for much of their lives and have become active consumers for the products and services that go along with increasing leisure. The old Puritan dictum that "For Satan finds some mischief still for idle hands to do" is being overthrown, but the Puritan influence still remains in the United States. People refer to "active" leisure rather than just "leisure"—the active disassociating leisure from the guilt-loaded idea of loafing.

FASHION   The role of fashion in American society has been growing in importance. With widespread ownership of television sets, not to mention rising circulations of magazines and newspapers and the increasing mobility of consumers, fashion news is disseminated in minimum time. The time span covered by the appearance of a new fashion, its adoption by a few pacesetters, its rise to popularity, and its subsequent decline is becoming progressively shorter. At the same time, expansions in discretionary income permit consumers to spend more in their attempts to satisfy the desire for change. Since there are increasing numbers of group-oriented people and fewer individualists, more importance has been placed on conforming to fashion changes. However, the "counterculture," including the "hippies," tends to emphasize nonconformance with fashion (and other) changes made by other segments of society.

POPULATION COMPOSITION   Most of the population growth throughout the world is in metropolitan areas, but in the United States it is in the suburbs rather than in the cities themselves. This trend has marketing significance because the suburbanite often represents a different market than the city dweller. The suburb retains much of the character of a small town—thus, neighborhood and local social groups strongly influence individual consumption patterns.

The population composition of the central core cities has been changing to a predominately low-income and poverty-level group of consumers. At the same time, an increasing proportion of central city residents are members of minority groups—from 1960 to 1980, for instance, New York's black population more than doubled. Low-income and ghetto groups are often served by different marketing institutions than those serving others; recent studies have raised questions as to whether such groups are being served adequately.[14] One countertrend should be mentioned: the "back-to-the-city movement," a social phenomenon evident in certain large cities that can be traced to the increased living inconveniences resulting from the extreme sprawling of suburban areas.

BUYER BEHAVIOR—INSIGHTS FROM PSYCHOLOGY

There have been three major approaches to the development of a psychological theory of human behavior: the experimental, the clinical, and the Gestalt. Experimental psychology has concentrated upon physiological tensions or body needs as motivational forces and has experimented with both human beings and animals. In clinical psychology, the basic physiological drives are examined as they are modified by social forces. Gestalt psychology, often called social psychology, regards the individual and his or her environment as an indivisible whole and considers individual behavior as being directed toward various goals. Each approach adds to our understanding of human behavior, but thus far no single psychological theory of consumer motivation is completely adequate or satisfactory in explaining buyer behavior. Consequently, marketing has borrowed those theoretical concepts which seem most applicable.

attitudes and learning

Studies of learning and the related areas of recognition, recall, and habitual response have furnished marketers with several keys to understanding consumer behavior. Concepts borrowed from learning theory help in answering such questions as these: How do consumers learn about products offered for sale? How do they learn to recognize and recall these products? By what processes do they develop buying and consuming habits?

[14] For example, see F. D. Sturdivant, *The Ghetto Marketplace* (New York: The Free Press, 1969).

The current trend in psychological thinking is to look at the total experience of the individual and to consider learning as a process in which total functions are altered and rearranged to make them more useful to the individual. Particular external stimuli do not always activate predictable responses, because motives and other factors internal to the individual also affect responses. What does this mean for the marketer? Simply that the buyer is influenced not only by external stimuli—for example, the marketer's promotion—but also by internal factors. [15]

1. *The Basic Factors Influencing Learning.* What are the basic factors influencing learning? One writer answers, "repetition, motivation, conditioning, and relationship and organization." [16]

Repetition is necessary for the progressive modification of psychological functions and, if it is to be effective, it must be accompanied by attention, interest, and a goal. Mere repetition of situations or stimuli does not promote learning; advertisers who depend on repetition alone waste both their efforts and advertising dollars.

The individual's **motivation** is the most important factor in initiating and governing his or her activities. Activity in harmony with one's motives is satisfying and pleasing; other activity is annoying at best and frustrating at worst. When, in a given situation, an individual has several motives, they may either reinforce each other, which promotes learning, or be in conflict, which hinders learning. Human motivation is a topic of considerable interest to marketing professionals, especially those concerned with preparing advertising and sales presentations. But neither marketers nor the psychologists have thus far been able to reach more than partial agreements about what constitutes even the most common or basic motives.

Conditioning is a way of learning in which a new response to a particular stimulus is developed. For example, seeing just any glass bottle does not evoke a standard response but seeing one particular type of bottle makes most Americans think of Coca-Cola. Through long advertising effort and continual exposure of this symbol, the Coca-Cola Company has conditioned the American public to recognize its bottle. The conditioned response, however, establishes a temporary rather than a permanent behavior pattern and, if it is not frequently reinforced by the original stimulus, the conditioned response eventually disappears. Furthermore, all persons do not respond equally to conditioning, nor are their responses generally predictable.

Relationship and organization are also factors facilitating learning. Or, to put it another way, learning effectiveness is enhanced if the thing to be learned is presented in a familiar environmental setting. Thus, a salesperson more effectively demonstrates a vacuum cleaner by using it on the customer's carpet in her home and showing her the dirt it has picked up than by

[15] Steuart H. Britt, "Applying Learning Principles to Marketing," *Business Topics,* Spring 1975, pp. 5-12.
[16] O. Mowrer, *Learning Theory and the Symbolic Processes* (New York: John Wiley & Sons, Inc., 1963), p. 225.

describing its capacity and cleaning power in a store. The housewife is interested in the machine's performance specifications only as they directly relate to the task of cleaning her own carpets. Thus, sales messages must relate the products to the consumer's needs and interests, if they are to attract the consumer's attention and lay the groundwork for purchase.

2. *Retention and Forgetting of Learned Information.* There is particular significance for the advertiser in the psychological explanation of retention and forgetting. Retention is explained in terms of impressions left in the nervous system as a result of learning. Forgetting, or negative retention, develops with the deterioration of these impressions. The more meaningful the material learned—that is, the more the learner completely understands it—the greater the rate of retention and the lower the rate of forgetting. [17] Retention curves for both meaningful and unmeaningful materials, plotted as functions of time, drop most rapidly immediately after learning and then gradually decline until the material is almost or entirely forgotten. This phenomenon is particularly important with respect to long-run promotion and advertising campaigns. Messages should be spaced closely enough to fortify the learning process. If they are too far apart, information learned from earlier messages will have been forgotten and must be relearned.

MOTIVATION—EXPLANATIONS OF BUYER BEHAVIOR FROM CLINICAL PSYCHOLOGY **Clinical psychology** has evolved from the pioneering work of Sigmund Freud. The principal motivation research techniques used in marketing trace to concepts originally developed by clinical psychologists. Among the most important of these concepts are the *unconscious, rationalization, projection,* and *free association.*

1. The **Unconscious.** This concept was championed by Sigmund Freud, the founder of psychoanalysis. According to him, the mind contains ideas and urges—some conscious and some beneath the threshold of consciousness but all influencing behavior. People are not consciously aware of all their motives, and this explains why consumers are often unable to articulate their real reasons for buying or not buying. Recognizing the existence of the unconscious mind, motivation researchers use indirect approaches, such as depth interviewing. More conventional research approaches, such as direct questioning, have been unsuccessful in providing data sufficiently reliable to justify predictions of consumer behavior. Practical marketers, of course, have long known that there are often wide discrepancies between what people say they will buy and what they actually do buy.

2. **Rationalization.** This concept relates to the mental process of finding reasons to justify an act or opinion that is actually based on other motives or grounds than those stated, although this may or may not be apparent to the rationalizer. In advertising, rationalization may often be capitalized upon by providing readers or listeners with a plausible, acceptable reason for buying in situations where they may be unwilling, con-

---

[17] B. Berelson and G. Steiner, *Human Behavior: An Inventory of Scientific Findings* (New York: Harcourt, Brace & World, 1964), p. 102.

sciously or unconsciously, to admit the real reasons. The prevalence of rationalization in our society explains why such direct questions as "Why did you buy this?" or "What were your reasons for buying?" so often fail to uncover the real buying motives. Thus, when it is suspected that rationalizing is a factor in consumer behavior, indirect research approaches, such as depth interviewing, are used.

3. **Projection.** This concept concerns the reaction that occurs when a person, seeing someone else facing a certain problem or situation, assumes the other person's reactions would be the same as his or her own. In other words, he or she ascribes his or her own motives to the other person. Putting the projection concept to practical use, motivation researchers have designed projective techniques (e.g., the stimulus picture) that provide a means for uncovering consumers' hidden or unconscious motives and attitudes.

4. **Free Association.** The principle of free association, which traces to Freud and is used extensively in psychoanalysis, has also been put to use by motivation researchers in their development of indirect research techniques. As Newman says, "The basic idea is that if a person gives up the usual logical controls he exercises over his thoughts and says whatever comes into his mind at the moment in the presence of a skilled listener, unconscious feelings and thoughts can be discovered.[18] Thus, an application of the principle of free association is found in depth interviewing, many of the techniques of which take the form of word-association tests, in which respondents are asked to give the first word that comes to mind for each of a list of unrelated words. Given the word *rain,* for example, the respondent might reply *drop.* Among the many marketing applications of word-association tests are those of screening possible names for new products, measuring the penetration of advertising appeals, and approximating the market shares of different competitors.

NEED SATISFACTION AND BUYER BEHAVIOR   Psychological studies indicate that human activity, including buying behavior, is directed toward satisfying certain needs. Not every individual acts in the same way in the effort to fulfill these **needs;** the actions of each not only depend upon the nature of the needs themselves but are also modified by the individual's particular environmental and social background. The motivation for any specific action derives from the tensions built up to satisfy needs, needs that frequently lie beneath the threshold of consciousness. Whatever action the individual takes is directed toward reducing these tensions.

Although clinical psychologists have not agreed on a single list of needs, the different lists available show more agreement than disagreement. In one list, illustrated in Figure 7-5, Maslow enumerates needs in their order of importance for most people with the most basic needs at the bottom of

[18] J. W. Newman, *Motivation Research and Marketing Management* (Boston: Division of Research, Harvard University Graduate School of Business Administration, 1957), p. 65.

Figure 7–5 Maslow's hierarchy of needs

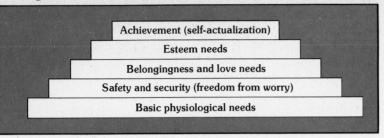

Source: A. H. Maslow, Motivation and Personality (New York:
Harper & Brothers, 1954), pp. 80–85.

the figure. According to him, an individual normally tries to satisfy the most basic needs first and, satisfying these, he or she is then free to devote his or her efforts to the next one shown on the list. Each category of need on the Maslow list is described as follows.[19]

1. *Basic Needs.* The needs to satisfy hunger, thirst, sleep, and so forth. These are the most basic needs, and until they are satisfied other needs are of no importance.
2. *Safety and Security Needs.* In modern society, these needs are more often for economic and social security rather than for physical safety.
3. *Belongingness and Love Needs.* The need for affectionate relations with individuals and a place in society is so important that its lack is a common cause of maladjustment.
4. *Esteem Needs.* People need both self-esteem, a high evaluation of self, and the esteem of others in our society. Fulfillment provides a feeling of self-confidence and usefulness; nonfulfillment produces feelings of inferiority and helplessness.
5. *Achievement Need.* This is the desire to achieve to the maximum of one's capabilities. Although it may be present in everyone, its fulfillment depends upon prior fulfillment of the more basic needs.

Often the marketing success of a brand depends on its ability to satisfy several needs at once; motivation research techniques are available to identify the strength or weakness of a product in terms of the needs it fulfills. The concept of needs and the theory that individuals normally try to satisfy them in some order are especially significant.[20]

PERCEPTION—HOW BUYERS PERCEIVE THEMSELVES AND THE PRODUCTS THEY BUY   Buyers see both themselves and the products they buy in terms of images. These images are the formalized impressions residing, consciously

[19] A. H. Maslow, *Motivation and Personality* (New York: Harper & Brothers, 1954), pp. 80–85.
[20] William J. McGuire, "Some Internal Psychological Factors Influencing Consumer Choice," *The Journal of Consumer Research,* March 1976, pp. 302–319.

or unconsciously, in the minds of individuals with regard to given subjects. Patterns of buying behavior are influenced by the images that consumers have of different products, particular brands, companies, retail outlets, and of themselves. Because images affect consumer buying behavior, marketers take them into account in drafting promotional plans and programs. Differences among individuals, products, brands, and the like result in different images, and motivation research is used not only to identify the nature of images but also to detect the implications for marketing action.

1. *Self-Image.* The **self-image** is the picture a person has of himself—the kind of person he considers himself to be and the kind of person that he imagines others consider him to be. Different people have different kinds of self-image, and this gives rise to market segmentation along psychological lines. For instance, the woman who sees herself primarily as a good housewife and mother exhibits a different total pattern of buying behavior from that shown by the woman who sees herself as a social leader or professional careerist. In many buying situations an individual prefers to buy those products and brands whose images appear consistent with his or her self-image. However, the power of the self-image as a buying influence varies from individual to individual and even within the same individual as he or she makes different buying decisions at different times.

2. *Brand Image.* The **brand image,** another stereotype, results from all the impressions consumers receive, from whatever sources, about a particular manufacturer's brand. In the minds of consumers familiar with a particular brand, there tends to be considerable consistency in the brand image or, as it is sometimes called, the *brand personality.* For competing brands there are in the minds of consumers distinctive images. Similarly, retail stores exhibit distinct images or personalities, as do corporations.

Consumers' appraisal of the distinctiveness of a brand's physical attributes not only affects the brand image but also has important implications for marketing. When consumers believe the brand is physically different from competing brands, the brand image centers on the brand as a specific version of the product. Depending on whether the marketer considers the image favorable or unfavorable, physical attributes of the product may be retained or changed, and marketing strategy may be directed toward reinforcing or altering the image. By contrast, when consumers believe a brand has no differentiating physical attributes, the brand image tends to be associated with the personalities of the people who are thought to buy it.

Through long-continued use of particular advertising and selling appeals, many brands have acquired definite images. In numerous cases, a brand image has developed without management's direction. Whether or not a particular brand image was shaped deliberately, management should identify its nature. Otherwise, ignorance of the brand image may result in poorly planned promotional programs. If the image is favorable, for example, inconsistent sales and advertising appeals may confuse or alienate existing customers. Before introducing a new brand to the market or an established brand to a different market, management should determine the sort of image it wishes to build.

COGNITIVE DISSONANCE   When a person makes an important decision, dissonance or discomfort will almost always occur, because the person making the decision knows that it has certain disadvantages as well as advantages. After making the decision, then, the person tends to expose him- or herself to information that he or she perceives as likely to support the choice and to avoid information that may favor the rejected alternative. [21] This theory was evidently intended to apply only to decisions involving postdecision anxiety, but it seems reasonable that it should also hold for situations involving predecision anxiety: a buyer may panic as the time of decision arrives and either rush into buying as an escape from the problem or delay it because of the difficulty in deciding among alternatives. In marketing, an important goal both of advertising and personal selling is to reduce **cognitive dissonance** on the part of buyers and prospects. Customers suffering cognitive dissonance may need reassuring that their decisions are or were wise ones. This can be accomplished by providing information that permits them to rationalize their decisions. For example, the owner's manual that accompanies a product when it is purchased usually begins by citing some important reasons why the buyer's decision to buy that product was an excellent choice.

BUYER BEHAVIOR—LIFE-STYLE

Economic, sociological, and psychological factors help us to understand buyer behavior, but they often lack the detail or richness of information required to provide optimal insights into human behavior. A new construct, life-style patterns, adds much of the lacking richness and dimensionality. A **life-style** is a distinctive mode of living in a dynamic society. Life-style research measures people's actions in terms of (1) their activities, (2) their interests, (3) their opinions, and (4) certain basic demographic characteristics. Table 7-1 lists the more important elements included in each of the four major dimensions of life-style. [22]

Life-style research answers questions such as: What do women think of the job of housekeeping? Do they participate in community activities? Are they interested in the future? If answers to these questions correlate significantly with product usage, magazine readership, or television program preference, a pattern emerges that is broader than product-specific measures, program ratings, or plain demographics. [23]

[21] L. Festinger, *A Theory of Cognitive Dissonance* (Evanston, Ill.: Row, Peterson & Company, 1957).

[22] Joseph T. Plummer, "The Concept and Application of Life-Style Segmentation," *Journal of Marketing,* January 1974, pp. 33-37.

[23] Kathryn E. A. Villani, "Personality/Life-Style and Television Viewing Behavior," *Journal of Marketing Research,* November 1975, pp. 432-439.

TABLE 7-1   LIFE-STYLE DIMENSIONS

Activities	Interests	Opinions	Demographics
Work	Family	Themselves	Age
Hobbies	Home	Social issues	Education
Social events	Job	Politics	Income
Vacation	Community	Business	Occupation
Entertainment	Recreation	Economics	Family size
Club membership	Fashion	Education	Dwelling
Community	Food	Products	Geography
Shopping	Media	Future	City size
Sports	Achievements	Culture	Stage in life cycle

Source: Joseph T. Plummer, "The Concept and Application of Life Style Segmentation,"
Journal of Marketing, January 1974, p. 34.

Life-style segmentation is concerned with people rather than products. It classifies them into different life-style groups, each with a unique style of living. The justification for this approach to segmentation is that the consumer, who is faced with hundreds of product choices in a given week, is not interested in the product per se but in its effect upon himself.[24]

BUYER BEHAVIOR—INDUSTRIAL USERS

Industrial users tend to be more "rational" in their buying than do ultimate consumers. (See Figure 7-6.) Industrial users buy to fill the needs of their organizations, and these needs are of a practical nature. But it is nonetheless true that organizations are composed of individuals, that one or more individuals do the buying, and that they all have personal needs that sometimes become enmeshed with their roles as buyers.[25] Thus, even industrial purchases may be made on emotional bases, as in the case of the purchasing agent who buys from a certain supplier because the sales representative is a good friend.

SUMMARY

Buyer behavior has been analyzed in this chapter through examining insights derived from economics and the behavioral sciences. In classical economic theory, financial self-interest explains buyer behavior; economic man acts rationally to maximize his financial well-being. Unfortunately, this explanation provides little help to marketers, whose customers confront them daily with apparently irrational behavior. So, searching for a clearer explanation, marketers next turned to psychology, which, in the main, explains individual behavior in terms of

[24] Lorraine Baltera, "Focus Selling Efforts on Life-Styles, Retailers Told," *Advertising Age,* January 26, 1976, p. 10.

[25] For an excellent discussion of this important matter, see Frederick E. Webster, Jr., and Yoram Wind, *Organizational Buying Behavior* (Englewood Cliffs, N.J.: Prentice-Hall, Inc., 1972).

Figure 7-6 A model of the buying organization

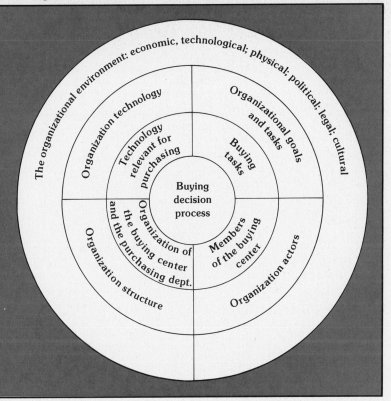

The organizational environment: economic, technological; physical; political; legal; cultural

Organization technology

Organizational goals and tasks

Technology relevant for purchasing

Buying tasks

Buying decision process

Organization of the buying center and the purchasing dept.

Members of the buying center

Organization structure

Organization actors

Source: Frederick E. Webster, Jr. and Yoram Wind, Organizational Buying Behavior *(Englewood Cliffs, New Jersey: Prentice-Hall, Inc., 1972), p. 54.*

basic needs common to all people. Psychological explanations of human motivation helped but, from the standpoint of marketers, fuzzy areas were still left where there were no satisfactory answers. More recently, marketing professionals, searching for added insights, combed the literature of sociology and anthropology, and it is now recognized that individuals, as social creatures, are strongly influenced in their buying by the social and cultural environments in which they live. Thus, each of the behavioral sciences—economics, psychology, sociology, and cultural anthropology—has helped fill in the missing pieces of what might be called the "jigsaw puzzle of buyer behavior." Recently, life-style segmentation has provided a more global look at buyer behavior. Yet so complex is human behavior in general and buyer behavior in particular that missing pieces in the jigsaw puzzle still remain; as of now, at least, no general theory of buyer behavior has received widespread acceptance among practical marketers. Nevertheless, if you have mastered the content of this chapter, you have the basic background material on buyer behavior relevant to marketing, which should help in analyzing practical marketing situations.

1 "The survival of a firm requires that it present, to some group of buyers, a differential advantage over all other suppliers." List some forms of differential advantage, and give examples of companies presenting each form.

2 Why do you suppose many advertisers have relied primarily on repetition to achieve customer recognition of their products, when learning is more easily achieved with proper motivation?

3 "In order to develop distinctive brand images, there must be clearly identifiable physical differences in products involved." Do you agree? Why or why not?

4 What is Festinger's theory of cognitive dissonance? Cite some instances where you personally experienced cognitive dissonance in buying situations. What, if anything, did the seller do to reduce your discomfort?

5 When an individual belongs to several peer groups, are his or her consuming activities likely to be affected equally by all groups? Why or why not? Explain.

6 What is an influential? How would you go about identifying influentials? Who would the influentials likely be in connection with the purchase of the following products? (a) golfing equipment; (b) plants and shrubs for landscaping; (c) musical instruments for teenagers; (d) office typewriters; (e) stereo components.

7 Explain how a marketer contemplating the introduction of a radically new type of product might use Rogers' model of the diffusion process in planning marketing strategy.

8 Why do you suppose some products have status connotations and others do not?

9 Need conflict is a situation in which an individual has more than one need and the satisfaction of one need causes other needs to remain unsatisfied. Using examples, explain how a person might go about resolving need conflict.

10 "Basically, the consumer is a problem solver." Comment.

11 Evaluate the ways in which the following contribute to a fuller understanding of buyer behavior: economics, psychology, sociology, anthropology. Give specific examples of how each discipline permits greater insight into buying behavior.

12 In what ways does perception contribute to the differences found among consumers? How does perception affect marketing strategy planning? Use examples.

13 Show how sorting theory can be used to explain the economic process whereby conglomerations are converted into assortments.

14 Why do you think a company selling tire-making machines might carry on an advertising campaign directed not to potential buyers of tire-making machines but to potential buyers of tires? Does this sort of strategy make sense for any company whose product has a derived demand? Why or why not?

15 Would you say that many consumers shut out (purposely do not see or hear) advertising to which they are exposed? Do many people discount a certain amount of advertising as "puffery" and, therefore, tend to be overly cautious in their acceptance of claims? Why? What are the implications for advertisers?

16 "Once a brand image has developed in the minds of the public, there is little that can be done to change it." Comment on this statement.

17 Identify and explain the factors that influence learning. Is buying behavior learned? Why or why not?

18 Explain, in your own words, the relationship between life-style and consumer behavior.

19 "Needs represent the foundation of consumer behavior." Comment. Does the failure of psychologists to agree on a common list of basic needs render it more difficult for the marketer to understand buyer behavior?

20 How does an individual's self-image affect his or her buying behavior? Give several examples.

21 | Would you classify consumer behavior as rational or emotional? Defend your position. Use examples.

22 | How has the changing role of women affected marketing? Be specific. Cite examples.

CASE PROBLEMS

Green Gables, a restaurant, had been operated for over 20 years by the Thornton family. It was located on the main street leading to the center of a small city in coastal New England. During the first 15 years, the restaurant was most attractively maintained. In fact, customers usually remarked about the decor and cleanliness of Green Gables. Its excellent seafood selection, along with moderate prices, made it a popular dining place among families and local business people. Sales surged during the summer, with the great number of vacationers and tourists visiting the area. However, the Thorntons failed to keep up the decor and had difficulty finding reliable kitchen help. As a result, restaurant sales dipped—slowly at first, then more rapidly. Repeat business became a thing of the past. No longer was Green Gables a favorite for family dining. Instead, only the irregular patronage of passing businesspeople and truckers made Green Gables' survival possible. With no prospect for things getting better and with no desire to "get started all over again," 68-year-old Nell Thornton sold out to the Pewter Platter, a small chain of family-style restaurants. New to the area, Pewter Platter completely renovated both the interior and exterior of the restaurant, restoring its charming atmosphere.

Opening of the Pewter Platter was preceded by extensive advertising in the local newspaper, which included a coupon for a free dessert with the purchase of a dinner. The new restaurant offered a more varied menu, with an equal number of meat and seafood dishes. Prices were slightly higher than they were prior to the takeover by Pewter Platter. Much to the new management's dismay, only a few local residents patronized the establishment during the first two months. It was mid-autumn, well past the booming summer season, and Pewter Platter needed to have increased business to justify staying open year-round. Several other area restaurants stayed open all year, and the trading area population was substantial. An opinion poll, conducted informally at a nearby shopping center, showed that many local residents viewed the restaurant as merely a "redecorated" Green Gables and still regarded it as a "rundown restaurant with greasy seafood," which it had become in its last years under Thornton management. In reality, though, it was now a well-run restaurant offering a varied menu of standard favorites. Management of the new Pewter Platter was puzzled as to what else they could do to counteract the unfavorable image that seemed to linger as a dark cloud over the restaurant. Even though it was past the big summer season, ways had to be found quickly to build up local repeat patronage, as this was the backbone of success for family-type restaurants such as the Pewter Platter. Pewter Platter needed considerably more business to justify staying open year-round. In fact, everything seemed made to order, except that initial market response to the new Pewter Platter was discouraging.

question:

1. What should Pewter Platter do?

When you have mastered the contents of this chapter, you should be able to:

1 Explain what is meant by "a product."
2 Distinguish consumers' goods from industrial goods.
3 Discuss the marketing characteristics of the three classes of consumers' goods.
4 Discuss the marketing characteristics of the four major categories of industrial goods and give examples of the types of goods included in each.
5 Discuss the marketing significance of each of the four stages of the product life cycle.
6 Illustrate how and explain why different kinds of products have different types of life-cycle curves.
7 Justify the need for product objectives and product policies.
8 Explain the nature of each of the three major phases in new product planning.

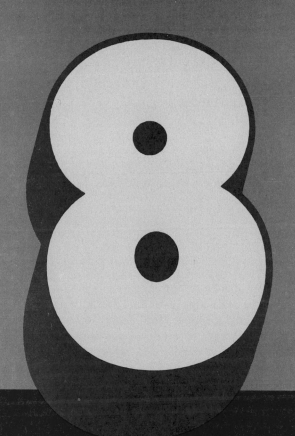

8

products:
marketing
characteristics,
life cycles, and
innovation

Successful marketing programs are built around two essential elements—products and markets. The essence of marketing, in other words, is the bringing together of products possessing want-satisfying capabilities with markets made up of potential customers having particular wants. Discussion in this and the following chapter focuses on the marketing significance of key aspects of product management.

WHAT IS A PRODUCT?   A **product** is both what a seller has to sell and what a buyer has to buy. Thus, any enterprise that has something to sell, tangible goods or not, is selling products. A laundry, for instance, sells the service of cleaning clothes and is just as surely engaged in selling a product as the retail stores that originally sold the clothes it cleans. Any firm that has something to sell, in fact, sells services as part of that something, even though we think of it as dealing in tangible goods rather than services per se. Furthermore, what a buyer buys is a mixture not of goods and services but, rather, of expected physical and psychological satisfactions. In other words, the buyer buys a total product, not merely the physical product itself.

Formally defined, then, *a product is a bundle of utilities consisting of various product features and accompanying services.*[1] The bundle of utilities (i.e., the physical and psychological satisfactions that the buyer receives) is provided by the seller who sells a particular combination of product features and associated services. When a man buys a suit from a clothing store, for example, he buys not only the garment itself but the clerk's assistance and advice, the store's alteration service, the prestige of the store's and maker's labels, perhaps charge and delivery services, and the privilege of returning

[1] Wroe Alderson, *Marketing Behavior and Executive Action* (Homewood, Ill.: Richard D. Irwin, Inc., 1957), p. 274.

156

157

products:
marketing
characteristics, life
cycles, and
innovation

the item for refund or allowance should it not yield the expected satisfaction. The clothing store sells not only men's suits but related services that customers regard as bundles providing both physical and psychological satisfactions during consumption.

In marketing, the term "good" is used as a synonym for "product." This is in line both with long-standing business usage and well-established academic practice. In the following discussion, as throughout this entire book, "good" and "product" are used interchangeably.

Depending upon the use for which it is destined, each good is classed as either a consumer or an industrial good. **Consumers' goods** are destined for final consumption by individuals (ultimate consumers) and households. Television sets, perfume and lipsticks, and boxed candy are all consumers' goods. **Industrial goods** are destined for use in the commercial production of other goods or in connection with carrying on some business or institutional activity. Iron ore, machine tools, and electronic computers are all industrial goods.

Actually, not many goods can be classified exclusively as consumer goods or industrial goods. Typing paper, for example, is used both for business and personal correspondence and, therefore, is both a consumer and an industrial good. Depending upon the circumstances surrounding its use, the same article can be either a consumer or an industrial good.

Why is this apparently artificial distinction important? Because consumers' and industrial goods are bought not only for different purposes but also—of greater marketing significance—characteristically, their purchasers take different approaches in making buying decisions. Consequently, the nature of marketing problems and appropriate marketing strategies also varies, depending upon whether the product is marketed as a consumer or an industrial good.

CONSUMERS' GOODS

The variety of consumers' goods is almost endless, literally ranging from A to Z—apples to zippers—and including such diverse items as candy bars, home swimming pools, grand pianos, and frozen TV dinners. There are so many different consumers' goods that it is impractical to analyze each individually. If these goods can be classified into a few general groups, common marketing strategies can be designed for each group. Several classification systems have been devised to facilitate analysis, but the traditional classification presented below is the most widely used.

traditional classification of consumers' goods

Melvin T. Copeland of the Harvard Business School, a pioneer marketing teacher, set up what is now known as the traditional system for classifying consumers' goods. Copeland based his classifications on differences in consumer buying attitudes and behavior. Under his system, three classes of consumers' goods are identified: convenience, shopping, and specialty.

CONVENIENCE GOODS Items the consumer buys frequently, immediately, and with minimum shopping effort are **convenience goods.** Examples include cigarettes, candy and chewing gum, magazines and newspapers, gasoline, drugs, and most grocery items. Note that these are all nondurables; that is, they are consumed or used up rapidly. Hence, consumers buy them frequently and normally neither postpone their purchases nor make them much in advance of the consumption time. Note, too, that in buying convenience goods, habit dominates the consumer's behavior. Habitual behavior makes it easy for the consumer to make buying decisions. In buying cigarettes and gasoline, for example, consumers know which brands they prefer, and they know the retail outlets where they generally buy them. Little or no conscious deliberation is required to decide each individual purchase, minimizing the time and effort devoted to buying convenience goods.

In buying most convenience goods, the consumer rarely bothers to compare competing offerings on the bases of price and quality. "It isn't worth shopping around for" expresses the typical consumer's attitude. However, if the item represents an important item in the consumer's budget, he or she may be willing to spend considerable time or effort getting the best buy. For example, a housewife may have a favorite brand of coffee and buy it habitually, but she may watch for "specials" and try to buy it then; she may even visit a store not usually patronized if it advertises a special price on her favorite brand. Also, if the price or quality of a convenience good, such as of a favorite brand of bread, gets too far out of line with competing brands, many consumers revise their buying habits. The consumer's possible gains in such situations outweigh the costs in time and effort.

Seeking to minimize shopping time and effort, the consumer buys convenience goods at conventional locations. A convenient location may be near the consumer's home, on the way to work, or near the place of work. Recognizing that consumers will not go far out of their way to buy, marketers of convenience goods make them available for sale in numerous and diverse outlets.

SHOPPING GOODS Items the consumer selects and buys after making comparisons on such bases as suitability, quality, price, and style are **goods.** Whenever a substantial number of consumers habitually make such shopping comparisons before they select and buy an item, it is considered a shopping good. Examples of goods that most consumers buy in this way include furniture, rugs, dress goods, women's ready-to-wear and shoes, and household appliances. Before buying these items, consumers shop around and compare different stores' offerings. Notice that the typical shopping good is bought infrequently, is "used up" slowly, and that consumers often are in positions to defer or advance the purchase date. Thus, they can afford to devote considerable time and effort to the buying decision. In other words, consumers believe that the possible gains from making shopping comparisons exceed the costs in terms of time and effort.

159

products:
marketing
characteristics, life
cycles, and
innovation

Not every consumer uses the same bases of comparison in buying shopping goods. In some cases, a consumer shops primarily to find something suitable—for example, the person who looks for drapes to match a particular carpet or upholstery fabric. In shopping for clothing, some women consider style the most important factor, whereas others are mainly "price shoppers." In shopping for childrens' shoes, these same women may consider quality the most important basis for comparison. The bases of comparison and the relative importance vary both with the product and the shopper, but the key word in identifying shopping goods is comparison.

Branding is much less important for shopping goods than for convenience goods. In some instances, the consumer undoubtedly is willing to pay more for a branded shopping good. For example, some women prefer certain brands of dresses, not because of styling or design characteristics, but merely because they have found they fit them with little alteration. But, in most cases, if the product is truly a shopping good, the consumer is unwilling to pay for the possible prestige of the brand name.

Because, typically, consumers devote considerable time and effort to the buying of shopping goods, shopping goods marketers can manage with fewer retail outlets than can convenience goods marketers. The shopping goods marketer places great emphasis on selling its goods in outlets where consumers are likely to look for such items rather than in every store.

SPECIALTY GOODS   Items for which significant numbers of consumers are habitually willing to make a special purchasing effort are known as **specialty goods.** Items in this category must possess unique characteristics or have a degree of brand identification or both. Examples of items usually bought as specialty goods are stereo components, fancy foods, stamps and coins for collectors, and prestige brands of men's suits. Consumers already know the product or brand they want; they are willing to make a special purchasing effort to find the outlet handling it. In reaching the buying decision, consumers do not compare the desired specialty good with others, as in the case of shopping goods. However, as specialty goods are often in the luxury price class, consumers may take considerable time in deciding to start the special search required.

Specialty goods are found in low as well as high price ranges. For instance, to obtain a stamp collection's missing stamp worth a dime or quarter may require nearly as much purchasing effort as to locate the rarity worth hundreds of dollars. Although less money is involved in one case than in the other, both prices are high relative to those of other articles without such unique characteristics. Consumers exert special purchasing efforts to locate such items, and prices are secondary considerations in buying decisions.

However, an item does not have to be difficult to locate to make it a specialty good. The consumer who wants to buy Bayer aspirin and will not accept a substitute can find the brand in nearly all drugstores and most grocery stores. An item is a specialty good if many buyers are willing to make a special purchasing effort, not that they always have to. Marketing practices of many manufacturers of specialty goods make it unnecessary for consumers to exert special purchasing efforts. They make their brands easy to locate, thus easy for consumers to buy.

A problem with the use of this or any method of classifying goods is the overlap between categories. Thus, different consumers might classify a particular product as a shopping or a specialty good.

INDUSTRIAL GOODS

Industrial users exhibit more uniform patterns of buying behavior than do ultimate consumers. Different industrial buyers are remarkably alike in the ways they go about making buying decisions for similar products. The automobile manufacturer's approach to the buying of machine tools, for example, closely resembles those taken both by its competitors and by other buyers of machine tools. Industrial goods, therefore, readily lend themselves to a classification system based on the uses to which they are to be put. There are four major categories: (1) production facilities and equipment, (2) production materials, (3) production supplies, and (4) management materials.

production facilities and equipment

This category includes installations, minor equipment, and plants and buildings.

INSTALLATIONS These are major items of capital equipment (such as factory turret lathes and commercial laundry dryers) essential to an industrial user's operations. Buying an installation involves investment of a comparatively large sum, so buying decisions generally require approval of both top management and the using department head. Because of this multiple purchase influence, persons selling installations commonly must convince several individuals before they actually get the orders, the negotiating periods often extending over considerable time. Some installations are designed and manufactured especially to buyers' specifications—for example, installations used in cane sugar processing and refining; sales personnel selling such items need technical background or training or both. Because of the characteristically high unit value, most installations are sold directly to industrial users by the manufacturers.

MINOR EQUIPMENT This subcategory includes pieces of equipment (such as work benches, lift trucks, and hand tools) that the industrial user utilizes in producing its product or service. Buying procedures are routine; ordinarily, the industrial user's purchasing executive orders according to specifications set by the department using the item. Because of the relatively high purchase frequency, marketers of minor equipment make certain that their salespeople call frequently on prospects. Listing in industrial catalogs, trade

161

products:
marketing
characteristics, life
cycles, and
innovation

journal advertising, and direct-mail promotion make up the usual program for maintaining representation at the buyer's plant between sales calls.

PLANTS AND BUILDINGS   These are necessary to an industrial user's operation and represent sizable capital investments. Thus, the plants and buildings subcategory somewhat resembles the installations subcategory; however, it also resembles the minor equipment subcategory since plants and buildings are supplementary to, rather than directly used in, the production of the industrial user's output. Plants and buildings are not usually marketed as complete units, although some construction engineering firms specialize in such products. In all major respects, industrial users approach the buying (or constructing) of plants or buildings in the same way that they go about buying installations.

production materials   This category includes raw materials, semimanufactured goods, and fabricating parts.

RAW MATERIALS   These are the basic products of farms, mines, fisheries, and forests that enter into the production of manufactured goods. Buying procedures for raw materials vary, depending upon the proportion their costs bear to total production costs and upon market conditions. If raw materials cost represents only a small part of total production costs, the suppliers are middlemen and the buying procedures routine. But when raw material cost accounts for a large part of a finished good's total cost, high-ranking purchasing executives deal directly with raw material producers. Similarly, if a raw material's market is characterized by stable supply and price conditions, relatively low-level executives use routine purchasing procedures. But, when raw material supplies and prices vary erratically, highly skilled and high-ranking executives do the buying and seek to adapt procurement procedures to changing market conditions.

SEMIMANUFACTURED GOODS   These are items—such as steel, glass, and lumber—that are one industry's end product and another's basic manufacturing material. Compared with raw material prices, semimanufactured good prices are relatively stable, so their purchase is more routine. Since most producers of semimanufactured goods are large companies, they sell direct to large industrial users. Where semimanufactured goods are also sold to numerous small industrial users, marketing channels contain one or more levels of middlemen.

FABRICATING PARTS   These are manufactured goods which, without any substantial change in form, are incorporated into or assembled into a more complex and finished product. Storage batteries, spark plugs, and tires for an automobile are examples. Industrial users buy fabricating parts, made to their own specifications, directly from the manufacturers. Single sales contracts are negotiated for periods of several months to a year, and the relationship between seller and buyer is generally a long-term one. These negotiations are directed by high executives of both buying and selling companies.

production supplies   These products are essential to industrial users' business operations but do not become part of finished products. Included are such items as fuel oil, coal, sweeping compound, and wiping cloths. Purchase of production supplies is a routine responsibility of industrial users' purchasing executives, and they usually buy them through middlemen rather than directly from makers. But when an item is used in large quantities, as a public utility uses coal in steam-plant generation of electricity, long-term purchase contracts, similar to those used in buying fabricating parts, are directly negotiated by top-ranking executives of buying and selling firms.

management materials   This category covers office equipment and supplies. Pieces of office equipment of high value, such as electronic computers and data-processing systems, are usually leased rather than bought outright but, in either case, decisions are reached in essentially the same way as those on production installations. Purchase or lease of major office equipment items involves substantial sums; hence, decisions require approval of both top management and the department head concerned, and the purchasing department merely handles the needed paper work.

Typewriters, desk calculators, and similar pieces of equipment are bought by the purchasing department as needed, on requisitions originating in the using departments, often with brands and models being determined by preferences of typists and clerks. Pencil sharpeners, staplers, and other low-unit-value articles of office equipment—as well as such office supplies as stationery and typewriter ribbons—are bought routinely, the purchasing department taking the initiative in ordering and generally carrying a stock on hand.

PRODUCT LIFE CYCLES   Products, like people, have a certain length of life during which they pass through certain identifiable stages. From the time a product idea is conceived, during its development and up to its market introduction, a product is in various prenatal stages (i.e., it is going through various product development phases). Its life begins with its market introduction; it then goes through a period during which its market grows rapidly; eventually it reaches market maturity; afterward its market declines; and finally its life ends.

Figure 8-1 is a visualization of a **product life cycle** for an industry (i.e., firms marketing directly competing items). Three curves are shown: (1) total market sales (this is the "industry product life cycle"), (2) total market profit (notice how this declines while sales are still rising, and (3) the relative number of competitors (notice how this continues to go up for a time after profits have turned down).

Figure 8-1 The industry product life cycle

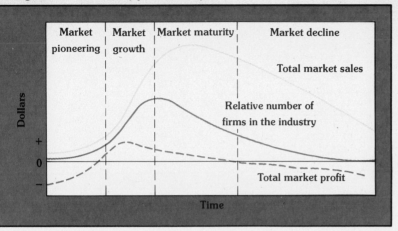

The exact path traced by the product life cycle varies. For some, like the "hula hoop," the product proves a fad and has a short life cycle, perhaps only a month or so. For others, such as plumbing fixtures, life cycles span decades. In between are most products with life cycles ranging from a few months (e.g., fashion apparel) to several years (e.g., washing machines and home freezers). All products are at some stage in their life cycles at any particular moment in time.

Life cycle curves also exist for each company's individual products. Figure 8-2 shows a life-cycle for a product's sales by the company doing the innovating. During the market pioneering stage of the industry product life cycle, one company—the innovator—may be the whole industry. But, by the market growth stage, the innovator shares the market with several competitors. Only coincidentally does the shape of an individual company's product life cycle resemble that of the entire industry, since after the market pioneering stage the industry cycle is a composite of several companies' experiences. Furthermore, managerial action can cause a particular company's product life cycle to vary from that of the typical company in the industry—for example, management may drop a product at any time, thus terminating its life cycle insofar as that company is concerned. The product-life-cycle concept can be a major factor in successful and profitable product management, from new product information to old product disposal.[2] For example, the change in industry profits as the product life cycle progresses is an important factor in the decision as to when to consider product abandonment.[3]

[2] For an excellent discussion, complete with several illustrations, on the use of the product life cycle in marketing strategy planning, see John E. Smallwood, "The Product Life Cycle: A Key to Strategic Marketing Planning," *MSU Business Topics,* Winter 1973, pp. 29-35.

[3] Bernard Catry and Michel Chevalier, "Market Share Strategy and the Product Life Cycle," *Journal of Marketing,* October 1974, pp. 29-31.

163

Figure 8-2 Product life cycle—innovating company

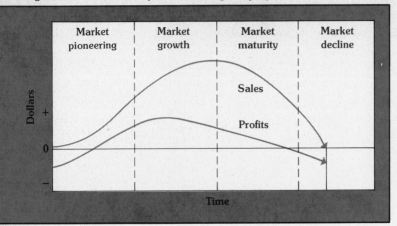

market pioneering   The market **pioneering** stage is one of heavy promotion, of securing initial distribution, and of identifying
and eliminating product weaknesses. Insofar as possible, marketing channels
are kept adequately stocked with the product. But, if the product is destined
for success, the innovator generally finds in this stage that demand exceeds
what it can bring to market.

market growth   During the market **growth** stage, competition increases rapidly, and manufacturing and distribution
efficiency are important keys to marketing success. Competing firms use
selective demand advertising, each emphasizing its own brand's advantages.
At first, personal selling is directed toward getting new outlets and keeping
them stocked but later shifts to selling against the competition. Ultimately,
competition becomes severe enough that if buyers cannot easily find favored
brands they can readily be persuaded to accept substitutes.

market maturity   During the market **maturity** stage, stiffening competition forces profits lower: prices come down and mar-
keting expenditures rise. Sales continue to increase for a while but at a
decreasing rate, eventually leveling off with market saturation. Supply exceeds demand for the first time, making demand stimulation essential, and
competitors heavily promote their brands, emphasizing subtle differences.
Because of the squeeze on profits and growing similarity of competing
brands, dealer support becomes increasingly critical while most dealers now
refuse to stock more than a few brands. During later phases of this stage for
durable goods, replacement sales dominate the market. Industry sales tend
to stabilize, causing the competitive structure to solidify.

The duration of the market maturity stage varies for different kinds of
products. While the product life cycle shown in Figure 8-1 indicates that

Figure 8-3 Industry product life cycle for product quickly consumed and repurchased

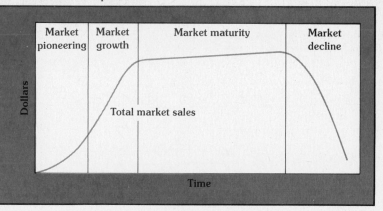

sales generally drop off right after the market saturation point, this does not always happen. Actually, in the cases of some convenience goods which consumers buy frequently and rapidly consume (nondurables), total market sales may level out, stabilizing there for several months or even years. Or, total market sales may slowly rise, reflecting perhaps the growth rate of the total population, as illustrated in Figure 8-3, which is a visualization of the life cycle typical of various broad categories of breakfast cereals and hand soaps.

Products characterized by long consumption lives after purchase (i.e., durable goods) have still a different type of life-cycle curve. Shortly after passing through the market growth stage, the life cycle for such products reaches a temporary market saturation point when everyone who would likely buy has already bought, and total market sales rapidly fall off for a while. But, as units of the product in the possession of consumers begin to wear out and people start buying replacements, total market sales again stabilize, perhaps staying at that lower level for a long period or even resuming a slow rate of growth. Figure 8-4 illustrates this type of product life cycle, typical, for example, of appliances such as refrigerators or dishwashers. Notice that the market decline stage for this type of product starts only after market sales begin to fall off permanently.

market decline   The market decline stage is characterized by either the product's gradual displacement by some new product or by any evolving change in consumer buying behavior. Industry sales drop off and the number of competitors shrinks. With production over-capacity, price becomes the main competitive weapon, and drastic reductions occur in advertising and other promotional expenditures, Under these conditions, most firms shift their attention to other products, gradually phasing out the declining product as its outlook grows increasingly bleak.

165

Figure 8-4 Industry product life cycle for a durable consumer good

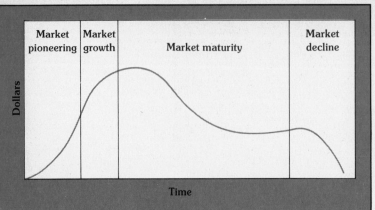

PRODUCT INNOVATION AND
PRODUCT LINE POLICY

Throughout modern industry, product innovation receives increasing emphasis and attention. The underlying reason is that markets are highly dynamic. What was a profitable product yesterday may not be tomorrow. Furthermore, successful new products command substantially higher profit margins than mature or declining products. Successful new products are profitable—at least for a while—mainly because it takes time for competitors to come up with their own versions, enter the market, and eventually compete on a price basis.

Most companies face the inevitable choice of product innovation and improvement or of gradually fading from the market. Most wagon and buggy manufacturers saw their market disappear as the automobile replaced the horse. Yet Studebaker, a wagon maker, recognized the need for change and successfully shifted to auto manufacturing and, much later, finding itself no longer able to compete profitably in the automobile market, moved into other product fields. Just as important as the continuing development of new products is the evaluation of existing products in the line and the judicious pruning of the line to eliminate unprofitable products or products less profitable than potential new ones.

need for product objectives

A company advances toward its overall objectives mainly through achieving acceptance of its products in the marketplace. Therefore, **product objectives,** derived directly from the company objectives, give direction to product innovation. They summarize the characteristics products should have in order that the company will actually be in the business it wants to be in. Yet, at the same time, they should not be so narrow or restrictive as to prevent adjustment to changes in the market. Product objectives, of course, apply to all products, both new and old, regardless of stage in the product life cycle.

167

products:
marketing
characteristics, life
cycles, and
innovation

Under the marketing concept, a company's product objectives are oriented toward the customers and their wants. They state explicitly that the company is engaged in servicing certain needs of specific types of customers. For example, one product objective reads, "To develop, manufacture, and market products meeting the heating and cooling needs of industrial and commercial establishments of all sizes." With this objective, note carefully, the company does not limit itself to specific products; rather, it limits its market to given types of customers with particular needs. As the market and its needs change, the company adjusts its products accordingly.

need for product policies

Product policies are the general rules management sets up to guide itself in making product decisions. They should derive directly from and be wholly consistent with product objectives. If a product objective, for example, states that "this company desires to make and market products requiring only a minimum of service after purchase," then a product policy is needed to spell out how this objective will be attained.

The important product objectives for most companies are sales volume, market share, and dollar profit. Yet, few companies bother to devise a formal method of using actual and anticipated performance characteristics in terms of these objectives when designing plans for the product line. Figure 8-5 illustrates a method of charting the performance of products in terms of sales, profit, and market share. Part A shows current position and projections for products 1 and 2. Part B positions the unidimensional analysis in A into a comprehensive scheme or product evaluation matrix. Product 1 is clearly a poor performer in a declining industry, with a low market share, and poor profitability. On the other hand, Product 2 is in a stable industry and is expected to increase its sales while maintaining stability in profit and market share. Analyses of this sort are necessary in firms where management thinks it important to continually reevaluate existing products in the line.

planning new products

While the details of new product planning vary with the company, generally they cover three major phases. Phase one involves the creation of new product ideas. The marketing concept advocates that a product planner start with a consumer need or needs (determined perhaps through marketing research and analysis of buyer behavior) and then appraise the extent to which present products fulfill these needs.[4] Once potential needs have been identified, a useful approach is to make a complete cross-sectional study of current usage patterns within the broad product category selected to determine customer reactions; such an approach is called benefit structure analysis.[5]

---

[4] Edward M. Tauber, "Discovering New Product Opportunities with Problem Inventory Analysis," *Journal of Marketing,* January 1975, pp. 67–70.

[5] For a description of this method, see James H. Myers, "Benefit Structure Analysis: A New Tool for Product Planning," *Journal of Marketing,* October 1976, pp. 23–32.

Figure 8-5 Incorporating sales, market share, and profit forecasts into the product evaluation matrix: a hypothetical example

PART A

Product	Current Position (C)				Unconditional Projection (P)				Conditional Forecast (CF)			
	Industry Sales	Company Sales	Market Share	Profitability	Industry Sales	Company Sales	Market Share	Profitability	Industry Sales	Company Sales	Market Share	Profitability
1	Decline	Decline	Av.	Below Target	Decline	Decline	Av.	Below Target	Decline	Decline	Marg.	Target
									Decline	Stable	Av.	Below Target
2	Stable	Decline	Av.	Target	Stable	Stable	Av.	Above Target	Stable	Stable	Dom.	Target

PART B

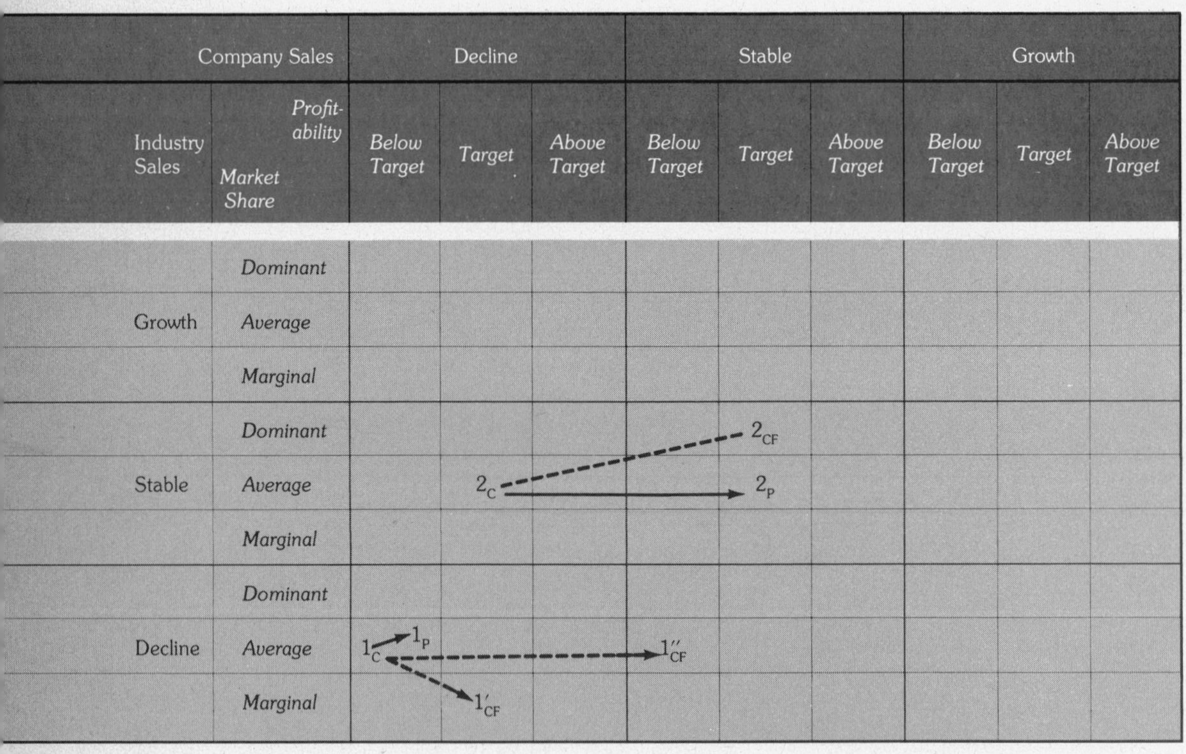

Company Sales		Decline			Stable			Growth		
Industry Sales	Profitability / Market Share	Below Target	Target	Above Target	Below Target	Target	Above Target	Below Target	Target	Above Target
Growth	Dominant									
	Average									
	Marginal									
Stable	Dominant						2_{CF}			
	Average		2_C			2_P				
	Marginal									
Decline	Dominant									
	Average	1_C → 1_P				$1''_{CF}$				
	Marginal		$1'_{CF}$							

Key: 1, 2, products; C, current; P, projected position; CF, expected position based on results of a conditional forecast analysis.

Source: Yoram Wind and Henry J. Claycamp, "Planning Product Line Strategy: A Matrix Approach," Journal of Marketing, January 1976, p. 6.

169

products:
marketing
characteristics, life
cycles, and
innovation

Phase two focuses on more thoroughly investigating the competitive market situation and company resouces with respect to each product idea developed in phase one. Market research is critical during this phase since market potentials and competitive marketing methods can reveal, among other things, the size and type of marketing organization required. Analysis of company resources indicates the adequacy of plant capacity, product service facilities, marketing channels, engineering abilities, and other human resources. This phase ends with selection among alternative product candidates, based on comparisons of each against specific project objectives, such as relative profitability, target market segment, and opportunity to attain product leadership. Several models have been developed to help the marketing manager decide whether or not to introduce a new product. Such models provide management with orderly bases for reaching new product decisions.[6]

Phase three relates to actual development of the new product. A program is put together for management and execution of the development project. This includes, among other aspects, an overall plan for the product's eventual marketing.

SUMMARY   Discussion in this chapter has focused on the product's critical roles in marketing, since all businesses that have something to sell sell a product of some sort. We have analyzed different kinds of products—emphasizing mainly the way in which buyers' attitudes, behavioral patterns, and buying procedures vary from one product category to another. We have also explored the product-life-cycle concept, indicating that products, like people, have a certain length of "marketing life," during which they pass through various identifiable stages, the cycle's nature varying somewhat for different kinds of products. Recognition of the existence of product life cycles underscores the need that marketers have for continuous programs of product innovation, thus providing replacements for dying products as well as opportunities for business growth.

[6] See Gert Assmus, "Newprod: The Design and Implementation of a New Product Model," *Journal of Marketing,* January 1975, pp. 16-31.

REVIEW
AND
DISCUSSION
QUESTIONS

1   Describe the nature of the product sold by each of the following organizations: a commercial bank, an architectural firm, a management consulting organization, a billiard table producer, a travel agency; a marketer of health foods, a daily newspaper, a museum of fine arts, a college or university, a manufacturer of lawn mowers.

2   What is the main basis used for distinguishing between a consumer good and an industrial good? Why is the distinction important? Explain.

3   Fully evaluate the "traditional" system for classifying consumer goods. Its advantages? Disadvantages? Why is it important to classify consumer goods in the first place?

4   The marketer of a fabricating part, such as automobile tires, often sells both to the OEM (original equipment market) and to the replacement market. Does such a marketer really sell the same product to both markets? Explain.

5	How do you account for the fact that the rate of product change (i.e., the speed of product innovation) varies so much from industry to industry? Why has it taken longer to approach market saturation with sewing machines than with television sets?
6	To what extent does product innovation provide an escape from price competition? Cite examples.
7	What is the purpose of a product objective? Of a product policy? How do they differ?
8	Refer to Chapter 2 on the marketing organization. Visualize a particular company serving a specific market and show how each company objective (that has marketing significance) could be the source of one or more product objectives.
9	How can a company tell what types of competition to expect for a new product?
10	Give some examples of products you regard as being in the market pioneering stage of their life cycles.
11	In what respects does an industry product life cycle differ from the life cycles for the individual products of competitors in the industry?
12	Appraise the product-life-cycle concept relative to its use in marketing planning.
13	Why is it that a product is called a "bundle of utilities?"
14	"The exact path traced by the product life cycle varies." Comment. Give examples.
15	For each stage of the product life cycle, explain briefly the main characteristics of the following:

a. Sales.
b. Competition.
c. Product policy.
d. Pricing.

e. Distribution.
f. Advertising.
g. Personal selling.
h. Marketing research.

16	New product planning may be thought of as a process involving several stages. Discuss.

CASE PROBLEMS

For most of the past 30 years, the Hopkins appliance brand had been among the market leaders in this highly competitive industry. The Hopkins reputation was built on quality, durability, and dependable service. Hopkins manufactured a wide line of household appliances, including gas and electric ranges, dishwashers, food-waste disposers, trash compactors, and gas barbecue grills. Recently, however, Hopkins' market leadership was deteriorating in the face of even more intense competition, particularly in the form of product innovation.

Ralph Lawson, the marketing manager for the past seven years, had a strategy of staying with proven products and introducing only minor styling changes each year. His philosophy was that maximum profits could be generated by staying with successful products and avoiding risks associated with new products' "uncertain market appeal." He did not want to disturb things. As a result, while leading competitors were rapidly introducing new features in their product lines and pioneering new concepts in appliance use, Hopkins Company found itself on the defensive on the innovation front. Often, Hopkins adopted improved product features a year or two after the competitors. Even with its wide line of appliances, Hopkins had not had a significant new product in over four years. It had been relegated to a role of follower.

Top management expressed concern over the loss of market leadership and believed that the way to turn things around was with an increased emphasis on new product development. Lawson, as marketing manager, was asked to present some proposals for organizing the new product effort, an effort aimed to generate successful new products. He was told that he would be responsible for guiding the new product development process from the initial stage of securing product ideas, through screening new product proposals for engineering and marketing feasibility, to developing the product prototype and market testing. He was undecided whether to rely on the product managers in each major appliance line to assume the responsibility for new product development in addition to their present roles, or to recommend setting up a department of new product planning.

He recognized that another possibility was to organize new-product venture teams within each company division. A venture team comprised of members from various operating departments could be formed specifically to bring a new product to market. After the new product was established, it could be turned over to the regular marketing organization.

Given the increasing competition, Lawson felt a need for fast action on his part. He wanted to find the most effective way of organizing a new product development program at Hopkins Appliance Company, one that would result in profitable new products. He also wanted to involve as much of the organization as possible in these processes. But, he did not know how to bring about this major change in company policy. He had several ideas but could not seem to put them all together. He did not know where to begin.

questions:

1. Identify and evaluate the alternatives open to Hopkins Appliance Company.
2. What course of action do you recommend?
3. Explain the importance of product innovation.
4. Who is responsible for new product planning and development in an organization?
5. Can new product development be thought of as a "process?"

When you have mastered the contents of this chapter, you should be able to:

1 Draw a grid illustrating the nine different product–market strategies aimed at improving a company's profitability.

2 Explain the meanings of product design simplification, greater integration, and reverse integration.

3 Identify the chief forms of remerchandising.

4 Discuss the factors management should consider in deciding to use (a) family brands or individual brands, (b) multiple brands for identical items, and (c) private branding.

5 Explain how a marketer should go about searching for new users and new uses.

6 Describe the three versions of the "product change—no market change" strategy.

7 Explain how a product customization strategy differs from a product systems strategy.

8 Differentiate trading up from trading down.

9 Outline the conditions under which a product replacement strategy is appropriate.

10 Explain the meanings of product line extension, diversification into related product lines, and product mix diversification.

product-market
strategies

Highly significant interacting relationships exist between products and their markets. Every product is aimed at some market, and its marketing success depends importantly on its "fit" with that market. Most companies are in business to make profits. They accomplish this through utilizing marketing's skills in matching products with markets and in effecting ownership transfers. In this chapter we consider how companies use different product-market strategies in attempts to improve their profitability.

There are two main ways to increase a company's profits: (1) through increasing its sales volume, and (2) through reducing its costs. Newly organized firms generally seek to increase profits through growth in sales. As a company grows—or as its size tends to stabilize—its management devotes increasing attention to the search for greater profits, through improving marketing effectiveness and reducing costs. Therefore, management must continually strive to improve the effectiveness and profitability of its product policies and strategies and, as uncertain economic conditions prevail, new complexities account for higher risks in product management and strategy.[1]

Figure 9-1 shows different combinations of product-market strategies that a company might use to improve its profitability. Notice that each product strategy is associated with some market strategy and that each has important implications for the other. Discussion in this chapter focuses on interactions of each product strategy with each market strategy, a total of nine different combinations. As you study this chapter, it is helpful to refer to this figure.

[1] Thomas A. Staudt, "Higher Management Risks in Product Strategy," *Journal of Marketing,* January 1973, p. 4.

Figure 9–1   Grid of possible combinations of
product–market strategies to improve profitability

Market strategy \ Product strategy	No product change	Product change	New product
No market change	Design simplification .... Greater integration— marketing, production, etc.—or "reverse integration"	Product line simplification and product discontinuance .... New models .... Planned obsolescence	Replacement of old product
Improved market	Remerchandising (e.g., branding change, change in guarantee, change in service policy, packaging change, etc.)	Product customization .... Product systems	Product-line extension .... Diversification (related fields)
New market	New uses .... New users	Market extension (e.g., trading-up or trading-down)	Product-mix diversification (unrelated fields)

NO PRODUCT CHANGE—
NO MARKET CHANGE

This is the least complex product–market strategy. There are two main versions: (1) simplifying the product's design, and (2) altering the amount of integration in the product's manufacturing and/or marketing. Both seek to improve profitability mainly through cost reduction, and both involve selling essentially the same product to the same market.

product design simplification

Simplifying a product's design may lower its manufacturing costs, thus contributing to greater profits. **Product design simplification**, strictly speaking, does not improve the product (from the user's standpoint) but makes the product simpler and cheaper to make. If a design simplification effort results in an improved design in the eyes of prospective buyers, then, of course, the product is no longer the same but now reflects product change in such terms as being easier to maintain or performing better. Improved designs, in other words, become easier to sell, while simplified designs remain unchanged both as to basic product features and salability.

PRODUCT FEATURES   Among the most important product features is product size. The chief consideration in determining product size is consumer need. Thus, when aspirin was first put on the market, tablet size was based

175

on normal dosages, minimum dosages, and a size small enough to achieve these dosages with multiples of a single tablet. Furthermore, each basis of market segmentation may affect size requirements: for example, when baby aspirin was introduced (to reach that age market segment), marketers offered a smaller size of tablet.

Size range and variation are also affected by inventory costs and stockturn, both for middlemen and for the manufacturer. This is especially evident with products such as clothing, where the range of possible sizes is very large. Although consumers' needs may dictate a large range of sizes, the costs of maintaining inventories and the low stockturn of the more extreme sizes may make it advisable to restrict the offering to sizes in the middle range.

In industries where standardized product size specifications have been established, most firms adhere to the standards because of the favorable effects on consumers and middlemen. The consumer's buying job and the middleman's buying and selling jobs are both simplified if they know, for example, that all size 10B men's shoes are exactly the same and need not be measured or tried on. Against these favorable effects must be weighed the possible disadvantages of reduced product differentiation and increased substitutability of competitive products.

Other product features—such as basic weights and measures, performance requirements, and chemical or technical properties—are determined in essentially the same manner as size. Each decision results from an evaluation of consumer needs, the effect on middlemen, comparative costs, and industry practice.

greater integration or reverse integration

Sometimes it is possible to reduce the costs (thereby increasing profits) of making and/or marketing a product through **greater integration** (i.e., by adding functions formerly purchased from others). An appliance manufacturer, for example, that formerly purchased plastic handles and other plastic components established its own plastic manufacturing operation, thus reducing manufacturing costs. Another manufacturer reduced its marketing costs by switching from distribution through wholesalers to direct distribution to retailers.[2]

In other situations, costs are reducible through **reverse integration** (i.e., by purchasing functions from others that were formerly performed by the company). Thus, a supermarket chain discontinued its integrated bakery operation and contracted with a large commercial baker for its requirements, thereby reducing the costs of supplying its stores with bakery products. And a large grocery products manufacturer cut its marketing costs by switching from direct distribution to retailers to an indirect system utilizing specialty wholesalers.

[2] M. T. Cunningham and C. J. Clarke, "The Product Management Function in Marketing," *European Journal of Business*, No. 2, 1975, pp. 129-149.

Decisions to change the degree of integration of manufacturing and/or marketing operations require thorough analyses of numerous factors. Among these are the relative costs, probable future sales, impact on product quality, the importance of secrecy, availability of needed resources and skills, and the likely reactions of middlemen and final buyers. Whenever the potential gains from capturing a bigger slice of the gross margin outweigh the associated disadvantages, greater integration may pay off. However, sometimes costs can be reduced by "farming out" more of the manufacturing and/or marketing operation—thus, reverse integration is also worth considering.

NO PRODUCT CHANGE— IMPROVED MARKET

This strategy aims to improve the product's market and profitability by increasing sales to present markets. This process of **remerchandising** is directed toward making the product more salable. Remerchandising, in other words, leaves basic features of the physical product unchanged but makes changes in the accompanying services. The following discussion analyzes the chief forms of remerchandising, proceeding generally from the more elementary to the highly sophisticated forms.

product quality

Different kinds of marketers have varying degrees of latitude in determining product quality. Marketers of the products of farms, forests, fisheries, and mines can exert little control over quality, defining it mainly through grading. Even for some manufacturers the limits of quality control are narrow: a chemical company, for example, cannot change basic compounds; it can affect quality only in terms of absences of foreign elements—that is, purity. But for most manufacturers a broad spectrum exists within which management can set and enforce standards over product quality—durability, uniformity, reliability, and similar characteristics.

Effective standardization of product quality provides the consistency and predictability in product performance so essential to building consumer brand preference. Buyers have a right to expect that all units of a product under a particular brand name will be alike. Consistency and predictability in product performance mean that more buyers who try the brand, if satisfied, will become steady customers. This indicated, then, that a manufacturer should assess market needs and preferences before it sets quality standards for its product. Generally, effective standardization of product quality is also a prerequisite to the profitable use of branding.

product service

For many products, service policies are important elements in marketing programs. For complex industrial products, such as computers, it is necessary to provide installation and repair services and also, in most cases, training for customers' personnel. In fact, in industrial markets, product service is often the most critical factor in selecting a vendor. For many products, though, especially consumer items, the need for service is not so clear-cut. Nevertheless, if an item is a consumer durable or semidurable with a comparatively high price and a relatively low purchase frequency, it may be difficult to consummate sales unless the manufacturer or dealer, or both, provide service.

Manufacturers, however, sometimes overestimate the importance of offering certain services. When discount houses were first developed, appliance makers were reluctant to sell through them, because these retailers did not provide repair and installation services. When these manufacturers learned, to their surprise, that many consumers were willing and able to handle both installation and servicing, their opposition to discount house distribution faded. The decision on what product services to offer customers should flow from an appraisal of their needs and expectations.

Appropriate service policies and practices not only facilitate initial sales but also help in keeping products sold, stimulating repeat sales, and building customer goodwill. Each product service offered (e.g., product installation, advice on operation, maintenance, and repair) should be evaluated against two criteria: the extent to which it accomplishes desired merchandising aims and whether it contributes to net profit.

product guarantees   Guarantees, express or implied, are promises made by a seller to buyers assuring them that they will receive certain services or satisfactions. Thus, a guarantee is part of the bundle of satisfactions a buyer receives when buying a product. The manufacturer expects its guarantee to serve one of two purposes: (1) to protect against abuses of the service policy, the **protective guarantee**; or (2) to provide an additional promotional element for selling against the competition, the **promotional guarantee**. For remerchandising, the promotional guarantee is of the most interest. If the estimated increases in sales are greater than the added costs involved, a promotional guarantee increases net profits. Promotional guarantees are most effective in stimulating sales when:

1. The product has a high retail price, and prospective buyers want assurance that it will perform as represented.
2. The product has a long useful life, and prospective buyers are concerned about the risk of product failure.
3. Buyers visualize the product as complex and costly to repair.
4. The product is not well known, and consumers need assurance to help them overcome uncertainty about it. [3]

packaging   Packaging changes are often key elements in remerchandising. There are many reasons for packaging a product—to protect it, to differentiate and identify it, to make it more salable, to allow greater ease in handling, to give greater convenience in use, or

---

[3] C. L. Kendall and Frederick A. Russ, "Warranty and Complaint Policies: An Opportunity for Marketing Management," *Journal of Marketing*, April 1975, pp. 36-37.

to provide information which helps the consumer make a purchase decision. Coal needs no protection against damage from the elements and handling, whereas photographic film needs protection from exposure to light; these are extremes, but the need of almost any product for protective packaging is usually just as clear.

If a product is packaged for brand differentiation and identification, it should remain packaged until purchased by the final buyer. Bulk packaging, removable before the final buyer buys, is for protection or handling convenience. Five-pound bags of sugar, for example, reach the supermarket inside a large paper bag—the small bags are for brand differentiation and identification, the large bag for protection and handling convenience.

When the brand name can be placed directly on the product, as with appliances, packaging for brand identification is not needed. But, if a product is hard to differentiate, as with nails, packaging may be the only way to differentiate it and secure some brand identification. For most consumer products, however, packaging is the main way to identify the brand at the point of purchase. The package, like a promotional display, relates the product to the producer's advertising and makes consumers aware of its availability in retail outlets. Beyond this, marketing executives expect the package to furnish consumers with needed product information and to provide the extra push so often required to propel consumers into buying.

PACKAGE DESIGN When packaging is primarily protective, design decisions are technical and involve comparative strengths, costs of materials, and shapes. When a package is primarily a promotional device, its elements must attract consumers' attention, hold their interest, and build their desire to buy. Package color, size, and shape are all important promotionally, so decisions on these elements should reflect the target market segment's preferences. With more and more products being sold through self-service outlets, the promotional aspect of package design becomes increasingly important, since in these stores the package carries the promotional burden it formerly shared with salesclerks. So much promotional emphasis, in fact, is placed upon the package that it is often referred to as the "silent salesperson."

Package design must also consider convenience in product handling by both middlemen and consumers. The shape should permit easy display on retail store fixtures. It should make it easy for the consumer to take the product home and to store it. In addition, package design must permit convenience in use and reuse.

PACKAGE SIZE The package-size decision evolves from appraisals of several factors, but the most important are the consuming unit and the rate of consumption. Cigarettes, candy bars, and toothbrushes are consumed by individuals and are packaged in units for individual rather than group consumption. Cake mixes and gelatin desserts are consumed by household or family units and are packaged for group consumption. Dry breakfast cereals are packaged both ways: in family boxes and in individual-serving packs.

Findings on the consumption unit and rate of consumption sometimes have to be modified when custom or habit strongly influences package size. For example, the housewife is so used to buying margarine in 1-pound (453.6-gram) units that it would be difficult to change to an unrelated unit, such as the pint or quart. She has learned to compare prices and to measure recipes on the basis of pounds and ounces of margarine and would resist buying in an unrelated unit of measure.

Package size sometimes affects total consumption. When consumers have plentiful supplies of a product on hand, they may consume more than if they have to make special buying trips to obtain it. The six-pack carton for soft drinks has demonstrated the success of this approach. So important is the package size/consumption rate relationship that a major base for market segmentation is that of product usage which, of course, has special meaning for package size. For example, it is often useful to segment markets on the basis of heavy, moderate, or light user characteristics, and to develop package sizes accordingly.

PACKAGE COST   The protection needed to deliver the item to the user in good condition determines the package's minimum cost, but consumer preference and convenience often make it advisable to exceed this minimum. A metal container may be less expensive but, because of strong consumer preference, the marketer may use a glass container for certain products, such as jellies. Likewise, a reclosable package, although more expensive than a throwaway, allows the customer to store the product easily until it is entirely consumed without having to transfer it to another container. Each such addition to the minimum cost should be justifiable in terms of its beneficial effect upon demand.

When a package is aimed at achieving brand identification or other promotional goals, its cost is usually higher than if it is solely for product protection. Nevertheless, most marketers of consumer items expect their packages to help in promotion and see cost differences as worthwhile. At a bare minimum, the package must carry the brand name, the marketer's name, a description of the contents, and other descriptive material (e.g., how to use the product). Once the cost of designing an attractive promotional label has been amortized, the cost per package may be no more than that of a purely protective-type container.

Therefore, packaging must perform different functions and meet diverse requirements. More specifically, the same consumer package must perform different functions and satisfy varied requirements and must do so in different environments. The marketer needs to recognize potential conflicts among package functions and resolve them in ways providing both consumer satisfaction and profits. For example, consider the product protection and salability functions. Thin plastic film is used to package apples, since consumers like to see what they are buying (salability). A package made of cardboard, while more protective, prohibits or makes more difficult visual inspection of the apples. Hence, a compromise is struck in the form of the thin plastic film which provides both salability and protection, although each function is performed adequately, rather than to its fullest degree.

branding   **Branding** is the use of a distinctive name and/or mark on a product to differentiate it from similar competitive products. Its use can insure the buyer of uniformity of quality or performance features of the product. The relative significance of branding as a means for enhancing a product's salability varies with the product and company. The truck farmer raising fresh peas competes for sales almost solely on a price basis, since buyers neither know nor care who grew the peas they buy. Yet the food processor, canning or freezing the same peas, can build consumer preference for its brand through differentiating and promoting it, convincing buyers of its superiority.

Branding's function is to bridge the gap between the manufacturer's promotional program and consummation of sales to final buyers. **Brand identification**, then, is essential for the firm wanting to differentiate its product, giving the company some degree of control over the product's resale by middlemen, and at the same time enhancing promotional effectiveness. Through brand identification, a company prepares itself to compete on a nonprice basis.

Some products lend themselves less readily to **brand differentiation** than others. Many products of farms, fisheries, forests, and mines are difficult to differentiate because of their unprocessed form but, even here, brand identification coupled with imaginative packaging and promotion frequently achieves some product differentiation, thus insulating the marketer from the full force of price competition. Swift (Esmark), for instance, achieved this with its "Premium Butterball Turkeys." Product differentiation through brand identification and promotion is easier to obtain for consumer than for industrial products; highly standardized industrial items, such as sheet steel, can be identified by brand name but appear impossible to differentiate effectively.

The branding decision is especially important for products where the potential effectiveness of brand identification to secure product differentiation is unclear. A few years ago, for instance, experts contended that branding women's dresses was of minimal value because women bought according to criteria unrelated to brand—such as color, design, styling, and fit. Today the dress industry not only uses brand names but promotes them heavily. Manufacturers learned, among other things, that variations in women's sizes and shapes, not provided for by differences in standard dress sizes, provided opportunities for real product differentiation and profitable branding. Brand identification has the highest potential payoff where it is possible to differentiate the product effectively in terms of features consumers consider important. But it also has payoff potentials where present products have features shoppers look for—brand identification reduces the searching time shoppers have to spend in finding products with desired features.

FAMILY BRANDS VERSUS INDIVIDUAL BRANDS   When a company sells more than one product it must decide whether to sell each under a separate brand or to use a family brand. Many situations exist where greater returns can be realized through making one choice rather than the other. Such decisions require evaluation of three factors: nature of the product line, promotional policy, and desired market penetration.

The nature of the product line is the most important. Similar products naturally related in consumers' minds, such as sheets and towels, benefit particularly from family branding. Favorable reaction to one item often leads buyers to buy others in the line. But this halo effect can also detract from a marketer's reputation, if unfavorable experiences with one item turn consumers against the entire line. Particular care must be taken that all items carrying the family brand conform to consumers' standards of acceptance.

Products lacking common marketing attributes are usually best marketed under individual brands, since little benefit comes from jointly associating them. There may even be adverse sales reactions from family branding; for example, associating a food item with a soap product may handicap sales of the food, since many consumers associate soap with an unpleasant taste.

All products do not lend themselves to sale under a family brand. The quality of family-brand products should be very similar so that no single item lowers the quality reputation of others. The product line should also be fairly compatible: a housewife may prefer a particular brand of soap, but she will not be at all interested in a new perfume carrying the same name because she is not convinced that experience in soap making will carry over to perfume making. However, some perfume manufacturers have been successful in selling soap under their labels, because of the use of similar scents coupled with skillful promotion. The products should also be sold to the same markets: little is gained from applying a family brand to one item sold to industrial users and to a second sold to ultimate consumers.

Promotional policy is important because using a family brand, rather than individual brands, makes possible a smaller total promotional budget. Under a family brand, much promotion can be directed toward the entire line, and even promotion emphasizing a single item increases recognition and demand for the entire line. With individual brands, separate and often duplicating promotional efforts are required. Thus, a family-brand policy permits the most effective use of limited promotional funds for similar products, yet family-brand promotional programs restrict opportunities for emphasizing individual differences in items.

The use of individual brands sometimes allows a greater total market penetration. For example, Procter & Gamble sells several brands of laundry detergent, each directed at a different market segment. Tide is directed toward the buyer with heavy cleaning needs—the very dirty clothing of mechanics or small boys. Cheer is directed toward the householders concerned with an extra white and attractive wash. One brand of detergent would not serve both of these markets completely, and Procter & Gamble finds that each product is more effectively differentiated by giving it a separate brand identity.

MULTIPLE BRANDS FOR IDENTICAL ITEMS   Makers of specialty goods often sell through a limited number of selected retail outlets to gain their dealers' cooperation in aggressively promoting the products. This has the effect of limiting the total sales potential because in any one market no single retailer or small group of retailers is normally in a position to attract all potential buyers. In such cases, market penetration may be increased by offering identical merchandise under a different brand name to a second group of selected retailers. This practice is known as **multiple branding**.

Frequently, mergers result in the use of multiple brands. The decision to retain the separate brands or to change to a single brand may depend on whether the different brands have developed dissimilar images that appeal to different market segments or on whether they have developed strength in different regional markets with well-known names that management is reluctant to abandon.

PRIVATE BRANDING   **Private brands** are those owned and controlled by middlemen rather than by manufacturers. Both manufacturers and middlemen face policy decisions on private branding. Manufacturers must decide whether to sell their products to middlemen for private branding. And middlemen must decide whether they can benefit from their own brands. The manufacturer's decision on the acceptance of private-brand orders should depend on the probable effect on the sales of its own brand, if it has one. A middleman's decision to promote private brands of its own should be based on the expectation of greater profits and/or greater control over the market.

NO PRODUCT CHANGE— NEW MARKET

This product-market strategy is particularly significant for companies with products already in, or about to enter, the market maturity stage in the life cycle. During this stage, industry sales tend to reach a plateau and then gradually fall off, but some companies explore the possibility of rejuvenating the product's sales and profit growth rates through finding new markets. In searching for new markets for a product that is approaching, or has already reached, the saturation level in its present market, management should consider both (1) possible new users, and (2) possible new uses.[4]

new users

The search for possible new users involves finding and evaluating untapped market segments. Management should start by reviewing the nature of the product's present market. One maker of crystal glassware, for instance, had for years focused its marketing efforts on the bride-to-be market, but its sales had topped out. After

[4] E. Raymond Corey, "Key Options in Market Selection and Product Planning," *Harvard Business Review,* September–October 1975, pp. 119–128.

studying the market more closely, management concluded that there were actually three market segments: (1) the bride-to-be, (2) the matron (women who had been unable to afford crystal at the time of marriage but could now), and (3) the "rich aunt" (the affluent relative who buys gifts for brides). Marketing efforts were redirected to tap the **new market segments,** and company sales and profits resumed their growth.

Management should also evaluate other groups of possible new users. Perhaps the most obvious is the different geographic market segment—that is, potential users outside the present market area. Products at near-saturation levels in industrial market segments sometimes find new markets among ultimate consumers (e.g., small power tools). Products used traditionally by men (e.g., cigarettes) sometimes have been marketed successfully to women, and the reverse has also happened (e.g., hair spray). Products initially aimed at one age group may be redirected to appeal to a different age group (e.g., baby foods for the elderly). And, of course, the new market most neglected by American marketers is the foreign market. Businesspeople who look beyond their national boundaries can tap rich new markets.

new uses   Detection and exploitation of new uses is a way to stretch a product's life. Fruit and vegetable processors, for instance, were found using small sewage pumps, originally developed for home use, to move items, such as peaches, along special water troughs during processing, thus preventing bruises and other damage. Such unusual applications are difficult to anticipate and sometimes are discovered by accident (e.g., a producer of lighter fluid accidentally found its product being used to remove road tar from automobiles). However, management should keep abreast of how its products are being used: sales people should ask dealers who is buying the product and for what purposes; marketing research should periodically survey buyers for the same reason.

PRODUCT CHANGE— NO MARKET CHANGE

The three versions of this strategy are (1) product line simplification and production discontinuance, (2) new models, and (3) planned obsolescence. Strategies involving product line simplification and product discontinuance envision profit increases through cost reductions. Those involving either new models or planned obsolescence seek profit increases through growth in sales volume.

product line simplification and product discontinuance   Reducing the number of models and/or products in a product line often affords opportunities for increasing profits.[5] Proliferation in a product line frequently traces to efforts to match every item offered by competitors or to satisfy salespersons' and dealers' pleas for more variety.

[5] Stanley H. Kratchman, Richard T. Hise, and Thomas Ulrich, "Management's Decision to Discontinue a Product," *Journal of Accountancy,* June 1975, p. 50.

Product proliferation is partially preventable through high selectivity in adding new products and models, but pressures always exist to offer greater variety. Marketing executives, in particular, push for more complete lines and more models, as this helps to satisfy widely varying market preferences. Production executives fight to keep product lines narrow and the number of models minimal, as this holds manufacturing costs down and simplifies production scheduling.

Under increasingly competitive conditions, market pressures force manufacturers to offer greater and greater product variety; increasing consumer sophistication and increasing market segmentation also contribute to product proliferation. Well-designed procedures for screening new product ideas improve the chances that additions will be profitable but do not ensure against product failures. Furthermore, today's successes become tomorrow's failures—products are born, grow, mature, and die, as the product-life-cycle concept indicates. Market and organizational pressures push in the direction of product proliferation; counterpressures are needed both to control new additions and to weed out tired products and models.

Product line simplification requires continual review of the line and the discontinuance of items not contributing directly (in their own right) or indirectly (e.g., as a repair part) to profits. However, simplification involves more than merely determining present profitability.[6] Sometimes a change in price, promotion, or marketing channels can make a currently unprofitable item profitable. At other times, dealers and customers expect, even demand, a full-line offering, preventing the weeding out of all unprofitable items. Some items, such as repair and replacement parts, may be unprofitable in their own right, yet have selling value and should be retained. Other unprofitable items must be kept in order to sell profitable items (e.g., when buyers regard a group of items as a "product system," as they do razors and blades).

Under some conditions, too, it is desirable to drop a profitable product. Management might choose **product discontinuance**, for instance, if the same resources would yield more profit if used in behalf of another item with a brighter future. Likewise, a profitable item might be dropped if it causes salespersons and/or dealers to divert their efforts from still more profitable items. In general, then, any item is a likely candidate for discontinuance if the company does not have the needed resources and/or talents to capitalize fully on its potential profitability.[7]

new models   Through introducing new models of old products, management seeks increased profits by stimulating sales volume. New models are not, strictly speaking, new products but rather variations of established products—new sizes, colors, designs, and the like.

---

[6] G. R. Barville and B. Pletcher, "The Product Elimination Function," *Journal of the Academy of Marketing Science,* Summer 1974, pp. 432-446.

[7] For an excellent discussion and evaluation of various approaches to product abandonment decisions, see Paul W. Hamelman and Edward M. Mazze, "Improving Product Abandonment Decisions," *Journal of Marketing,* April 1972, pp. 20-26.

Management's hope in bringing out a new model generally is that it will come closer to fitting what present buyers really prefer.

Introducing new models is a regular feature of product strategy for many producers, the regularity and frequency of model switching varying among industries and individual firms.[8] Some switch models only when justified by significant product improvements. Others introduce new models on a regular, periodic basis even though changes are superficial. In competing with the American automobile industry, strongly committed to annual model changes, the Volkswagen has been marketed successfully under a strategy of changing the model only when technological improvements justify it.

planned obsolescence   **Product improvement,** whether real or contrived, provides a means for accelerating the rate of obsolescence of products in consumers' possession. This is most important in mature industries whose markets have reached, or are approaching, saturation. In these industries, a manufacturer competes not only with other manufacturers, but with the products sold in the past. If a marketer depends solely on physical obsolescence, gradual wear, and deterioration, its prospects for sales and profits are limited.

Products in consumers' possession can be made obsolete in two ways: by improving performance characteristics of new models and by altering consumers' concepts of the acceptability of models they already own. The auto industry's introduction of automatic transmissions exemplifies the first type of created obsolescence, and the annual change in auto body style is an example of the second. The term **planned obsolescence** describes both types.

Planned obsolescence of the second type is highly controversial. Some writers charge that it is economically wasteful, and many business executives call it wasteful and contrary to the country's best interests. Proponents defend it as a necessary support to a high-level economy and point out that the criticisms are based on the moral judgment that a desire for the latest thing is socially bad. Supporters feel that wanting something new and different is socially good. From the consumer's standpoint, creation of obsolescence through real product improvements is generally acceptable, but shifts in standards of acceptability (as in appearance) are more controversial. Yet fashion, having been part of western culture for centuries, is not the creation of marketers.

PRODUCT CHANGE—   The two main types of this strategy are (1) product
IMPROVED MARKET   customization, and (2) product systems. Both aim to
                   improve profitability through increasing sales volume.

[8] Frederick A. Webster, "A Long-Run Product Diversification Growth Model," *American Journal of Small Business,* April 1977, pp. 20-27.

product customization   Product customization involves tailoring product specifications very closely to buyers' needs in order to make profitable sales to those who would otherwise not buy. The mildest form is to offer a wide choice of models to make it easier for buyers to decide in favor of some model made by the company rather than by its competitors; this form of customization is often used in shopping goods, situations, such as with ladies' shoes or men's shirts. A stronger form of customization involves offering a basic line of standard products but allowing customers to write their own specifications for certain product features; this is common, for example, in marketing grinding wheels to industrial users and in selling custom-designed insurance policies to business buyers. The most extreme product customization occurs in situations where labor looms very large in total production costs, and unusual craftsmanship and scarce technical skills can command premium selling prices. Thus, small firms, such as custom tailors, turn out products more or less meeting customers' exact specifications, while large firms, such as the aerospace companies, turn out items, such as moon vehicles, meeting buyers' specifications within extremely close limits.

product systems   Product systems strategies seek greater profitability through increasing the utility of products to buyers, thus stimulating sales volume. The automatic washing machine is an example of a product system that combines functions formerly performed by hand and by a washboard, pails, tubs, a scrub brush, a hand wringer, and so on. By combining these functions, it solves more of a household's washing problems than any of the items it replaced and is worth more (i.e., has greater utility) to the household since it also provides greater convenience, eliminates unpleasant tasks, and saves time.

Product systems sold to industrial markets, such as the baggage-handling systems used in airports, like those sold to consumer markets, provide added utility to users by relating and automating various necessary tasks formerly performed separately. Generally, too, they provide cost savings and accomplish the entire task more effectively.

PRODUCT CHANGE—
NEW MARKET   This strategy seeks increased profitability through additional sales volume generated by changing certain features of the product and selling it to a new market segment. Very few products wholly satisfy the needs of more than one market segment, so companies often must change certain product features to match them better with the individualized needs of new target market segments. Trading up and trading down are the main forms of this strategy.

trading up and trading down   Both trading up and trading down involve bringing out changed versions of a product and altering the nature and direction of promotion. Generally, companies trading up or down do one or the other, but not both at the same time.

187

A company **trades up** when it adds a higher-priced, more prestigious product version with the main goal of increasing sales of a present lower-priced version. Thus, while trading up involves cultivating a new market segment, the emphasis is on increasing sales to an old market segment—an old one and a new one. Ford Motor Company, for example, introduced the Thunderbird (a prestigious, relatively high-priced car) hoping to increase sales of the lower-priced Ford. Thunderbird was promoted separately but in ways that made certain that prospective buyers of lower-priced cars would know it was Ford-made. Companies trading up anticipate that a halo effect will carry over from the new prestige item to the older lower-priced and less prestigious item.

A company **trades down** when it adds a lower-priced product version in the hope that buyers who would not, or could not, buy a higher-priced version will now buy the new version because it carries some of the prestige. In trading down, then, emphasis is on tapping a new market segment, one not tapped effectively earlier because the original version had too high a price. For example, Ford Motor Company, after successfully trading up with the Thunderbird, saw an opportunity to tap a market segment of "people who would have liked to have a Thunderbird but could not afford it." The traded-down version was the Mustang, a car resembling the Thunderbird but much lower-priced, which became an outstanding success.

NEW PRODUCT— NO MARKET CHANGE

This strategy seeks increased profitability through selling a new product to the same market segment, the new product replacing an older product sold for the same general purpose. Thus, **product replacement** strategy aims at retaining the level of sales now coming from a particular market segment where an older product's sales are being endangered by competitor's new products serving the same uses. Examples of new products that replaced old ones are numerous. A few of them are: automobiles replaced carriages, diesel locomotives replaced steam locomotives, jet planes replaced piston-driven aircraft, the transistor is replacing the vacuum tube, and the ballpoint pen nearly replaced the fountain pen. For companies having products in the market maturity stage, new products should be waiting in the wings, ready for market introduction at the proper times.

NEW PRODUCT— IMPROVED MARKET

This strategy aims to increase profitability through adding sales volume gained from new products sold to the same market segments. Often the new products are extensions of the present product line; for example, the ready-to-eat cereal added to a line of regular cereals, or the addition of new flavors to an old product line, as was done by Ovaltine.[9] Sometimes the new products are

[9] Kevin V. Brown, "How to Make a New Product from an Old Product," *Product Management,* December 1976, pp. 26-31.

members of related product lines sold to the same market segments as present products; for example, the pet food added by a marketer of breakfast cereals.

product line extension When final buyers regard several products as a related group or line, management must decide whether to produce a partial or complete line. Consumers, for example, buy both kitchen and laundry appliances in the same retail outlets and sometimes shop for several appliances at the same time. The manufacturer's decision to extend its offerings within a product line should result from evaluation of several factors. It must be financially able to add new items. Management should analyze the likely effect of adding to the line on the profits of existing line members. If management finds that numerous buyers prefer to buy two or more products at the same time (as often happens with matching appliances), a more complete line may increase sales of present products. Similarly, as a company extends its line, each item's marketing costs should be reduced, since little more promotion or selling effort is needed to sell the line than to sell an individual item.

Against these potential gains should be balanced the new items' probabilities of success. Does the company have the production, engineering, and general management knowhow to develop and produce new products as good as its present products? Management must also evaluate the effect of the proposed additions on the reputations of present products; if buyers consider a new item inferior to those already in the line, the entire line's reputation may suffer.

diversification into related product lines Companies add related product lines for two main reasons: (1) to capitalize further on company knowhow in serving particular market segments, and (2) to reduce the risk of obsolescence in the present product line. Market segments do not disappear suddenly, but demand for a product line sometimes does.

How far a company should diversify into related product lines depends on various considerations. Will related product diversification reduce unit sales and distribution costs? Can the sales force sell the related line effectively? What promotional expenses are required? Who are the new competitors, what strategies do they employ, and what advantages do they have? Will a beneficial halo effect from the present line carry over to the related line? Can the items in the new line actually be developed, produced at reasonable cost, and differentiated in ways attractive to potential buyers? This type of analysis should permit management to estimate the profitability of adding a related product line.

NEW PRODUCT— NEW MARKET This strategy seeks to increase profitability through greater sales volumes obtained from selling new products in new markets. Thus, it involves **product-mix diversification**—selling unrelated product lines to entirely different markets. Companies adopt this strategy for reasons such as unexpected research breakthroughs or discoveries of profitable opportunities to develop products for new markets.

This strategy involves considerably greater risk than any other product-market strategy. Both the product and the market are totally new to the company, so proposals for unrelated product diversification merit the most careful investigation. Generally, a company is well advised first to fill out its present line then diversify into related lines sold to the same markets, and finally (after other profit-increasing possibilities are exhausted) to diversify into new markets with new products.

A final note pertaining to all new product strategies is appropriate. In a competitive economy, in some industries, new product introductions are necessary for a firm's survival. In such cases, there should be a comprehensive method for analysis of the new product introduction program. In addition to the traditional economic criteria (profitability, sales volume, product line compatibility, etc.), the evaluation procedure should include social and environmental factors. Such factors include environmental and production compatibility, environmental and user compatibility (in use and after use), recycling potential, and social and moral impact. [10]

SUMMARY   Analysis in this chapter has focused on the nine different combinations of product-market strategies and their main forms. Each form of each product-market strategy represents a potential opportunity for improving profitability. Most product-market strategies (all but pure product design simplification, and product line simplification and product discontinuance) seek to increase profitability mainly through increasing sales volume. But achieving increased profits through increased sales involves more than simply deciding on a product-market strategy. As Figure 9-2 shows, the particular product-market strategy chosen requires integration with appropriate distribution, promotion, and price strategies into an overall marketing strategy. Matching products with markets is essential to marketing, but so is effecting ownership transfers (i.e., making sales). While well-chosen product-market strategies can help in making sales by making a product more salable, to capitalize on potentially profitable product-market opportunities management must also formulate and implement parallel distribution, promotion, and price strategies.

You now have the needed background on the marketing significance of key aspects of product management. From Chapter 8, you have gained an understanding of how products vary in their marketing characteristics, how they move through life cycles, and the need marketers have for continuous programs of product innovation. From Chapter 9, you have gained understanding of how companies use different product-market strategies in efforts to improve their profitability. Thus, we are now ready to consider the next major component of overall marketing strategy—distribution.

[10] Dale L. Varble, "Social and Environmental Considerations in New Product Development," *Journal of Marketing,* October 1972, pp. 11-15.

Figure 9-2 Product–market strategy and overall
marketing strategy

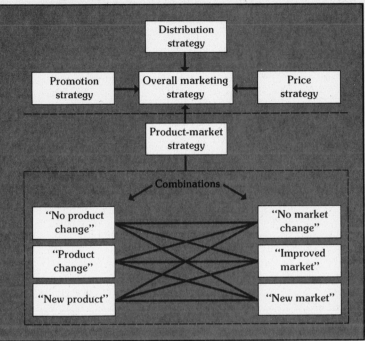

1. Consumers buy a "total" product rather than the physical product alone. Explain this statement, using several examples.

2. In what ways can a new product be "new?" Explain fully. Give an example for each.

3. The starting point in the new product development process is searching for ideas. What are the possible sources of new product ideas? Which are the best sources? Why? And, who should screen the ideas to select those that should be further investigated?

4. How would you recommend that each of the following organizations go about finding new users for its products?
   a. A manufacturer of small, hand-operated paper cutters and hole punchers.
   b. A producer of talcum powder for babies.
   c. A manufacturer of office furniture.
   d. A maker of pots and pans for restaurants and institutions.

5. "A company operating under the marketing concept must let its products proliferate. Otherwise, how can it provide all dealers and customers with what they want?" Agree or disagree? State your reasoning fully.

6. Under what conditions should a company consider discontinuing unprofitable products? Profitable products?

7. "The advantages of using a family brand clearly outweigh those of using individual brands on different products." Agree or disagree?

8. From the viewpoints of the manufacturer, the retailer, and the consumer, what do you see as the role of packaging (for consumer goods)? In your opinion, how effective is consumer goods packaging?

9 | Why might a company diversify into related product lines rather than extending its present product line?

10 | The "new product–new market" strategy involves considerably greater risk than any other product–market strategy. Why?

11 | How would you respond to the frequent criticism of marketing that there are too many products, resulting in consumer confusion and a large number of failures? Support your position.

12 | Prepare a list of all the product–market strategies discussed in this chapter, including major variations of each strategy. Then identify those that seek increased profitability through (1) cost reduction, (2) increased sales, (3) both cost reduction and increased sales, and (4) some other means. Also, evaluate each strategy in terms of its potential effectiveness.

13 | Describe the importance of branding from the viewpoints of the manufacturer, the retailer, and the consumer.

14 | Regarding branding, what types of policy decisions are faced by manufacturers and middlemen?

15 | Are you satisfied with the level of product quality found today? Why or why not? Who or what determines the level of product quality?

16 | Has the package effectively replaced the salesperson in retail stores? Be specific.

17 | The "no product change–new market" strategy is especially significant for companies with products already in or about to enter the market maturity stage in the life cycle. Explain fully.

18 | Would it be sensible to use a rule of thumb that no package is justifiable if it increases the cost of the product by more than 10 percent? Why?

19 | What reasons would companies with large market shares, such as Coca-Cola and Pepsi-Cola in the cola market, have for entering new markets with changed products? For instance, why did these two companies enter the market for low-calorie soft drinks? Cite other examples.

20 | Explain remerchandising. Use examples.

CASE PROBLEMS

Marathon Shoe Company manufactured a wide line of athletic shoes and had been a sales leader in the industry for over 20 years. Marathon produced shoes for all sports and jealously guarded its reputation for high quality. Shoes were distributed nationally by manufacturers' agents who sold to what Marathon management called the "best" sporting goods stores, department stores, and shoestores. Although the company had received many requests, Marathon shoes were not sold to "discount" stores. The company strongly encouraged premium pricing of its shoes at the retail level, convinced that the brand image was enhanced because Marathon shoes were priced higher than most competitive shoes.

In 1977, Marathon entered the market for running shoes in an attempt to capitalize on the running for physical fitness boom in the United States. Sales of running shoes exceeded company expectations, and evidently were riding on the coattails of the Marathon name. The line of running shoes consisted of three models: the Elite, priced to retail at $39.95; the Star, retailing at $35.95; and the Top-Performer, retailing at $31.95. During the past year two different magazines devoted to running selected the Elite as the best running shoe.

A substantial advertising program backed the Marathon distribution effort. Media used included national TV, and general consumer and special-interest magazines. For example, *Runner's World, Running Times, Marathon, Sports Illustrated, Sport, Time,* and *Fortune* were among the magazines used. Every advertisement played heavily upon the Marathon name.

Katherine Ostheimer, vice-president of marketing operations, recently came across some statistics showing that over 30 percent of total running-shoe sales were in the $15–24 retail price range, a price range in which Marathon had no entry. Ostheimer began wondering whether Marathon should add a fourth model to its line, one aimed to compete in this price range. The company had the know-how and the capability of producing a "good shoe for the money," but Ostheimer wanted to check out a few things with the sales manager before formally proposing the new product idea.

In the ensuing discussions that took place over a three-week period, several issues were identified concerning the proposed new running shoes, but few answers resulted. Ostheimer wanted the answers before she developed a new product proposal for evaluation by Marathon's new product screening committee. Among the unanswered questions were these:

1. Would sales of the new shoe, tentatively named the Marathon "26.2," merely substitute for sales of other Marathon models?
2. Would the lower price affect the price/quality relationship that existed in people's minds?
3. Should "26.2" advertising emphasize the Marathon name?
4. Should the new product be sold through established retail outlets?
5. Would the manufacturers' agents take on the additional item?
6. What appeals should be stressed in the advertising?

The more Ostheimer thought about the matter, the more she was convinced of the need for a quick decision because of intense competition in the running-shoe market. The longer the company stayed out of this price range, the more it would lose, as people were in a buying mood. At the same time, however, Ostheimer knew she needed answers to the questions that had arisen. She asked her assistant, William Tulloch, to organize a committee to study the issues, and to pin down other questions requiring answers before the proposal should be forwarded to the new product screening committee.

questions:

1. How should Ostheimer answer the questions raised?
2. What other special problems might arise?
3. Should Marathon market the new running shoe?

PART FOUR

DISTRIBUTION

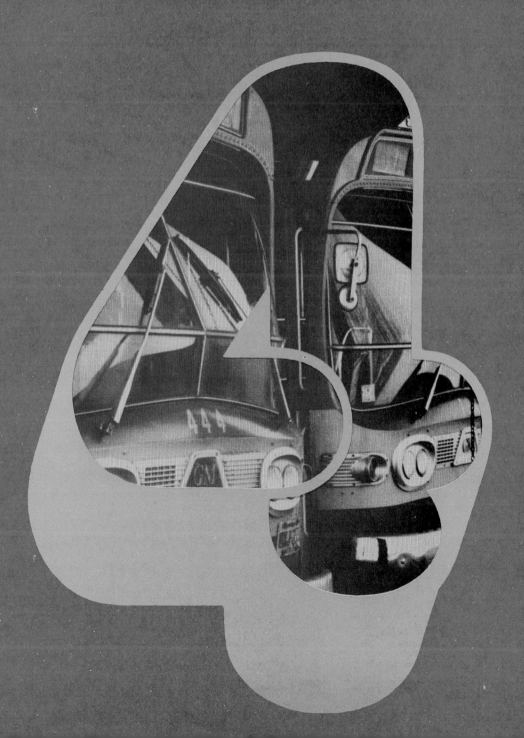

When you have mastered the contents of this chapter, you should be able to:

1. Explain the relationship of distribution decisions to other major marketing decisions.
2. Define important terms used in distribution.
3. Discuss key relationships between the management of physical distribution, marketing institutions, and marketing channels.
4. Explain the various factors influencing decisions on size of inventory.
5. Contrast the relative strengths and weaknesses of each of the three decision alternatives on geographic deployment of inventory.
6. Outline the conditions under which a marketer should (a) operate its own branch warehouse, or (b) use public warehouses.
7. Explain how the marketer should make decisions on modes of transportation.
8. Discuss the marketing significance of decisions on materials handling, order size, and order processing.
9. Explain the total cost approach to the management of physical distribution.
10. Summarize the inputs and decisions that comprise distribution strategy.

10

the field
of distribution

Distribution is concerned with the activities involved in transferring goods from producers to final buyers and users. It includes the physical activities, such as transporting and storing goods, and the legal, promotional, and financial activities performed in the course of transferring ownership. Since a succession of enterprises is generally involved in the distribution process leading up to the final sale to the consumer or user, to understand distribution one must analyze both the different kinds of marketing institutions and the marketing channels in which they operate. Your overall learning objective, then, in this and the following three chapters (all of Part Four) is to gain this broad understanding of distribution. In Part Four, analysis focuses first on the actual physical distribution of products from producers to final buyers; second, on the various types of distributive institutions (including producers, wholesalers, and retailers) that bring products into contact with markets and effect ownership transfers; and third, on marketing channels and channels policy.

SOME BASIC DEFINITIONS IN DISTRIBUTION [1]

middlemen

Middlemen specialize in performing activities directly related to the purchase and sale of goods in the process of their flow from producers to final buyers. As the name "middleman" suggests, such institutions are situated in marketing channels at points between producers and final buyers. Producers regard middlemen as extensions of their own marketing organizations, because if there were no middlemen their own organizations would have to carry on all negotiations leading up to sales to final buyers. Final buyers—ultimate consumers and industrial users—consider middlemen as sources of supply and points of contact with producers.

[1] Unless noted otherwise, the definitions in this section and the remainder of Part Four are those compiled by the Committee on Definitions of the American Marketing Association. See Committee on Definitions, *Marketing Definitions* (Chicago: American Marketing Association, 1960).

merchants and agents   Middlemen fall into two broad classifications: merchants and agents. A **merchant** takes title to (i.e., buys) and resells merchandise. An **agent** negotiates purchases or sales or both, but does not take title to the goods in which it deals. Thus, the chief distinguishing characteristic relates to whether the middleman takes title to the goods it handles. If it does, it is a merchant. If it does not, it is an agent. Also, the merchant always both buys and resells, whereas the agent may specialize in negotiating only buying or only selling transactions.

retailers and wholesalers   Middlemen may also be separated into two other major categories: retailers and wholesalers. The principal basis for distinguishing retailers and wholesalers relates to whether the business sells in significant amounts to ultimate consumers. If it does, it is a retailer. If it does not, it is a wholesaler.

A **retailer** is a merchant, or occasionally an agent, whose main business is selling directly to ultimate consumers. A retailer is distinguished by the nature of its sales rather than by the way it acquires the goods in which it deals. It usually sells in small lots, but this condition is not essential. The dealer who sells the furniture and floor covering for the initial outfitting of a large home, for instance, may make a sale of several thousand dollars, but it is still a retail sale if the buyer (i.e., the homeowner) is an ultimate consumer.

Wholesalers buy and resell merchandise to retailers and other merchants and to industrial, institutional, and commercial users, but do not sell in significant amounts to ultimate consumers. Notice that this definition does not specify that wholesalers must deal in large lots, nor does it require that they habitually make sales for purposes of resale. Most wholesalers do sell in large lots, but many do not. Similarly, most wholesalers do sell for purposes of resale, but there are many who sell directly to industrial users. The one essential distinguishing feature of the wholesaler is that it must be a middleman, who usually does not sell to ultimate consumers.

retailing and wholesaling[2]   **Retailing** consists of the activities involved in selling directly to the ultimate consumer. It makes no difference who does the selling; but, to be classified as retailing, selling activities must be direct to the ultimate consumer. Retailers, of course, are engaged in retailing, and so is any other institution that sells directly to ultimate consumers. Manufacturers engage in retailing when they make direct-to-consumer sales through their own stores, by house-to-house canvass, or by mail order. Even a wholesaler engages in retailing when it sells directly to an ultimate consumer, although its main business may still be wholesaling. If the buyer in a transaction is an ultimate consumer, the seller in the same transaction is engaged in retailing.

Wholesaling involves selling to buyers other than ultimate consumers. These buyers may be wholesalers and retailers who buy to resell. They may

[2] The Committee on Definitions of the American Marketing Association does not provide a definition for "wholesaling."

be industrial users (manufacturers, mining concerns, or firms in other extractive industries), institutional users (schools, prisons, or mental hospitals), commercial users (restaurants, hotels, or factory lunchrooms), government agencies, or farmers buying items for their agricultural operations. Wholesaling is carried on not only by wholesalers but by manufacturers, other producers, and other business units that make sales to buyers who are not ultimate consumers. If the buyer in a transaction is buying for resale or to further its business or other operations, the seller in that transaction is engaged in wholesaling. All sales not made to ultimate consumers are wholesale sales.

THE PROCESS OF DISTRIBUTION AND ITS ELEMENTS

Figure 10-1 shows the relationship of distribution strategy to the other elements of marketing strategy—product, promotion, and price. Distribution strategy is composed of three main elements: (1) physical distribution (Chapter 10), (2) institutions (Chapters 11 and 12), and (3) marketing channels (Chapter 13). Chapter 10 serves also as an introduction to the entire field of distribution.

physical distribution

Physical distribution, a critical element in distribution strategy, is concerned with the actual movement and storage of products after their production and before their consumption. All producers and final buyers and most middlemen (i.e., all except for one type of merchant wholesaler—the drop shipment wholesaler, and several types of agents) in varying degrees perform physical distribution activities. Total costs of physical distribution bulk large, generally ranking third in size in the overall cost of goods and exceeded only by the costs of raw materials and labor.

Efficiency in physical distribution significantly influences a company's chances for marketing success. In this chapter discussion focuses on (1) various interrelated facets of physical distribution management including inventory control, storage, transportation, materials handling, order size control, and order processing; and (2) the total distribution system.

producers and wholesalers

In any marketing channel, the producer is the seller in the first of the sequence of marketing transactions that occur as the product moves toward its market. Such producers include enterprises engaged in manufacturing, in mining and the extractive industries, and in farming. Of these, manufacturers, with their capabilities of differentiating their products from those of competitors, possess the greatest power to influence the total sequence of transactions in distributing their products.

The second type of institution in the sequence of transactions that move the product toward its market is often a *wholesaler.* Consumer products are often sold by producers directly to retailers, or occasionally direct to consumers, but in many instances wholesalers serve as important links be-

Figure 10-1 Distribution strategy and overall
marketing strategy

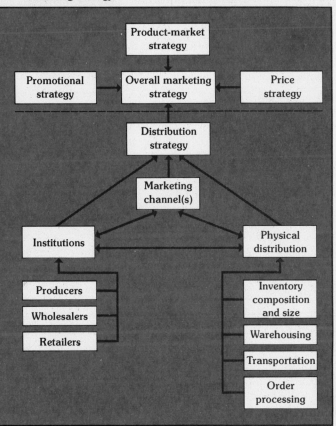

tween producers and retailers. Industrial products are most often sold directly to the user, but in some cases the producer uses wholesale middlemen to reach final users. Even though wholesalers are not present in all marketing situations, the wholesaling field is large, with over 300,000 establishments operating in the United States alone.

There is tremendous diversity in wholesaling establishments. Both merchant and agent middlemen types are important in wholesaling. Some wholesale middlemen have long-standing relationships with the producers they represent; others may serve a particular producer only once. Some receive, store, and even process goods; others never see the goods they sell. Some provide a wide range of services; others provide none. Each type of wholesaler evolved to serve the needs of a unique market segment.

retailers *Retailing* occurs in all marketing channels for consumer goods because, by definition, it consists of the activities involved in selling directly to ultimate consumers. While a few producers of consumer products handle their own retail distribution, most

201

rely on separately owned retail institutions to distribute their outputs to ultimate consumers. Although you, as a consumer, already know a great deal about retailers, to understand retail distribution you must know more, especially about the operating methods of various retail institutions.

Marketers and consumers view the roles of retailers somewhat differently. Producers and wholesalers regard retailers as intermediaries providing contacts with target consumer market segments, while consumers think of them as sources of supply for all types of products. Actually, retailers serve both roles—they buy and assemble consumer products (either directly from producers or through wholesalers) and resell them to ultimate consumers. Because both roles are so basic, retailers are the most numerous of all marketing institutions—wherever there is more than a handful of people, there are retailers.

marketing channels   A **marketing channel**, or channel of distribution, is a path traced in the direct or indirect transfer of ownership to a product, as it moves from a producer to ultimate consumers or industrial users. Every marketing channel contains one or more transfer points, at each of which there is either an institution or a final buyer; during marketing, in other words, legal ownership of the product changes hands at least once. (This bare minimum occurs in situations where producers deal directly with final buyers and there are no intervening middlemen.) Generally, legal title to the product passes from the producer to and through a series of middlemen (distributive institutions) before the consumer or industrial user finally takes possession. Transfer of ownership may be direct, as when the producer sells the product outright to a wholesaler or retailer, or it may be indirect, as when an agent middleman does not take legal title but simply negotiates its transfer. From the producer's standpoint, such a network of institutions used for reaching a market is a marketing channel. We think it logical to examine the building blocks—that is, the institutions (Chapters 11 and 12)—before we look at the different ways they can be joined together in marketing channels (Chapter 13).

PHYSICAL DISTRIBUTION

The managerial function of physical distribution requires decisions on size of inventory, storage and inventory location, modes of transportation, materials handling, order size, and order processing. The total physical distribution decision, to be most efficient, must optimize the combination of the individual inputs.

decisions on size of inventory   Inventories are, in effect, reservoirs of goods held in anticipation of sales—that is, of filling demands from farther along the marketing channel. Incoming quantities of the product ready for sale arrive, usually at irregular intervals, and are added to the inventory reservoir. The outgoing product flow is more continuous but still fluctuates considerably. The volume in the inventory reservoir pulsates but not always with a regular rhythm; for day to day, changes occur in the rates and quantities of input and output. Therefore, in deciding inventory size, management must determine both maximum and minimum allowable limits. Setting these upper and lower limits involves both sales and cost considerations.

SALES CONSIDERATIONS   The main objective in maintaining any inventory is to meet market demands, that is, to make sales and to fill customers' orders. Inventories are kept in anticipation of market demand, so the upper and lower control limits should be attuned to forecasted sales. The more accurate the sales forecast is, the greater the opportunity is for gain from economical inventory operations. The less accurate the forecast is, the greater the need is for substantial buffer stocks over and above normal inventory levels.

Two additional factors need consideration. One is management's concept of an **acceptable level of customer service.** Experience indicates that, in a typical business, about 80 percent more inventory is needed to fill 95 percent of customers' orders from stock on hand than to fill just 80 percent of such orders.[3] Each firm, then, must strike a balance between what it considers reasonable customer service and costs, in line with overall marketing objectives.

The other factor is **distribution system responsiveness**—the ability of a system to communicate needs back to the supplying plant and get needed inventory into the field. The amount of responsiveness determines how quickly management can adjust inventory to demand changes. Thus, distribution system responsiveness directly influences the lower inventory limit.

COST CONSIDERATIONS   Three types of costs are associated with the inventory. **Holding costs** include warehousing and storage charges, costs of capital tied up in inventory, costs of adverse price movements, obsolescence, spoilage, pilferage, and taxes and insurance on inventory. **Costs of shortages** include special clerical, administrative, and handling costs and, most important (because of stockouts), losses of specific sales, of goodwill, and even of some customers. **Costs of replenishing** inventory differ in composition depending upon whether a business does its own manufacturing or buys from outside sources.

Inventory decisions should seek to balance the three types of costs. Whereas holding costs rise as inventory increases, the costs of both shortages and inventory replenishment decrease. Holding, shortage, and replenishment costs are all related, then, to inventory size; total costs are a function of the amount stored. Determining how much to store to minimize total costs requires balancing inventory-holding costs against either costs of shortage or costs of replenishment or both.

[3] J. F. Magee, "The Logistics of Distribution," *Harvard Business Review,* July-August 1960, p. 62.

decisions on storage and inventory location   Decisions on storage and inventory location are linked to decisions on inventory size. For instance, a decision to restrict inventory size drastically, so as to operate almost from hand to mouth, reduces total need for storage space. Marketers make three important storage decisions: geographic deployment of inventory, ownership of warehouse facilities, and number and location of warehouses.

GEOGRAPHIC DEPLOYMENT OF INVENTORY   There are three decision alternatives on **geographical deployment of inventory:** (1) concentration at or near the plant or at some other central location, (2) dispersion at several distribution points located in or closer to the main markets, and (3) concentration of substantial inventories at a few distribution centers and redistribution to a larger number of distribution points dispersed throughout the market. The first two alternatives are opposite extremes; the third is a compromise between them.

Comparison of **inventory concentration** and **inventory dispersion** reveals opposite sets of strengths and weaknesses. The company that concentrates its inventory minimizes the number of customers' orders unfilled because of stockouts; but in so doing it may increase total transportation costs and delay customer service. The firm that disperses its inventory needs a larger total inventory investment and, in effect, commits each subinventory to sale only in a particular market area; but it reduces total transportation charges and speeds up customer service. The concentration decision permits more rapid adjustment to changes in the makeup of incoming orders because unexpected demands originating from only a few markets usually can be met at once; the dispersion decision requires either the maintaining of a large enough reserve stock at each branch to meet most emergencies or some provision for moving stocks among branches. Thus, the dispersion decision requires the greater inventory investment because the sum of many small reserve stocks scattered over the whole market is greater than one large reserve stock held at a single location. If the product line consists mostly of bulky and low-unit-value items, total transportation costs are lower when decentralized warehouses are used, because railroads and truckers charge less for moving full carloads than less-than-carload lots. Both alternatives, then, have general strengths and weaknesses, and whether a marketer chooses one or the other—or adopts the third as a compromise—depends upon its evaluation of each factor's relative importance. These evaluations, in turn, are influenced by the nature of the product line, target markets, marketing channels, promotional strategies, pricing policies, and competitors' practices.

WAREHOUSE OWNERSHIP   Manufacturers deciding to disperse their inventories choose between operating their own branch warehouses or using public warehouses. This choice depends upon the amount of sales volume originating in particular markets, the preference for fixed or variable warehousing costs, the degree of flexibility desired in making changes in the pattern of inventory deployment, relative warehousing efficiency, and marketing channel(s) used. There is relationship and interaction among these factors. If a substantial volume of goods with little seasonal fluctuation is moved, a good case can be made for branch warehouses owned and operated by the manufacturer. Branch warehousing costs are mainly fixed and, with a large steady flow-through of goods, costs per unit of product moved are low. Because public warehouses base their charges on the space and labor actually used, the scales generally tip in their favor only when a small volume is to be handled or when a large volume with great seasonal fluctuations is to be stored. The variable costs associated with the use of public warehouses also provide greater flexibility in changing the geographical deployment of inventory. Because most cities have many public warehouses, the manufacturer can easily close out stocks in some locations and place them in others.

The chief economic justification for the **public warehouse** is that it dovetails local small storage needs of many manufacturers, which, in turn, results in a large enough storage facility to make efficient use of storage space, warehousing labor, and mechanized handling equipment. However, with a large and steady sales volume of its own, an individual manufacturer realizes comparable efficiencies in its own branch warehouses. Furthermore, if its product requires either specialized handling and technical service or special storage facilities, it may be forced to own and operate branch warehouses, because such facilities are not available everywhere.

NUMBER AND LOCATION OF WAREHOUSES   The decision as to the number and location of warehouses is influenced by several important variables, including customers' buying patterns and delivery expectations, freight rate structures, service characteristics of alternative transportation media, warehouse operating costs, location of factories, production capacities and product mix of individual factories, and costs of building or renting suitable warehouses in different cities. It is possible to secure data on each of these variables, but the number of possible combinations of the many sets of complex, and to some extent interrelated, variables is staggering. Thus, in the past, largely because of the mountain of work involved in calculating the probable results of each combination of variables, most decisions on number and location of warehouses were intuitive. With the advent of the high-speed digital computer, such computations became more routine.

Operations researchers have devised simulation techniques that permit mathematical representations of a company's distribution system, present and proposed, to be programmed on a computer. In a comparatively short time, a computer provides the probable operating results under many different combinations of numbers and locations of warehouses. Such simulations furnish marketing executives with much additional information needed for decisions on related problems.

decisions on modes of transportation

Significant improvements are being made in **transportation** services. Truck transportation is improving with the construction of more superhighways and the use of large trailers. Rail freight transportation is improving as more roads provide *piggyback* service (rail movement of loaded tractor trailers), "unitized" trains, and other service innovations. Air freight transportation is improving with the larger jet air carriers and the use of "containerized" (giant containers holding many smaller shipments) loading and unloading systems. These improvements are indicative of the general trend toward providing shippers with more rapid and efficient transportation services.

Too often, decisions on modes of transportation are made solely in terms of comparative shipping costs. In these cases, management ignores the fact that transportation is only one part of what should be a totally integrated physical distribution system. When transportation decisions are made in isolation, shipping costs may be minimized but total physical distribution costs are usually not. Shipping decisions that aim only to reduce transportation cost may be more than offset by increases in warehousing costs, costlier packing, and the costs of carrying larger-than-necessary inventories.

Transport time—the time required for moving goods from warehouses, for example, to customers—is a major determinant of efficiency in the distribution system. Reductions in transport time, although commonly accompanied by increased shipping costs, often result in significant savings in warehousing costs, packing costs, and inventory investments. For instance, switching from a distribution system composed of surface transportation and branch warehouses to one involving air transportation direct to the customer normally results in higher transportation costs but much lower storage costs. Net savings often flow from such changes, largely because of reductions in storage and inventory costs.

However, physical distribution costs can sometimes be cut through using slower and lower cost modes of transportation. For instance, Westinghouse Electric Corporation switched from air to surface transportation for deliveries of rush orders. By making improvements in all the distribution steps before shipment, Westinghouse saved so much time that it could use the slower surface transportation and benefit from the lower cost. Generally, transportation decisions should be based both on cost and transport time, and the relative significance of each depends on their combined relationship to the overall efficiency of the total physical distribution system.

materials-handling decisions

Materials handling is the physical distribution area that has experienced the greatest change and improvement in recent decades. One major improvement was the elimination of "manhandling" of goods. Thirty years ago it was common to use manpower to transfer goods from storage to transportation and back to storage. Today, most goods are not handled by human labor at all until they reach the retail or final buyer level. Improved conveyor systems and forklift equipment make possible almost total mechanization.

A second improvement was **containerization**—the development of methods by which a large number of units of a product are combined into a single compact unit for storage and transportation. Containerization has evolved from the simple pallet to complex and special-purpose containers. Containerization cuts both materials-handling costs and time, because it allows goods to be moved greater distances in bulk form, increasing mechanized handling and reducing manhandling.

Materials-handling decisions and costs are interrelated with other decisions and costs. Improved materials handling not only cuts the cost of handling goods, it also improves the relative effectiveness of transportation and storage. For example, containerization so drastically reduces the "loading turnaround time" for ships that it has greatly lessened their "comparative speed" disadvantage. At the same time, improved materials handling makes for more effective utilization of storage space and, hence, a reduction of investment in facilities. Improved materials handling may increase the utilization of warehouse storage space by 50 percent or more, since it makes possible "ceiling-high" stacking of goods. Similarly, improved materials handling, by speeding up the processing of orders and movement of shipments, contributes to improved customer service.

order-size decisions   Order-size decisions are also complicated because of the interrelationships of order sizes to other facets of physical distribution. For example, when orders are for quantities less than the contents of a normal pallet or container, the goods must be handled by hand instead of by machine. Manhandling raises costs appreciably. Less-than-pallet-size orders also increase the costs of storage and inventory control and add to their complexity. The size of an order may also affect the level of shipping costs, since bulk or carload shipping rates are lower than rates for smaller quantities. Management must, therefore, make decisions concerning minimum order sizes, units of increment in order sizes, and preferred order sizes so that customers' orders are of sizes consistent with the objective of optimizing total physical distribution costs.[4]

order-processing decisions   The methods a marketing organization uses for processing customers' orders affects its service to them in terms of reorder time and consistency of delivery time. Variations in these two time variables exert influences upon the buyers' profits by changing their minimum investments in inventory, altering their ordering costs, and changing the probability that they will be out of stock. Because of these considerations, buyers tend to shift their orders to suppliers who provide superior order-processing service. In a study of 700 retailers, it was found that store buyers could discriminate among even small differences in order

[4] A good discussion of order-size decisions, complete with examples, may be seen in Arthur J. Schomer, "An Approach to Inventory Management," *Journal of Accountancy,* August 1965, pp. 75-77.

service time and that their rating of this factor influenced their overall rating of a supplier.[5] Even small improvements in order-processing service provide a supplier with competitive advantages; thus, it is worthwhile exploring possible avenues leading to greater efficiency in order processing.

the total distribution system   Physical distribution is intimately related to other aspects of marketing. Consider what takes place as products move through marketing channels, over time and through space, from production to consumption. Inventories are held by manufacturers, by middlemen at each distribution level, and by ultimate buyers at the end of the channel. In the distribution of consumer goods, for example, consumers add to their stocks by buying from retailers. This reduces retailers' inventories and the retailers place replenishing orders with wholesalers, who, in turn, replenish by placing orders with manufacturers. Thus, while products are flowing forward to final buyers, there is a reverse flow of orders, causing alternating subtractions from and additions to inventories at each level. Each time a manufacturer ships an order, it initiates this chain reaction in the performance of transportation, inventory control, storage, and other physical distribution activities.

Even though the way total distribution costs are divided among physical distribution activities varies widely from one company to another, it is possible to generalize about the relative cost of each activity. Table 10-1 shows the average division of physical distribution costs in a sample of 26 large companies. Carrier (transportation) charges were the largest cost element (44 percent of the total), while warehousing and handling costs, including storage charges and materials-handling costs, were the second largest cost element (20 percent of total physical distribution costs).

From the manufacturer's standpoint, physical distribution management demands integrated planning of all transportation, storage, and supply requirements, plus implementation of inventory policy. This requires decisions on the deployment and size of inventory at specific times and places, ensuring that the right products are in the right quantities at the right places at the right times. The solution should strike an optimal balance between physical distribution costs and the expectations of end buyers and users of the product.

A manufacturer works toward optimum performance of the total distribution system by coordinating its inventory policies and practices with those of other channel members. How middlemen manage their inventories definitely affects the manufacturer's costs and profits. Their actions also determine the quality of service and product availability at the times and places desired by final buyers. If middlemen are overstocked, they may cut prices to make sales, thus jeopardizing future sales at normal prices, possibly damaging the manufacturer's reputation for product quality, and perhaps

[5] R. P. Willet and P. R. Stephenson, "Determinants of Buyer Response to Physical Distribution Service," *Journal of Marketing Research,* August 1969, pp. 280-283.

**TABLE 10-1 PHYSICAL DISTRIBUTION: MAJOR
ELEMENTS OF COST IN 26 LARGE COMPANIES**

Cost Element	Total Distribution Cost* (%)
Carrier charges	44
Warehousing and handling	20
Inventory carrying cost	18
Shipping room and administrative (includes order-processing costs)	18
Total	100

*Averages for survey sample as a whole, based on available company data
and/or author's estimates. Percentages assigned to various items vary as much
as ±20 percent among the 26 individual companies.

making themselves less enthusiastic about relationships with the manufacturer. If middlemen follow unintelligent inventory practices, such as "hand-to-mouth" buying, the manufacturer is forced to enlarge inventories and, consequently, to increase costs. Furthermore, the manufacturer and the middlemen suffer hidden costs from being out of stock and unable to fill orders when buyers want them. Unfortunately, out-of-stock costs are not recorded by conventional accounting systems, but profits and sales are both reduced when customers go away empty-handed.

Estimates of physical distribution costs indicate that they account for as much as one-third of the manufacturer's selling price and from one-fifth to one-fourth of the price the final buyer pays. Any area accounting for so much of total costs is a prime target for management's efforts to increase efficiency. Gains in physical distribution efficiency cause improvements in net profits. Most estimates of the cost of physical distribution are based upon selling in domestic markets. In international markets (where distances are greater and inventories often must be larger) physical distribution costs generally account for even larger shares of the final prices of products.

SUMMARY   Distribution is a major marketing decision area embracing physical distribution management, management of marketing institutions, and management of marketing channels. The institutions participating in the process of moving products to consumer and industrial buyers are producers, wholesalers, and retailers. Channel decisions focus upon selecting the kinds and numbers of institutions that are to participate in moving goods from the producer to consumers and/or industrial users. Physical distribution activities are performed in moving the product through time and space from the producer to the final buyer. Products often do not reach final buyers until months after their production, and this makes inventory control and storage necessary, sometimes at several different distribution levels. Marketing also requires moving products from points of production to points of consumption, sometimes many thousands of miles, and this makes transportation, materials handling, and order processing necessary and important.

Recognition that all facets of physical distribution should be treated as a unified managerial responsibility reduces the possibility of emphasizing certain facets at the expense of others. Awareness of opportunities for cost savings in physical distribution has become greater with more widespread understanding of the total cost approach to physical distribution management.

Physical distribution decisions are major decisions, as difficult to make on rational bases as they are to reverse or change. They require considerable market information, both qualitative and quantitative, and, in using this information, decision makers must clearly conceptualize the nature of the total physical distribution system, each of its facets, and the relationships each facet bears to others and to the total system.

REVIEW AND DISCUSSION QUESTIONS		
	1	Explain the relationship between distribution strategy and the other elements of marketing strategy—product, promotion, and price.
	2	What is physical distribution "efficiency"? How does a company achieve it? Discuss.
	3	"Managing physical distribution involves balancing distribution costs against an acceptable level of customer satisfaction." Explain.
	4	Comment on this statement: Viewed from the position of the manufacturer, physical distribution management requires logistical planning.
	5	What kinds of costs are associated with the inventory? Explain how inventory costs are "balanced" in making inventory decisions. How does a middleman's management of inventories affect the manufacturer's costs and profits?
	6	Contrast and compare inventory concentration and inventory dispersion from the standpoint of their respective strengths and weaknesses.
	7	Explain fully the various decisions relating to storage and inventory location.
	8	Why is it that manufacturers cannot completely "control" (i.e., direct and regulate) physical distribution?
	9	"Each time a manufacturer ships an order, it initiates a chain reaction in the performance of physical distribution activities." Explain in detail.
	10	Describe the role of transportation in an integrated physical distribution system.
	11	What is meant by a "total cost" approach to physical distribution?
	12	For a "Manager of Physical Distribution," outline and describe the duties and responsibilities of such a position, including the person's relationship to the chief marketing manager.
	13	Describe, in your own words, what is meant by the "total distribution system." What is the value of thinking of it as a "system"?

CASE PROBLEM

Onondaga Distributors, Inc., manufactured and sold a wide line of industrial parts. In going over sales records for the past two years, Bob Borgman, sales manager, noted a substantial increase in the number of small orders. John Fleming, assistant sales manager, was asked to conduct a detailed investigation of the order size of sales.

Fleming's research revealed that nearly 30 percent of the orders were clearly unprofitable, falling well below the $22.50 per order needed to break even. Average order size of unprofitable orders (30 percent of the total) was $10.35.

Borgman recognized that Onondaga Distributors was losing money on some orders, and he knew that distribution costs directly affected the company's profitability. But he was mindful of the fact that many small, unprofitable orders were from established customers who had long dealt with Onondaga and were used to ordering in small lots. Borgman did not want to jeopardize the company's position with this group of loyal customers. At the same time, he knew something had to be done, but he was uncertain how to proceed.

questions:

1. What alternatives are available to Onondaga?
2. What should be done to correct the small-order problem?

When you have mastered the contents of this chapter, you should be able to:

1   Discuss the relative power different kinds of producers have in influencing the total sequence of transactions involved in marketing their products.

2   Explain the operating nature of the producers' cooperative marketing association.

3   Contrast the marketing roles played by general merchandise wholesalers, general line wholesalers, and specialty wholesalers.

4   Compare the operating methods of the service wholesalers and the different limited-function wholesalers.

5   Compare the operating methods of the main agent wholesalers.

6   Outline the circumstances under which producers should include each type of wholesaler in their marketing channels.

11

distribution :
roles of producers
and wholesalers

Producers and wholesalers play important roles in distribution. In any marketing channel, the *producer* is the first in the succession of enterprises involved in the distribution process. The producer, in other words, is the first seller in the sequence of marketing transactions that takes place as the product moves toward its market. For the marketing channels in which they participate, *wholesalers* play roles as both buyers and sellers of products moving toward their final destinations in the marketplace. Although wholesalers generally buy directly from producers, many wholesalers obtain much of what they sell by buying from other wholesalers. A considerable number of marketing channels feature both producers and wholesalers, and in these channels both types of institutions serve as partners in distribution—performing distribution activities necessary to move the producers' output to the points of ultimate sale.

PRODUCERS   Different types of producers enjoy different degrees of power in controlling the flow of their product through marketing channels to final markets. In general, manufacturers of tangible products have the most power and can (within limits) use channels containing the number and type of middlemen (wholesalers and/or retailers) that they regard as appropriate for the product and market. In general, too, enterprises engaged in providing services, such as insurance protection or air transportation, have considerable power in selecting and using channels designed to fit their needs—although many such enterprises have their distribution decisions "hedged in" by legal restrictions of one sort or another. Firms engaged in the extractive industries (agriculture, forestry, mining, and fisheries) generally have a more difficult time in directing the flow of their products to market. In many cases, the outputs of extractive industries flow to market through more roundabout channels than with most manufacturers—marketing channels serving the extractive industries tend to develop in an unplanned way, the way a river cuts its own course. However, even in agriculture one can find many exceptions to this—Central Soya Company, for instance, has a fully integrated operation devoted to the production of broiler chickens and exercises a high degree of control over their flow to consumer and institutional markets.

manufacturers and service enterprises

How much power a given manufacturer or service enterprise has to influence the sequence of transactions depends on how much opportunity it has for differentiating its product or service from those of competitors and on its success in capitalizing on the opportunity. If the product or service can be differentiated and final buyers (ultimate consumers or industrial users) can be convinced that differentiating features make the item a better buy than competing items, the marketer has the power to gain a significant marketing advantage. The automobile manufacturer, for example, has considerable opportunity to differentiate its product in appearance, performance, and operating characteristics. The manufacturer of common nails, by contrast, has little opportunity to make the product much different from those of competitors.

Capitalizing on a product or service differentiation opportunity requires more than simply convincing final buyers of the superiority of the product or service. It must be possible for them to obtain the item from suppliers at prices they are able and willing to pay. Different middlemen vary in their willingness to support the manufacturer in terms of promoting and actively selling the product or service. Middlemen also vary as to what it costs the manufacturer or service enterprise to use them as components in the marketing channel; and this affects the price that final buyers ultimately have to pay.

Balancing the need for support with the costs involved, the manufacturer or service enterprise tries to put together a distributive network that gives final buyers ready access to outlets handling the product or providing the service at prices they consider reasonable. If the product or service can be differentiated in ways important to final buyers, the "channel captain" (manufacturer or service enterprise) can exercise considerable discretion in selecting members for its "channel team"; that is, it has considerable power to control the sequence of transactions as the item moves to market. If little opportunity exists for differentiating the product from like products, the manufacturer or service enterprise is not a channel captain and has little power to control the sequence of transactions, and the sequence may instead be controlled by middlemen or by final buyers. The firm attempting to control the marketing channel devotes its primary attention to the market— the final buyers of its product. Starting with the market, a manufacturer, for instance, attempts to detail the sequence of steps required to supply prospective buyers with its product. Even before this, however, the manufacturer should have identified and evaluated final buyers' needs and the strength of market demand and, in its research and product development effort, should have designed a product that meets these needs.

The sequence of steps required for moving the product or service to market may or may not call for the services of middlemen at one or more distribution levels. Even after deciding on this sequence—that is, the marketing channel—the marketer often devotes considerable effort to assuring that the planned series of transactions takes place. Through its advertising and other promotional activities, for instance, a manufacturer may work to build demand to the point where final buyers insist that suppliers stock and sell the product. Or, as another example, the manufacturer may use advertising to final buyers as a vehicle for directing prospective customers to outlets where the product is on sale. In these and similar ways a marketer seeks to assure that its distribution network functions according to plan.

enterprises engaged in extractive industries

Enterprises engaged in the extractive industries, such as those in mining and farming, generally have less power to exert significant influences over the total sequence of marketing transactions involving their products. Usually, they can do little about differentiating their products to meet final buyers' needs more closely. Furthermore, they generally find it very difficult to stimulate demand. Demand for the mining company's output, for instance, derives from the demand for products manufactured by its customers. Demand for aluminum, in other words, depends upon the demand for products fabricated by customers of aluminum mining companies, that is, products such as aluminum beach chairs, pots and pans, golf carts, and siding and sash used in building construction. It might seem logical, then, for the mining company to direct its efforts toward stimulating the demand for its customers' products. Individual mining companies, however, are often too small to finance and mount promotional programs of the required magnitude.

The situation confronting farmers is similar to that of the mining company, for, unless they sell their crops through cooperatives, they are generally unable to support the extensive promotion needed to exert significant influences on their products' demand. Moreover, the demand for farm products commonly derives from the demand for products of processors of agricultural commodities. When certain food processors, for instance, began making oleomargarine out of "100 percent pure corn oil" and successfully promoted the new product's health benefits to consumers, increases in demand for corn followed increases in demand for corn-oil margarine. Furthermore, unlike most manufacturers, who find it relatively easy to drop or add products as demand conditions change, many farmers—such as orchardists, cattlemen, and grain farmers—are limited to a single crop by virtue of their land, equipment, and experience. Thus, they are unable to do much about adjusting the nature of their outputs to fit the market's changing needs and preferences.

producers' cooperative marketing associations   Hoping to improve the efficiency with which their output is marketed, some groups of producers, chiefly in agriculture but sometimes in other extractive industries, organize and operate **producers' cooperative marketing associations**. These associations represent the collective effort of small producers who desire to gain more control over the distribution of their output in the hope of reducing distribution costs and exerting favorable influences on demand. Such cooperative endeavors tend to put their members more on a par with manufacturers as far as control over marketing channels is concerned.

The agricultural cooperative marketing association, with its relatively large size and the specialized attention its management gives to marketing activities, can, if it chooses, bypass one or more levels of middlemen present in more conventional marketing channels. Some cooperatives succeed in eliminating only the assembler or broker of agricultural products. Others extend their marketing operations even to such activities as maintaining sales offices in important marketing areas—as is done by Sunkist Growers, Inc., a cooperative marketer of California and Arizona citrus fruits. Most agricultural cooperative marketing associations are set up primarily to handle the packing and grading of their members' crops, usually managing to perform these activities at lower costs than members would incur individually. Some, such as Sunkist Growers, go so far as to affix brands to the product and to conduct massive promotional programs designed to build and maintain consumer recognition for the brand and to expand its demand. The cooperative marketing association often provides its members with enhanced power in controlling the flow of their products through marketing channels to final markets.

USE OF POOLING   One operating practice unique to cooperative marketing associations is called **pooling**. This is the practice of mixing the outputs of members and, after deducting average expenses, paying them the average price received during the marketing season, usually on the basis of established grades. Among the arguments advanced in support of pooling are that (1) it is difficult or impractical to keep each member's output segregated in storage and en route to market, and (2) shipments are made at different times during the marketing season at different prices for comparable qualities and grades of produce.

USE OF CASH ADVANCES   Typically, the producers' cooperative marketing association provides its members with **cash advances** when they deliver their crops to the packing house. As sales are made, members receive further advances. Checks for the remaining proceeds of sales are often delayed until six to nine months after closing the pool. Some cooperatives do not use cash advances, instead issuing warehouse receipts to members; these can be used as collateral for loans from commercial banks.

FORMAL MEMBERSHIP CONTRACTS   Most cooperative marketing associations believe it necessary to require members to execute written **formal membership contracts.** This helps to assure the association of a continuous volume of business and enables management to draft firmer plans for future operations, especially when such plans require financial commitments. At one time provisions of membership contracts were stringent, often giving the association the right to enforce specific performance by injunction. The recent trend has been toward more liberal contracts as, increasingly, associations rely on their own satisfactory performance to hold members' loyalty.

PURCHASING SERVICES   Many producers' cooperative marketing associations provide their members with purchasing services. Many buy such items as seed, fertilizers, tools and implements, and gasoline and oil for resale to members, and a few also deal in various consumer goods. Some, such as Agway, not only market crops grown by their farmer-members but also operate stores to supply members and others with items used on farms, as well as such diverse goods as grass seed, lawn mowers, automobile tires, and food for wild birds.

WHOLESALING

Wholesaling is a very large business, both in terms of the total number of establishments and of their total sales volume. In the United States, as Table 11-1 shows, almost 350,000 wholesale establishments transact over $680 billion in sales annually. During the period 1954 to 1972 (the latest date for which data are available), as this table also shows, the number of wholesale establishments rose by nearly 40 percent. In the same period, wholesale sales made by wholesale establishments increased even more spectacularly, rising by nearly 200 percent.

How the chief types of wholesale establishments are classified on the basis of ownership is shown in Figure 11-1. By far the most important, both

TABLE 11-1   U.S. WHOLESALERS:
NUMBER OF ESTABLISHMENTS AND
TOTAL SALES, SELECTED YEARS

Year	Number of Establishments	Sales (billions)
1972	348,200	$683.7
1967	311,000	459.5
1963	308,000	358.4
1958	287,000	285.7
1954	250,000	234.0

Source: U.S. Department of Commerce, Bureau of the Census, Statistical Abstract of the United States, 1976, p. 809.

Figure 11-1   Wholesale establishments classified by type of ownership.

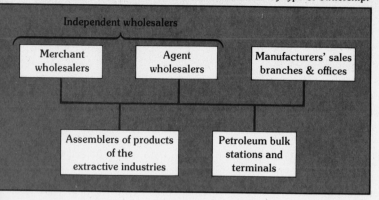

in terms of total number of establishments and total sales volume are the merchant wholesalers, which are independently owned establishments. However, the operating expenses of this group as a whole tend to be higher than those of other wholesalers. The second most important type—manufacturers' sales branches and offices—are separately identifiable wholesaling establishments owned and operated by manufacturers and functioning in ways similar to the independently owned establishments. The agent wholesalers, a group composed of diverse kinds of agents and brokers, are the third most important type. The two remaining types—assemblers of products of the extractive industries and petroleum bulk stations and terminals—may either be owned by merchant wholesalers, agent wholesalers, or manufacturers (or other producers). These last two types are rather specialized operations; the petroleum bulk stations and terminals, the bulk of which are refiner-owned, devote themselves exclusively to storage, transport, and sale of petroleum products; the assemblers of products of the extractive industries include wholesale fish buyers, buyers of uncut precious stones, country grain elevators, dairy and produce stations, fruit and vegetable packing houses, livestock concentration yards, and other establishments primarily engaged in purchasing from individuals and organizations engaged in extractive industries.

MERCHANT WHOLESALERS   Merchant wholesalers, by definition, buy and resell goods on their own account; that is, they take title to the products they handle and convey title directly to those with whom they deal. In consumer goods marketing, their principal customers are retailers, but they also sell to industrial users and to institutional and commercial users. Merchant wholesalers are also active in industrial marketing, serving as intermediaries between the supplying manufacturers and the industrial users; here they are known by such names as mill supply houses, mining supply distributors, machinery dealers, and oil well equipment houses.

219

TABLE 11-2   SALES OF MERCHANT WHOLESALERS,
DURABLE GOODS AND NONDURABLE GOODS
(excluding farm products, raw materials), 1968–1977
(millions of dollars)

Year	Durable Goods	Nondurable Goods	Total
1968	$110,861	$139,286	$250,147
1969	122,290	149,064	271,354
1970	127,214	160,096	287,310
1971	140,941	174,145	315,086
1972	161,088	195,925	357,013
1973	195,869	245,992	441,861
1974	237,044	312,792	549,836
1975	220,094	315,502	535,596
1976	246,752	334,162	580,914
1977	285,729	356,554	642,283

Source: U.S. Department of Commerce, Bureau of the Census,
Census of Business Wholesale Trade, December 1977, p. 2.

Table 11-2 shows the sales of merchant wholesalers for 1968 to 1977. Over the 10-year period, total sales increased by nearly 160 percent, with durable goods sales increasing by 160 percent and nondurable goods sales by 155 percent.

Table 11-3 shows sales of merchant wholesalers by kind of business for 1977. Machinery, equipment, supplies wholesalers, and motor vehicles—automotive equipment wholesalers were the most important categories of durable goods wholesalers, accounting for 32 percent of total durable goods sales. In the nondurable goods category, groceries and related products, although still the most important category, accounted for only 31 percent of the total, down from 41.7 percent in 1972. This reduction reflects the increasing vertical integration in grocery marketing.

There are two primary ways of classifying merchant wholesalers. First, according to the range of merchandising they handle, there are (1) general merchandise wholesalers, (2) general line wholesalers, and (3) specialty wholesalers. Second, according to method of operation, there are (1) service wholesalers, and (2) limited-function wholesalers.

classification by range of merchandise handled

GENERAL MERCHANDISE WHOLESALERS A **general merchandise wholesaler** is a merchant wholesaler who carries a general assortment of products in two or more distinct and unrelated merchandise lines. For instance, such a wholesaler may stock and sell dry goods, hardware, furniture, farm implements, electrical equipment, sporting goods, and household appliances. With the gradual disappearance of the retail general store came a decline in the importance of general merchandise wholesalers until today there are compara-

TABLE 11-3   SALES OF MERCHANT WHOLESALERS BY KIND OF BUSINESS, 1977

Kind of Business	Sales (millions)
Total sales (excluding farm products, raw materials)	$572,213
Durable goods, total	285,729
Motor vehicles, automotive equipment	54,139
Electrical goods	31,763
Furniture, home furnishings	30,763
Hardware, plumbing, heating equipment, supplies	22,425
Lumber, construction materials	26,166
Machinery, equipment, supplies	82,052
Nondurable goods, total	356,559
Groceries and related products	110,743
Beer, wine, distilled alcoholic beverages	23,386
Drugs and allied products	10,867
Paper, paper products	15,473
Other nondurable goods	48,623
Farm products (raw materials)	70,071
Merchant wholesalers, grand total	$642,285

Source: U.S. Department of Commerce, Bureau of the Census, Monthly Wholesale Trade Report, December 1977, p. 2.

tively few left. However, particularly in predominantly rural sections of the West and South, general merchandise wholesalers still serve as suppliers to hardware stores, electrical supply stores, auto accessory dealers, drugstores, and smaller department stores. General merchandise wholesalers are much less important in terms of both number of establishments and sales volume than either general line or specialty wholesalers.

GENERAL LINE WHOLESALERS A **general line wholesaler** carries a broad assortment of goods within a single merchandise line, but it may also handle limited stocks of goods in closely related lines. Thus, a general line grocery wholesaler usually carries not only a broad stock of canned fruits and vegetables, cereals, tea and coffee, but also razor blades, soaps and detergents, toothpaste, school supplies, and other items commonly sold in retail grocery stores. Measured in terms of total volume of sales, general line wholesalers are more important than either general merchandise wholesalers or specialty wholesalers. General line wholesalers are important distributors of groceries, drugs, and hardware to independent retailers in these fields. General line wholesalers also sell such industrial goods lines as electrical, plumbing, and heating equipment and supplies to both large and small industrial users.

The importance of the general line wholesaler in consumer goods marketing declined with the rise of corporate chains and other mass retailers that prefer to buy directly from producers. There is a similar trend among industrial users toward direct buying from producers, and this is reducing operations of general line wholesalers of industrial goods. But, since small-scale independent retailers continue to exist, and because industrial users continue to need some items in quantities too small to justify direct purchase, general line wholesalers are still important marketing intermediaries in both consumer and industrial goods markets.

SPECIALTY WHOLESALERS   A **specialty wholesaler** carries only part of a merchandise line but, within its restricted range of offerings, it has a very complete assortment. In the wholesale grocery trade, for instance, specialty wholesalers specialize in such partial lines as canned foods; coffee, tea, and spices; dairy products; frosted and frozen foods; or soft drinks. The specialty wholesaler represents an advanced step in what seems a universal trend among merchant wholesalers to specialize merchandise offerings.

Specialty wholesalers pride themselves on the strong promotional support they provide for the restricted number of manufacturers' brands they handle. They provide this strong support by concentrating on relatively few items. It is possible for the specialty grocery wholesaler's sales people, for instance, in the routine performance of their duties to push every item handled on every sales call and to perform on behalf of manufacturers' brands such promotional activities as erecting special displays, handling in-store product demonstrations, and arranging for the distribution of samples. Sales personnel working for general line grocery wholesalers, by contrast, cannot give a special push to more than a handful of the many thousands of items in stock or to any one manufacturer's brand.

However, the narrowness of the specialty wholesaler's merchandising offering, together with the need to provide strong promotional support for all items handled, causes it to concentrate on market areas where there are large numbers of retail outlets. Selling only a few items and strongly promoting each one, it can make economical use of sales personnel only where there are numerous retailers to call on and relatively little travel time is required between stops. The specialty wholesaler's sales force makes frequent calls on retailers, but, because this makes it possible for retailers to carry smaller stocks, the average size of orders is small. Specialty wholesalers are concentrated in the heavily industrialized and thickly populated parts of New England, the Middle Atlantic states, the Midwest, and the Pacific Coast. In other areas (such as most of the Rocky Mountain states and much of the South), where population is sparse, cities and towns are far apart, and retail outlets are widely scattered and few in number, relatively few specialty wholesalers exist.

classification by method of operation   Merchant wholesalers perform many marketing activities for their suppliers and customers. Those who perform all or most of the activities generally associated with wholesale trade are **service wholesalers.** (These activities are buying and assembling, selling, storage, transportation, marketing risk bearing, marketing financing, and marketing information.) General merchandise and general line wholesalers perform these activities and, therefore, are also service wholesalers. Some specialty wholesalers perform only a few of these activities; others perform more. Depending on the extent of its service, a specialty wholesaler may be classed either as a service wholesaler or as a **limited-function wholesaler** who performs only a few of the activities normally associated with wholesaling operations. Remember, however, that all merchant wholesalers—limited-function as well as service wholesalers—take title to the goods they handle and resell to those with whom they deal. Thus, all perform the buying and assembling and selling activities. The main types of limited-function wholesalers are described in the following discussion.

TRUCK WHOLESALERS   Combining selling, delivery, and collection in one operation, **truck wholesalers** (also known as "wagon jobbers") carry only a limited range of stock, although the selection within that range may be rather complete. Thus, the nature of a truck wholesaler's merchandise offering also makes it a specialty wholesaler. Truck wholesalers call mainly on retailers, although some, such as those in the grocery trade, also sell to restaurants, hotels, and other food service establishments. Because the items they handle are often perishables or semiperishables, truck wholesalers make frequent calls on customers. Their ability to make fast and frequent deliveries is their main appeal to both their customers and the manufacturers they represent.

RACK JOBBERS   A **rack jobber** markets specialized lines of merchandise to retail stores and provides certain special services. The merchandising policies of most rack jobbers cause them also to be specialty wholesalers. The original rack jobbers evolved after World War II to serve the special needs of supermarkets, which, in increasing numbers, were then adding nonfood lines.

Rack jobbers serving supermarkets and other grocery retailers usually specialize in one or both of two lines—toiletries and housewares. Managers of retail stores served by rack jobbers are relieved of the merchandising problems involved in handling what are for them sundry items, and are left free to concentrate their merchandising efforts on their major lines. The rack jobber may or may not furnish its own display racks but, basically, all that it requires of the retailer is some selling space, which the rack jobber stocks with a selection of items priced for immediate sale. Occasionally, rack jobbers supply merchandise on consignment: that is, they retain legal title to the merchandise up to the time the retailer sells it, the retailer paying only for the goods sold (and, incidentally, for shoplifted items) and retaining a portion of the profit for itself. Through aggressive merchandising and effective use of displays, rack jobbers have built up large volumes of nonfood sales in grocery stores. Manufacturers of nonfood lines find that rack jobbers provide an effective means of achieving low-cost distribution through retail food stores.

CASH-AND-CARRY WHOLESALERS   **Cash-and-carry wholesalers** pursue at the wholesale level the same sort of service policy that characterizes cash-and-carry retail operations. Whereas service wholesalers send their sales personnel to retailers to solicit orders, later deliver these orders, and grant credit to retailers, allowing them to pay at later dates, cash-and-carry wholesalers require retailers to come to the wholesale warehouse, pick their own orders, pay cash, and carry away their own purchases. By restricting the services it performs and lowering its operating costs, the cash-and-carry wholesaler is able to price its goods lower than those of service wholesalers. Price, then, is what attracts retailers to the cash-and-carry wholesaler. But, because retailers must perform additional services for themselves, they often find that by the time the order gets to the store, its cost is every bit as high as if it were purchased from a service wholesaler. However, cash-and-carry departments do provide an economical means for service wholesalers to use in reaching many small retailers who customarily buy in lots too small to justify the wholesaler's sending sales personnel, providing delivery, and extending credit, but since travel time and distance are important, they only operate in large cities.

DROP SHIPMENT WHOLESALERS   **A drop shipment wholesaler** does not physically handle the goods it sells but leaves the performance of storage and transportation activities to the manufacturers whom it represents. When goods are ordered, the manufacturer ships them directly to the retailer but bills the drop shipper at factory prices. Subsequently, the drop shipper collects from the retailer. This distribution system makes possible reductions in transportation and storage costs. It eliminates the necessity for double hauling (i.e., from the factory to the wholesaler and then on to the retailer), and no costs are incurred for handling the goods in a wholesaler's warehouse.

However, customers buying through drop shippers often order in small lot sizes and, because freight rates are higher for small lots than for large lots, some of the savings from eliminating double hauling are offset by higher freight rates.

The retailer, to make economical use of drop shipments, must both order in larger than normal quantities and adjust its operations to allow for longer periods during which the goods are in transit. These adjustments are necessary inasmuch as most retailers are located farther from the manufacturers' plants than from the wholesalers serving as alternative supply points. The need for ordering in larger-than-normal quantities also forces the retailer to invest additional funds in inventory. Despite these unattractive features, however, retailers often find cost savings sufficient to justify drop shipments. This is especially true with standard, fast-selling items that sell regardless of season and that offer little risk that the retailer will be unable to resell them.

Drop shipment wholesalers are also much used in industrial marketing. They are important distributors of such items as sand, clay, coal, and lumber—all commodities of low value, relative to transportation costs incurred in their distribution, and all involving situations where any interruption of deliveries, causing breaks in customers' production operations, may lead to significant cost increases. Industrial users purchase these items in such large quantities and with such great regularity that it pays them to have several shipments in transit at any one time, each spaced to arrive before it is needed and always allowing some margin of safety for late-arriving shipments. Thus, the industrial user manages to work around the long period during which drop shipments are in transit. Furthermore, customers generally buy these commodities in lots large enough to gain freight rates as low as those a service wholesaler might secure.

MAIL-ORDER WHOLESALERS   A **mail-order wholesaler** substitutes mail-order catalogs and order forms for a sales force and passes on to retailers some of the savings in the form of lower prices. This limited-function wholesaler is mainly active in selling such staple consumer items as hardware and dry goods. However, with successive improvements in transportation and communication services, the importance of mail-order wholesalers has declined. One basic weakness of this type of operation is that it does not provide the seller a really adequate substitute for a strong promotional push by sales personnel. Moreover, its success rests on the willingness of retailers to take the initiative in placing orders, something that cannot always be counted on, especially when competitors' sales forces make personal calls on retailers.

AGENT MIDDLEMEN

Agent middlemen—most of whom engage in wholesaling rather than in retailing—assist in negotiating sales or purchases or both on behalf of their principals (buyers or sellers or both). Usually, the agent does not represent both buyers and sellers in the same transaction, and it is ordinarily paid by commission or fee. Agent wholesalers differ from merchant wholesalers in that they do not take title to the merchandise and generally perform only a few wholesaling activities.

Agent wholesalers as a group operate in many fields, but individual agents customarily concentrate on such lines as foods, grain, copper, steel, machinery, electronic supplies, or textiles. The main types of agent wholesalers are brokers, commission houses, manufacturers' agents, selling agents, resident buyers, and auction companies.

brokers

A broker is an agent who represents either buyer or seller in negotiating purchases or sales without having physical control over the goods involved. The broker is more often the agent of the owner of goods seeking a buyer than of a buyer searching for a source of supply. Each broker tends to specialize in arranging transactions for a limited number of products, and this causes the broker to be well informed concerning conditions in these particular markets.

Acting strictly as an intermediary, the broker has limited powers as to prices and terms of sale, and possesses little or no authority to bargain on behalf of its principal. The broker's main service is to bring buyer and seller together. Representing either the seller or the buyer, the broker relays the buyer's offer to the seller and the seller's counteroffer to the buyer, and continues this process until the terms are satisfactory to both parties, at which time the exchange takes place. The broker never has direct physical control over the goods but sells by description or sample. Whenever the broker arranges a sale, the seller ships the goods directly to the buyer. The broker receives its commission from the principal who sought its services.

Brokers are most used by producers who sell their products at infrequent intervals and find it uneconomical to establish standing sales forces of their own or even to establish long-term relationships with other types of agent wholesalers. Although an individual producer may use the same broker year after year, each transaction is considered completely apart from every other. There is no obligation on the part of either the broker or the seller to maintain this relationship in future transactions. Small canners, whose outputs are too small to justify developing and promoting brands of their own and whose entire pack may be put up in two or three months, often rely solely on brokers. Similarly, farmers harvesting one major crop a year often find it economical to use brokers.

Sometimes brokers are used by larger manufacturers who want to extend the distribution of their products. In such instances, brokers serve as the key middlemen in arranging initial distribution of the product among other types of middlemen. Thus, a broker may be instrumental in opening up a new market for the producer or in gaining access to outlets that have previously not stocked the product.

commission houses

A **commission house** is an agent who customarily exercises physical control over and negotiates the sale of goods belonging to principals. The commission house enjoys broad powers as to prices, methods, and terms of sale, although it must also obey its principals' instructions. Generally, it arranges delivery, extends necessary credit, collects, deducts its fees, and remits the balance to its principal. Thus, except for the fact that it does not take title, the commission house performs activities very similar to those of service merchant wholesalers—more so, in fact, than any other agent wholesaler.

Most commission houses are engaged in the distribution of fresh fruit and produce. The relationship of the commission house and its principals covers a harvest and marketing season. A truck farmer, for instance, signs a seasonal agreement with a commission house situated in a market center; as the crop is harvested, it is shipped to the commission house. The commission house is authorized to sell each shipment on arrival at the best price obtainable without checking back with the farmer. Although legal title to the goods never passes to the house, it sells in its own name, bills buyers, extends credit, makes collections, deducts its fees, and remits the balance to the truck farmer. The farmer might prefer to hold his product off the market at times and bargain for higher prices, but the factor of perishability makes any delays in selling costly. The commission house's operation is especially geared for rapid sale of perishable commodities, and this is the main reason this type of agent is important in agricultural marketing.

manufacturers' agents   Four main features characterize the operations of a **manufacturers' agent:** (1) it has an extended contractual relationship with its principals, (2) it handles sales for each of its principals within an exclusive territory, (3) it represents manufacturers of noncompeting but related lines of goods, and (4) it possesses limited authority with regard to prices and terms of sale. Some manufacturers' agents have physical control over an inventory but most do not. Ordinarily, the manufacturers' agent arranges for shipments directly from the factory to the buyer. Because its principal activity is selling, the agent maintains a sales staff large enough to provide adequate coverage of its market area. It sells at prices, or within a price range, stipulated by its principal and receives a percentage commission based on sales.

Manufacturers' agents are generally used either when a manufacturer finds it uneconomical to have its own sales force or when it is financially unable to do so. Some manufacturers, for instance, find that certain market areas do not provide enough business to justify assigning their own sales personnel. Yet manufacturers' agents, each representing several principals, operate profitably in the same areas. Thus, it is common for manufacturers to use their own sales force in areas with large potential sales and to use manufacturers' agents elsewhere. Other manufacturers use agents to open up new market areas, then replace them with their own sales personnel as the sales volume grows. Still other manufacturers, particularly those who are small and have narrow product lines, use a network of manufacturers' agents to avoid altogether the problems and expenses of maintaining their own sales forces. Manufacturers also find manufacturers' agents useful in selling in foreign markets because of their familiarity with local customs and markets.

Manufacturers' agents are most important in the marketing of industrial goods and such consumer durables as furniture and hardware. In industrial goods marketing, such as in the marketing of electronic components, agents employ sales representatives who have considerable technical competence and who contact industrial users directly. In marketing consumer durables, sales personnel employed by manufacturers' agents generally call on and sell to retailers. Numerous furniture manufacturers rely on manufacturers' agents to sell their entire outputs. In many cases, in both industrial and consumer goods marketing, the manufacturers' agent can, because of its intimate contact with the market, offer advice to the manufacturer on a wide variety of matters, including styling, design, and pricing.

selling agents   A **selling agent** operates on an extended contractual basis, negotiates all sales of a specified line of merchandise or the entire output of its principal, and usually has full authority with regard to prices, terms, and other conditions of sale. Thus, it differs from the manufacturers' agent in that it is ordinarily not confined to operating within a given market area, has much more authority to set prices and terms of sale, and is the sole selling agent for the lines it represents.

Some selling agents render financial assistance to their principals. This practice traces back to early selling agents who were usually much stronger financially than were their principals. Many textile mills, for instance, were started with the initial financial backing of selling agents, who saw this as a way to increase their own business volumes and hence their commissions. Today, selling agents do not provide investment capital for their principals, but many help their principals in financing current operations. Because many modern selling agents continue to have higher credit ratings than their principals, it is common for them to endorse their principals' short-term notes at banks and other lending institutions. Occasionally, too, a selling agent assists its principal financially either by making direct loans on accounts receivable or by guaranteeing these accounts so that a lender will advance needed funds to the principal. There is, however, a trend away from this type of financing activity by selling agents. The trend has accelerated with the growth of financial institutions known as "factors," who specialize in discounting accounts receivable—that is, in making short-term loans with accounts receivable as the collateral.

The manufacturer who uses a selling agent, in effect, shifts most of the marketing task to an outside organization. This frees the manufacturer to concentrate on production and other nonmarketing problems. In addition, because the selling agent is in close contact with buyers, it is often in a position to guide the manufacturer on styling, design, and pricing matters. Often, too, it assists the principal with or takes over sales promotion and advertising. Sometimes, in the textile and apparel trades, the selling agent even specifies the features that the principal should build into the product and how much to manufacture. Since the selling agent works for a straight commission, the principal's selling costs vary proportionately with sales made, and no fixed selling costs are incurred. For all these reasons, small manufacturers with neither the managerial talent nor the financial strength to market their own products use selling agents.

The manufacturer who uses a selling agent should realize, however, that it is "placing all its marketing eggs in one basket." Because the selling agent is the manufacturer's only contact with the market, the bulk of the bargaining power rests with the agent, not with the manufacturer. Recognizing this, selling agents may resort to price cutting instead of exerting a reasonable effort to sell the manufacturer's output. In such situations, the manufacturer, cut off from the buyers by the selling agent and having dealt with them only through this intermediary, is literally "over the barrel." If it is weak financially and needs loans that cannot be obtained without the selling agent's help, it may not even be able to break with the selling agent in order to obtain another agent. The moral is clear: If the manufacturer is going to use a selling agent, its first choice should be a good one.

resident buyers   A **resident buyer** differs from most other agent middlemen in that it represents buyers only. Specializing in buying for retailers, it receives its compensation on a fee or commission basis. The resident buyer operates in lines of trade, such as furniture and apparel, where there are well-defined market centers to which retailers travel to make their selections. Resident buyers maintain offices in market centers and, whenever retailers are unable to make the trip to market, they serve as retailers' contacts with the sources of supply.

Resident buyers are independent of their principals. They should not be confused with the resident buying offices, maintained in such market centers as New York, which are owned by out-of-town stores. Nor should they be confused with the central buying offices maintained by chain-store organizations. The resident buyer is purely and simply an independent agent specializing in buying for principals who are retailers.

auction companies   As its name indicates, an **auction company** uses the auction method of catalogs and competitive bidding by prospective buyers to sell its principals' products. Auction companies are important in selling products of varying quality and those that cannot be efficiently graded—situations frequent in agricultural marketing. In the fresh fruit and vegetable trade, auction companies are in central markets—that is, in cities that are important distributing points for such items. In the marketing of livestock and of agricultural crops such as leaf tobacco, auction companies are located in principal producing areas and at shipping points. An auction company has physical control over the lots consigned to it, arranges for their display, conducts the auction, makes collections from the buyers, and remits the proceeds, less its commissions, to the principals.

The auction method of selling leaf tobacco dates back to Civil War days. Until then tobacco leaf was spread on sidewalks for display, and growers had no option whatever but to accept the prices offered by buyers. This exploitation of the growers caused the Virginia legislature to give some attention to the marketing situation, resulting first in provisions whereby tobacco was graded by professionals on the basis of intrinsic value and later in the establishment of warehouses using the auction method of selling.

other agents   Other types of agent middlemen evolved to serve special marketing needs. Whenever a large enough group of buyers or sellers needs some special marketing service, there are always enterprising individuals who set up in business to provide it. There are export and import agents in leading port cities who serve the needs of principals seeking foreign markets or overseas sources of supply. There are purchasing agents, which are independent businesses, specializing in locating sources of supply for buyers of industrial goods. They all have the same basic economic purpose—they all help to bring buyers and sellers together in return for fees or commissions.

SUMMARY   Producers and wholesalers play important roles in distribution. In any marketing channel, the producer is the seller in the first of the sequence of ownership transfers that occur as the product moves toward its market. If the producer can differentiate its product in ways important to final buyers, it has considerable power to control the entire sequence of ownership transfers; but if it has little opportunity for product differentiation, it has little power to control this sequence; instead, middlemen or final buyers may control it. Producers of farm products can increase their marketing impact by joining producer cooperatives. Manufacturers and service enterprises, in general, have more power than other kinds of producers and are more able to use marketing channels containing the type and number of transfer points that they desire.

Wholesalers occupy positions in marketing channels somewhere between producers and final buyers. Merchant wholesalers, the most numerous type, take title to the products they handle and convey title directly to their customers, who may be (depending on the situation) retailers, industrial users, or institutional and commercial users. Merchant wholesalers differentiate their operations both as to the type and range of merchandise handled and the nature of services provided—both for the producers who supply them and for the customers they serve. Agent middlemen, who assist in negotiating ownership transfers without actually taking title themselves, take many different forms, tailoring their operations to meet the needs of the principals they represent (sellers, buyers, or both). Generally, too, agent middlemen perform fewer wholesaling activities than do merchant wholesalers.

You should now, therefore, be thoroughly familiar with the first two building blocks in marketing channels—producers and wholesalers. You should understand the ways in which producers can affect the distribution of their products or services and the extent of their potential impact. You should have a good knowledge of the numerous different types of merchant wholesalers and agent middlemen, particularly with respect to the ways they differentiate their operations and the services they provide. If you know these things well, you understand "wholesale distribution."

REVIEW
AND
DISCUSSION
QUESTIONS

1 | "You can eliminate the wholesaler but not its functions." Comment, and include in your discussion the likely impact upon total distribution costs elimination of the wholesaler would have.

2 | Define the following:
   a. Merchant wholesaler.
   b. Agent wholesaler.
   c. General merchandise wholesaler.
   d. General line wholesaler.

    e. Specialty wholesaler.
    f. Service wholesaler.
    g. Limited-function wholesaler.
    h. Truck wholesaler.
    i. Rack jobber.
    j. Cash-and-carry wholesaler.
    k. Drop shipment wholesaler.
    l. Mail-order wholesaler.
    m. Broker.
    n. Manufacturers' agent.
    o. Selling agent.
    p. Resident buyer.
    q. Auction company.

3   Describe the role of wholesaling in distribution. Use several examples.

4   What particular advantages are offered by specialty wholesalers?

5   Shouldn't it be to the advantage of a retailer to deal only with a very limited number of general line wholesalers instead of a much larger number of specialty wholesalers? If so, how can you explain the greater growth of specialty wholesalers?

6   Discuss the major differences between service wholesalers and limited-function wholesalers. Give examples.

7   Limited service retailers have captured an increasingly important share of the market in recent years. Why, then, haven't limited-function wholesalers managed to do the same thing at the wholesale level? Explain.

8   Explain the major differences between agent wholesalers and merchant wholesalers.

9   Describe the basic operations of a broker. Do you regard brokers as essential to the marketing process, or are they collectively just another example of the excess in middlemen, who do little, if anything, toward increasing a product's value as it travels through the distribution channel? Explain.

10   How do selling agents differ from manufacturers agents?

11   Explain the conditions most likely to surround a manufacturer's decision to use a manufacturers' agent instead of its own sales force.

12   What type of agent middleman would be most appropriate for the following situations?
    a. A small manufacturer of golf clubs.
    b. A manufacturer of a limited line of high-quality men's clothing.
    c. A small manufacturer of household cleaning brushes to be distributed through supermarkets.
    d. A manufacturer of industrial equipment (for which it has its own sales force), which is adding a line of home swimming pools.
    e. A small manufacturer of unbranded men's work clothes.

13   Producers who can differentiate their products have greater control over the channel through which their products are sold. Is there any advantage to such control?

14   Analyze the factors that determine the extent of a manufacturer's power and influence in the channel of distribution.

CASE PROBLEM

Quality Crafts was a dynamic young consumer products company which over the last six years had developed three diversified lines of goods. The Quality Modes Line included quality leather and vinyl goods such as wallets, key cases, attaché cases, and handbags. The Luster-Life jewelry line included attractive gold- and silver-toned costume pieces coordinated with the latest women's fashions. The Quality-Ware appliance line contained a small group of hair dryers, can openers, coffee makers, and toasters. All three product lines were sold nationwide by a sales force of 85 people to department stores, discount chains, and some specialty shops.

Alice Bickford, marketing manager, was eager to continue the company's expansion into new market areas. She was planning to introduce a line of office equipment and supplies the next spring. This line initially would include leather- and vinyl-bound business planning calendars and memo pads, blotters, and desk top accessory sets. Small office equipment would follow.

The major problem with launching this new line was to find an effective distribution plan. Major emphasis would be on securing distribution through office supply dealers, and this was a new market for Quality Crafts. Bickford wanted to assign responsibility for selling the new line to the present sales force, believing that would cost less than hiring a new sales force.

Steve Warner, the sales manager, opposed Bickford's plan. He felt that the present sales force was hard pressed to promote the company's three existing lines and could not assume the task of building relationships with business supply outlets. Even though the customer accounts would be the same in some cases (department stores, for example), Warner thought it would be preferable to get new salespeople to sell the office supply line. He contended that a sales force devoting itself exclusively to the new line would speed its introduction and eventual acceptance.

However, Bickford strongly objected and noted that the company could not afford another large financial commitment for the coming year. She suggested using a manufacturers' agent to establish distribution in the office supply field. Hiring what amounted to a specialist in the field of office supplies would be an efficient way to penetrate this new market rapidly and with a minimum fixed investment. The company would not have to overburden the present sales force and it would not have to hire and train new salespeople.

Warner objected that Quality Crafts would lose much control over distribution. He said it was this very matter of control that led to rejecting a manufacturers' agent proposal when the Quality-Ware appliance line was introduced four years ago.

Bickford replied that a business friend had used a manufacturers' agent to improve his distribution of auto parts, with great success. The sales manager would be responsible for directing and coordinating the agent's efforts. Distribution goals and strategy would be developed by the sales manager, although the agent could supply guidance based on his experience. Bickford was convinced that a manufacturers' agent would exert adequate sales effort, if motivated sufficiently with commissions and given adequate advice concerning Quality Crafts desired product image.

Bickford had contacted a manufacturers' agent, National Office Supply, whose general manager she had recently met. National Office Supply offered to act as Quality Crafts' agent. Its extensive national sales force already sold related business supplies. Under terms of the tentative agreement, Quality Craft would pay National Office Supply a 7 percent commission on sales.

Warner and Bickford both preferred using a company-controlled sales force to sell Quality Craft products exclusively. However, the young company was in no position to have everything at once. A decision had to be reached soon, as other marketing plans for new lines were nearing completion.

questions:

1. Identify and evaluate the alternative distribution plans for Quality Crafts, Incorporated.
2. Do you agree with Bickford or with Warner regarding the use of manufacturers' agents?

When you have mastered the contents of this chapter, you should be able to:

1   Discuss house-to-house selling as a retailing method.

2   Compare the different types of independent stores as to operating methods and competitive advantages and disadvantages.

3   Explain the three main ways in which retail institutions grow.

4   Compare mail-order houses, department stores, and chain-store systems with respect to their development, operating methods, and competitive advantages and disadvantages.

5   Compare retailer cooperatives and wholesaler-sponsored groups as to their organization and operating methods.

6   Discuss the nature of consumer cooperatives, their operating policies, and the settings conducive to their success.

7   Contrast supermarkets and discount houses as to basic characteristics, operating philosophy, and buying practices.

8   Analyze the conditions under which a marketer should seek to have its product sold through automatic vending machines.

9   Evaluate franchising as a method of retail distribution.

10   Discuss the implications of shopping centers for central city shopping districts and for manufacturers.

11   Explain the "wheel of retailing" hypothesis.

12

distribution :
retailing

Retailers play their basic roles in many different ways. Each adjusts to the expectations of both its suppliers and its customers through the merchandise selection it handles, the size of its operation, its pricing, its location, and its selling methods—as well as through other operating policies and practices. Because of the many choices of this sort open to retailers there is tremendous variety among retail institutions. Retailers range all the way from the roadside fruit stand to the multibillion-dollar corporate chain.

While we tend to think of retailing as being confined to fixed retail locations, it may take place wherever an ultimate consumer and seller get together. In fact, fixed retail locations are a relatively recent development. Retailing in ancient times was carried on mostly by traveling peddlers or from temporary stalls situated in town or village markets. The outdoor public market is still a feature of the retailing system (through a relatively unimportant one), and the peddler has evolved into the house-to-house selling organization.

The highly competitive nature of retail distribution makes for tremendous variety and frequent change in types of institutions and retailing methods. From time to time, both in the United States and abroad, new or different types of retail institutions and retailing methods appear on the retail scene and those that succeed have an impact upon older types of institutions, which, in order to survive, modify their ways of doing business.

THE RETAIL FIELD: SIZE AND IMPORTANCE

Retailing is a large business, both in total establishments and sales volume. In the United States, as Table 12-1 shows, more than 1,900,000 retail establishments transact over $650 billion in sales annually. In the 28 years from 1948 to 1976, the number of retail establishments grew fairly modestly (up by 150,000), but retail sales increased by over five times. The average yearly sales per establishment was $340,000 in 1976. Despite the relatively small average yearly sales of retail stores, there are some giant retail organizations,

Figure 12-1   A Framework for Retailing

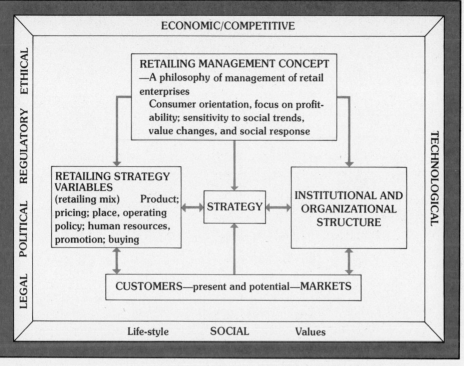

Source: J. Barry Mason and Morris L. Mayer, Modern Retailing (Dallas: Business Publications, Inc., 1978), p. 6.

as shown in Table 12-2. Notice that these large retailers had higher profits as a percent of their invested capital than as a percent of sales—this is true of nearly all retail businesses, small or large.

TABLE 12-1   RETAILERS: NUMBER OF ESTABLISHMENTS AND TOTAL SALES, SELECTED YEARS

Year	Number of Establishments	Sales (billions)
1976	N.A.	$651.9
1972	1,913,000	459.0
1967	1,763,000	310.2
1963	1,708,000	244.2
1958	1,795,000	200.4
1954	1,722,000	170.0
1948	1,770,000	130.5

Source: U.S. Department of Commerce, Bureau of the Census, Statistical Abstract of the United States, 1977.

TABLE 12-2   THE 10 LARGEST U.S. RETAILERS, 1976

Retailer	Sales (thousands)*	Profit	
		As Percent of Sales	As Percent of Invested Capital
1. Sears Roebuck	$14,950,208	4.6	11.7
2. Safeway Stores	10,442,531	1.0	12.4
3. S. S. Kresge	8,483,603	3.1	18.5
4. J. C. Penney	8,353,800	2.7	11.9
5. Great Atlantic & Pacific Tea	6,537,897	0.1	1.0
6. Kroger	6,091,149	0.8	10.6
7. Marcor (includes Montgomery Ward)	5,280,280	2.9	10.4
8. F. W. Woolworth	5,152,200	2.1	10.0
9. Federated Department Stores	4,446,624	3.8	13.2
10. Lucky Stores	3,483,174	1.3	18.6

*Net sales include all operating revenues and revenues from discontinued operations when they are published. For companies not on a calendar year, the figures are for fiscal years ended no later than January 31, 1977. Sales of subsidiaries are included when they are consolidated.

Source: By courtesy of Fortune, July 1977, pp. 168–169.

Figure 12-2 shows the relative importance of different lines of retail trade. Retailers in the food group (grocery stores, meat and seafood markets, and bakery products stores) transact the largest volume of sales, annually accounting for over $140 billion. Automotive group retailers (automobile dealers and tires, batteries, and accessories dealers) rank second to the food group retailers, with over $125 billion sales, followed by general merchandise retailers (including department stores, variety stores, and mail-order houses), who have over $105 billion sales. Together, in 1976, these three groups accounted for 72 percent of all retail sales in the United States, up from 57 percent in 1973.

HOUSE-TO-HOUSE SELLING   Modern **house-to-house** salespeople are descended from "Yankee peddlers," who, on foot, on horseback, and in wagons, traveled from farm to farm and from settlement to settlement, selling various manufactured articles to pioneers and frontier families.[1] Today's house-to-house salespeople differ from the peddler in two important ways. First, they are seldom the independent operators that their predecessors were. Most house-to-house salespeople are either semiindependent agents or employees of large manufacturers or distributors utilizing this retailing method. Among these large concerns are Avon Products (cosmetics

[1] For a fine historical account of house-to-house selling, see Harry Golden, *Forgotten Pioneers* (Cleveland, Ohio: World Publishing Company, 1963).

Figure 12-2　Retail store sales, by kind of business, 1976

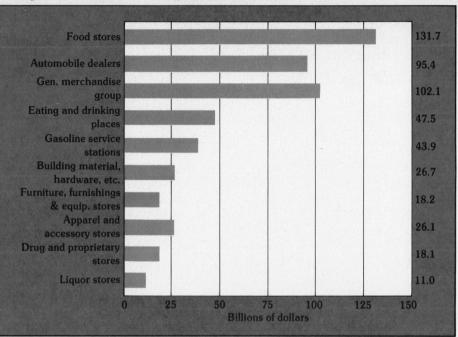

Source: U.S. Depart. of Commerce, Bureau of the Census.

and toilet articles), Wearever Aluminum (cooking utensils), Tupperware (plastic housewares), and The Fuller Brush Company (cleaning and household articles). Second, today's house-to-house salespeople tend to restrict their offerings to a small number of articles within a single merchandise line. They may specialize in encyclopedias, lawn and garden stock, vacuum cleaners, china, cosmetics, or household cleaning materials. The salespeople affiliated with the large house-to-house organizations are almost equally divided between men and women, more than half working part-time. Thus, it is not unusual for a direct-selling company to have from 5,000 to 10,000 salespeople, nearly all working on a commission basis. Avon Products has more than 350,000 people, principally women, selling part-time in its worldwide operation.

House-to-house selling eliminates the expenses of retail store operation, but it is not a low-cost retailing method. It requires travel and personal contact, and these are substantial costs for recruiting, maintaining, and managing sales staffs large enough to transact a profitable sales volume. These cost conditions affect the operating methods of direct-selling companies. To cover the high cost, they strive for high average order size, either by handling items of high unit value or by selling large assortments. Some, such as Avon Products, make more effective use of salespeople's time by establishing steady customers. Others, such as Tupperware, use *party plan selling,* in which a group of potential buyers are brought together in one of their homes for a product demonstration; several orders often result at one time.

The commissions paid to house-to-house salespeople range from 25 to 40 percent of the amount of the sale and the total costs of house-to-house selling run to approximately 60 percent of sales. This appears high, and it is for retailing. But companies using house-to-house selling do not have to allow for wholesalers' and retailers' margins, nor do they generally have large fixed selling and administrative expenses. Whether house-to-house selling is an expensive distribution method depends on the manufacturer's alternatives. If the alternative is to use wholesalers and retailers and field a full-time permanent staff of salaried salespersons, it may well be that house-to-house selling is economical by comparison.

House-to-house selling sometimes is an appropriate solution to a manufacturer's retail distribution problems. It may be the only way that a radically different new product can be introduced, particularly if a company has limited finances. For example, the early manufacturers of vacuum cleaners found it impossible to secure distribution among conventional retailers because of difficulties in convincing consumers of the merits of the product. The manufacturers discovered that by demonstrating their cleaner's superior cleaning power in the home on the housewives' own carpets, it was easy to overcome sales resistance. Once vacuum cleaners were generally accepted by consumers, it was possible to abandon house-to-house selling for regular retailers. Certain other products, too, such as sewing machines and rug cleaners, seem to sell more easily when demonstrated in the home. Still others, such as encyclopedias and Bibles, are items that most consumers will not shop for in retail stores but that they will buy if approached in their own homes.

INDEPENDENT STORES   An **independent store** is a retailing business unit controlled by its own individual ownership or management. Although there are both large and small independent stores, most large-scale independently owned stores are classified as supermarkets, department stores, and discount houses. In this discussion, we consider an independent store as any individually owned or managed retail business unit, small or large, which cannot be readily classified as a supermarket, department store, or discount house. We use this working definition to side-step the academic problem of distinguishing small-scale from large-scale retailers. How does one, after all, decide where small ends and large begins? The sales volume yardstick is the one most used, but number of employees, square feet of floor space, and inventory dollar size have all been tried. One big difficulty with all these measures is that the dividing line must still be chosen arbitrarily; furthermore, the criteria for largeness are constantly being revised upward. But, because at any given time some retailers are smaller than others, in the following discussion we refer to independent retailers as being relatively small or large.

small independent retailers   Today, most small independent stores are concentrated in fields where it is easy to set up in business. Usually, this means that no great amount of capital is needed or that easy financing is available. Probably, this is why there have been so many small independent gasoline retailers until recently[2]—a fairly small investment in inventory turned over rapidly results in a sales figure many times the value of the inventory. Many small retailers, of course, are well financed, but they are the exceptions.

Small independent retailers meet strong competition from large retail chains, supermarkets, discount houses, and department stores. The small independent generally buys its inventory from wholesalers or other middlemen, rather than directly from producers, so its merchandise costs are higher than those of large, direct-buying competitors. Thus, it has to charge higher prices (to cover its costs) than its competitors.

Small independents must use something other than the price appeal to attract trade. The more successful find some way to differentiate their stores in their customers' minds. They may achieve this with a unique selection of merchandise, or through personalized service and friendly relations with customers. Or the independent may stay open longer hours than larger competitors and offer such extra services as credit and delivery. A convenient location, too, may be attractive to customers. As long as substantial numbers of ultimate consumers consider such things important, small independent retail stores are likely to stay in business.

large independent retailers   Large independent stores are most important in retail fields, where corporate chains, department stores, and other integrated retail institutions either have no operating advantages or are at a competitive disadvantage. In retailing women's clothing, for instance, the independent store buys most of its merchandise directly from manufacturers, the same source from which the chain women's clothing store and the women's clothing departments of the department store must buy. Whereas the chain may buy larger quantities than the independent, any quantity discounts it receives are generally too small to permit it to use the lower-price appeal effectively.

Of even greater significance is that most items of women's clothing are not at all standardized, either in appearance or construction. In large towns and cities, several women's clothing outlets handle the same manufacturer's line, but, because they handle very few identical garments, the consumer has little opportunity to make price comparisons. In small towns there is even

[2] After the energy crisis in the 1970s it became evident that the number of gasoline stations was excessive, and many independents were squeezed out by company-owned stations.

less likelihood that competing retailers will represent the same manufacturers, or sell identical garments if they do, so it is virtually impossible for the consumer to make direct price comparisons. This makes merchandise selection of key importance in retailing women's clothing; the local independent can offer dresses and sportswear in tune with consumer preferences in its own locality; chain organizations, with their centralized buying, find it hard to adjust to unique preferences of local markets. Other lines that offer similar competitive advantages to the independent retailer are men's clothing and furniture.

Some large independent stores are successful because their owners have specialized knowledge that enables them to "run rings around" larger competitors. Examples abound in the retailing of such goods as Oriental rugs, musical instruments, and sports equipment. Numerous consumers hesitate to buy such items without professional advice. Chain stores and department stores sell these items, but usually they have to use less well-informed personnel than those who staff independent specialty stores.

Another group of large independent retailers has succeeded in building local reputations as *quality stores*. Some handle large assortments of related merchandise—for example, men's or ladies' apparel—and feature the latest fashions. Others deal in lines, such as jewelry, where the store image is as important as merchandise quality. Independents often find it easier to build prestige reputations than their chain-store or department store competitors. Furthermore, many independent quality stores are old and well established; it is not easy for competitors to acquire quality reputations locally in the space of a few months or years.

competitive advantages of
independent stores

In comparison with their competitors, successful independents, both large and small, possess significant advantages. The most important is that they can more easily adapt their operations to fit the unique needs of the communities in which they do business. Furthermore, the owner-managers of many successful independent stores often are more able and more aggressive than the hired managers of department store and chain-store units. Also, many consumers are loyal to locally owned and operated stores and look askance at stores controlled from out of town.

The competitive strength of the independent retailer varies from one line of retailing to another (as well as from one location to another). In retailing lines, where chains and other mass retailers can gain little price advantage through volume buying and where the independents can adjust more nearly to market needs, independents account for important market shares.

LARGE-SCALE INTEGRATED RETAILERS

The large-scale or mass retailers achieve their growth in three ways. First, some grow by increasing the physical size of their operating units to cater to more customers. As a store becomes larger, its power to attract customers increases because of the greater variety of merchandise offered for sale; moreover, up to a certain size, its costs per dollar of sales decrease. Beyond the optimum size, costs increase faster than sales. Optimum size of a retail establishment is also limited by the geographical extent of its market. For example, a department store that has its market limited to a single trading area does not have the growth potential of a mail-order retailer, whose market area may be as broad as the reach of the postal system or the United Parcel Service.

A second way that a retailer can expand is through acquiring additional stores in different market areas. These multiple outlets are operated in any of three ways: (1) a branch store operation may be established, with the parent store servicing the branches' merchandising and operating needs; (2) the outlets may be operated independently, being tied to the parent organization solely on a financial basis: or (3) a central management office may be responsible for all aspects of the retail stores' operations.

A third way to achieve retail growth is through integration. An integrated retail institution reduces marketing costs by eliminating, simplifying, or consolidating various activities involved in the marketing process. When a retailer bypasses a wholesaler to buy directly from a producer, some part of that wholesaler's activities are taken over by the retailer. If the retailer performs these activities more efficiently than the wholesaler, its costs are reduced accordingly. Most large-scale retailing operations grew through some combination of larger outlets, additional outlets, and integration.

mail-order houses　　MAIL-ORDER RETAILING OF GENERAL MERCHANDISE
Although a majority of their sales are through retail outlets, **mail-order houses** such as Ward's, Sears, and Penney's, which have sales in their mail-order divisions in the tens of millions of dollars annually, offer wide assortments of articles within each of a large number of merchandise lines. They buy directly from the producer, often contracting for a large share or even all of a producer's output. Many small manufacturers are completely dependent on one or the other of the large mail-order houses for distributing all they produce. Most of the over 20,000 sources of supply for Sears, for instance, are small manufacturers. Indeed, the company is on record as stating that "it prefers to work with smaller factories, which concentrate on production, and look to it for a substantial part of their distribution." [3] In the case of Sears, such small manufacturers are the main suppliers of Sears' own brands—Kenmore, Homart, Craftsman, Silvertone, J. C. Higgins, Charmode, and others.

OTHER TYPES OF MAIL-ORDER RETAILING　　The mail-order method is also used for retailing more limited selections of merchandise. Small manufacturers use this method to sell much or all of their output. Among the items retailed directly by such manufacturers are shirts, men's and women's apparel, toys, bird houses and feeders, and rugs. Some of these manufacturers distribute catalogs to consumers, but more often they use direct-mail promo-

---

[3] "How Sears Stays on Top," *International Management,* Vol. 23, April 1968.

tion and small advertisements in magazines and newspapers. Mail-order retailing is important, too, for many growers of trees, shrubs, plants, and seeds, who distribute their catalogs to homeowners.

Mail-order retailing is also used by the many "of-the-month" clubs. Typically, these clubs provide the service of preselected merchandise, thus relieving their members of the need for choosing their purchases from numerous alternatives. Book-of-the-Month Club, for instance, informs its members of monthly selections, which must be rejected by members if they do not wish to receive them. Because of their operating scheme, the clubs provide automatic distribution for products chosen as monthly selections. Most clubs are true middlemen, for they make their purchases from producers and resell them to consumers. The book clubs are the longest established in the field, but similar organizations engage in mail-order retailing of such items as food, fruit, toys, gifts, and foreign imports.

department stores NATURE OF OPERATIONS Formally defined, a **department store** is a large retailing unit handling a wide variety of shopping and specialty goods—including women's ready-to-wear and accessories, men's and boys' wear, piece goods, small wares, and home furnishings—and organized into separate departments for purposes of promotion, service, and control. Thus, the two main features of the department store are a broad merchandise offering and departmental organization. Responsibility for buying and selling is decentralized to individual departments, each carrying different lines of goods, and each under the control of a buyer or department manager. Buyers are relatively free to operate their departments as they see fit, provided that their operations produce profits considered adequate by the store's top management and their merchandise lines fit into the overall store image in terms of price and quality. In addition to supervising merchandising activities, the store's central administrative organization operates and maintains the physical facilities, provides such services as credit and delivery for the customers, and assists the merchandising division with such activities as advertising and promotion.

Originally, department stores relied on the great breadth of their merchandise offerings to attract customers. Gradually, however, the more aggressive stores, seeking to build their trade, broadened the range of services offered to customers. Today, it is a rare department store that does not provide charge accounts, installment plans, home delivery, and other customer services. Some offer elaborate restaurants and tearooms, nurseries to care for small children, and interior decorating advice. Some services are self-supporting; others are not. But even though some services may show an accounting-type loss, they are retained because of their proven power to pull in customers.

By nature, the department store is a horizontally integrated retail institution. It brings together under one roof a range of merchandise offerings comparable to the combined offerings of many stores specializing in single or fewer merchandise lines. This exposition-like character is the source of much of the department store's drawing power, but it is not without disadvantages, particularly in purchasing. Some departments do enough business to justify direct buying from manufacturers, but many do not. The small-volume departments, particularly in individually owned stores, are often unable to buy in large enough lots to qualify for quantity discounts from manufacturers and, hence, must buy through wholesalers and agents, resulting in high merchandise costs.

DEPARTMENT STORE BUYING GROUPS Because of the disadvantages they encounter in purchasing, some independently owned department stores join **buying groups.** Member stores cooperatively own, maintain, and use the services of resident buying offices located in such market centers as New York and Chicago. Through consolidation of the orders of member stores, the buying office achieves savings by placing orders for lots larger than any member could buy individually. Furthermore, the combined bargaining power results in lower price quotations by suppliers. A secondary, though important, activity of the resident buying office is to provide member stores with current information on prices, availability of new items, and fashion trends.

DEPARTMENT STORE OWNERSHIP GROUPS Many previously independent department stores have been absorbed into **ownership groups.** Most of these groups were put together originally by financiers rather than by merchandisers. They were intended to result primarily in immediate profits for the organizers through the flotation of new issues of common stock not in improved operating efficiency. But, over time, central managements of the ownership groups abandoned their solely financial orientations and focused upon improving and standardizing operating policies and procedures. One early development was the centralized buying offices, enabling stores in the group to buy many standard stock items and some fashion goods at lower costs. Nevertheless, many types of merchandise are still bought by stores individually. Among these are high-fashion items (where speed of procurement and direct contact with the producer are critical), and articles needed to satisfy purely local demands. Top managements of the department store ownership groups have also worked toward greater uniformity in nonmerchandising activities, such as in the standardization of personnel policies and store-operating systems and records.

Each store in an ownership group plans its merchandise offerings to cater to classes of trade in its own selling area. Because the inventory is mainly shopping goods (items customers shop around for and compare before buying) and specialty goods (items customers spend considerable time searching for), and because consumer preferences vary from one area to another, most department stores, whether or not they belong to ownership groups, find it difficult to standardize the merchandise offerings of stores in different locations. Furthermore, stores in the same ownership group often attract different classes of trade in different cities.

The uniqueness of the merchandise offering and of the classes of trade catered to results in each store's having a distinctive image. Thus, most department store ownership groups continue to operate stores under the names they had when they were independently owned. Allied Stores Corporation, for instance, operates, among others, Jordan Marsh in Boston, Titche-Goettinger in Dallas, the Bon Marché in Seattle, Dey Brothers in Syracuse, and Joske's in San Antonio and Houston. Federated Department Stores operates, among others, Filene's in Boston, Shillito's in Cincinnati, the Boston Store in Milwaukee, Bloomingdale's in New York, Abraham & Strauss in Brooklyn, Rich's in Atlanta, Burdine's in Miami, and Bullock's in Los Angeles. Each of these stores has a distinct image in its own trading area.

chain-store systems   A **chain-store system** is a group of retail stores of essentially the same type, centrally owned and with some degree of centralized control of operation. This definition is broad enough to include not only the well-known A & P and Woolworth chains, but also Ward's and Sears' retail stores and the department store ownership groups. Thus, basically, the distinguishing feature of a chain-store system is that it owns and controls a group of stores. The department store ownership group is one type of chain-store system, the retail stores of Montgomery Ward are another, and the K-Mart stores represent still another type. However, by long-established and customary usage, the term "chain-store system" refers to a multiunit retailing operation that cannot be categorized as a department store ownership group or the retail outlets of a mail-order house, and where some element of central control is exercised over merchandising.

The relative importance of chain-store systems is shown in Table 12–3. Chain-store systems made up of 11 or more stores collectively account for over 30 percent of the nation's total retail sales. Notice, too, that since 1966, chain stores have increased their proportion of total retail sales.

Table 12–4 indicates the relative importance of chain-store systems in various retail fields. They are of the most importance in the department store field, where they account for almost 90 percent of that field's total sales. In the nation's largest retail field—groceries—they transact more than half of the total sales. They hold relatively small shares of the market in retail fields such as furniture and appliances and men's and boys' wear.

STRENGTHS FROM HORIZONTAL INTEGRATION   Certain strengths of the chain-store system trace to its **horizontal integration** (i.e., its operation of multiple stores). With each new store, the system extends its reach to another group of prospective customers. Also, each store added means greater sales volume and, consequently, increased opportunity to effect economies through buying in larger lots. It means, too, that the costs of central administration and of providing highly specialized merchandising, buying, and promotional services can be spread over more stores. Thus, these costs are reduced for each store in the system. Furthermore, other economies are

**TABLE 12-3 TOTAL SALES OF RETAIL STORES AND
CHAIN-STORE SYSTEMS WITH 11 OR MORE STORES,
1966-1976**

Year	Sales of All Retail Stores (millions)	Total Sales of Chain-Store Systems* (millions)	Chain-Store System Sales of All Stores Sales (%)
1976	$651,900	$199,600	30.6
1975	584,400	188,100	31.3
1974	557,800	169,400	31.5
1972	448,379	137,650	30.7
1970	375,527	110,848	29.5
1968	339,324	94,194	27.8
1966	303,956	80,323	26.4

*Based on sales of organizations operating 11 or more retail stores.

Source: U.S. Department of Commerce, Bureau of the Census, Statistical Abstract of the United States, 1977, p. 830.

affected through standardizing store systems and procedures and adopting uniform personnel policies. These strengths, all due primarily to horizontal integration, are reflected in lower costs for the merchandise handled and in generally lower operating expenses than those incurred by most independent retailers.

MERCHANDISING AND OPERATING ECONOMIES Relative to most of its competitors, particularly those that are independent stores, the chain realizes significant savings in merchandising and operating expenses. Some are secured through eliminating or limiting such customer services as credit and delivery. Others are obtained by limiting merchandise variety—by stocking, for example, only three different brands of canned peas in each of two sizes rather than three brands in four sizes.

Other economies are realized through application of the basic merchandising philosophy of the chain, which is to squeeze the maximum sales out of each dollar invested in inventory. The chain, in other words, gears its operation so that it has a small inventory relative to its sales volume. One aspect of this philosophy relates to decisions on composition of inventory; the chain seeks to maximize the number of fast-selling items and to mimimize the number of slow movers. The chain attempts to build a large sales volume by pricing its merchandise lower than many of its competitors, with a comparatively lower profit per item. Thus, the chain stresses high sales volume and low unit profits, while many competitors are satisfied with low sales volume and high unit profits.

BUYING POLICY Because the chain-store system is a high-volume operation, it buys directly from producers or through their agents. Rarely does a chain buy from merchant wholesalers, for the system usually buys in larger

**TABLE 12-4 SALES OF CHAIN-STORE SYSTEMS IN
VARIOUS RETAIL FIELDS, 1976***

Kind of Business	Sales in 1976 (millions)	Total Sales in 1976† (%)
Total sales	199,600	30.6
Durable goods stores‡	11,600	5.4
Tire, battery, accessory dealers	2,300	23.0
Furniture, home furnishings	N.A.	N.A.
Nondurable goods stores‡	188,000	43.0
Apparel and accessory stores	7,000	24.5
Men's, boys' wear stores	N.A.	N.A.
Women's apparel, accessory stores	2,600	23.4
Shoestores	1,700	38.6
Drug and proprietary stores	8,200	41.6
Food stores‡	74,400	52.8
Grocery stores	73,500	56.1
Department stores	60,700	89.3
Variety stores	6,600	79.5

*Data based on sales of organizations operating 11 or more retail stores.
†Multiunit sales as percent of all retail sales.
‡Includes data not shown separately.

Source: U.S. Department of Commerce, Bureau of the Census, Statistical
Abstract of the United States, 1977, p. 831.

quantities and with larger discounts than the wholesalers can. Thus, by
operating its own warehouses, the chain-store system effectively becomes its
own wholesaler. Chain-store systems, therefore, are also **vertically integrated;** they take over and perform for themselves marketing activities that
would otherwise be performed by separate wholesale institutions.

WEAKNESSES   Most weaknesses of the chain-store system stem from its
horizontal integration and its merchandising philosophy. Centralized decision making means that individual chain units cannot react to changing
local conditions as quickly as alert local competitors. When individual units
lag behind the independents in making new products and brands available—
and frequently they do—centralized purchasing is usually at fault. Furthermore, in keeping with the high sales volume and low-profit merchandising
philosophy, the chain economizes on other costs and often dispenses with
such services as charge accounts and delivery. In doing this, it, in effect,
concedes to competitors the patronage of consumers desiring these services.
Moreover, because of its integrated nature, the chain has many stores and
requires many managers. Recruiting, training, and retaining managers in the
numbers needed are formidable tasks. Individual chains, of course, have
found ways to deal with, or minimize, these inherent weaknesses; nevertheless,
these weaknesses, together with the impersonal and cold character of most
chains, offset many competitive advantages chains have over independents.

DISTRIBUTION OF CONVENIENCE GOODS Chain-store systems are important links in the distribution system for many *convenience goods*. Both large and small manufacturers of food products (where chains account for over 50 percent of total volume) and drug products (where chains account for more than 40 percent of total volume), for instance, know that their brands cannot be made sufficiently available to consumers unless chain outlets stock them. Manufacturers of items sold largely through department stores of variety stores find that, to achieve meaningful sales volume, they need chain-store distribution.

Offering producers of convenience goods the tempting prize of widespread and high-volume retail distribution at a relatively low selling cost, skilled chain-store buying specialists drive hard bargains. They push for and usually obtain the lowest prices and most advantageous promotional allowances (which are payments made by manufacturers for advertising and otherwise promoting products at the retail level). Chains handling convenience goods expect most suppliers to promote their own products with heavy consumer advertising to minimize the in-store selling effort needed. In the absence of such promotion, the chain often prefers to handle its own store brands, packed for it either under contract by outside manufacturers or by captive (i.e., owned by the chain) canning or processing plants.

DISTRIBUTION OF SHOPPING GOODS Chain-store systems are also important retailers of some *shopping goods*. Chains are active, for instance, in retailing men's and women's apparel, dry goods, and shoes. In contrast to many of their independent competitors in these lines, however, shopping-goods chains tend to concentrate on low-priced and fast-selling items. In other words, chains that specialize in shopping goods seek items that resemble convenience goods as closely as possible. To obtain them, chains often pass up high-fashion merchandise in favor of more staple items. Because of this, as well as because of the need for large sales volumes, shopping-goods chains generally cater to middle- and lower-income consumer groups.

Commonly, shopping-goods chains have manufacturers under contract to supply them with goods according to the chain's own specifications. The supplying manufacturers need not be especially large, but they must be large enough to fill the chain's requirements.

Some shopping-goods chains are the retail arms of the manufacturers who own and control them. Bond Clothes, a retailer of men's and boys' clothing, makes its own suits and coats. The Thom McAn stores are operated by Melville Shoe Corporation. Other manufacturers, such as Genesco, sell part of their output through their own retail outlets and the rest through other types of retailers. But even when chain-store systems are controlled by manufacturers, there is a need for outside sources of supply. Thus, a manufacturer-controlled shoe chain, such as Thom McAn, retails not only shoes but related items, such as hosiery and shoe polish, bought from outside sources.

RETAILER COOPERATIVES

With the expansion of chain-store systems in the 1920s, independent stores suffered serious patronage losses. Independent retailers began to devise schemes for reducing their own wholesale costs, and there evolved the retailer-owned cooperative, an enterprise owned and controlled by retailer-stockholders, who patronize it and share in any savings in proportion to their patronage. The retailer cooperative has a warehouse, carries inventory in stock, and employs a manager. Even more significantly, it renders advice and assistance on retail merchandising problems, such as store layout and location, store operation, record systems, advertising methods and layouts, and personnel policies. Often, too, the retailer cooperative persuades its members to adopt a uniform name, store front, and sign, and to engage in cooperative advertising. The net effect is an organization more in the image of a chain-store system. However, most retailer cooperatives place more emphasis on group buying than on group promotional activities. Experience indicates, nevertheless, that heavy group promotion is an important key to success. When retailer-owned cooperatives emphasize group promotion, their members generally become more effective competitors of chain-store outlets.

WHOLESALER-SPONSORED GROUPS

In other instances, wholesalers have taken the initiative in organizing independent retailers into voluntary groups. Each retailer affiliating with a voluntary group owns and operates his or her own store but is associated with the sponsoring wholesaler for buying and merchandising. The retailer members agree to concentrate their purchases with the sponsoring wholesaler. They also agree to operate their stores under the group name and to display uniform store signs, thus maintaining identity among their stores and in their promotional efforts. The wholesaler, in turn, agrees to supply the retailer members with merchandise at the lowest possible prices. In addition, the wholesaler prepares and places advertising in local media and provides advice and assistance on merchandising, store layout and operation, cost control, and other problems. Retention of a wholesaler's profit as a part of the total cost structure makes it a neat trick for the sponsor to offer its affiliated retailers lower prices than would be available from competing wholesalers. Therefore, the wholesaler-sponsor often makes its main contribution and justifies its role through providing promotional assistance and management advice.

Whereas the early voluntary groups admitted any independent retailer of any size, the more recent trend is to restrict membership to large retailers. In the most successful groups, the sponsoring wholesaler and the retailer members pay considerable attention to advertising and store-operating efficiency. The largest voluntaries are in the food industry, where there are such nationwide organizations as *I.G.A.*, *Red and White*, and *Clover Farm Stores*. However, voluntaries in other fields, such as in hardware and drugs, are of some importance.

CONSUMER COOPERATIVES   A **consumer cooperative** is a retail business owned and operated by ultimate consumers to purchase and distribute goods and services primarily to its members. The operating policies used by most American cooperatives are (1) open membership—any consumer is free to join; (2) democratic control—each member has but one vote regardless of the number of cooperative shares held; (3) limited interest is paid on capital invested by members; (4) all sales are made at prevailing market prices and for cash only; and (5) members receive patronage dividends proportionate to their purchases.

There are some large consumer cooperatives in the United States, but their total impact on American retailing has been negligible. They have been very successful in some European countries, but not as successful in the United States because other types of retailing institutions grew up here and provided the strongly competitive setting that kept retailing costs and profits low. Most U.S. consumer cooperatives are in the grocery retailing field because their organizers have been impressed with the large part that food purchases play in total consumer spending, but consumer cooperatives have more chance for success in the United States when they handle other merchandise lines than groceries. For instance, they have been highly successful in operating college and university bookstores. The consumer cooperative in this field is often more efficient than its privately owned competitors, mostly small independent stores. In marked contrast to grocery retailing, where low unit profit margins are the rule, the book and school supply trade is characterized by relatively high margins. This combination of favorable factors has enabled cooperative college stores to pay patronage dividends of as much as 12 to 13 percent of members' purchases.

SUPERMARKETS   The basic characteristics and operating philosophy of the **supermarket** are indicated in its definition: a large retailing business unit selling mainly food and grocery items on the basis of the low-margin appeal, high turnover, wide variety and assortments, self-service, and heavy emphasis on merchandise appeal. Originally, when supermarkets were first introduced in the early 1930s, they were devised as purely food-retailing businesses. They continue to emphasize the mass selling of food and grocery items, but in order to widen their merchandise appeal and improve their profit potentials, increasing numbers of supermarkets add such nonfood lines as drugs, household utensils, hardware, and garden supplies. This trend toward **scrambled merchandising,** together with the spreading habit of many consumers to shop only once or twice per week for groceries, has enabled the supermarket to increase the dollar value of the average order sold each customer on each trip to the store.[4] To stimulate store traffic, the supermarket typically promotes its low prices through heavy advertising and mass merchandise displays; many also feature premium and

[4] G. H. Snyder, "New Slant on Non-foods," *Progressive Grocer,* August 1971, pp. 52-58.

251

trading stamp plans. Because the supermarket needs a high sales volume for profitable operation, large merchandise stocks are displayed on the selling floor to achieve maximum merchandise exposure. Readily accessible reserve stocks and adequate checkout counters, along with check-cashing facilities and a parking lot large enough to handle peak volumes of business, also make for high volume.

Many buying practices of supermarkets are routine. Certain staples and nationally advertised items are carried by nearly all supermarkets. The responsibility for buying varies with the company's size and organizational structure. Large supermarket chains have specialized buyers who bargain with and make purchases from suppliers, and store managers requisition most items from warehouses. In smaller companies, a single executive negotiates and makes all purchases. Managers of produce and meat departments often have authority to buy for their own departments. Supermarkets affiliated with retailer cooperatives and voluntary groups generally make most of their routine purchases through the wholesaling units of such organizations. Ordering and shelf-stocking of perishable items, such as crackers and cookies, are often handled by manufacturers' sales representatives under supervision of the owner, manager, or other individual responsible for buying. The ordering and stocking of nonfood lines are often taken care of by rack jobbers, with minimum supervision by supermarket personnel.

DISCOUNT HOUSES

A **discount house** is a retailing business unit that features a large selection of general merchandise (often including food), competes on a low price basis, and operates on a low markup with minimum customer service. Most discount houses today are full-line, limited-service, promotional stores that actually are department stores. In fact, the term "discount house" is used increasingly to refer to any retail establishment whose main promotional emphasis is on selling nationally advertised merchandise at prices below those of conventional dealers.

In the late 1940s and early 1950s circumstances were ripe for the establishment and growth of discount houses. Traditional appliance outlets, such as department stores and small dealers, had grown accustomed to high markups—often 35 to 40 percent of the retail price—and they were also used to selling at manufacturers' full "list" prices. Furthermore, appliance manufacturers had promoted their brand names to the point where consumers no longer depended on retailers to guarantee the product. Every reputable manufacturer stood behind its products regardless of the outlets that sold them. Discount-house operators could sell appliances and other consumer durables profitably at prices as much as 30 percent below those of conventional outlets. Because the conventional retailers first maintained their own total sales and profits, for a few years they did not put up much of a competitive battle. By the time they realized that they had to meet or undercut discount-house prices, discount houses had won strong customer loyalty.

By the 1960s, the selection of merchandise offered by discount houses had broadened appreciably. To the original lines of **hard goods** (appliances, furniture, and other consumer durables), broad lines of **soft goods**—including clothing for men, women, and children, linen and bedding, and gift-wares—had been added. Today, soft-goods lines occupy roughly half of the selling floor space in the typical large discount house. The early hard-goods discount houses depended strongly upon brand, attracting customers by offering well-known brands at discount prices. Since brands are far less important in soft-goods lines, today's discount houses with broadened lines of merchandise find it more difficult to prove that their prices are really lower. Instead, they must build consumer confidence in their pricing structures.

In the 1960s and 1970s, discount houses continued to grow, both in terms of number of outlets and total sales.[5] This growth came partly from continuing expansion by the pioneer discounters and partly from invasions of the discount field by other types of retailers. Table 12-5 shows the kinds of retailers and some of the leading retail organizations currently operating discount houses. Increasingly, companies operating conventional department stores, variety stores, or food stores have invaded the field, setting up separate discounting divisions. Among companies in the variety store field,

[5] "Discounters Coming on Stronger Than Ever," *Publishers' Weekly*, July 12, 1971, p. 63.

TABLE 12-5 KINDS OF RETAILERS AND SOME LEADING RETAIL ORGANIZATIONS ENGAGED IN DISCOUNTING

1. The Prepioneers (who were discounting before the discounters)
   Klein Department Stores, Inc.
   Ohrbach's
2. The Pioneer Discounters
   Vornado, Inc.
   E. J. Korvette
   Spartan Industries
   Gibson Products Company
3. Department Store Operators
   Allied Stores Corp.—Almart Stores
   J. C. Penney Company—Treasure Island Stores
   Mangel Stores Corp.—Shoppers Fair
   Federated Dept. Stores—Richway
4. Variety Store Operators
   S. S. Kresge Co.—K-Mart
   F. W. Woolworth Co.—Woolco Division
5. Corporate Grocery Chain Operators
   Grand Union—Grand Way Division
   Stop and Shop—Bradlee's Division
   Kroger
6. The Catalog Discounters
   Service Merchandise Company
   Unity Buying Service, Inc.

for example, S. S. Kresge Company has its K-Marts and F. W. Woolworth, its Woolco stores. Discount retailing has increasingly become an industry of giants.

Discount houses buy their merchandise stocks both from wholesale distributors and directly from manufacturers. Early in their growth, they did nearly all their buying from distributors, but as discount houses grew larger and became important outlets for many consumer durables, and as chains of discount houses such as E. J. Korvette were organized, more and more manufacturers made direct sales to them. Large discount houses now have as many direct-buying privileges as the largest chains. In fact, discount chains count among some of the largest retail chains today.

Discount houses are hard buyers, but they are also fast buyers. Manufacturers appreciate a fast buyer when they find themselves with unexpectedly large inventories that more conventional retail outlets seem incapable of moving. In fact, one of the most distinguishing characteristics of the modern large, broad-line discount house is its strong emphasis on specially priced "distress" merchandise offered on a "one-time" basis.

comparison of supermarkets and discount houses The supermarket and the discount house have much in common. Both rely on the appeal of low prices, wide variety and assortments, self-service, and the handling of well-known brands of merchandise. Both keep their prices down by combining operating expense economies with a high-volume business in fast-selling items. However, the supermarket is, by definition, a large retailing business, whereas the discount house may be any size—from very small to very large.

The larger discount house is the one most resembling the supermarket—as a matter of fact, some large discount houses feature grocery departments and offer tough competition to supermarkets. Because a discount house, like a supermarket, must transact a large total sales volume if it is to offer low prices, many operate their grocery departments at no profit or even at a loss, regarding them as a means of getting people into the store and of obtaining the required overall level of sales. Nearby supermarkets find it difficult to match the discount house's nonprofit grocery pricing policy—tough competition indeed!

AUTOMATIC SELLING Automatic selling or, as it is more commonly known, **automatic vending**, involves the sale of goods or services to ultimate consumers through coin-operated machines. Whereas most automatic vending machines are still coin-operated, machines that make change for one-dollar bills see expanding use. The change-making machine is overcoming a long-time disadvantage of automatic vending—the inability to serve customers who do not have the proper change. Automatic selling is not a new retailing method; the Tutti-Frutti Company installed chewing-gum machines at elevated railroad stations in the 1880s. Historically, the major portion of vending machine volume has come and still comes from soft drinks, cigarettes, and candy. Two out of every 10 candy bars sold are sold through vending machines, as are 16 out of 100 packs of cigarettes and more than one out of four soft drinks.

Among the many attempts that have been made to use vending machines for products other than soft drinks, candy, and cigarettes, those with packaged milk and ice cubes have been most successful. One area of considerable success in vending is in the sale of "fast foods." Vending machines are located in areas where large numbers of people congregate, such as office buildings, factories, schools, sports, and entertainment areas. They offer a selection of hot and cold foods and beverages that can make up a meal.

Although automatic selling still accounts for only a small percent of all retail sales—only $6.9 billion out of an estimated $448 billion total in 1972—vending machines are increasingly important as outlets for many products. The National Automatic Merchandising Association (N.A.M.A.) estimates that there are 6,100 vending machine operators in the United States with more than 6.5 million machines, selling products that literally range from soup to nuts. Vending machine volume expands with each new technological improvement in machine design and operation. The first coffee vending machine, for instance, was installed in 1946 and by 1972 such machines were selling coffee at an annual rate of $432 million. N.A.M.A. states that the average person spends about $22.50 annually on purchases from coffee machines. [6] The association reports that annual vending volume more than doubled (from $2.1 billion to $4.5 billion) from 1958 to 1967 and that it had increased by more than that amount in the next five years (to $6.9 billion in 1972).

FRANCHISING   A franchise is a conditional right given to a retailer to market the franchise company's products or services under the banner of the franchiser. Generally, franchise companies have a product or service that has been successful locally, but they lack sufficient capital to expand their own retail outlets. The recent and rapid growth of franchising leads some to regard it as a new retailing concept, but franchising started early in the twentieth century. Most pioneer automobile manufacturers, for instance, were too financially weak even to handle their own wholesaling (let alone their own retailing), so they turned to independent wholesale distributors, who, in turn, granted retailing franchises to dealers throughout their territories. As manufacturers grew larger and improved their finances, they absorbed the distributors and granted franchises direct to auto retailers. Another early user of franchising was the petroleum industry, which has been using the method almost as long as there have been gasoline service stations. As a company using franchising gains financial strength, it often moves to reduce the number of its franchised dealers through buying out the most profitable ones and converting them to a retail chain operation;

[6] "Census of the Industry, '73," *Vend,* May 1973, pp. 61-80.

**Figure 12-3 Some franchising companies that achieved
rapid growth during the 1960s and 1970s**

Robo-Wash—automatic car wash
Western Auto—automobile parts and accessories
Budget Rent-a-Car—car rental
Snap-on Tools—auto repair tools and equipment
Long John Silver's—fish and chips
Dunkin' Donuts—doughnut shop
McDonald's Hamburgers—hamburgers and soft drinks
International House of Pancakes—pancakes
Colonel Sanders Kentucky Fried Chicken—chicken dinners
Burger King—hamburgers and drinks
Dairy Queen—soft ice cream, sandwiches, and soft drinks
Shakey's Pizza Parlor—pizzas and soft drinks
Mr. Steak—restaurants specializing in steak dinners
Arby's Restaurants—roast beef sandwiches
One Hour Martinizing—fast cash-and-carry dry cleaning
Culligan Soft-Water Service—water-conditioning service
Mary Carter Paint Company—paint and painting supplies
Manpower, Inc.—temporary office help at low cost
General Business Services—bookkeeping and tax service for all small business
A to Z Rentals—tools and household equipment
Convenient Food Mart—convenience food stores
Aero-Mayflower—moving and trucking service
Servicemaster—carpet and furniture cleaning
Howard Johnson—restaurants and motels
Wendy's Old Fashioned Hamburgers—hamburgers

this tendency has been particularly evident throughout the petroleum industry since the "Arab oil crisis" of the 1970s.

Until the 1960s franchising accounted for a small share of total U.S. retail sales, but during that decade many new industries, particularly service industries, adopted the franchising concept and its total impact increased enormously. By 1976 there were more than 445,000 franchised retail outlets in the United States whose total sales (some $212 billion) accounted for nearly one-third of all U.S. retail sales.[7] Recently, the growth of franchise retailing has slowed considerably. Nevertheless, franchise retailing is still very much an important part of the total retail scene. Figure 12-3 lists some better-known franchise companies. As is evident in this figure, franchising has expanded greatly in fields such as prepared foods, dry cleaning, and equipment rentals. But automobiles and gasoline are still the two most important products sold mainly through franchised dealerships, and fast foods is third.

[7] U.S. Department of Commerce, Bureau of the Census, *Statistical Abstract of the United States,* 1977, pp. 830, 837.

The main attraction of franchise retailing to the franchising company is that this is a way to secure many of the advantages of having its own outlets without having to finance them. If a manufacturer, for example, sells its products through completely independent dealers, generally it has little or no control over their promotion or how they are retailed. If the same manufacturer, however, sells through franchised dealers, it retains control over marketing practices and can specify retailing procedures in detail. This aspect of franchising can be an advantage for both parties, since a large manufacturer can afford to hire experienced professionals to design highly effective retail operating systems and procedures.

One disadvantage of franchising is that it is difficult to adjust to unique local conditions. An additional disadvantage is that it is next to impossible to control managerial performance within the franchised dealerships. Standardized operating procedures and professional advice are not enough to compensate for sloppy or ineffective local management, as demonstrated by the high failure rate among franchised dealers nearly everywhere. [8]

SHOPPING CENTERS

A **shopping center** is a group of stores and other commercial establishments, planned, developed, owned, and managed as a unit, with off-street parking provided on the property and related in location, gross floor area, and type of shops to the trading area served. [9] Shopping centers are classified according to their size, which is determined by the trading area served and which, in turn, determines the kinds and variety of stores included.

neighborhood centers

The **neighborhood** center is the smallest and most common type of shopping center. A supermarket is usually its focal point, with the smaller stores geared to supply convenience goods and services (drug and hardware stores, beauty and barber shops,

[8] Other problems have arisen in the franchise system of distribution, among them: (1) franchising has come under increased attack from the courts as being "anticompetitive," (2) some franchisors treat their franchisees unfairly, and (3) certain franchisors engage in deceptive practices in selling franchises and in negotiating franchise agreements. For an excellent analysis of these and other aspects of franchising, including whether or not franchisees need protection from deceptive selling practices and an evaluation of some legislative proposals designed to protect franchisees, see Shelby D. Hunt, "Full Disclosure and the Franchise System of Distribution," in *Marketing Education and the Real World,* Boris W. Becker and Helmut Becker, eds., Proceedings of the American Marketing Association, 1972 Fall Conference (Chicago; American Marketing Association, 1972), pp. 301-304.

[9] The American Marketing Association defines a shopping center as "a geographical cluster of retail stores, collectively handling an assortment of goods varied enough to satisfy most of the merchandise wants of consumers within convenient travelling time, and, thereby, attracting a general shopping trade." The A.M.A. definition includes both planned and unplanned shopping areas. Unplanned shopping areas, usually called "shopping districts," are nonintegrated (i.e., they have no overall plan with respect to the merchandise stocked by each retailer). In contrast, the shopping center defined by the Urban Land Institute is an integrated planned unit. For that reason, the definition used here seems more relevant to this discussion.

laundry and dry cleaning establishments, gasoline stations) to some 7,500 to 20,000 people living within 6 to 10 minutes' driving distance. Neighborhood centers may have only a dozen stores, but the total area occupied, including parking space, is likely to range from 4 to 10 acres. Generally, a neighborhood center is well located if there are no strong competitors within about two miles.

community centers   The **community center** is a large operation and usually features a variety store or a small department store in addition to the supermarket and small stores also found in the neighborhood center. Thus, the community center provides a merchandise offering that includes a selection of shopping goods, such as clothing and home furnishings, as well as convenience goods. The community center serves a market of from 20,000 to 100,000 persons and occupies from 10 to 30 acres. According to experts, a community center should not have strong competitors within a radius of three to four miles.

regional centers and   The **regional center** is the largest of all. Two or more
shopping malls   large department stores provide its main drawing power, further enhanced by 100 or more smaller stores. The newer regional centers have increasingly been designed as shopping malls with from two to four department stores serving as anchor stores and providing the convenience to shoppers of moving from store to store under covered passageways. Many older regional centers have also been converted to shopping mall operations. Shoppers, therefore, in the regional centers and shopping malls are exposed to a very wide range of goods. Regional centers are usually set up to serve 100,000 to 250,000 people living within a radius of five to six miles. Such centers, more closely resembling central city shopping districts than the smaller centers, are slowly but surely changing consumer shopping habits, especially because they reduce the need or urgency to go to the central city to shop.

implications for central city   Because of their relatively generous parking facilities,
shopping districts   easy accessibility by automobile, and nearness to the suburban middle-income market, regional centers and shopping malls in many cities have weakened, or even almost eliminated, both the central city's downtown shopping district and the older "main street" suburban business district. It is estimated that there were roughly 375 regional shopping centers in 1978. Central city merchants press for measures to alleviate traffic congestion and for improved parking facilities, but they are not likely ever to match the convenience of the outlying regional shopping centers and malls.

Figure 12–4 shows the evolutionary development of shopping centers in a rapidly growing medium-sized American city—Austin, Texas. The shopping centers are numbered in order of their dates of completion. Center 1, a moderate-sized community center, was built in 1958 as a small commu-

Figure 12-4 Austin, Texas: city and major retail shopping centers

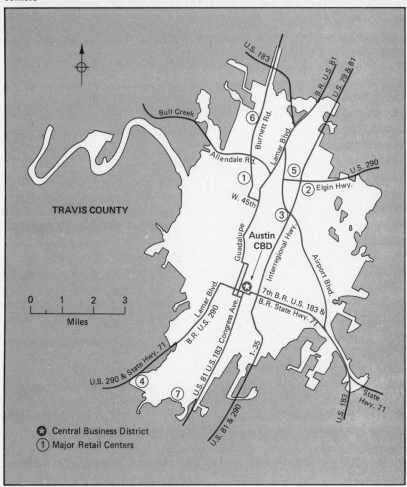

Source: Department of Commerce. Bureau of the Census.

nity center and enlarged in 1963. Centers 2 and 3, moderate-sized regional centers, were built in 1959 and 1963, to serve northern areas of the city, which were experiencing rapid population growth. Center 4, a large community center, was built in 1970 to serve southern areas of the city, which were experiencing moderate population growth. Center 5, a large regional center with three large department stores, was completed in 1971 and has considerably more square feet of retail floor space than the downtown central business district. Center 6, a regional center with two large department stores, and Center 7, a smaller regional center, were opened in 1975. During the 17 years from construction of the first community center to construction of the newest regional center, Austin's population grew from 170,000 to 300,000 and the main direction of growth was toward the north, so that four of the five regional centers are nearer the city's population center than is the central business district. This pattern of retail growth is typical of most small- to medium-sized cities that have experienced recent rapid growth—usually, the central business district regresses to the position of an unplanned shopping center for nearby residents and downtown employees, while outlying and suburban shoppers increasingly patronize the regional centers.

In addition to competing with central-city shopping areas and smaller centers, expanding regional centers and shopping malls have increasingly become competitive with each other. Driving time to the center is highly influential in determining consumer shopping preference.

implications for the manufacturer   For the manufacturer, the main marketing significance of the planned shopping center is that it is an integrated retail unit. Consumers view the center as a single large shopping convenience and not as a conglomeration of individual stores, each going its separate way. [10] Recognizing this, shopping center developers sometimes restrict the classes of merchandise individual stores are permitted to handle. But, in large centers, controlled competition among stores handling similar merchandise lines is allowed. A manufacturer of lighting fixtures, accustomed to selling its line through both hardware stores and department stores, encounters three different distribution situations in shopping centers: (1) in some, the line is restricted to the hardware store; (2) in others, it is restricted to the department store; and (3) in still others, both the hardware store and the department store are free to handle the line. This same manufacturer even finds instances where shopping center branches of department stores are not permitted to handle its line even though the parent stores have stocked it for years. The great need for information about such situations explains why manufacturers maintain close contact with their dealers operating, or planning to operate, stores in shopping centers. In addition, the extensive use of self-service in shopping centers has caused many manufacturers to redesign product packages and add more information to the labels. And, with the growing importance of the regional centers and shopping malls, manufacturers are reexamining their advertising practices, especially with respect to advertising in media that are aimed specifically at the trading areas of shopping centers.

THE WHEEL OF RETAILING HYPOTHESIS AND TRENDS OF FUTURE GROWTH   Changes in retailing evolve gradually over the years. According to the wheel of retailing hypothesis, advanced by M. P. McNair, new forms of retailing institutions obtain a foothold on the retail scene through emphasizing a price appeal made possible by low operating costs inherent in the new form of institution. Over time the new institutions upgrade their

[10] Bert Rosenbloom, "The Trade Area Mix and the Retailing Mix: A Retail Strategy Matrix," *Journal of Marketing,* October 1976, pp. 58-59.

facilities and services, necessitating added investments and higher operating costs. At some point they emerge as high-cost, high-price retailers, vulnerable to competition from newer forms of retailers, who, in turn, go through a similar metamorphosis. Mail-order houses and department stores, for example, were originally low-cost retailers soliciting business mainly through use of the price appeal, but eventually the wheel turned and they became vulnerable to chain-store systems, discount houses, and other newer institutions.[11] As another example, conventional supermarkets in the late 1960s encountered new competition from the new food discount stores, which, in line with the wheel notion, were featuring lower prices made possible by lower operating costs due to stripped-down services.[12]

There is a marked trend toward giantism in retailing in the United States today. Only in the case of the highly specialized, single line stores can a small entrepreneur still start on a shoestring, and even here much of the new growth has been in franchised outlets. Electronic data processing made possible the central management of multiple-unit retail organizations, such as chains, with greater efficiency than previously was thought possible. In the sector of retail merchandising, however—that is, in the selection of what is to be sold—many a small retailer still enjoys a clear-cut advantage over its larger competitors.

SUMMARY   Retailing occurs in all marketing channels for consumer goods, with most producers of consumer products relying heavily on separately owned retail institutions to distribute their outputs to ultimate consumers. Retailers serve as marketing intermediaries for producers and wholesalers and as sources of supply for ultimate consumers. Because of the many possible ways of adjusting to the expectations of suppliers and customers, retailers are the most diverse, as well as the most numerous, of all marketing institutions.

[11] See M. P. McNair, "Significant Trends and Developments in the Postwar Period," *Competitive Distribution in a Free, High-Level Economy and Its Implications for the University,* A. B. Smith, ed. (Pittsburgh, Pa.: University of Pittsburgh Press, 1958), pp. 17-18. See also S. C. Hollander, "The Wheel of Retailing," *Journal of Marketing,* July 1960, pp. 37-42. Hollander concludes: "The wheel of retailing hypothesis is not valid for all retailing. . . . [It] does, however, seem to describe a fairly common pattern in industrialized, expanding economies."

[12] For a most provocative analysis that bears directly on the wheel of retailing hypothesis, see Arieh Goldman, "The Role of Trading Up in the Development of the Retailing System," *Journal of Marketing,* January 1975, pp. 54-62. Goldman cites evidence which indicates that, while many new retailing institutions have penetrated the retail system using a price appeal, some (e.g., department stores, discount stores, and supermarkets) have entered combining low prices with a regular level of services and appearance (rather than the "no-service, low-status" profile suggested by the wheel of retailing hypothesis). Goldman's conclusion is that the wheel of retailing hypothesis correctly identifies the low price factor as the major aspect of the appearance of new retailing institutions, but does not provide an adequate explanation of "why."

House-to-house selling, one of the most ancient retailing methods, is important today in only a few lines of trade, even though several large concerns rely upon it for their retail distribution. House-to-house selling eliminates the expenses of retail store operations, but it is generally a high-cost retailing method. Nevertheless, some manufacturers find retail distribution through house-to-house selling appropriate, especially those with products that benefit from demonstration in the home or that consumers will usually not shop for in retail stores.

Independent retailers, both small and large, take a variety of forms. The general store, perhaps the oldest type, has disappeared in many sections of the country. Small independent retailers, generally concentrated in fields requiring small capital investments, usually do not try to compete on a price basis but find ways to differentiate their stores in the eyes of their customers. Large independent retailers are important in fields where integrated retailers either have no operating advantages or are at competitive disadvantages.

The large-scale integrated retailers achieved their growth in different ways. The large mail-order houses, capitalizing on several environmental changes, integrated wholesaling and retailing for a wide range of merchandise and made effective use of catalog selling and the price appeal; later, capitalizing on further environmental changes, they also became important operators of retail stores. The department stores, featuring broad merchandise offerings and departmental organizations, relied both on their exposition-like character and various customer services to attract trade. Chain-store systems, applying a basic philosophy of small inventory relative to sales volume, capitalized on their integrated nature, horizontally and vertically, and made effective use of competitive prices; today, chains are important distributors of convenience goods sold to mass markets and shopping goods sold to middle- and lower-income market segments.

You also now know the operating methods and characteristics of retailer cooperatives, wholesaler-sponsored groups, consumer cooperatives, supermarkets, discount houses, automatic vending, franchise distribution, and the different kinds of shopping centers. These institutions and retail distribution methods—in their present forms, at least—represent relatively recent innovations in retailing. All developed as responses to changes either in the competitive environment or in consumer markets or in producers' marketing requirements. With the background knowledge that you now have of both wholesale distribution and retail distribution, you are ready to move on to an analysis of marketing channels—the subject of the next chapter.

1   How do you explain the high failure rate among independent retailers, particularly small ones?

2   In what ways can a small retailer compete effectively with large retailers? Discuss.

3   Give your assessment of the present state of retailing in terms of its efficiency and ability to serve consumers effectively. Justify your position. What changes would you suggest? Why?

4   Identify and analyze the advantages of large-scale retailing over small-scale retailing. Which advantage do you think is most important? Why?

5   Discuss and analyze the evolution of the chain-store system, its strengths derived from horizontal integration, the merchandising and operating economies it can achieve, buying policy, and weaknesses. Cite several examples.

6   What are the reasons underlying "scrambled merchandising"? Explain.

7   "Several years ago it was easy to distinguish between a discount house and a department store. Today, however, the lines of distinction are much less clear and, in some cases, it is impossible to tell the difference between these two types of retail institutions." Agree or disagree? Why?

8   Distinguish between the three types of shopping centers—neighborhood, community, and regional.

9   Does the evolution of large, planned shopping centers spell the ultimate elimination of downtown shopping centers? In what ways do downtown merchants have an advantage over merchants in the shopping centers? What can downtown do to bounce back?

10   It has been said that the retailer is in a very advantageous strategic position—dealing directly with the consumer. What advantages does this have for the retailer? Are there any disadvantages?

11   Describe the significance of franchising, its advantages and disadvantages.

12   Compile a listing of "Ten Rules for Successful Retailing" which you would adhere to if you were engaged in retailing.

13   What do you see as the retailer's social responsibilities to the community being served?

14   What is the role of marketing research at the retail level? Why do so few retailers do any marketing research?

When Landon's Department Store was founded in 1921 by Jane Landon, the town of Keeton was a shopping center for surrounding farms and the state college of 400 students. The store grew along with the college (now a state university) and the further development of Keeton as a business center for the surrounding rural area. Landon's Department Store had an established reputation as a source of good-quality clothing for the entire family and moderately priced household accessories and sporting goods.

Several developments dramatically changed the character of Keeton and the surrounding area. A 20-mile turnpike was opened connecting Keeton with the state capital and the major industrial area to the north. University enrollment grew to 15,000 students, with prospects that this figure would continue climbing. Several large housing developments were being constructed on the town's outskirts and were attracting fashion-conscious suburbanites who worked in the state capital.

The biggest marketing challenge to Keeton's old, established businesses occurred when a large shopping mall (with branches of two major department stores) opened along the turnpike five miles to the north. Landon's management felt that new marketing approaches were needed. The store's reputation as a reliable source of basic product needs would no longer be sufficient. Landon's had a convenient location in an attractive business district near the new residential areas and the university. What it needed was a new image in keeping with the times. The major obstacle was Landon's image as a small-town operation. Assuming Landon's could make the desired physical changes, how could the store communicate its new image as a fashion store to townspeople, especially older residents?

Landon's considered opening several boutiques within the store, each geared to specific target markets. For example, a gourmet cooking and household accessories boutique, and a giftwares department featuring unique imported and handcrafted items, both aimed to attract young suburbanites. If these boutiques were properly publicized with a grand opening featuring visiting experts, management felt that many new families would be attracted into the store and see the new fashion image permeating it. Perhaps courses, such as gourmet cooking, could also be offered. To attract the university market, an improved record department could be opened with a visit from a new music group and campus clothing boutiques could offer 5 percent discounts to students presenting I.D. cards. Another possible strategy was to feature a larger stock of fashionable clothing. While Landon's welcomed college student business, it had never done much to appeal directly to young adults. Intensified radio and newspaper ads might stress the theme that Landon's "has something special for most everyone, students, children, sports enthusiasts, young working people, homeowners, people on the move." Care could be taken to assure long-time customers that Landon's still offered fine-quality merchandise at reasonable prices.

Landon management generally agreed that the several changes in the market area served by the store, including what promised to be formidable competition from the two new department store branches nearby, meant that something had to be done to keep the department store in the mainstream of Keeton commerce. The major problem was what to do and how to go about attracting more customers.

questions:

1. What alternatives does Landon's Department Store have?
2. Is it feasible for a medium-size store to appeal to so many diverse market segments?
3. Design a basic communications plan (set of guidelines) for a department store seeking to generate a new image.
4. What should Landon's do?

When you have mastered the contents of this chapter, you should be able to:

1   Outline the conditions under which producers find it appropriate to use each main type of marketing channel.
2   Explain the various factors influencing channel usage.
3   Illustrate the two types of "dual distribution."
4   Identify the key problems producers face in the initial determination of marketing channels.
5   Demonstrate the use of *trade-off analysis* in the determination of marketing channels.
6   Discuss the three general degrees of distribution intensity and the factors influencing the distribution intensity decision.
7   Analyze the problems producers have in obtaining channel usage initially and in building and maintaining middlemen's cooperation.

marketing channels

Analysis in the two preceding chapters focused on the middlemen who operate on the wholesale and retail levels of distribution. These middlemen constitute the building blocks that producers seek to link together into marketing channels to bridge the gap between themselves and the target markets. Marketing channels are the distribution networks through which producers' products flow to market. More formally defined, a **marketing channel,** or channel of distribution, is a path traced in the direct or indirect transfer of ownership to a product, as it moves from a producer to ultimate consumers or industrial users. As emphasized throughout Part Four, to understand distribution, you must understand both marketing institutions and marketing channels. Discussion in this chapter focuses on (1) the different types of marketing channels, (2) factors influencing their usage, and (3) producers' problems in determining and using them.

TYPES OF MARKETING CHANNELS

Marketing channels vary widely, from the simple one employed by a spark plug manufacturer selling its entire output to one automobile manufacturer to the long and complex channels employed in moving nonperishable farm products to market. Marketing channels are made up of different kinds of building blocks, including producers, consumers, or industrial users; wholesale institutions (both agent and merchant wholesalers), and retail institutions. Thus, the possible number of different channels is large. Figure 13-1 illustrates the more commonly used marketing channels and shows that the channel building blocks bear a hierarchical relationship to each other. For example, if agent middlemen are present in a marketing channel, they are generally situated farther back in the channel than wholesalers and/or retailers.

Figure 13–1   Marketing channels commonly used in the
distribution of industrial and consumer goods

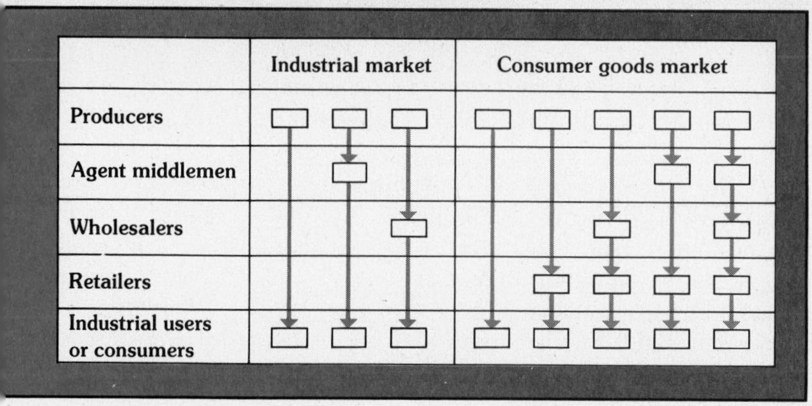

	Industrial market			Consumer goods market				
Producers	☐	☐	☐	☐	☐	☐	☐	☐
Agent middlemen		☐					☐	☐
Wholesalers			☐			☐		☐
Retailers					☐	☐	☐	☐
Industrial users or consumers	☐	☐	☐	☐	☐	☐	☐	☐

manufacturer to consumer or user   There are two levels in the shortest marketing channel. They are the producer and either the ultimate consumer or industrial user. The direct producer-to-industrial-user channel is the most common way of marketing industrial goods. There are several reasons for this: many industrial products have markets composed of few potential users; the users of particular industrial products are clustered together in only a few market areas; some industrial products have special servicing and installation requirements which the manufacturer can best provide; others are so technical that manufacturers deal directly with prospective users; and, in many cases, industrial users insist on buying directly and buy in quantities large enough to make direct sales by producers economically feasible.

The direct producer-to-ultimate consumer channel is not nearly so common. But some farmers deal directly with consumers at roadside stands or from stalls in public markets. Some small businesses, such as bakeries and dairies, and some larger businesses, such as tire manufacturers, sell directly to consumers, either through their own retail outlets or on a house-to-house basis. There are even a few manufacturers, in such lines as shoes and shirts, who sell directly to consumers through mail-order departments. However, not many manufacturers of consumer products rely wholly or even principally on the producer-to-ultimate consumer channel, because ultimate consumers are numerous, widely scattered, and accustomed to buying in very small quantities.

manufacturer through agent middleman to consumer or user   Some producers use agent middlemen as intermediaries between themselves and the next level of distribution. Agent middlemen, who generally operate at the wholesale level, are much used in marketing agricultural produce, partly because most farmers are too small to handle their own distribution efficiently and partly because the main growing areas are separated geographically from the larger markets.

In marketing both industrial and consumer goods, agent middlemen are used usually, although not exclusively, by manufacturers who want to rid themselves of much of the marketing task. A manufacturer's entire output is turned over to one or a small number of agent middlemen for marketing, in which case the manufacturer, in effect, delegates the formulation of overall marketing strategy to one or a few outside organizations, the manufacturer's participation being limited to the selection of the agent(s). In other instances, the manufacturer uses agents to market its product in some areas—generally ones with limited sales potentials—and either uses its own sales force or merchant middlemen in other market areas.

When agent middlemen are used, they negotiate the transfer of legal title to the producer's merchandise with institutions active on the next distribution level. In marketing consumer goods, they negotiate with either merchant wholesalers or retailers or both, or the agent arranges for further negotiations to be handled by other agent middlemen situated farther along the marketing channel and nearer the ultimate consumer. For products sold through a limited number of retail outlets, such as furniture, the agent negotiates directly with retailers. For products sold through numerous retail outlets, such as most grocery items, the agent negotiates with merchant wholesalers, who, in turn, sell to retailers. However, in marketing grocery products, agents may also deal directly with such large-volume retailers as grocery chains and retail cooperatives. In marketing industrial goods, agents usually negotiate directly with industrial users; but in some lines, such as small hand tools, it is common for them to negotiate with merchant wholesalers, such as industrial distributors or mill supply houses, which, in turn, sell to industrial users.

manufacturer–retailer–ultimate consumer

This is one of the most common marketing channels for consumer products. Manufacturers using it have some compelling reason for avoiding wholesale middlemen: their products may be perishable, either physically or fashionwise—hence, speed in distribution is essential; the retailers involved may be predominantly large (such as chains, department stores, and mail-order houses) and, as a policy matter, refuse to buy through wholesalers; the retailers handling the product may be located near each other, thus making it convenient for the manufacturer to sell to them directly; the available wholesalers may be unable or unwilling to provide the promotional support that the manufacturer feels its product requires; or the manufacturer may desire closer contact with ultimate consumers than that afforded through channels containing more distribution levels.

Manufacturers who distribute their products directly to retailers must finance the inventories that would otherwise be carried by merchant wholesalers. Furthermore, they need either a product line wide enough to permit their sales representatives to write large orders or a narrower line ordered by retailers in large quantities. If individual retailers do not ordinarily buy in large quantities, a manufacturer should have some other compelling reason for selling to them directly.

One important reason for distribution direct to retailers is the manufacturer's desire to use franchising.[1] A franchise is a continuing relationship between a manufacturer (or an expert in the performance of some service) and a retailer in which, for a consideration, the manufacturer supplies the retailer with manufacturing and marketing techniques, a brand image, and other know-how. This method of operation, which has existed for many years in such fields as petroleum marketing, has increased enormously in importance during the past decade. The franchisor-franchisee relationship requires continuing close contact so that the franchisor can provide advice, supervision, and help when needed. The manufacturer-to-retailer-to-ultimate-consumer marketing channel meets this requirement.

manufacturer–merchant wholesaler–retailer–ultimate consumer

The manufacturer–merchant wholesaler–retailer–ultimate consumer channel is often called the traditional or orthodox channel. A manufacturer finds it suitable under some or all of these conditions: it has a narrow product line; it is unable to finance distribution direct to retailers or can put the funds to more productive use elsewhere; retail outlets are numerous and widely dispersed; wholesalers are able and willing to provide strong promotional support or the product does not require such support; the products are staples, not subject to physical or fashion deterioration; the manufacturer's advertising to ultimate consumers exerts a strong pull in causing retailers to stock the product. Manufacturers using this channel but desiring closer contact with retailers often employ "missionary" sales personnel who, while calling on retailers, refer any orders they obtain to local wholesalers for filling and delivery.

manufacturer–merchant wholesaler–industrial user

The manufacturer–merchant wholesaler–industrial user marketing channel is used by many producers of industrial items such as small tools and other standard pieces of equipment. These are products of small unit value used by numerous and diverse industrial establishments. Merchant wholesalers serving the industrial market, although their operations in many ways resemble those of consumer goods wholesalers, sell directly to industrial users and are known as industrial supply houses, mill supply houses, industrial hardware distributors, or equipment distributors.

[1] Mel S. Mayes and Neil M. Whitmore, "An Appraisal of the Marketing Channel for Automobiles," *Journal of Marketing,* July 1976, pp. 39-40.

FACTORS INFLUENCING CHANNEL USAGE

the product   The product's nature, its technical characteristics, its degree of differentiation from competitive products, whether it is perishable, whether it is a staple or a nonstaple—these and other product characteristics limit the possible channel alternatives. Individually or in combination, they restrict the alternatives to those in a given line of trade, or to those containing a certain number of distribution levels, or to those where middlemen are equipped to provide technical service and repair, or to those where middlemen have specialized storage facilities (e.g., for frozen foods) or are specialists in some phase of marketing (e.g., fashion merchandising). The crucial marketing needs of a given product, of course, may be unique. For example, the marketing needs for a line of power garden tools are quite different from those for a line of imported children's clothing.

The product's characteristics also determine the length of the channel (i.e., number of distribution levels). The product's unit value sets the limit as to how short the channel can be—a unit value in the thousands of dollars indicates a short direct-sale type of channel; a unit value of a few cents (unless a large number of units make up the average sale) indicates a longer channel. Perishability of the product influences channel length—perishable items must move through short channels to get them to final buyers quickly. The product's complexity is a determinant—highly technical products requiring specialized selling and/or servicing talent move through the shortest channel available. The degree of product standardization is a factor—highly standardized items can be marketed through long and complex channels; custom-made items are best distributed direct to the user.

the market   Market factors exert powerful influences on channel usage. Customer buying habits are the most important; when customers are used to buying a particular product from a particular source, for instance, it is difficult to switch them to a different source. Market size and location are also important: If the number of final buyers is large, then the channel is likely to contain at least one layer of middlemen; if the final buyers are widely dispersed geographically, generally the product moves through a channel containing one or more layers of middlemen.

DUAL DISTRIBUTION   Certain market factors cause products to move through multiple marketing channels. In some instances, the factor is average order size—a manufacturer sells direct to a large chain organization because of its large purchases but uses wholesalers to reach smaller retailers. In other instances, the factor is that the product has both an industrial and a consumer market—a manufacturer of carburetors sells original equipment direct to automobile manufacturers but replacements through retailers to ultimate consumers.

Dual distribution involves selling through two or more marketing channels either a single brand or two brands of essentially the same product. An example of the first type of dual distribution is the practice in petroleum marketing of selling a single brand of gasoline and related products both through franchise independent outlets and through company-owned stations. An example of the second type of dual distribution is the practice of some appliance manufacturers who sell a nationally advertised brand through a network of wholesalers and retailers and an almost identical product under a private brand through a large chain or mail-order retail organization. Dual distribution enables a manufacturer to achieve deeper penetration of a market than it could obtain through a single marketing channel. However, there is a risk of alienation of channel members in either or both of the channels if they encounter strong competition from the other.

Many large manufacturers use multiple channels because of two market factors: variations in average order size and a product with both a consumer and industrial market. For instance, Figure 13-2 shows the multiple-channel system a typewriter manufacturer uses in selling direct to large users and mass retailers and through wholesalers and retailers to other industrial and consumer market segments.

the producer   Factors within the producer's own organization influence channel usage. Management's experience and ability are important—unless management is capable of setting up and controlling a direct sales force, channels including middlemen or agents are needed. Financial strength is important—short channels require a larger outlay for fixed selling expenses than do long channels. The producer's desire for control over the product's sale to end buyers also influences channel length; if, for example, management wants to ensure the product's aggressive promotion, it chooses the shortest available channel.

Figure 13-2   Multiple marketing channel system of a typewriter manufacturer

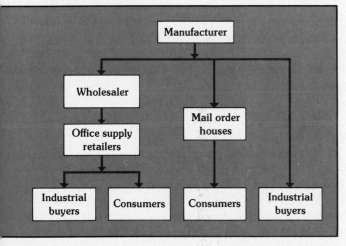

The reputation of the producer and/or its products also influences channel usage. Middlemen accept a well-known product line but hesitate to take on unknown items made by unknown companies. In other words, the better and more favorably known a manufacturer and its products are, the more freedom its management enjoys in putting together the combination of middlemen it wants.

The width of the manufacturer's product line also influences channel length. If a wide line of related products is to be sold to the same general class of buyers, a short channel is feasible. The manufacturer with a wide product line can sell directly to the retailer, or sometimes even to the consumer, and still secure orders large enough to be profitable. When the product line is narrow, by contrast, or consists of items sold to different markets, the distribution network is likely to include one or more levels of middlemen.

the middlemen   Marketing channels are often dictated by the middlemen available, their willingness to represent particular manufacturers, and the relative costs of using them. A manufacturer may be restricted in its choice of channel by the availability of particular middlemen; thus, if middlemen of the type it wants are not available or those it wants are unwilling to take on its product line, it may have to take second choices. Some middlemen may be willing to take on the manufacturer's product line but unwilling to accept its distribution policies, with respect to price, required promotional effort, and the like. Furthermore, the cost of using different middlemen relative to its own sales and profit goals influences the manufacturer's channel choice.

PRODUCERS' PROBLEMS IN CHANNEL DETERMINATION AND USAGE

Producers face several key problems both in the initial determination of marketing channels and later in using them. Those faced in making the channel decision include (1) adjusting to buyers' needs and expectations, (2) determining the best channel alternative(s), and (3) determining distribution intensity (i.e., deciding on how many middlemen should handle the product on each distribution level). Problems faced by producers later on include (1) obtaining initial channel usage, and (2) building and maintaining middlemen's cooperation.

adjusting to buyers' wants and expectations   A producer's main role in the determination of marketing channels is that of adjusting to buyers' wants and expectations on each distribution level. In consumer goods marketing, for instance, the final buyers are ultimate consumers, and they buy from those retailers who best serve their needs. This is illustrated in the early history of discount houses, when certain manufacturers of nationally advertised products refused to permit discounters to handle their lines. Nevertheless, discount houses managed to obtain these products (through "bootleg" channels) or to obtain competitive lines from producers less particular about their retail outlets. Ultimate consumers, in ever-increasing numbers, demonstrated that they preferred to buy such items from discount houses rather than from conventional retailers. Manufacturers, realizing the hopelessness of trying to keep their products out of discount houses—and the potential loss in sales volume if they succeeded—relented, many actively seeking retail representation through discount houses.

At other distribution levels, too, buyers' wants and preferences are important. Once the producer determines which kinds of retailers are most acceptable to ultimate consumers, it must find out the type of supplier from which these retailers prefer to buy the product. Retailers may customarily buy directly from manufacturers, or they may buy from merchant wholesalers, or they may buy through agents of some sort. Whatever the normal buying pattern of retailers, a producer should make its product available through the same sources. Similarly, the producer must analyze the wants and expectations of buyers at other distribution levels.

determining the best channel
alternative(s)

From the producer's standpoint, determining the best channel alternative(s) involves (1) recognizing what "best" means, and (2) comparing the various alternatives in terms of this meaning. If, as in most cases, best means most profitable, the producer estimates for each channel alternative both the sales volume potential and the costs of channel usage, and then compares the alternatives in terms of their relative contributions to long-run profit.

Certain market statistics are required for making such comparisons. The most basic relate to the potential market. The producer needs long-run estimates of market potential and from these, perhaps by applying some "target share-of-the-market percentage," its management must derive long-run estimates of the firm's sales potentials. After considering these sales potentials, together with data on the "reach" of outlets at each distribution level, management determines whether a single channel or a number of channels are needed.

Marketing cost analysis is used to determine probable costs of performing required marketing activities under each arrangement. In each channel there is implied some scheme for dividing up performance of marketing activities, apportioning some to the producer and others to different channel members. The costs of performing each activity at each distribution level and the total costs of accomplishing the entire marketing task must be estimated for each channel.

Then the two sets of estimates—sales and costs—are combined, generally in the form of a **trade-off analysis**. Figure 13-3 shows a hypothetical trade-off analysis, comparing the projected results of selling direct to retailers and using a selling agent. As indicated, channel usage costs rise with sales volume for both alternatives but at different rates. The costs of using a selling agent are mostly variable, while those incurred in selling direct (through the company's own sales force) to retailers are mostly fixed (assum-

Figure 13-3 Trade-off analysis—selling agent vs. direct sales to retailers

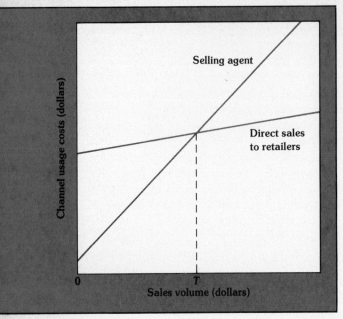

ing that sales personnel are paid mainly on a straight salary basis). Under this set of conditions, channel usage costs rise more rapidly with additional sales through the selling agent than they do through a company sales force.

Notice that at sales volume *T* (the trade-off point) channel usage costs are identical for both channels. This indicates that the selling agent is the best alternative at any sales volume lower than *T*, while the direct-to-retailer channel is the best at any sales volume higher than *T*. If the manufacturer believes that in all likelihood sales will be less than *T* (and assuming no other important considerations), then it should use the selling agent; otherwise, it should sell direct to the retailers.

determining distribution intensity   Not only must the manufacturer decide the kind of middlemen it needs on each distribution level, it must decide how many middlemen are needed on each level. If it decides to sell directly to retailers, it must choose from among many different kinds of retailers; if it decides to use wholesalers, it must choose from among the different kinds of wholesale institutions. Then it determines how many retailers of the chosen types are needed to reach the consumers it wants to reach; and, assuming that it decides to use wholesalers also, how many wholesalers of the chosen types are required to reach all the retailers it desires to use. The manufacturer decides not only the kinds of building blocks to include in its marketing channel(s), but the number of each kind.

Decisions on the number of middlemen relate to distribution intensity.

There are three general degrees of **distribution intensity**: mass, selective, and exclusive. These are arbitrary classifications since there are many intermediate gradations. Distribution intensity should be regarded as a broad band with mass distribution at one end and exclusive distribution at the other. Within this broad band, a large number of points represents different degrees of selective distribution.

EXTREMES OF DISTRIBUTION INTENSITY   The two extremes are mass and exclusive distribution. **Mass distribution** provides maximum sales exposure for a product, whereas **exclusive distribution** involves using a single middleman—a retailer, for example—in each market area. Generally, a manufacturer must use multiple channels, and frequently some rather long channels, to achieve mass distribution intensity. By contrast, a manufacturer using exclusive distribution tends not only to use a single channel but also to sell directly to the chosen outlets.

SELECTIVE DISTRIBUTION   Most manufacturers have neither complete mass distribution nor complete exclusive distribution but, rather, some form of **selective distribution**. Voluntarily or involuntarily, in pursuing a policy of selective distribution, manufacturers restrict the number of outlets at each distribution level. Voluntary restriction occurs when a manufacturer decides—in a given market area, for instance—to use not every conceivable outlet for its product but only a few desired outlets. Involuntary restriction occurs either when certain desired outlets refuse to handle a manufacturer's product or when the available outlets in a given market are fewer than the number that the manufacturer would like to have.

Sometimes the number of middlemen is limited to those that can best serve the manufacturer (i.e., that can be the most profitable). But the more modern view is that the number of outlets should be limited to those that can best serve sufficiently large numbers of ultimate buyers (i.e., not necessarily including only those outlets most profitable to the manufacturer but also other outlets, such as those situated in locations more convenient to ultimate buyers).

If skillfully implemented, selective distribution results in greater profits for each channel member. The manufacturer gains because it sells to a smaller number of accounts (thus reducing selling expenses), and at the same time it sells more to each account. The middlemen gain because fewer of their competitors handle the manufacturer's product, permitting them to attract trade that might otherwise go elsewhere.

Better merchandising practices also augment the profits of manufacturer and middleman alike. There are fewer out-of-stocks because more adequate inventories are handled. More valuable retail display space is used. At all levels there is increased desire to cooperate in coordinating promotional efforts. Even the manufacturer's small order problem disappears almost entirely.

DECIDING DISTRIBUTION INTENSITY Particularly important in deciding distribution intensity are a product's marketing characteristics. The more frequently final buyers purchase a product, the stronger the argument is for mass distribution or for an extensive form of selective distribution. The greater the gross margin is for the middlemen, the more persuasive the argument is for something closer to exclusive distribution. The amount of product service expected by final buyers may vary from none at all (a point in favor of mass distribution) to a large amount (an argument for exclusive distribution). If the useful life of a product is long, distribution should be quite selective or even exclusive. Similarly, the more searching time final buyers are willing to devote to finding a product outlet, the fewer outlets a manufacturer can afford to have.

The anticipated or actual market position of a brand also influences the decision on distribution intensity. If a brand has consumer preference, the manufacturer can use some degree of selective distribution. If a brand is so fortunate that final buyers insist on it and refuse substitutes, highly selective distribution is feasible and exclusive distribution possible.

Other factors also influence the decision on distribution intensity. A manufacturer must take into account the strength of its desire to control price at each distribution level and its relation to the size of the policing problem. Management must appraise the market risk inherent in each alternative—for example, exclusive distribution is like putting all the marketing eggs in a limited number of baskets, and in a specific market area, it is like putting all the eggs in one basket. Management must know the attitudes of distributive outlets: some actively seek and enthusiastically support exclusives, others want no part whatever of exclusives, and still others accept exclusives chiefly to deprive competitors of them. The manufacturer must compare the alternatives in relation to its advertising program—both as to probable waste circulation (i.e., appearance of its advertisements in geographic areas other than those where it contemplates having distributors) and as to problems in coordinating middlemen's promotional efforts with its own. Management's attitudes toward competition must also be considered. Someone has to decide whether it is more desirable to have competition inside or outside retail outlets and the amount of protection that should be sought from in-store competition and in-market competition.

obtaining channel usage Obtaining channel usage requires that approaches be made to individual members of the prospective channel team. The producer's proposal must be sold to the managements of channel members and, once this is done, there is need to follow through and sell the team members' sales staffs. In other words, for each channel member's organization, someone must convince both the executives and those who do the actual selling of the marketing worth of the product.

The decision each prospective channel member makes—either to accept or to reject the manufacturer's proposal—is a product selection decision. Such decisions are made at each distribution level. To put it another way, while the manufacturer thinks of the situation as that of putting together a marketing channel, each middleman (i.e., prospective channel member) thinks of it in terms of "Should I add or not add this product to my stock?" If a consumer product, for instance, is to be marketed through wholesalers and retailers, such decisions are made at three levels—wholesale, retail, and consumer. Before the consumer can decide to accept or reject the product, the retailer must have already decided to accept it; and, before the retailer can make this decision, the wholesaler must have decided to accept it. [2]

building and maintaining middlemen's cooperation   Building and maintaining middlemen's cooperation is a critical matter. When a manufacturer determines its marketing channels and obtains middlemen to assist in the distribution process, it is, in effect, casting its lot with them. If they succeed in selling the product, the manufacturer succeeds; if they fail, it fails. Middlemen make the payoff sales—unless the supply of product finally flows through to final buyers, the marketing channel becomes clogged, and all previous marketing efforts are wasted. It is important, then, for the manufacturer to recognize that middlemen are customers for the product, even though they are not final buyers. At least as much attention should go toward securing and maintaining a harmonious working relationship with the middlemen as to building a good reputation among final buyers.

Whether middlemen actively promote, simply recommend, or just handle the manufacturer's products depends largely upon their attitudes toward the manufacturer and its salespeople. If they value these associations, the manufacturer's chances of obtaining satisfactory cooperation are good. If they stock the product line merely for their customer's convenience, the manufacturer finds it more difficult to capitalize on market opportunities. Sometimes, despite the adverse attitudes of middlemen, it is possible, through heavy advertising and promotion to final buyers, to pull a product through the marketing channel. But forcing middlemen to handle a product generally involves high marketing costs—it is both less costly and more effective to win and hold middlemen's loyalty and cooperation.

Situations in which middlemen are not merely apathetic but outwardly hostile to the manufacturer and its products are serious. Many manufacturers who experience this type of difficulty have little personal contact, such as through salespeople, with their middlemen, relying instead on the pull type of advertising to final buyers. Middlemen who stock products only because the number of calls generated through advertising forces them to do so may put the product under the counter, keep it in the backroom, or provide it with the least desirable shelf or counter positions. If they handle competing

---

[2] Adel I. El Ansary and Robert A. Robicheaux, "A Theory of Channel Control: Revisited," *Journal of Marketing,* January 1974, p. 7.

brands, they may attempt to sell substitutions when their customers ask for the manufacturer's brand—this, of course, is all the more serious when the brand possesses few features differentiating it from competitors.

APPRAISAL OF MARKETING POLICIES   The manufacturer seeking to build and maintain mutually beneficial relations with its middlemen should make critical appraisals of the product, the services rendered in connection with it, and other policies followed in its marketing. The manufacturer should ascertain how well or how poorly the product matches middlemen's merchandising requirements and the extent to which it conforms to their evaluations of their customers' wants. Manufacturer-performed services, such as installation and repair, should be offered in response to recognized needs of middlemen and their customers. All of the manufacturer's distribution and promotion policies and practices must be intelligently conceived, uniformly and fairly applied, and fully understood by middlemen; otherwise, the manufacturer's marketing efforts cannot begin to approach full effectiveness.

Similarly, the manufacturer should closely examine its pricing practices. When a manufacturer uses unwise pricing, such as granting excessive discounts for large orders, its product may become a "price football" for large middlemen competing on the basis of price. This frequently happens after the product becomes well known and is in strong demand because of continued heavy advertising to final buyers. In these circumstances, smaller dealers may not even try to meet their larger competitors' resale prices, instead devoting their efforts to promoting substitutes for the manufacturer's brand. The underlying difficulty here, as in most cases of unwise pricing, is that some middlemen believe they receive inadequate compensation for handling the product. Often, the solution to problems traceable to unwise pricing is found through revising decisions on marketing channels and distribution intensity.

ANALYSIS OF COMMUNICATIONS WITH MIDDLEMEN   Lack of or insufficient personal contact of middlemen with the manufacturer often contributes to their failure to give the manufacturer their wholehearted cooperation. Particularly when the marketing channel includes several layers of middlemen, when personal selling plays little or no part in the promotional program, or both, defects are likely to exist in the manufacturer's communications system with its distributive network. Although its product, distribution, promotion, and pricing policies may all appear fundamentally sound, a manufacturer's remoteness, institutionally if not geographically, from certain middlemen and their problems may cause certain of its policies to be inappropriate for them. When competitors have closer personal relationships, such as through salespeople with these same middlemen, they may regard the manufacturer as too distant to deserve their attention or cooperation. They may continue to handle the manufacturer's product, but mainly because of its already established demand among their own customers. To improve such a situation, the manufacturer must improve its communications with its middlemen.

There are many ways to improve communications with middlemen. Sometimes drastic changes in channel policy are required—for example, a manufacturer may switch from the use of wholesalers to direct-to-retailer selling, thereby obtaining closer personal contact with retailers. Or it may be sufficient to supplement wholesalers' efforts with a force of "missionary" sales representatives. A program of occasional visits to middlemen by sales and other executives may do wonders in improving communications and in cementing relationships; similar benefits may come from company sponsorship of national or regional conventions for middlemen. Such inexpensive methods as personal letters or telephone calls from marketing executives, circulation of specially edited dealer magazines, or advertising to the trade sometimes prove effective not only in improving communications, but in building and retaining dealer cooperation.

SUMMARY

Marketing channels are the distribution networks through which direct and indirect ownership transfers are effected as products move from producers to final buyers. Except where producers deal directly with target markets, all channels represent cooperative arrangements of producers and middlemen toward the end of making products available for purchase by final buyers. In all cases, the particular channel used is influenced by factors related to the product, the market, the producer's own organization, and the middlemen—the relative influence of each factor varying with the situation.

In the determination of marketing channels, the producer's main role is that of adjusting to the wants and expectations of buyers on each distribution level. Generally, the producer regards the best channel alternative(s) as the most profitable and, consequently, must estimate and compare for all alternatives both sales potentials and channel usage costs. As management decides on the type of channel and the kinds of middlemen to use on each distribution level, it must also decide on distribution intensity, that is, determine how many middlemen should represent the manufacturer on each level.

In implementing the channel aspects of its distribution strategy, the producer faces problems both at the outset and later. In obtaining initial channel usage, it must recruit the individual members of the prospective distribution team, convincing them of the merits of its proposal. After the producer succeeds in linking its chosen middlemen together into a marketing channel, it faces problems in building and maintaining cooperative relationships with them; in resolving these problems, the producer must appraise all aspects of its overall marketing strategy and its system for communicating with the distributive network. Any producer using a marketing channel that includes middlemen needs their cooperation to achieve marketing efficiency.

You should now understand how decisions on marketing channels and their implementation fit into distribution strategy. You should know not only the main types of marketing channels but, more important, the reasons for using each type. You should know both the factors influencing channel usage and the problems producers face in determining and using channels. If you know these things, you understand the channel aspects of distribution strategy.

SUMMARY ON DISTRIBUTION

Part Four (Chapters 10 through 13) has covered the inputs and decisions that comprise distribution strategy. Figure 10-1 shows the four main elements of overall marketing strategy (product-market, promotion, distribution, and price strategies). This figure also shows a graphic representation of the various aspects of distribution strategy. Physical distribution (covered in Chapter 10) deals only incidentally with ownership transfers, focusing mainly on the physical movement of goods both through space and through time.

Marketing institutions—wholesalers and retailers—not only constitute the building blocks producers seek to link together into marketing channels, but also play important roles in implementing distribution strategy, including making critical decisions on physical distribution. In the two chapters on marketing institutions (Chapters 11 and 12) we placed particular stress on their dynamic nature. In the past 200 years the rate of institutional change has greatly accelerated. New institutions have appeared, scored great successes, and settled back as significant but not dominating features of the scene; others have gradually faded away. Traditional institutions have had to modernize their operating methods to stay in business. Many of these changes in marketing institutions and their operating characteristics represent a continuation of long-range trends; a few represent a reversal of previous trends. They have come about, in almost all cases, as the result of attempts to adjust operating methods more closely to the needs and expectations, often changing, of the market.

Chapter 13 dealt with marketing channels—the distribution networks through which direct and indirect ownership transfers are effected as products move from producers to final buyers. Major emphasis in this chapter was on the relationships of channel members to one another and to final buyers. Channel usage, as well as producers' choices of channels, is determined by diverse factors, including the products' nature, the target market(s), the producer itself (its financial strength and know-how), and the middlemen available.

The three elements of distribution strategy illustrated in Figure 10-1 are interrelated and interdependent. Marketing channel decisions and physical distribution decisions are made by marketing institutions—producers, wholesalers, and retailers. Furthermore, marketing channels assume the movement of goods, and the movement of goods assumes eventual transfers of ownership. Various combinations of these elements constitute the distribution strategy input to overall marketing strategy.

1 | Describe the several types of marketing channels available to the manufacturer.

2 | Explain the meaning and significance of each of the following statements:
a. The producer does not always enjoy complete freedom in selecting marketing channels.
b. Manufacturers make channel selection decisions, whereas middlemen make product selection decisions.
c. A manufacturer should consider the middlemen on its channel team as extensions of its own marketing organization.

3 | Analyze the relationship of sales forecasting and marketing cost analysis to the determination of marketing channels.

4 | "The longer the distribution channel, the greater the chance for mistakes and the greater the inefficiency." Agree or disagree? Why?

5 | What factors cause manufacturers to use dual marketing channels?

6 | What influence does each of the following factors have on the choice of marketing channels? (a) the product; (b) the market; (c) the manufacturer's organization; (d) the middlemen.

7 | What is the producer's main role in the determination of marketing channels? Discuss.

8 | How is trade-off analysis used in determining the best channel alternatives? Explain.

9 | Identify and explain fully the various degrees of distribution intensity. What conditions would lead a manufacturer to select each particular distribution intensity? Discuss.

10 | How should a manufacturer go about building and maintaining middlemen's cooperation? Discuss.

11 | What factors determine the extent of a manufacturer's power and influence in the channel of distribution?

12 | Which of the following are engaged in wholesaling? In retailing?
a. A manufacturer of power saws who sells to building contractors and homeowners.
b. A dairy farmer who sells to schools and restaurants.
c. A clothing manufacturer who sells through a catalog to ultimate consumers.
d. A retail sporting goods store that sells to the athletic departments of high schools and colleges.
e. A hardware wholesaler who sells to retail hardware outlets.
f. A tire manufacturer who sells through its own retail stores.
g. A furniture wholesaler who sells to homeowners.

13 | Describe the role of communication in a channel of distribution.

CASE PROBLEM

The M. L. Scott Toy Company made a wide line of games and toys and had a favorable reputation in the industry. The product line was top quality and the retail prices were higher than the industry average. Sales had increased steadily over the past several years, with the company surpassing the $120 million mark recently.

Scott games and toys were distributed by a sales force numbering 173. The products were in every conceivable type of retail outlet, as Scott had always believed in a policy of intensive distribution. The company provided extensive national advertising support, and did considerable cooperative advertising with the retail dealers.

Although sales were satisfactory, management was increasingly concerned over several developments surfacing in the last six months. In many cases, communications and instructions issued by central management were either disregarded or improperly handled. For example, the number of situations in which suggested retail prices were not used increased markedly, with Scott products often becoming loss leaders. This bothered management because the loss leader pricing was believed to damage the company's quality image.

Many salespeople reported annual difficulty in "selling" merchandising ideas and plans to dealers. And, when it appeared that the dealers were in agreement over the use of certain ideas, they failed to use them. Company policy was to use the sales force to communicate ideas, instructions, and policy changes to dealers, and in the past this had been an effective communications channel. But this smooth communication existed no longer.

M. L. Scott Toy Company prided itself on doing everything possible to maintain a solid, hard-hitting retail network, but clearly this solidarity was not what it had been. There was less evidence that a distribution "team" existed, as one Scott executive commented. Retail dealers seemed to be going their own way, independently doing their own thing. The one aspect of this team remaining was dealer participation in Scott's cooperative advertising program.

While management agreed that the lack of cooperation was not an overwhelming problem now, the fact that problems existed represented a sharp change from the past and was a source of concern. Scott wanted to nip it in the bud to prevent things from getting further out of hand. Not having had to deal with this type of problem before, Scott management was not sure where to start.

questions:

1. How does a manufacturer achieve teamwork and cooperation among members of the channel of distribution?
2. What are Scott's alternatives?
3. What action should the company take?

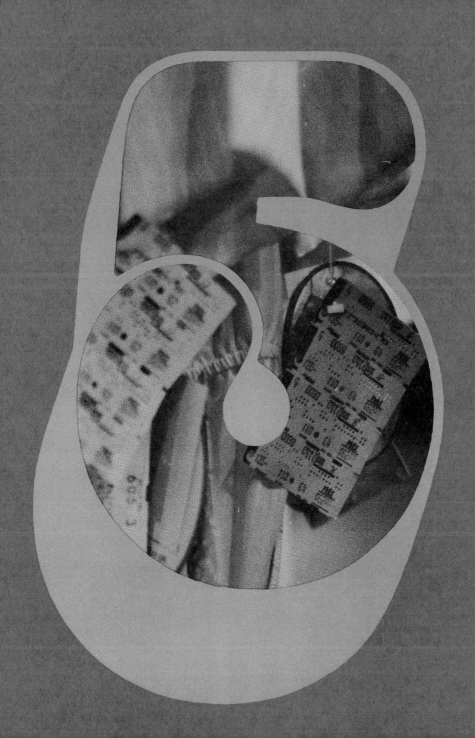

When you have mastered the contents of this chapter, you should be able to:

1   Discuss the various internal and environmental factors influencing pricing decision.
2   Calculate break-even points, given the necessary data.
3   Analyze the relationship of costs and competition to pricing decisions.
4   Identify the main types of long-run pricing objectives.
5   Explain the three policy alternatives concerning pricing relative to the competition.
6   Differentiate between full-cost pricing and contribution pricing.
7   Define the following terms: one-price policy, variable-price policy, quantity discount, trade discount, F.O.B. pricing, delivered pricing, freight absorption.
8   Describe the policy decisions involved in pricing a product line.
9   Outline the reasons why certain marketers use or do not use: (a) suggested resale prices, (b) a guaranty against price decline.

14

pricing
management

Without prices there is no marketing. Products may be matched with markets, but only when buyers and sellers agree on prices do ownership transfers occur. Either a buyer or a seller may propose a price, but it does not become one until accepted by the other.

Generally, the seller, regarding pricing as a controllable, makes the offer and the buyer decides whether to accept it. Modern marketers, except in rare instances, enjoy considerable freedom in making pricing decisions. This freedom comes from their success in manipulating other controllables (products, distribution, and promotion) so as to improve their ability to compete on a nonprice, rather than on a price, basis.[1] In other words, only when pricing is a controllable (made so by successful manipulation of other controllables) can a marketer compete on a nonprice basis. Nevertheless, in most marketing situations, pricing decisions, both individually and collectively, do influence the relative ease with which "ownership transfers" are affected. While pricing is not usually the most critical element in marketing, it is an essential element.

Discussion in this and the following chapter (all of Part Five) focuses on pricing's role as a controllable and its place in overall marketing strategy. This chapter covers (1) factors influencing pricing decisions, (2) long-run pricing objectives, and (3) price policies.

FACTORS INFLUENCING PRICING

Factors both internal and external to the firm affect the price at which a product is offered on the market. Internal factors include the interaction of the other marketing controllables (product, distribution, and promotion) and cost. The influence of the marketing controllables on pricing is analyzed in Chap-

---

[1] See J. C. Udell, "How Important Is Pricing in Competitive Strategy?" *Journal of Marketing*, January 1964, pp. 44–48.

ter 15. External factors include competitors' prices, buyer behavior, the economic climate, and governmental actions. Thus, deciding a product's price is a complex process, influenced by many variables.

costs   The extent to which costs can or should enter into pricing decisions varies, but generally there is a tendency for management to overemphasize the cost factor. One reason is that "hard" cost data are readily available to price setters, but they may only be able to guess about competitors' actions and reactions, the behavior of buyers, and changes in economic conditions. Thus, some price setters base pricing decisions entirely on cost.

Over the long run sales revenues (i.e., prices × unit volumes) must be sufficient to recover all costs, but short-run prices do not necessarily have to cover all short-run costs. Equally important, cost should not set a ceiling on price; market demand ultimately determines the "best" price.[2]

NATURE OF COST DATA   Cost figures are often not as accurate as they appear on the surface. Although costs are expressed in exact dollar amounts, their computation requires many subjective judgments. Production cost accounting involves numerous arbitrary allocations of overhead costs to arrive at unit cost. Marketing cost accounting requires even more arbitrary allocations.

Furthermore, cost data adequate for accounting purposes are often not suited for pricing decisions. Accountants work mostly with historical costs and are mainly concerned with controlling current operating costs. Pricing decisions are more related to future costs than to either present or past costs. Thus, pricing decision makers are more interested in estimated than in known costs.

Estimating production costs is particularly difficult for joint-cost products. A manufacturer making several products in the same plant, often on the same machinery, may find it impossible to allocate total costs among them except on a wholly arbitrary basis. The unreliability of the resulting cost data leads to pricing individual products according to "what the traffic will bear," using cost data only as a general guide to ensure that total sales revenue on all products is enough to cover total costs.

COST CONCEPTS   The two cost concepts most relevant to pricing decisions are fixed costs and variable costs. Fixed costs, often called "overhead costs," do not vary with the amount of sales and include salaries, rent, heat, light, depreciation, property taxes, bond interest, and the like. By contrast, variable costs vary somewhat automatically with the amount of sales and include such costs as raw materials, labor paid on a piece rate or hourly basis, salespeople's commissions, and packaging, packing, warehousing usage, and shipping.

[2] Douglas G. Brooks, "Cost-Oriented Pricing: A Realistic Solution to a Complicated Problem," *Journal of Marketing*, April 1975, pp. 72-74.

Figure 14-1 Typical break-even chart

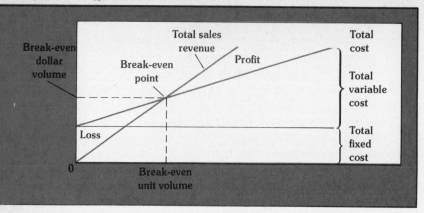

BREAK-EVEN COMPUTATIONS   Because the interrelationship of costs and sales volume determines the amount of profit (or loss), break-even analysis helps in estimating the effects of different prices on profits.[3] Figure 14-1 is a typical break-even chart. Notice that the break-even point occurs where total costs equal total sales revenue, indicating the number of units of product that must be sold at a particular price to cover total costs. If sales volume goes beyond this point, each additional unit sold brings in some profit; each sale before reaching this point is at a loss.

If we want to determine the break-even point mathematically, rather than graphically, there are three steps. First, compute total *fixed costs for the operating period* (at a predetermined volume of output) and *variable costs per unit* (calculated by dividing total variable costs by the number of units made or sold). Second, compute the **unit contribution to fixed costs** as follows:

$$\begin{array}{c} \text{Unit Contribution} \\ \text{to Fixed Costs} \end{array} = \left(\begin{array}{c} \text{Selling Price} \\ \text{per Unit} \end{array} \right) - \left(\begin{array}{c} \text{Variable Costs} \\ \text{per Unit} \end{array} \right)$$

Third, compute the **break-even point** itself—that is, the total number of units which must be sold to cover total fixed costs—as follows:

$$\begin{array}{c} \text{Break-even Point} \\ \text{(units)} \end{array} = \frac{\text{Total Fixed Costs}}{\text{Unit Contribution to Fixed Costs}}$$

Then if we multiply *break-even unit volume* by the *selling price per unit*, we determine the dollar sales volume needed to reach the break-even point.

[3] Break-even analysis is also used to evaluate the effects on profits of alternative solutions to other marketing problems. It is used, for example, to show the effects on profits of altering the amounts invested in advertising, of changing the sales compensation method, of adding a new product, or of changing a marketing channel. Break-even analysis helps in analyzing any marketing problem in which alternative solutions differ as to their impact on costs and/or sales volume.

To illustrate, suppose that a marketer has total annual fixed costs of $40,000, variable costs per unit of $1.50, and is thinking of pricing its product (assume that it has only one product) at $3.50 each. Unit contribution to fixed costs is $3.50 minus $1.50, or $2.00 per unit, and break-even unit volume is

$$\frac{\text{Total Fixed Costs}}{\text{Unit Contribution}} = \frac{\$40,000}{\$2} = 20,000 \text{ units}$$

To obtain the break-even volume in dollars, multiply break-even unit volume (20,000 units) by selling price ($3.50), which yields $70,000. To check this, add total fixed costs ($40,000) to variable costs per unit multiplied by break-even unit volume ($1.5 × 20,000, or $30,000), which means that total dollar costs are also $70,000. At the break-even point, total costs equal total sales dollars.

Suppose, now, that the marketer wants to determine the different effects on the break-even point of pricing its product at $3.00 and $4.00. At the lower $3.00 price, break-even unit volume rises to 26,666+ units; at the higher $4.00 price, break-even unit volume falls to 16,000 units. The marketer, in deciding which of the three prices to use, would estimate the potential sale volume at each price to determine which price would produce the most sales above break-even—and thus the most profit.

Thus, in using break-even analysis in pricing decisions, it is not enough to compute only the different break-even points. The effect of each alternative price on demand must be considered.[4] Furthermore, in many cases changes occur in fixed costs and unit variable costs at different output levels, requiring adjustments in break-even computations. The seller, in other words, is more interested in the sales and profits it can expect at different price levels than in break-even points as such. Prices, sales volume, and costs all have effects on profits.

competitors' prices and likely reactions

Most modern marketers seek to compete on a nonprice basis to the utmost extent by keeping their prices essentially the same as competitors' prices. In such instances, the marketer seeks to gain partial control over a market segment as, for example, through product differentiation or selective distribution. This may enable the marketer to obtain higher prices than competitors. However, when competitors' prices change, the firm must keep its own prices generally in line; otherwise, its control over the particular market segment gradually slips away.

Furthermore, in making price changes, a marketer must consider competitors' likely reactions. Will they follow a price rise? A price cut? How soon? A price change is the easiest switch in marketing strategy to copy, and

[4] D. Frank Jones, "A Survey Technique to Measure Demand Under Various Pricing Strategies," *Journal of Marketing*, July 1975, pp. 75-77.

copying can be almost instantaneous. That, perhaps, is why most marketers prefer nonprice competiton—product, distribution, and promotion changes are neither easy to copy nor can they be followed quickly. The first competitor making a profitable nonprice move gains more than a temporary advantage.

buyer psychology and behavior

The effectiveness of relative price as a factor in making sales varies with buyer psychology and behavior. Buyers shopping for high-fashion items often regard prices as of secondary importance and frequently are more interested in quality or prestige. In shopping for a dress to wear on a special occasion, for example, a woman may regard price—within limits, of course—as less important than cut or styling. Similarly, in industrial marketing, buyers of machine tools first consider such product attributes as quality and durability, price being important only in choosing among two or more comparable makes. Moreover, the relative prestige of certain products in the consumer goods field varies directly with their prices; for instance, many buyers of prestige automobiles, such as the Continental, buy mainly because others will know they paid a high price. However, low price is an important aid in selling products difficult to differentiate (e.g., sugar, gasoline, and certain industrial raw materials), and a price slightly below competitors' may produce large increases in sales volume.

The frequency with which the typical buyer purchases a product also influences pricing decisions. Products ultimate consumers buy frequently, for instance, are sold profitably by middlemen at low markups because of fast inventory turnover. When sales are high relative to inventory investment, a small profit per sale returns a large annual profit. High-turnover products, such as most grocery items, are profitably retailed at 15 to 20 percent markups, whereas slow-turnover products require higher retail markups—hardware, for instance, carries a 35 to 40 percent retail markup. The typical buyer is much more price-conscious with frequently purchased items, such as coffee. For such products, price and price promotions are particularly important strategy inputs.

The quantity of a product usually bought at one time by a typical buyer may affect offering prices. The larger the quantity bought at a time, the lower the marketing cost is per unit. For instance, it costs a retailer little more to sell six of an item than to sell one, so cost savings make possible profitable price reductions for quantity purchases. Purchases in larger quantities tend to increase the buyer's total consumption because possession of extra quantities often causes him or her to use more.

The relative bargaining power of potential buyers influences pricing decisions. A marketer of a consumer product, for instance, may be "bargained into" giving special low prices to large buyers, such as corporate chains, in order to get them to handle its product at all. Similarly, marketers of industrial products make price concessions to large customers to gain, or retain, their patronage. However, the giving in to buyers' demands for special prices is limited in the United States by legislation outlawing price discrimination among like buyers (see Chapter 19).

economic climate   Because of the stickiness of administered prices (i.e., ones set by management and held stable over time), the company emphasizing nonprice competition adjusts slowly to changing economic conditions. This causes delays in price reductions at the beginning of a recession, causes inventories to build up to abnormally high levels, and necessitates larger price cuts later. Similarly, during periods of rapidly rising costs (characteristic of business upturns), increases in administered prices lag behind the need, resulting in cost-price squeezes. Therefore, the company emphasizing nonprice competition should be alert to impending economic changes and make needed and timely price adjustments.

legislation and governmental pressures   Practically every country has legislation that influences pricing alternatives, and the marketer must be informed about those laws in each country where it sells. In the United States, for instance, at the federal level, the Clayton Act, as amended by the Robinson-Patman Act, prohibits several pricing practices that discriminate among like buyers: cumulative quantity discounts, noncumulative quantity discounts in excess of actual cost savings, "dummy" brokerage payments, and discriminatory promotional allowances. At the state level, some states have Unfair Trade Practices Acts prohibiting sales at prices below cost (or cost plus some designated markup).

The possibility that governmental pressures will be brought to bear is a factor that decision makers, particularly in basic industries where price increases might be regarded as inflationary, should consider. In industries whose members produce less basic and more differentiated products, the likelihood of governmental intervention is more remote but still possible. Governmental intervention in pricing decisions is likely to become increasingly frequent and more influential in the future, especially during inflationary periods.

PRICING OBJECTIVES   Long-run pricing objectives derive directly from company objectives. They provide guidance to decision makers in determining price policies, formulating pricing strategies, and setting actual prices. Most companies have profit as a main pricing objective, although other objectives, such as market share, a target annual rate of growth, or keeping out competition may be more important to some companies.

Occasionally, a company "charges what the traffic will bear"—this may maximize short-run profit but it is not usually the way to maximize long-run profit. Most experts suggest, in fact, that companies should refrain from maximizing short-run profits in order to maximize them in the long run. But it is impossible to prove that a short-run pricing strategy leads to maximum long-run profits. We agree with one writer who concludes, "Long-run profit maximizing is elusive and perhaps unmeasurable." [5]

Profit maximization is more an ideal than a usable pricing objective. Recognizing the elusiveness of profit maximization, realistic decision makers focus on other long-run pricing objectives related, in one way or another, to securing, if not the maximum, at least a satisfactory long-run profit.

target return pricing objectives

Many companies have pricing objectives aimed to achieve a certain target **return on investment** (ROI), a certain return on net sales, or simply some targeted dollar profit.

TARGET ROI In working toward a target ROI objective, pricing decisions are made so that anticipated total sales revenues exceed total costs by enough to provide the desired rate of return on the total investment. Since the objective is to secure the targeted return on the total investment, pricing decisions for specific products, groups of products, or company divisions need not be individually designed to produce precisely the specified ROI; rather, the objective is for the company's entire operations to earn, on the average, the specified ROI.

Additionally, "on the average" means *standard sales volume*—that is, the average sales level experienced over several years' operations. ROI pricing objectives are more common among manufacturers than middlemen and among large companies than small ones. [6]

TARGET RETURN ON SALES Numerous middlemen set their pricing objectives as a targeted return on sales, stated as some percentage of dollar sales. Then they price their inventories with sufficiently high markups so that sales revenues will cover total costs and yield a desired profit on the year's operations. Different items in the inventory carry different markups—some priced to return more than the targeted return, some less.

TARGETED DOLLAR PROFIT In many small businesses, particularly small manufacturers, the pricing objective is a targeted amount of dollar profit. Typically, such companies are managed by their owners, who simply want to earn a good living. Consequently, they set prices to return that dollar profit which represents in their minds "a good living."

price stabilization as an objective

Some companies seek to keep their prices relatively stable over long periods, hoping to smooth out, possibly even to eliminate, cyclical price fluctuations. During periods of depressed business, they work to keep prices from falling too far; during periods of good business, partially perhaps out of a sense of social responsibility, they try to keep prices from rising to "what the traffic will bear." A **price**

[5] R. A. Lynn, *Price Policies and Marketing Management* (Homewood, Ill.: Richard D. Irwin, Inc., 1967), p. 99.

[6] Michael Deakin, "Pricing for Return on Investment," *Management Accounting*, December 1975, pp. 43–44.

stabilization objective is often paired with a target ROI objective; both are typically long-run pricing objectives.

Price stabilization is also an important pricing objective in other situations. Marketers of products vulnerable to price wars, such as tires, regard price stabilization as desirable. Companies promoting their products through national advertising in which prices are featured also attach considerable importance to price stabilization.

target market share as a pricing objective

Pricing products to obtain a **target market share** is nearly as common as target ROI pricing. A dominant company in an industry may set a target-market-share pricing objective defensively—that is, to emphasize the importance of holding the market share it already has, or to restrain itself from becoming too dominant in the industry (which might increase its vulnerability to antitrust prosecution). Smaller and younger companies set target-market-share pricing objectives offensively—that is, to establish benchmarks for their growth in the industry. Some giant retailers, such as Sears, Roebuck and Safeway, also have aggressive target-market-share objectives, generally trying to increase their market share both geographically and for individual product lines.

meeting or keeping out competition as a pricing objective

In certain industries, meeting or keeping out **competition** is an important pricing objective. If a company is its industry's price leader, for instance, it may set prices designed to discourage new competitors from entering the market. Similarly, companies that are price followers set their prices to meet competitors' prices, including those of the price leader. The meeting-competition pricing objective is often used with the target market share objective—thus, a company working to retain a given target market share might have to meet competitors' price cuts in order to hold that share.

PRICE POLICIES

Price policies constitute the general framework within which management makes pricing decisions. They provide the guidelines within which management formulates and carries out pricing strategy. Although price policies should be reviewed continually, they form an important part of the company's image and should be changed only infrequently. Each company needs a "bundle" of price policies appropriate not only to company and pricing objectives but to its overall marketing situation.

pricing relative to competition

Every company adheres to some policy, either explicitly or implicitly, regarding the prices of its products relative to those of competitors. If competition is mainly on a price basis, then each company generally prices its products at the same level as its competitors. If there is nonprice competition, each marketer chooses from among the three alternatives discussed below.

MEETING COMPETITION This is the alternative usually chosen. Marketers competing on a nonprice basis meet competitors' prices, hoping thereby to minimize the use of price as a competitive weapon. A "meeting competition" price policy does not mean meeting every competitor's prices, only the prices of important competitors—important in the sense that what such competitors do in their pricing may lure customers away.

PRICING ABOVE THE COMPETITION This is a less common policy but appropriate in certain circumstances. Sometimes higher-than-average prices convey an impression of above-average product quality or prestige. Many buyers relate a product's price to its quality, especially when it is difficult to judge quality before buying. In these instances, buyers may pay a little more for an item whose higher price implies higher quality. [7]

Sometimes, too, a manufacturer suggests higher-than-average resale prices in the hope of improving middlemen's cooperation. If the manufacturer wants middlemen to exert aggressive selling and promotional efforts, it may set relatively high "list" prices at which it suggests that they resell the product to secure above-average markups. The higher markups are passed on to final buyers in the form of higher prices, but the increased cooperation of the middlemen may more than offset the sales-depressing tendency of the higher prices and may even increase total sales. Generally, for a product to compete successfully at a price above the market, it must either be so strongly differentiated that buyers believe it superior to competitive brands or middlemen must enthusiastically and heavily promote it.

PRICING UNDER THE COMPETITION Many firms price under the market. Some have lower costs because their products are of lower quality. Others substitute lower prices for the promotional efforts (which also cost money) of their competitors. Marketers following this policy must either have low costs or accept a low profit per unit of product sold.

pricing relative to costs

Every company has a policy regarding the relationships it seeks to maintain between its products' prices and the underlying costs. Long-run sales revenues must cover all long-run costs, but short-run prices do not have to cover all short-run costs. Management needs some policy to guide short-run pricing decisions toward attainment of long-run pricing objectives. There are two main alternatives.

FULL-COST PRICING Under a policy of **full-cost pricing**, no sale is made at a price lower than that covering total costs, including both variable costs

---

[7] For some excellent analyses of the price-quality relationship, see Benson P. Shapiro, "Price Reliance: Existence and Sources," *Journal of Marketing Research*, August 1973, pp. 286-294; Kent B. Monroe, "Buyers' Subjective Perceptions of Price," *Journal of Marketing Research*, February 1973, pp. 70-80; David M. Gardner, "An Experimental Investigation of the Price/Quality Relationship," *Journal of Retailing*, Fall 1970, pp. 25-41; and Zarrell V. Lambert, "Product Perception: An Important Variable in Pricing Strategy," *Journal of Marketing*, October 1970, pp. 68-71.

and an allocated share of fixed costs. The reasoning is that if prices cover short-run costs, they will also cover long-run costs. Nevertheless, rigid adherence to this policy is difficult: the price buyers are willing to pay bears little or no relationship to the seller's costs. Also, there are complex problems involved in determining real costs. Furthermore, prices on items already on hand often must be cut below full cost in order to sell at all. Such "clearance sales" are a regular and necessary business practice. While businesses should try to keep prices above short-run costs in most situations, they should permit below-cost prices when necessary. A full-cost pricing policy should be regarded only as a flexible guide to decision making.

CONTRIBUTION PRICING   A company with a **contribution pricing** policy uses full-cost pricing whenever possible but will price, under certain conditions, at any level above the relevant *incremental costs*. Suppose, for example, a seller is offered a special contract to supply a large buyer, who will not pay the going price. The buyer may argue that the price differential is justified because of savings to the seller in selling time, credit costs, handling expenses, and the like. Still, the demanded price concession may exceed the likely savings, so that total income from the proposed transaction is not enough to cover total costs. Emphasizing the short-run aspects, most economists would advise the marketer to accept the order if the resulting revenues cover all incremental costs and make a contribution to fixed costs and/or profits. After all, current sales at established prices may already be large enough to cover the fixed costs, and the proposed sale at a special price will not raise fixed costs (assuming the incremental costs are all variable costs), so this sale need not bear an allocated share of fixed costs to yield net revenue. In other words, they argue that as long as the proposed price more than covers the out-of-pocket costs of the transaction, then the excess over these costs represents profit.

Economists, however, often do not clarify all the conditions under which they make this recommendation. The major purpose of a contribution pricing policy, is to specify the conditions under which offers at prices under full cost will be considered. Two important conditions should both be present for such offers to be accepted: (1) the company has the capacity and can put it to no more profitable use, and (2) the portion of the output sold below full cost is destined for a different market segment so that specially-priced product will not undercut the existing market. Both conditions are important but the second is critical to the continuance of prices at full cost or above for the bulk of the output.

uniformity of prices to different buyers

Every marketer should have a policy outlining the conditions under which it will charge different buyers identical prices and those under which it will allow price differentials. A contribution pricing policy, as just explained, details one set of conditions under which it might charge differential prices. But the question of uniformity of offering prices arises in still other circumstances.

ONE-PRICE VS. VARIABLE-PRICE POLICY   Generally, marketers prefer to sell
on a one-price basis—that is, by asking all like buyers to pay exactly the
same price. In the United States, the one-price policy is used in selling most
consumer products and many industrial products. Elsewhere, especially in
the developing countries, sellers commonly use variable pricing even for
most consumer items.

Sellers regard the one-price policy as attractive for three reasons: (1) it
provides a uniform return from each sale, simplifying the forecasting of
profits; (2) selling costs are lower, since time is not wasted in negotiating
prices with individual customers; and (3) there is less risk of alienating
customers because of preferential prices given others.

Variable pricing, however, is common where individual sales are large.
It is hardly worth a customer's or retailer's time to bargain over the price of
a pound of coffee, and the loss of an individual sale is not important enough
to a retailer to cause it to reconsider its price. But, in buying an auto, many
a customer exerts considerable effort to obtain a lower price, and the sale is
important enough to the dealer for it to hesitate to lose a sale because of a
few dollars.

The bargaining power of individual buyers varies with the transaction
size. In the industrial market, a large buyer represents a greater potential for
future business than a small buyer so a seller may make concessions to gain
or retain the large buyer's patronage. In addition, some buyers have greater
bargaining power because of their ability to pay cash. For these reasons,
negotiated pricing (under variable price policies) exists in many industrial
markets and even in some consumer markets. Reluctant as many sellers of
consumer durables are to admit that their prices are not fixed, often they
hold to one price and negotiate on the value of "trade-ins" instead.

price differentials   Most marketers vary their prices under certain conditions even though they generally adhere to one-price
policies. Price differentials may be based on size of purchase, type of customer, or buyers' geographical locations. The marketer using these kinds of
price differentials extends them to all buyers meeting the specified requirements.

QUANTITY DISCOUNTS Granting price reductions on large purchases is
common. Through such reductions, called quantity discounts, sellers try to
increase sales by passing on to buyers part of the saving resulting from large
purchases. These can be substantial savings, for it may take little, if any,
more of a sales representative's time to sell a large order than a small one.
And the same holds for order processing, order filling, billing, and transportation costs (because quantity rates are offered by carriers).

Firms using quantity discounts in the United States must keep two
legal restrictions in mind (both included in the Clayton Act): (1) the price
reduction can be no greater than the actual savings resulting from the larger
quantity order, and (2) discounts must be made available on proportionately

equal terms to all like purchasers. Within these restrictions, quantity discounts provide a way to reduce marketing costs and increase sales volume.

TRADE DISCOUNTS   A marketer often sells the same product to different classes of buyers. A paper manufacturer, for instance, sells typing paper to wholesalers, to retail chains, and to businesses buying for their own use. Some buyers in each class buy approximately equal quantities on each order, and one might expect the manufacturer to sell at the same price. But other factors may cause the manufacturer to offer different trade discounts from the list price to each class of buyer. Assume that it makes 70 percent of its sales through wholesalers: this marketing channel is essential to its success, and it hesitates to do anything that might antagonize or threaten the existence of its wholesalers and the retailers they serve. If the manufacturer gives a corporate chain the same price that it gives wholesalers, the chain's outlets may underprice the independent retailer competitors served by the wholesalers. For this reason, some manufacturers extend lower prices to wholesalers than to retail chains regardless of the amounts purchased.

OTHER TYPES OF DISCOUNTS   Many marketers grant other types of discounts. Some give cash discounts for prompt payments by buyers. Others allow special promotional discounts to middlemen providing local advertising or other promotional support, although generally such discounts are not offered continuously but periodically, as for a few weeks during the spring and fall. Still others use seasonal discounts to persuade buyers to place their orders in advance of the normal buying season, so as to even out seasonal sales peaks.

geographical price differentials   The policy a marketer adopts with respect to "who should pay the freight" bears directly upon its price quotations to buyers in different geographical locations. In general, the farther away the customer is from the factory, the higher the freight charge is for a given size of shipment. There are three major policy alternatives: (1) "F.O.B." or "free on board" pricing, (2) delivered pricing, and (3) "freight absorption."

F.O.B. PRICING   The marketer using an F.O.B. pricing policy quotes its selling prices at the factory (or other point from which it makes sales), and buyers pay all the freight charges. Buyers in different places have different "landed costs"—each pays the price at the selling point, plus the freight from there to its location, thus determining its total costs for the delivered shipment. Not only do buyers' costs vary but resale prices of the product in different parts of the country also vary. This prevents the marketer from advertising the resale price nationally except in a general way, such as "Priced at $19.95—prices at your local dealer may vary slightly." The main attraction of F.O.B. pricing for the manufacturer is that it simplifies price quotations to those with whom it deals directly.

DELIVERED PRICING   The marketer using a **delivered pricing** policy pays all freight charges but, of course, builds them into its price quotations. In effect, it averages total freight charges for all customers and incorporates some amount, which may or may not be the exact average, into the price quoted. Prices quoted buyers are really F.O.B. destination prices—and the marketer's net return varies with the buyer's location. Delivered pricing is appropriate when freight charges account for only a small part of the product's selling price or when a marketer attempts to maintain "suggested" resale prices or to advertise them throughout its market. Standardized resale prices are most likely to be obtained when the marketer assures middlemen of uniform markups regardless of their locations.

FREIGHT ABSORPTION   Some marketers use a **freight absorption** policy to counter stiff price competition from sellers located closer to prospective buyers. This policy takes the form of quoting a price to the buyer that is the usual F.O.B. factory price plus an amount equal to that which the competitive marketer located nearest to the customer would charge. Thus, freight absorption pricing is often adopted to lessen the competitive disadvantages of F.O.B. pricing, especially where strong locally based competition is met in certain markets.

policy on price leadership   All marketers should decide whether, as a matter of policy, they will initiate or follow price changes. In some industries there are well-established patterns of **price leadership**. In basic industries, such as steel and cement, one company is the price leader and is usually the first to raise or cut prices; other industry members simply follow—or, sometimes, fail to follow with price increases, thus causing the leader to reconsider and perhaps to cancel the announced increase. Similar patterns exist in marketing such consumer products as gasoline and bakery goods, where, usually in each market area, one company serves as the price leader while others follow. Generally, price leaders have the largest market share in the industry.

Even when final buyers are not price-conscious, producers know that the middlemen handling their products are sensitive to price changes. In response to even very small price changes, up or down, they will consider switching suppliers. Thus, even the marketer of a consumer product competing on a nonprice basis must be alert to impending price changes—the important policy question is whether to initiate or simply to follow price changes. The answer depends largely upon the marketer's relative market position and the image of leadership it desires to build.

product line pricing policy   Pricing the individual members of a product line calls for certain policy decisions. The different items in a product line tend to compete with each other—that is, a buyer who wants one member of the line usually does so to the exclusion of others. One policy decision concerns the amount of **price space** that should exist between the prices of individual members of the line. Having the proper amount of price space is critical—too little may confuse buyers and too much may leave gaps into which competitors can move and make sales. Determining the proper amount of price space requires thorough knowledge of the market, of buyers' motivations, and of competitors' offerings and prices.

Other important policy decisions concern the pricing of the top (highest-priced item) and the bottom (lowest-priced item) of the line. Generally, companies try to price the in-between members of the line so that they account for the greatest sales volume, using the bottom of the line as a **traffic builder** and the top of the line as a **prestige builder**. As the traffic builder, the lowest-priced item affects the line's total sales far more than the price of any other item in the line—thus, price changes on it often have a magnifying effect on sales of other line members. As the prestige builder, a change in the price of the top of the line also influences sales of other line members.

other policy questions   SUGGESTED RESALE PRICES   Some manufacturers wish to influence the resale prices at which middlemen sell their products. This involves suggesting prices to middlemen— perhaps by printing the price on the package or through suggestions by the manufacturer's sales representatives.

Manufacturers adopt **suggested resale prices** for different reasons. One wants to establish a customary resale price for its product, a price that consumers can become familiar with, one that they can normally expect to pay; without some control, resale prices among different retailers vary considerably. Another wants to prevent its products from being used as price leaders, so it suggests resale prices to protect its dealers from the competition of price cutters. Still another suggests its products' resale prices because it believes that they bear on consumers' evaluations of the products' quality.

Most manufacturers, however, do not have suggested resale price policies. One group is not bothered by resale price differentials on their products and welcomes any pricing action by resellers that increases sales. Another group recognizes that a suggested resale price policy is difficult to administer and enforce, particularly when marketing channels are long and/or the product is mass distributed.

GUARANTY AGAINST PRICE DECLINE   Some marketers, whose products are subject to frequent price fluctuations, have policies guaranteeing the stability of the price for a specified period after the sale. Sugar refiners and coffee roasters, for instance, sometimes grant **guarantees against price declines** to their middlemen because their selling prices tend to parallel price fluctuations in the sugar and coffee commodity markets. Buyers' fears, therefore, that they are buying at the wrong time are alleviated by the manufacturer's promise to refund an amount equal to the price change on all unsold stock left in buyers' hands.

POLICY ON USING PRICING AS A PROMOTIONAL DEVICE   Some companies have formal policies concerning the extent to which they will use **pricing as a promotional device**. Many follow a policy of temporarily reducing prices for promotional purposes under certain conditions, such as in introducing a new product, or to counter the effects of competitors' increases in promotional activity. Others, as a policy matter, refrain from even temporary price reductions, relying instead upon increased advertising and other promotion.

SUMMARY   You should now know and understand the many factors influencing pricing decisions, the various pricing objectives, and the different kinds of price policies. Most marketers enjoy considerable freedom in pricing, yet in making nearly all pricing decisions management must consider numerous internal and environmental factors. Management must make certain that its pricing decisions are consistent with the company's objectives and image and, in addition, it must take into account such factors as the other strategic components of the marketing program (product-market, distribution, and promotion), costs, the competition, buyer psychology and behavior, the economic climate, and legislation and governmental pressures.

Pricing objectives derive directly from company objectives. But the general elusiveness of the profit-maximization objective forces management to set other pricing objectives related to securing, if not the maximum, at least satisfactory long-run profits. These include such objectives as achieving a target return on investment or sales, stabilizing prices, holding or obtaining a target market share, and meeting or keeping out competition.

Price policies, collectively making up the framework within which management makes pricing decisions, should be consistent with, and contribute to the achievement of, pricing and company objectives. Accordingly, marketers need price policies for such matters as company prices relative to the competition, the relationships of price to costs, uniformity of prices to different buyers, use of price differentials, price leadership (or followership), product line pricing, suggested resale prices, guaranteeing buyers against price declines, and the use of pricing as a promotional device.

1 During which stage of the product life cycle does management have the most discretion in making pricing decisions? The least discretion? To what extent is pricing a marketing controllable? Explain.

2 Why are marketers generally more reluctant to use price than promotion as a competitive weapon?

3 The problem of finding the optimum combination of product, marketing channels, promotion, and price is extremely complex. Explain how, for purposes of planning short-run operations, it is possible to go about solving this problem.

4 Distinguish among the following:

   a. Quantity discounts.
   b. Trade discounts.
   c. Cash discounts.
   d. Promotional discounts.
   e. Seasonal discounts.
   f. Market price.
   g. Administered price.
   h. One-price policy.
   i. Variable price policy.
   j. Price leader.
   k. Full-cost pricing.
   l. Contribution pricing.
   m. Price objective.
   n. Price policy.

5 Give some examples of items in a product line that "compete" with each other. What pricing problems do such items present?

6 Would you agree that manufacturers' suggested resale prices are to the disadvantage of consumers? Why or why not?

7 Explain the role of price (its importance, whether it is uncontrollable or controllable by the marketer, etc.) in the following instances:

   a. A bicycle manufacturer.
   b. A commercial photographer.
   c. An indoor ice skating rink.
   d. A newspaper publisher.
   e. A bus system.
   f. A professional baseball club.
   g. A radio producer.
   h. A children's museum.
   i. An electrical utility.
   j. An apple grower.

8 "The effectiveness of price as a factor in a product's sales varies with buyer psychology and behavior." Comment on this statement.

9 Identify and evaluate the different pricing objectives.

10 What factors determine whether a company should be a price leader or a price follower? Explain. How important is competition in a marketer's pricing strategy?

11 What is the relationship between product innovation and the degree of pricing freedom of a marketer? Give examples.

12 Evaluate the impact of legislation and governmental pressures on pricing by a manufacturer.

13 Explain how an administered price differs from a market price.

303

14   What "trade-offs" exist between price and (a) the nature of the product, (b) marketing channels, and (c) promotional strategy?

15   Why do you suppose that so many marketers rely primarily on cost rather than market factors as the basis for setting prices on their products?

16   "Despite what one might want to believe, it is competition, and competition alone, that determines a marketer's price." Comment.

CASE PROBLEM

Photo-Systems, Inc., known as PSI, had established a stable niche for itself over the past 15 years. PSI, a medium-size company in the photography field, now held a 15 percent market share for still cameras and a 10 percent market share for motion picture cameras. The product line also included projectors and photographic supplies. After years of steady growth, PSI's market share for the cameras had leveled off in the past three years.

Thomas McMurtry, marketing manager, reviewed the marketing mix in an effort to find the cause for the lack of growth. PSI's product line had been redesigned and improved each year, and every item in the line compared favorably with competing items offered by the two photography industry leaders. While PSI did not offer as many product variations as the leaders, its line covered the entire range of needs for amateur and professional photography. The PSI distribution system was considered strong, with a force of 136 salespeople calling nationwide on a variety of distributive outlets. Likewise, the promotion campaign over the past five years had been considered effective. Industry research showed that 78 percent of commercial photographers and 61 percent of amateur photographers were "familiar" with the Photo-Systems brand name.

McMurtry noted, however, that in the past two months, the two market leaders had engaged in heavy price competition and were giving higher discounts to wholesalers and large retail accounts. This change was noteworthy because little variation in pricing practices had existed in the industry. In the past, PSI set its suggested retail prices so as to meet those of the two leading firms. Now competition offered larger-than-usual trade discounts, and frequently their products were retailing for less than Photo-Systems' suggested retail prices.

The sudden emphasis on price competition by the two market leaders came as a surprise to McMurtry. He was puzzled whether or not to try to match the prices of the competition. On the one hand, he was afraid that if prices were not cut business would be lost. He believed there was brand loyalty toward Photo-Systems cameras, but he did not know how much. On the other hand, if prices to distributors were cut, he thought the cut would be reflected in lower retail prices (which he really did not want).

McMurtry did not know what the competitors were planning. He did not know whether the price cuts were permanent, or whether this was a temporary battle among the two leaders. Many uncertainties surrounded issues that McMurtry had not dealt with previously. He felt compelled to take some action soon.

questions:

1. What are the alternatives for Photo-Systems?
2. What should McMurtry do?
3. How would you describe the relative effectiveness of price competition v. nonprice competition?

When you have mastered the contents of this chapter, you should be able to:

1   Illustrate the pricing strategy of a marketer whose product has lasting distinctiveness.
2   Outline the conditions under which a marketer with a product in the market pioneering stage should use (a) price skimming, or (b) penetration pricing.
3   Contrast the pricing strategies during market growth of (a) the innovating marketer, and (b) its competitors.
4   Compare pricing strategy during the market maturity stage under conditions of (a) oligopolistic competition, and (b) monopolistic competition.
5   Explain the meaning of "run-out" strategy.
6   Discuss how price-setting procedures vary under different competitive conditions.
7   Explain cost-plus pricing, and markup pricing.
8   Demonstrate the *practical* use of break-even analysis for price setting.
9   Discuss the two main approaches to estimating demand.

15

pricing strategy

Marketers seek to attain their long-run pricing objectives through price policies and pricing strategies. Management uses price policies as general guidelines in making pricing decisions over long periods. The pricing decisions management makes to fit the changing competitive situations encountered by specific products are its **pricing strategies.** Thus, price policies are general and long-run, while pricing strategies are specific and short-run. Setting the price itself is a key element in the formulation of pricing strategy and, as the competitive situation changes with different stages in the product's life cycle, the relative freedom management has in setting prices also changes. Discussion in this chapter focuses first on pricing strategies as they relate to other marketing strategies, on price strategies under different competitive situations, and then on price-setting procedures.

INFLUENCE OF MARKETING CONTROLLABLES ON PRICE

Many factors, both internal to the company and environmental, as Figure 15-1 indicates, influence pricing decisions. Among the internal factors are the company's desired public image and the other strategic components of overall marketing strategy (product-market, distribution, and promotional strategies). The environmental factors, most of them "uncontrollables," include the competition, buyer psychology and behavior, economic climate, and legislation and governmental pressures. Interacting in complex ways, both the internal and environmental factors influence the setting of pricing objectives, the determination of price policies, and the formulation of pricing strategies.

desired public image

Pricing decisions must be consistent with the desired public image. Unwise pricing can damage, or needlessly alter, a favorable image that has taken years to build. Pricing objectives derive directly from company objectives (which, as a composite, reflect

Figure 15-1 Factors influencing pricing decisions and relationship of pricing strategy to overall marketing strategy

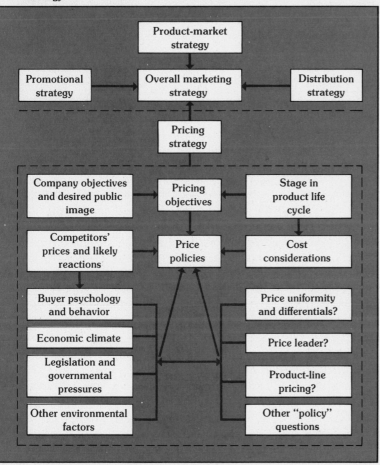

top management's vision of the kind of company it is trying to build). Similarly, price policies should be consistent with pricing objectives. And pricing strategies (i.e., the ways in which policies are implemented) should be in line with both price policies and pricing objectives.

product–market factors STAGE IN PRODUCT LIFE CYCLE The freedom management has in making pricing decisions varies with the stage in the product life cycle. During market pioneering, the innovator enjoys wide discretion ranging from setting the initial price very high to skim the market to setting it very low to achieve market penetration quickly. Competitors enter during the market growth stage, but nonprice competition prevails and, at first, individual companies (because of differentiated products) have considerable freedom in pricing. During the later phases of market growth and early phases of market maturity, different competitors see opportunities to widen the market, and price reductions become key factors in securing further market expansions. Sometime during market maturity, however, the market approaches saturation and price reductions no longer expand sales, emphasis shifts from selling to new users to making replacement sales to present users, usually through introducing new models or using other forms of product differentiation, and prices stabilize. Finally, during market decline, sporadic price reductions occur as different companies clear out stocks and discontinue the product.

PRODUCT DIFFERENTIATION   Competing on a nonprice basis depends not only on the amount of product differentiation but also on its relative importance to prospective buyers. Customers who consider product differentiation important do not ignore price completely, but they do not buy competing brands solely because of small price differences. A prospective new-car buyer with a strong preference for Chevrolet, for example, will not buy a Ford or a Plymouth because of a price difference unless it is substantial. Price is not unimportant to such buyers, and they may shop around among several Chevrolet dealers to get the best terms; but, in selecting the make, they regard product differences as more important than small price differences. The particular characteristics differentiating a brand may range from fashion and styling to quality and durability to product service. To the extent that members of target market segments regard such features and services as important, the marketing significance of price in attracting buyers is lessened and price becomes more of a controllable.

THE PRODUCT'S PRICE ELASTICITY OF DEMAND   Price elasticity—the relative sensitivity of a product's sales volume to changes in its price—varies widely among different products. Demand for fresh strawberries is price elastic, since a relatively small price change increases (or decreases) their sale considerably. Demand for coal is price inelastic, since a relatively small price change has little effect on the amount sold. These generalizations, of course, hold only within certain limits. A substantial increase in the price of coal, for instance, may cause buyers to switch to less expensive fuels or to conserve fuel.

When a product has a price inelastic demand, its marketer has little incentive to cut the price, since sales revenue per unit of product decreases more rapidly than unit sales increase. The marketer is much more tempted to raise prices, as sales revenue per unit of product increases faster than unit sales decline. However, the availability and prices of substitute products limit the profitability of any sizable price increase.

When a product's demand is price elastic, pricing decisions are no less difficult. Unless a company has no strong competitors at all (a rare situation except during market pioneering), it cannot hope to take business permanently away from competitors through a price cut, since they can quickly match or better the reduction. Price reductions in such cases are profitable to individual companies only if they expand the industry's total sales so that the increase in the quantity the industry sells more than offsets the loss of sales revenue per unit. If close substitutes exist, declines in their prices may cancel out or reduce anticipated sales increases. Price hikes are no more attractive unless competitors follow; but even if they do go along, availability and prices of substitute products limit the profitability of any sizable price increase.

OTHER PRODUCT-MARKET CHARACTERISTICS   Other characteristics of a product's market may affect pricing decisions. The size of the potential market makes a considerable difference: if a marketer can anticipate a large sales volume, it can realize substantial economies in physical distribution and promotion, thus reducing total marketing costs, and it may use an accordingly low price to improve the chances of attaining that sales volume. The relative density of the potential market (i.e., the degree of concentration of possible buyers) also affects marketing costs and, consequently, offering prices. Any factor that may change marketing costs affects pricing, since it shifts the level at which the price can be set and still be profitable.

distribution strategy   Distribution strategy influences pricing decisions. Specifically, the producer's pricing decisions must take into account the size of the gross margins that middlemen expect. Such expectations reflect individual middlemen's costs and their profit objectives as well as the scope and importance of the activities each is to perform for the manufacturer. In fact, each middleman's costs and the services it performs are related; that is, services involve costs. A wholesaler carrying an inventory and handling repairs, for instance, has higher costs and expects more gross margin than one who neither carries an inventory nor handles repairs. If the channel includes more than one level of middleman, the gross margin requirements and services performed by each level need considering.

Similarly, if the marketer follows an exclusive or highly selective distribution policy, there are implications for pricing. Companies that have such policies generally expect dealers to provide additional services, such as local advertising and product service. Dealers, in turn, expect larger margins. The manufacturer using mass distribution bears such costs himself; consequently, its dealers obtain lower gross margins on the product.

promotional strategy   Promotional strategy affects pricing decisions. If a manufacturer, for example, uses massive advertising to "pull the product through the channel," it will probably allow middlemen somewhat less than normal gross margins. If it expects them to assume some of the advertising burden, they will expect greater than normal gross margins. If the manufacturer minimizes its use of advertising and other promotion, it may then offer middlemen lower prices (and higher gross margins) to get them to provide needed promotional support.

PRICING STRATEGY AND THE
COMPETITIVE SITUATION

Pricing strategy varies with the competitive situation. At one extreme, pricing is an uncontrollable, and forces outside management's control determine prices. For example, some farm prices are determined by the relationship between available supply and market demand, as explained in classical economic theory. Lettuce growers have no need for a pricing strategy—their only pricing decision is to accept or reject the current market price. At the other extreme, in those rare cases where the marketer has a long-term monopoly, pricing is almost 100 percent a controllable. Generally, the monopolist, so economic theory indicates, sets its price to maximize profits by "charging what the traffic will bear," but, in the "real world," various external pressures prevent it from obtaining a pure monopoly-type price. Nevertheless, a monopolist's price is the purest example of an administered price—one set by management and held stable over a long period.

In the vast majority of the in-between cases, pricing is a controllable but hardly ever to the extent that it is with the monopolist in economic theory. Pricing becomes a controllable through a combination of marketing skill and luck. Most modern marketers differentiate their products, hoping to reduce the incentive prospective buyers have for choosing competitors' offerings solely on a price basis. Most use promotion in an effort to differentiate their products further in prospective buyers' minds. Similarly, they differentiate other aspects of their "total offerings" through their individualized choices of marketing channels and middlemen, physical distribution systems, and the like. Most modern marketers, in other words, manipulate the other controllables to enhance their ability to use pricing as a controllable—only when pricing is a controllable does management need to formulate pricing strategy and set specific prices.

Joel Dean identifies three kinds of competitive situations met by particular products as those where the product has (1) lasting distinctiveness, (2) perishable distinctiveness, or (3) little distinctiveness.[1] A product has "distinctiveness" to the extent that it can be sold at a price above or below those of competitors without causing changes in their prices or sales.

The relative distinctiveness of most products varies with the stage of the product life cycle. Few products have lasting distinctiveness—except for items as diamonds and ermine furs in certain market segments—if lasting means more than 10 years, and distinctiveness means that no acceptable substitutes exist.[2] Most products in the market pioneering stage have perishable distinctiveness, which gradually diminishes in the market growth and market maturity stages. This happens as competitors introduce their own versions, which become progressively closer approximations of the innovator's product, and as their overall marketing strategies come more and more to resemble that of the innovator. Products of perishable distinctiveness

[1] J. Dean, *Managerial Economics* (Englewood Cliffs, N.J.: Prentice-Hall, Inc., 1951), p. 402.
[2] Ibid., p. 403.

ultimately become products of little distinctiveness sometime during the market maturity stage and continue as such during their market decline. Since both the product's relative distinctiveness and overall marketing strategy vary with the stage of the product life cycle, so does pricing strategy.

PRICING STRATEGY FOR PRODUCTS OF LASTING DISTINCTIVENESS

Few products have lasting distinctiveness, so this type of competitive situation is rare. But when it occurs, the marketer essentially enjoys the monopolist's pricing freedom. Figure 15-2 shows the "pricing model" that economists say the monopolist should use. According to this model, the marketer of a product of lasting distinctiveness would select the price for its product by drawing a vertical line from the point of intersection of its marginal cost (MC) and marginal revenue (MR) curves to the demand curve (D). This point of intersection would determine the optimal price and quantity to be sold. The rectangle defined by points P and Q and the demand curve shows total revenue, and the shaded part of the rectangle (above the intersection of the average total cost curve with line Q) represents the profit at price P and quantity Q.

But in the real world the marketer of a product of lasting distinctiveness is not likely to use price P in an attempt to maximize its profits. Other factors cause it to choose some price lower than P: possible adverse public

Figure 15-2   Pricing a product of lasting distinctiveness to maximize profit (monopoly pricing)

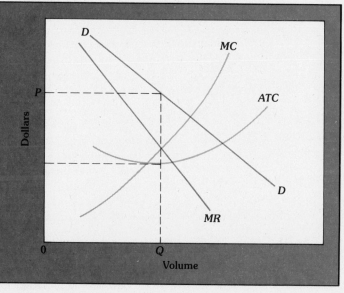

reactions to monopoly pricing, the threat of governmental intervention, and the possibility of weakening its bargaining position with organized labor. Even when a monopolist starts out with a profit-maximizing price (P), sooner or later it is almost certain to encounter outside pressures that force it to lower this price.

PRICING STRATEGY DURING MARKET PIONEERING

During market pioneering, the marketer's appropriate pricing strategy depends both upon how distinctive its new product is and how long it expects this distinctiveness to last. The more distinctive the new product is, the more freedom the marketer has in pricing it. If it is highly distinctive—that is, a revolutionary new product with no close substitutes, such as the hand-held electronic calculator when it was introduced on the market—the marketer can choose from a wide range of possible profitable prices. If it is only slightly distinctive—that is, if it represents only comparatively minor changes from existing and substitute products—the marketer's range of possible profitable prices is restricted, the most likely price being very slightly above those of the competitive substitutes. Similarly, the longer the period during which a marketer expects its new product's distinctiveness to last, the wider the range of possible profitable prices.

Most new products, however distinctive they are initially, have only a limited period free from competition. The length of this period is determined by factors such as the relative uniqueness of the product innovation, its patentability, the rate at which it gains market acceptance, and potential competitors' product development capabilities. During the market pioneering stage, the innovating marketer generally enjoys considerable pricing discretion, but rarely can it count on more than three years of freedom from competition. For most products, then, the marketer must formulate pricing strategy during the market pioneering stage on the assumption that product distinctiveness will deteriorate in a relatively short time as competitors enter the market. Such was the pricing strategy for electronic calculators. The original price of simple models was over $100. Similar models today retail for $10.

price-skimming and penetration-pricing strategies

During the market pioneering stage, the marketer has a choice between two pricing strategies—price skimming or penetration pricing. A **price-skimming** strategy uses a high introductory price to skim the "cream" of demand (as was done with electronic calculators), while a **penetration-pricing** strategy uses a low introductory price to speed up the product's widespread market acceptance. Neither of these strategies is intended to maximize profits—both aim toward achieving other short-range pricing objectives, price skimming to recoup product development costs quickly and penetration pricing to capture a certain market share before competitors enter the market.

Whether to use price skimming or penetration pricing during the product's market pioneering stage depends on its price elasticity of demand (i.e.,

Figure 15-3   Pricing products of perishable distinctiveness: skimming versus penetration strategies

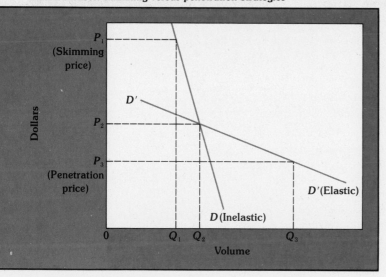

on the relative sensitivity of the product's sales to its price). Figure 15-3 shows two contrasting demand curves—*DD* for a new product with an inelastic demand and *D'D'* for one with an elastic demand. For the product with an inelastic demand, the marketer's best strategy is a skimming price (such as P_1) and to plan on selling a volume of Q_1 since the quantity that can be sold at the much lower price (P_3) is only slightly more. For the product with an elastic demand, the best strategy is a penetration price (such as P_3) and to plan on selling a volume of Q_3. An intermediate price, such as P_2, is too low a price for the product with an inelastic demand and too high for that with the elastic demand. At price P_2, in both cases a volume of Q_2 would be sold, and sales revenues would be lower than if price skimming had been used for the product with the inelastic demand and penetration pricing had been used for that with the elastic demand.

attractions of price skimming   Five factors make price skimming an attractive strategy for many marketers. First, if the product is highly distinctive, it tends to have a more price inelastic demand at first than it will have later, because advertising and personal selling generally have more influence on sales than price does during a product's market pioneering stage. Second, a high introductory price divides the market into segments according to their responsiveness to price—the skimming price taps the market segment insensitive to price, later price reductions reach more price-conscious market segments. This pricing procedure was followed in the introduction of computers, of television, and of electronic calculators; in each instance the later segments were reached with prices as low as 10 percent of original introductory prices. Third, if an introductory price is too high it is

315

easy to cut it, but if it is too low, it is difficult and awkward to raise it. Fourth, a high introductory price often generates greater *dollar* sales and profits than a low introductory price—thus, price skimming provides funds the marketer can use later in expanding sales to other market segments. Fifth, price skimming gives the innovating marketer a chance to recoup its product development expenses before competitors, whose product development expenses should be lower, enter the market.

conditions making penetration pricing appropriate

Management should consider using penetration pricing under any or all of four different conditions: (1) when the new product's demand is highly price elastic, even early in the market pioneering stage; (2) when the marketer can realize substantial manufacturing and marketing economies if it obtains a large sales volume (such economies, of course, bring down average total costs); (3) when the marketer expects strong competition soon after introducing the product—that is, when it expects the product's market pioneering stage not to last long; and (4) when there is little or no elite market for the product—that is, a market segment made up of buyers who will probably buy regardless of price.

competitors' likely reactions

The innovating marketer's single most important consideration in choosing between price skimming and penetration pricing is the relative ease and speed with which competitors can launch their own versions of the new product. For revolutionary new products with large potential markets, penetration pricing is the most appropriate strategy. This is because the existence of a large potential market is certain to attract large competitors soon after introduction of the innovation. Penetration pricing discourages prospective competitors by making the market appear less attractive (i.e., less profitable) than if the innovating marketer uses a price-skimming strategy. If the marketer expects that competitors will need considerable time and will encounter great difficulties in coming up with their own versions of the product type, then, of course, price skimming is appropriate strategy. If the marketer's new product is only slightly distinctive, then, the best choice is penetration pricing—at a price either at or slightly above those of competitive substitutes.

PRICING STRATEGY DURING MARKET GROWTH

innovating marketer's pricing strategy

During the market growth stage for a product of perishable distinctiveness, the innovating marketer's pricing strategy must increasingly take direct account of the pricing strategies of its competitors as, one by one, they enter the market. If the innovator used price skimming during the market pioneering stage, it may either switch to penetration pricing when significant competition appears or, alternatively, reduce its price in several successive steps as more competitors enter the broadening market. If the innovating marketer used penetration pricing during market pioneering, it is likely to continue that strategy during market growth. In either case, during market growth, the innovator's main pricing objective is to retain a particular market share.

pricing strategies of competitors entering during market growth stage Competitors new to the market take note of the innovator's pricing strategy, and price with the objective of gaining and holding some target market share. If the innovator has been price skimming, the first few competitors to enter the market seek to underprice the innovator slightly and, as it steps down its price, some try to time their price cuts (also in steps) so as to precede the innovator's price cuts. Competitors entering the market later during market growth use penetration pricing all along, new competitors have no choice but to do the same, though, as will be explained later, it is not necessary that all use identical penetration prices.

nonprice competition during market growth During the market growth stage, while each marketer's pricing strategy becomes increasingly dependent upon those of its competitors, nonprice competition also increases. Different competitors seek to gain advantages through promotional efforts, changing or improving the product, extending its distribution, and the like. Those that succeed in becoming leading brands often also succeed in pricing their entries at a "price above the market"—that is, they use a **premium-pricing strategy**. Those that do not succeed in becoming leading brands must generally price either at competitive levels or under the market. Each competitor in formulating its pricing strategy considers not only the nonprice components of its own overall marketing strategy but also those of its competitors. As market growth proceeds, all competitors find that both their pricing and overall marketing strategies are increasingly interlocked.

PRICING STRATEGY DURING MARKET MATURITY

During market maturity most products of perishable distinctiveness lose their distinctiveness at an increasing rate. Brands become more and more alike, and there is increasing substitution among brands. Market shares tend to stabilize and, in the contest to maintain market shares, leading brands cannot command as high a price as before. As production methods stabilize and as individual manufacturers develop excess production capacity, private-label competitors enter and secure important market shares, usually by offering private labels at under-the-market prices.

The ballpoint-pen industry provides a typical example of the changing role of price as an industry moves to market maturity. Although a very small portion of the market continued to go to a handful of distinctive, high-priced brands, the vast bulk of the market shifted to a group of barely differentiated brands with relatively low and stable prices. Private and unbranded products became important, and market shares became fairly stable.

The net effect of these developments on pricing strategy depends upon the ease of market entry and upon the number of competitors. If market entry is difficult and the number of competitors small, an oligopolistic pricing situation may develop (if it has not done so during market growth). If market entry is easy and the number of competitors large, then monopolistic competition prevails and governs individual marketers' pricing strategies.

oligopolistic pricing

For products of perishable distinctiveness, an oligopolistic pricing situation may develop either during a late phase of market growth or an early phase of market maturity. An oligopoly, by definition, is a market that has such a small number of sellers that each has a significant effect on the market price. Each, therefore, in making price changes must consider this likely effect on competitors and how they may react.

Oligopolists are reluctant to use price as a competitive element in their marketing strategy because of the shape of their demand curve. If an oligopolist raises his price unilaterally, the demand becomes highly elastic; that is, the quantity sold at the higher price is considerably less. If, however, the oligopolist's price increase is followed by the industry, the demand curve remains relatively inelastic, so that the quantity sold at the higher price is only a little less than before. Assuming that price changes are independent, and not collusive, the oligopolist must take care only to raise its prices when it is almost certain that competitors will follow suit (i.e., when the new prices reflect higher costs).

What will happen when the oligopolist cuts its prices? If the price cut is not followed by the industry, the price cutter's demand becomes highly elastic, and it gains a large increase in quantity sold. However, other oligopolists cannot afford to let this happen, and, since the number of competitors is small enough so that each firm is quickly aware of the others' actions, price cuts are immediately copied throughout the industry. Under these conditions demand remains relatively inelastic, and quantity sold only increases a little, so that dollar revenue for the industry decreases. Consequently, under oligopolistic conditions both increases and decreases in price are likely to result in decreased revenue, so all industry members tend to refrain from making price changes and turn to other marketing controllables to gain a competitive advantage.

pricing under monopolistic competition

Under monopolistic competition, market entry is easy and the number of competitors is large. According to economic theory, each competitor attempts to maximize profits by setting its price at the point where marginal revenue and marginal cost are equated. With products in the market maturity stage, demand is highly price elastic, and each firm is more concerned with its own costs as a basis for setting price than with competitors' prices. The ease of market entry makes each competitor concerned about market share, so that the range of prices narrows. Some manage to obtain premium prices provided that their brands retain some distinctiveness (and/or if they succeed in keeping various nonprice advantages gained during the market growth stage). But the amount of a marketer's price premium cannot exceed the average price by much or the marketer loses market share, as its fringe buyers switch to lower-priced substitutes. If a marketer's brand loses its distinctiveness to the extent that it becomes indistinguishable from many competing brands, the marketer may be forced to lower its price to or below the market's average.

Greater flexibility in pricing strategy is possible under monopolistic competition than under oligopolistic competition. The number of competitors is large, and a price change by any one affects each of the others only slightly. If one competitor, for example, cuts the price, it may increase its sales, while each of its competitors loses only a small amount of business. Therefore, unlike under oligopolistic competition, the chances are against a price cut's inviting instant retaliation by competitors. Nevertheless, a marketer contemplating a price cut must consider the ever-present possibility that too drastic a reduction may set off a *price war*, with the impact spreading from one company to another throughout the entire industry.

PRICING STRATEGY DURING MARKET DECLINE

A product in the market decline stage is of little or no distinctiveness. By the time this life-cycle stage is reached, the number of competitors has dwindled considerably, with only a few remaining. Why do some competitors remain? A marketer may keep such a product in its line for any of several reasons: the marketer may need it to round out its line, it may have a hard-core market that continues to insist on buying it, it may still be profitable, and so on. Marketers of products in the market decline stage generally price them competitively, hoping to secure a sales volume large enough to return a profit. But if the product has a sizable hard-core market, the marketer may even raise its price a bit, thus obtaining a slight premium price; at this point the marketer also cuts promotional costs to the bone, and thus may realize considerable profit through this run-out strategy.

PRICE-SETTING PROCEDURES

Procedures for setting prices vary with competitive conditions. At one extreme, pricing is an uncontrollable, market prices being determined by the forces of supply and demand. For some commodities, organized commodity exchanges exist and provide the mechanism that determines market prices— for example, cotton, coffee beans, raw sugar, wool, potatoes, corn, wheat, oats, soybeans, eggs, copper, and silver. For other commodities, such as tobacco and most livestock, prices result from auctions, where prospective buyers make bids and prospective sellers decide whether to accept them. For other farm commodities, such as fruits and vegetables, no formal price-making mechanism exists and buyers and sellers arrive at prices through individual negotiations. Sellers of most commodities, in other words, have very little power in setting the prices on their outputs: market prices are determined by interactions of supply and demand and vary from day to day, even from one sale to another. At the other extreme, where monopolies exist, pricing is largely a controllable, purely administered prices being set and held stable by management.

However, for *products of perishable distinctiveness*—that is, for those that go through more-or-less normal life cycles, marketers enjoy varying amounts of freedom in setting specific prices. Management has considerable price-setting freedom in the first two stages of product life cycles. This freedom diminishes if oligopolistic competition develops and an industry price leader emerges (as often happens), in which case other industry members set their prices at or near the leader's price. If monopolistic competition develops instead, an industry price leader is less likely, although most competitors set their prices close to the industry average. Sometime, then, either late in a product's market growth or during its market maturity stage, management's freedom in setting specific prices lessens—with most competitors keeping an eye on other competitors' pricing moves. During the market decline stage, the few remaining marketers tend to price competitively but an occasional one lucky enough to retain a sizable hard-core market regains some pricing freedom.

One situation in which a marketer may or may not have much pricing freedom is that involving the price-setting procedure known as **competitive bidding**. If the product is of little or no distinctiveness, then, of course, the marketer must submit a bid price that is not only close to but also under those of competitors if it wants to secure the business. However, if the product is highly unique or somehow involves an input of scarce talents (e.g., the scientific know-how that goes into the design of space exploration equipment), a particular marketer may have considerable leeway in setting its "bid price."

cost-plus pricing   Surveys show that **cost-plus pricing** is the most common price determination procedure. Cost-plus pricing involves making a cost estimate and adding a margin to cover marketing expenses and profit. Thus, a manufacturer, for example, might set the price for a new product by estimating the product's per unit total costs (at some predicted level of production and sales) and, then, adding a certain percentage to provide a gross margin (i.e., expenses + net profit). With per unit total costs of $5.00 and a 40 percent add-on markup, for instance, the manufacturer would set the new product's price at $7.00 (i.e., $5.00 + $2.00).

In using cost-plus pricing, however, manufacturers generally apply different markups to each cost component, as illustrated in Table 15–1. Cost-plus pricing applies various rules of thumb to set a price. The particular costs management considers and the percentages (or multipliers) it uses vary with its understanding of the behavior of different kinds of costs. Each company using cost-plus pricing, through experience and trial and error, derives its own rules of thumb.

TABLE 15-1   ILLUSTRATIONS OF COST-PLUS PRICING

	Product A	Product B
Labor cost/unit..................................	$ 5.00	$ 2.00
Materials cost/unit.............................	1.00	8.50
Factory overhead (at 150% of labor).........	7.50	3.00
Total cost/unit..............................	$13.50	$13.50
Markups:		
On labor (100% of cost)	$ 5.00	$ 2.00
On materials (20% of cost).................	.20	1.70
On factory overhead (10% of cost)........	.75	.30
Total markup/unit.........................	$ 5.95	$ 4.00
Price = (cost + markup)	$19.45	$17.50

	Product C	Product D
Labor cost/unit..................................	$ 5.00	$ 2.00
Materials cost/unit.............................	1.00	8.50
Total labor and materials/unit.............	$ 6.00	$10.50
Markups:		
Labor cost/unit times 5.....................	$25.00	$10.00
Materials cost/unit times 2	2.00	17.00
Total markup/unit.........................	$27.00	$27.00
Price = (labor & materials/unit + markup)	$33.00	$37.50

Users of cost-plus pricing generally regard the formula-determined price as only a starting point, since, in most cases, it needs adjusting for the competitive situation. One exception is that 100 percent cost-plus determined prices are appropriate during the market pioneering stage, especially when the product is radically new and different; this life cycle stage, as you will recall, is the only one where the innovator is free of direct competition—but the innovator must consider the probable entry of competition in setting the introductory price. During the three subsequent life-cycle stages, competitors' prices and their possible reactions are important considerations in setting prices; hence, the need for adjusting cost-plus determined prices.

markup pricing by middlemen   Markup pricing is the middleman's counterpart to the manufacturer's cost-plus pricing. In pricing an item, the middleman typically thinks of cost as the base and adds a markup (an amount believed sufficient to cover both estimated expenses and desired profit). Management applies different percentage markups to different items, depending upon, among other factors, the rate of stockturn, competition, trade custom, and the manufacturer's suggested resale prices. Each middleman, however, attempts to secure the overall average markup needed to cover both anticipated expenses and desired profit; consequently, some items receive above-average markups, others average, and still others below average. Furthermore, the middleman adjusts markup-determined prices for various reasons; for example, a book dealer who buys books at a cost of $7.50 each may first apply a 25 percent markup on the selling price to arrive at a tentative price of $10.00 each but, considering this as a psychologically bad price, the dealer adjusts the price downward to either $9.95 or $9.98 each.

IMPLICATIONS FOR THE MANUFACTURER'S PRICING   The fact that middlemen generally use markup pricing affects the way the manufacturer sets its prices. A manufacturer whose products are distributed through middlemen, *if* it wants to influence their resale prices on its products, must take their customary markups into account in its own price setting. Thus, if a manufacturer believes its product should retail at $5.00 and if the customary retail markup on this type of product is 30 percent of the retail price, it may then set the price to retailers at $3.50. If the manufacturer uses wholesalers to reach retailers and their customary markup is 10 percent, it may set its price to wholesalers at $3.15. Therefore, this manufacturer's price setting goes beyond merely setting its own prices and has strong influences on both its wholesalers' and retailers' resale prices.

using break-even analysis in pricing   In using **break-even analysis** for price setting, management goes beyond break-even computations and estimates probable sales at alternative selling prices. To illustrate, assume the date shown in Table 15-2, where a marketer has variable costs per unit of $50, total fixed costs of $20,000, and is considering four different possible selling prices: $75, $100, $130, and $150. At each price, the contribution per unit is shown in column (3), and the break-even point in column (5).

To complete the analysis, the marketer needs the additional data shown in Table 15-3. Specifically, estimates are required of the sales at each price (column 2). Then the marketer calculates total revenues (column 3)

TABLE 15-2   COMPUTATION OF BREAK-EVEN POINTS AT FOUR DIFFERENT PRICES

(1) Price/ Unit	(2) Variable Costs/Unit	(3) Contribution/Unit (1) − (2)	(4) Total Fixed Costs	(5) Break-even Point (units) (4) ÷ (3)
$ 75	$50	$ 25	$20,000	800
100	50	50	20,000	400
130	50	80	20,000	250
150	50	100	20,000	200

TABLE 15-3 ESTIMATED SALES, TOTAL REVENUES, TOTAL COSTS, AND TOTAL PROFITS AT FOUR DIFFERENT PRICES

(1) Price/ Unit	(2) Estimated Sales (units)	(3) Total Revenue (1) × (2)	(4) Total Costs*	(5) Total Profits (3) − (4)
$ 75	750	$56,250	$57,500	− $1,250
100	600	60,000	50,000	10,000
130	440	57,200	42,000	15,200
150	375	56,250	38,750	17,500

Computed from data in Table 19-2.
Total Costs = Total Fixed Costs + (Variable Cost/Unit × Estimated Sales, units).

and total costs (column 4) at those sales volumes which, in turn, makes it possible to estimate the total profits at each price (column 5).

Perhaps the greatest strength of the break-even analysis method of pricing is its dependence upon demand analysis as an element in the pricing decision, instead of depending solely upon cost. It is not uncommon to read news announcements such as: "General Motors Announces a Price Increase of 10% to Reflect Increased Costs," or "U.S. Steel Passes on Costs of New Union Contract in a 6% Price Increase." When no attempt is made to relate such higher prices to demand, the price increases may result in loss of revenue. In the GM and U.S. Steel cases, one result was that buyers turned toward alternative sources of supply—lower-priced foreign imports—which had not previously been considered by many.

ESTIMATING DEMAND Clearly, using break-even analysis together with estimates of sales at alternative prices is the ideal price-setting procedure. However, the "catch" is in "estimating how much buyers will buy at different prices," that is, in ascertaining the shape and nature of the "demand curve." Nevertheless, despite numerous difficulties, there are ways to approximate demand schedules.

There are two main approaches to estimating demand. One is to offer the product at various prices until the shape and nature of its demand curve is approximated; although these trial-and-error data may not represent the real demand curve, the marketer can use this experience in the market to arrive at a specific price, hopefully near the optimum. The other approach is to use formalized market tests to gauge demand at different prices—the marketer systematically offers the product at different prices in different markets (or at different prices at different times in the same markets) under controlled conditions. Analysis of the results of the market tests leads to a usable demand schedule. Demand schedules arrived at through properly designed market tests provide closer approximations of the real demand curve than those derived from trial-and-error market experiences.

SUMMARY   You should now, after completing Part Five, thoroughly understand pricing's role as a controllable and its place in overall marketing strategy. From Chapter 14 you gained needed knowledge of the many factors influencing pricing decisions, the various long-run objectives, and the different kinds of pricing policies. Building on this foundation, from this chapter you should have gained important perspectives on different pricing strategies, learned the conditions under which each is appropriate or necessary, and developed understanding of price-setting procedures.

Only when pricing is a controllable does management need to concern itself with formulating pricing strategy and setting specific prices. Pricing is a controllable when management succeeds in manipulating combinations of the other controllables (product, distribution, and promotion) in ways that make it so. Of the other controllables, management's manipulation of the product has the most influence in converting price from an uncontrollable to a controllable. Most modern marketers market products of perishable distinctiveness (ones that go through more-or-less normal life cycles), so formulating appropriate pricing strategy (i.e., manipulating price as a controllable) is of considerable importance. During the product's market pioneering stage, the innovating marketer may skim the market at a high price or penetrate it at a low price. During the product's market growth stage, competitors invade the market, and both they and the innovator must take direct note of each other's pricing behavior in formulating pricing strategy; thus, price skimming becomes inappropriate and each competitor tends to set prices aimed to gain or retain some target market share. During the product's market maturity stage, it loses its distinctiveness at a faster rate, both price and nonprice competition intensify, and the range of competitors' prices narrows and moves toward stability. During the product's market decline stage, most companies price competitively, but a few obtain a slight premium through successful pursuit of "run-out" strategies.

Price-setting procedures vary with competitive conditions. The more that pricing is a controllable, the greater is the marketer's freedom in setting prices. However, sole reliance on cost-plus pricing is appropriate only during the market pioneering stage of a radically new and different product (i.e., for one that has no close competitive substitutes). At other stages in the product life cycle, cost-plus pricing is used appropriately only as a starting point, because of the increasing need to consider competitor's behavior in setting prices. Markup pricing—the middleman's counterpart to the manufacturer's cost-plus pricing—affects the manufacturer's price setting if management desires to influence their resale prices on the manufacturer's products. Price-setting procedures that combine break-even analysis with demand estimation are ideal, assuming that maximizing profits is the main pricing objective.

You now have the needed understanding of the third controllable—pricing. Coupling this understanding with what you previously learned about the other three controllables—products, distribution, and promotion—you are ready to move on to Part Six: Promotion.

1   How does a pricing strategy differ from a pricing policy? Explain.

2   How does pricing a product of lasting distinctiveness differ from pricing one of perishable distinctiveness? Give examples.

3   Under what conditions is a price-penetration strategy most appropriate? A price-skimming strategy? Use examples.

4   How does pricing under an oliogopolistic situation differ from that encountered under monopolistic competition? Explain in detail.

5   Why should cost-plus pricing be regarded as only a starting point in price determination?

6   How might a management go about approximating the shape of the demand curve for a particular product? Of what significance would this be for pricing that product?

7   Fully describe the role of price in each stage of the product life cycle.

8   "Pricing decisions must be consistent with a marketer's desired public image." Comment.

9   How does a product's price elasticity of demand affect pricing strategy? Be specific.

10 What is the relationship between distribution decisions and pricing decisions? Between promotion and pricing?

11 Why is break-even analysis important in pricing?

12 What is your opinion as to the importance of price in determining the success of a product? A service? Explain your position.

13 How does pricing under an oligopolistic situation differ from that encountered under monopolistic competition?

CASE PROBLEM

Henderson Tool Company was the fourth largest manufacturer of home power tools in the United States, with annual sales over $50 million. The product line included various sizes of drills, sanders, jigsaws, and circular saws. The Henderson brand enjoyed a fine reputation for quality, durability, and precision performance. Henderson products were priced higher than most competitive lines, and this caused complaints from several retailers, who regarded the price structure as unnecessarily high.

Company management, in justifying the pricing policy, pointed out that production costs were much higher than the competition due to continuing extensive engineering efforts to improve the product line and use of the finest steel and other raw materials. In addition, Henderson offered more services to dealers, including handling complaints, advising customers on special problems and guaranteeing tools for two years against any manufacturing defects, the industry's most comprehensive warranty. A substantial advertising program backed up the dealers' efforts. The level of personal service provided to dealers by the Henderson sales force was also high. Salespeople called at least twice a month on each account. During these contacts, salespeople handled complaints, explained product quality, and offered substantial training on product uses as well as numerous merchandising suggestions. The sales force was a real company asset.

With an extensive network of regional warehouses, reorders of basic tools or replacement parts were handled quickly. Henderson also offered repair service at each warehouse. The guarantee terms were so liberal that most repairs were handled at no charge if the tool had been purchased less than two years previously.

While all these manufacturer-supplied services and high-quality standards added to total costs, management considered them essential to maintain the company's reputation. Company philosophy was to make superior-quality products and to maintain a position of "distinction" in the industry, even though market shares might have been increased with lowered prices.

Many dealers, however, believed that a much larger volume of Henderson power tools would be sold with a 10 to 15 percent cut in price, even if the lower prices resulted in lower levels of warranty protection and dealer service. Henderson management wondered if pricing policy should be reevaluated now that the product line was well known and established.

question:

1. What should Henderson Tool Company do?

When you have mastered the contents of this chapter, you should be able to:

1   Explain the relationship of overall marketing strategy to marketing communications.
2   Describe the five stages in the communications process.
3   Define the following terms: noise, feedback, source effect, promotional mix.
4   Contrast the nature and distinctive characteristics of the following forms of promotion: personal selling, advertising, point-of-purchase display, packaging, direct mail, trading stamps, premiums, sampling, and couponing.
5   Analyze the various factors influencing the "inputs" that should be incorporated in particular promotional mixes and strategies.
6   Explain the relationship of promotional objectives to the total appropriation for promotion.
7   Discuss the relationship of promotion to demand stimulation in terms of each of the three general promotional objectives.

16

promotional
strategy

Promotional strategy is the second key element in overall marketing strategy. **Product-market strategy,** the first key element, focuses upon fitting the product and its features to the target market's needs and wants. **Promotional strategy**—the subject matter of Part Six—focuses upon making the product flow through the marketing channels to the target market. Thus, promotion concerns the marketer's activities in communicating both with members of the product's target market and the middlemen to increase the chances that the planned sequence of sales (i.e., ownership transfers) takes place smoothly and efficiently.

Discussion in this chapter covers (1) the role of communications in overall marketing strategy, (2) the nature and distinctive characteristics of different forms of promotion, (3) the factors involved in blending different forms of promotion into promotional mixes and strategies, and (4) the total promotional appropriation.

OVERALL MARKETING STRATEGY AND MARKETING COMMUNICATIONS

Figure 16-1 shows the relationship between overall marketing strategy and promotion as a means of communication. Management combines the four controllables—product-market, promotion, distribution, and price strategies—into an overall marketing strategy. Establishing and maintaining communications with target market segments is the main mission assigned to promotion. Thus, promotion involves sending messages to target markets and intervening middlemen through various marketing communications media—advertising, personal selling, point-of-purchase materials, packaging, and other media, such as samples and coupons. The "messages sent" relate to various aspects of the overall marketing strategy that management feels might contribute to favorable buying responses on the parts of middlemen and members of target market segments. However, as implied in this figure, the "messages received" are not necessarily identical to the "mes-

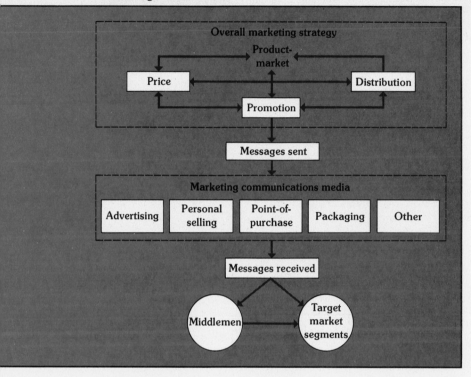

sages sent," thus emphasizing the fact that successful promotion comes
about only through effective communications! This flow of messages in a
communications mix is illustrated in Figure 16-2.

COMMUNICATIONS AND
PROMOTION

Communications requires a sender (or source), a message, and a receiver. Unless a sender's message is received by someone, no communication takes place.
And, clearly, a marketer's promotional message must be received by middlemen and/or those making up target markets, if it is to achieve its objective.

the communication process

The communication process, as Figure 16-3 shows,
consists of five stages.[1] At the first stage the source
originates the communication. In the second stage—encoding—the idea to
be communicated is translated into a language or medium of expression
suitable for transmission. During the third stage, the message carrying the
idea flows or moves from the source toward the receiver. In the fourth stage,

[1] E. Crane, *Marketing Communications* (New York: John Wiley & Sons, Inc., 1965), p.
11, builds communication around only three stages—source, message, and receiver.

Figure 16-2   The communications mix and message flows
in an integrated marketing program

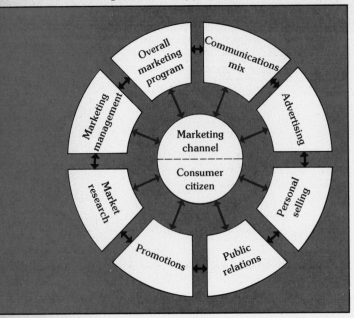

Source: Eugene J. Kelley, Marketing Planning and Competitive
Strategy (Englewood Cliffs, New Jersey: Prentice-Hall, Inc., 1972), p. 99.

decoding takes place; in other words, the message is interpreted. In the fifth
stage, the decoded message reaches the receiver, the target of the communication.

Figure 16-3 also shows two other elements affecting the communication process—noise and feedback. Noise consists of extraneous interferences
with communication, thus making it less effective. It can be actual noise,
such as the sound of an airplane interfering with a salesperson's presentation, or other kinds of interference, such as "snow" or a double image dis-
turbing a television commercial. Even a distracting remark or action by
another that interferes with the message's reception is considered noise. Any
sort of distraction vying for the receiver's attention or interfering with the
reception of the message is noise. In all communication processes, noise is
present to some degree or another.

Feedback is the other element and, normally, it is essential for effective
communication. Communication without feedback is called one-way communication, and it is rarely as effective as two-way communication. Feedback is important to the information source (the sender of the message)—to
determine the effectiveness of the communication, the source needs feedback
to tell whether the "message sent" was actually the "message received," or
whether the receiver interpreted the message entirely differently. Feedback

Figure 16-3 The communication process

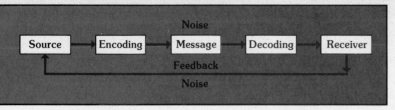

takes many forms: it might consist of a nod, an expression of interest, or a smile from the listener or reader; it might consist of a marketing research report or a returned coupon from the receiver of an advertising message. Marketing management needs effective feedback in order to identify and rectify the causes of communication breakdown. [2]

Numerous factors may interfere with effective communication. A breakdown at the message stage may mean that no communication whatever takes place. An error in encoding or decoding may mean that the message received differs from the message sent. The source might say "What a place!" intending to mean "How nice it is!" The receiver may hear it as "How dreadful it is!" A receiver's different background and way of thinking may cause him or her to interpret the message's meaning in a way not intended by the source. Therefore, for example, in oral communications, such as in salespersons' presentations or those conveyed through radio or television, semantics are important. An expression or word may convey different meanings in different parts of the country, and such differences may be even wider between nations. Words such as "closet" and "napkin" have considerably different meanings in the United States and Great Britain, differences that could prove embarrassing to the message source. Often, differences are even more marked when a message is translated into a foreign language. [3]

source effect   When communication is direct from sender to receiver, it is called one-step. When it goes through an intermediary or third party (frequently a marketing opinion leader), it is called two-step. In either case, whether the source is the sender or the intermediary, it is important to recognize the effect of the source's reputation upon the way a message is received. The audience's feeling about the message source (e.g., concerning its credibility) helps determine the message's effectiveness in persuading receivers to take some action or change an attitude. If the source is highly prestigious or credible, the message is much

[2] Claes Fornell, "Efficiency in Marketing Communication," *Marquette Business Review,* Summer 1975, pp. 80-89.

[3] For a detailed discussion of communications theory, see C. I. Hovland and L. Janis, eds., *Personality and Persuasibility* (New Haven, Conn.: Yale University Press, 1959), pp. 229-240.

more likely to influence the audience. For example, for most people an article in *Fortune Magazine* about the future role of business is more credible and, hence, more influential than the same article published in a daily newspaper. This phenomenon is known as source effect. The source may exert as strong an influence on the receiver as the message itself. The more familiar and prestigious a source is, the more it is likely to influence the receiver with its promotional message.

FORMS OF PROMOTION

Personal selling and advertising are the two best-known forms of promotion. They are also the most important forms in terms of cost and market impact. Personal selling is almost always an important part of promotional programs, and it is commonly supported by advertising. Other forms of promotion are far less important in terms of total dollars spent but often make important contributions to successful promotional programs. Individual firms, depending upon their needs, may allocate large sums to other methods of promotion and depend heavily on them for success.[4] These promotion methods include point of purchase display, packaging, and direct mail, to name the more important. Public relations, an unpaid form of promotion, is difficult to control but is frequently effective.

personal selling

The mission of personal selling is to match up specific products with specific customers on a person-to-person basis to secure ownership transfers. In other words, personal selling seeks to pair the right products with the right customers. Basically, it consists of communicating product and service features in terms of benefits and advantages to the buyer and of persuading him or her to buy the right kind and quantity of the product. Its effect is to push the product through the distribution channel.

Since most people do not like to admit that they have been "sold" anything, most ultimate consumers underestimate the influence of personal selling on their patterns of buying behavior. This is in marked contrast to the sale of industrial products where buyers generally admit that they rely heavily on sales people as sources of product information and advice. Personal selling, however, plays an important role in marketing even the most heavily advertised and promoted consumer products, such as detergents. The consumer buys detergents on a self-service basis and generally without the help of a salesclerk: however, what is often forgotten is that a considerable personal selling effort is required to persuade retailers to stock the particular detergent and to ensure it adequate display and shelf space. Ultimate consumers are not exposed directly to the detergent producer's personal selling effort; nevertheless, it plays a critical role in promotional strategy.

[4] V. Kanti Prasad and L. Winston Ring, "Measuring Sales Effects of Marketing Mix Variables and Their Interactions," *Journal of Marketing Research,* November 1976, pp. 391-396.

Personal selling is potentially both the most effective and the most costly form of promotion. Its effectiveness traces to its personal one-to-one approach. The salesperson directs his or her message to a single prospect, so it can be tailored specifically to fit that prospect's needs. The flexibility inherent in personal selling is a great advantage favoring its use. In addition, in interpersonal communication, there is maximum opportunity for feedback. When the prospect has a question about the sales representative's message, he or she can ask for clarification, and the representative then has a chance to adapt the message accordingly. Clearly, however, this personal one-to-one relationship results in a high cost per message received.

advertising   Advertising is an impersonal form of promotion and involves transmitting standard messages to large numbers of intended receivers. Its effect is to pull the product through the distribution channel by appealing directly to the product user. The advertiser has a wide choice of message media, including purely visual media, such as newspapers and magazines; purely aural media, such as radio; and combined aural and visual media, such as television. Although the same message is used, it can be targeted specifically to selected prospects through appropriate media choices. For example, an advertising message can be directed primarily to housewives by placing it on daytime television or in a homemakers' magazine, such as *Good Housekeeping.*

One noteworthy weakness of advertising is the great difficulty in obtaining accurate feedback to evaluate message effectiveness. There is no automatic feedback mechanism, as with personal selling, and the mechanisms most advertisers use for obtaining feedback are not very sophisticated or effective. In addition, advertising is relatively inflexible compared with personal selling, since the same message must be directed to large numbers of prospects (some may not even be bona fide prospects, and reaching them is wasted promotional effort).

Advertising's importance in marketing is frequently overrated. Since advertising is mainly directed toward consumers, and since the typical consumer is exposed to a large number of messages each day, many are more aware of it. Also, there is a tendency to be impressed with the importance of advertising and with its apparent costs, which might be $50,000 for a single magazine advertisement, or $100,000 for the advertising on a television program. However, while an advertising budget of $1 million a year may appear very large, companies with that kind of advertising effort often have sales forces of 500 or more each costing $20,000 per year, representing a total personal selling cost of $10 million.

Advertising costs are actually relatively low per promotional message received. A television commercial may be seen by hundreds of thousands, or even millions, of viewers, so even though the total cost seems high, the cost per message received may be only a few cents. However, because of its impersonal nature, advertising can seldom move the prospect to buying action as well as can personal selling. Generally, the role most effectively served by advertising is to acquaint prospects with the product and its strengths so that they will be more favorably disposed toward it in later buying situations. Because of advertising's low cost per message, it is highly useful for developing initial product awareness or acceptance, which makes the final selling job easier. Also important to remember is that advertising is an out-of-pocket cost; a commitment to spend $100,000 on an advertising campaign is made without any guarantee of return on the investment.

point-of-purchase display   The **point-of-purchase display** (e.g., in a retail store) is the silent salesperson that calls the prospective buyer's attention to the product and, hopefully, makes the prospect decide to buy. Some research indicates that promotion at the point of purchase is more effective than any other.[5] Retailers rely heavily on in-store displays to familiarize customers with products and their features and to allow them the opportunity to examine them. Some displays even make it possible for the customer to try out the product.

Displays vary widely, ranging from a showing of new automobiles with promotional literature and pricing information in a dealer's showroom to a display rack for candy and chewing gum beside the cash register in a super-market. The automobile showroom display makes it easy for prospective buyers to familiarize themselves with the different features of cars on display and to do so at their leisure. Display plays a similar role in the promotion of many other large, complex, and "big ticket" (i.e., expensive) items, such as home appliances, furniture, and musical instruments, and for numerous soft goods, such as clothing, piece goods, and linens and bedding. The candy display by a cash register has a different objective—that of reminding customers to buy.

Display, as a form of promotion, is not restricted to retail stores or, for that matter, to consumer products. Merchandise marts provide display booths for manufacturers or distributors to show their product lines to retailers who visit the mart to buy. Display is also an important form of promotion at trade shows and expositions, where industrial buyers are provided with opportunities to examine and test products too bulky for a salesperson to demonstrate on the prospect's own premises, before making their buying decisions.

Marketers rarely use display as their only form of promotion. Even with products sold in self-service stores, the product's ability to sell itself with the help of a point-of-purchase display depends importantly upon brand recognition, which is generally built up rather slowly through frequent exposures of prospective buyers to advertising messages over long periods. And, as mentioned previously, the manufacturer's sales representative must convince the retailer to handle the product before it can be put on display in the store. In fact, it is usually also necessary for the manufacturer's sales representative to persuade the retailer to erect the display! The situation is similar for most big ticket items such as automobiles: not many

[5] R. T. Peterson, "Experimental Analysis of Theory of Promotion at Point of Consumption," *Journal of Marketing Research,* August 1966, pp. 347–350.

people buy a car without examining it in the showroom (and in most cases even test-driving it), but few buy *solely* because of what they see and do in the showroom. Advertising is generally necessary to get the prospective car buyer sufficiently interested to visit the showroom. And, most important, it generally takes a live salesperson to clinch the sale. Display serves as a reminder of the product's existence, an opportunity to examine the product, and as a trigger for buying decisions. However, for maximum effectiveness, display must generally be used in combination with personal selling and/or advertising.

packaging   Packaging, besides serving to differentiate or protect a product, is also an important form of promotion. The package plays two critical promotional roles. First, it calls shoppers' attention to the product in retail stores, an especially critical role in self-service stores where the package and the display (if any) are the only ways the manufacturer has to communicate with shoppers. Second, it carries selling messages and other items of information that many shoppers need to make buying decisions. As mentioned earlier (in Chapter 9), the package essentially must provide product protection, ease of handling, selling ability (in the absence of a salesperson), convenience, and information.

Good package design, from a promotional standpoint, must be capable of attracting the shopper's attention away from other products and brands also competing for attention. If three competing brands are located side by side on the same retail shelf, the attention of most shoppers is drawn to the best-designed package. Good package design involves a proper blend of color, design, and type style, but the proper blend varies in different situations. For example, research has demonstrated that certain combinations of color are most effective in attracting the attention of shoppers; but, if the packages of the leading competitive brands already carry these color combinations, a particular marketer will find it advantageous to use a different combination to set its brand apart and divert attention away from the competitive packages.

direct mail   While direct-mail promotion serves much the same purpose as printed advertising, it allows greater precision in selecting target receivers. For the same cost, a single newspaper advertisement might reach 10,000 readers and direct mail only 100 prospects. But if the mailing list is compiled carefully, the 100 direct-mail messages may reach more real prospects than the newspaper advertisement.[6] For example, an art gallery with a $1 million Van Gogh painting to sell might be better off if it sent a direct-mail piece to 100 carefully screened individuals than if it advertised in *The New York Times* with its large readership. Direct mail also contrasts with most advertising in that it can be made more personalized. Even a form letter, when individually typed on an

---

[6] For an excellent example of the variety of mailing lists that may be purchased by marketers, see *Catalog of Mailing Lists* (New York: Fritz S. Hofheimer, Inc., annual).

automatic typewriter, can convey the impression of person-to-person communication. When the number of prospects is small, each can be sent an individually designed message, thus increasing the potential impact.

Direct mail, like other forms of promotion, is rarely used alone. Its main use is as a supplement to other forms of promotion. It provides an excellent way to maintain contact with customers of industrial products between sales calls. Also, like advertising, it can help develop the product awareness or acceptance that increases purchase probabilities when buyers are contacted by salespersons or see displays.

other forms of promotion   There are many other forms of promotion which, although used less frequently than those already mentioned, are effective in certain situations. Special forms of promotion are often designed to get consumers to try a new product. **Sampling** is one widely used form of special promotion. Sampling of new food products is often conducted in retail stores. Other samples of consumer products, such as detergents or personal care and grooming products, are mailed or delivered to residences. Pharmaceutical manufacturers rely heavily on sampling to doctors to make them aware of new products. **Couponing** plays a similar role in stimulating purchases of new or improved products. Coupons offering a price reduction on purchases of various brands of products are made widely available to prospective buyers, inserted as "tear-outs" in magazines or newspapers, through the mail, or by distribution in stores and other public places. **Trading stamps** provide powerful promotion in situations where it is difficult to develop strong customer store or brand preferences. **Special premiums** are used for similar reasons. For example, breakfast cereal manufacturers use premiums, usually choosing varieties that are attractive to children, their largest market segment.

The variety of forms of promotion is nearly as broad as man's ingenuity. When a special promotional need arises, it seems a new form of promotion (or a new twist on an old form) is developed to serve it. While these special forms of promotion are relatively unimportant in terms of the total promotional dollars spent by business, they play key roles in the overall marketing strategies of individual companies.

PROMOTIONAL MIXES AND STRATEGIES

Most promotional strategies use various combinations, types, and amounts of different forms of promotion—marketing professionals use the term **promotional mix** to refer to the combination, types, and amounts used by a marketer. Generally, a combination is needed, because most forms of promotion used alone are seldom effective and/or efficient. Advertising by itself, for instance, is not usually effective in actually making sales; generally, its effectiveness is increased when it is used with personal selling or display. Even personal selling, which can sometimes produce sales without the support of any other form of promotion, often proves an expensive way to make

Figure 16-4 The promotional mix, promotional strategy, and overall marketing strategy

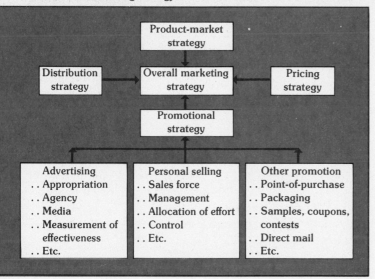

sales when it is used alone—a small expenditure for advertising to pave the way for the salesperson may enormously increase sales productivity and thus reduce the selling cost per sales dollar.

Figure 16-4 shows the relationship of the promotional mix, promotional strategy, and overall marketing strategy. Various combinations, types, and amounts of personal selling, advertising, and other forms of promotion are brought together into a promotional mix that becomes the promotional strategy. For each component of the promotional mix—personal selling, advertising, and so forth—management sets objectives, determines policies, and formulates strategies. These individual strategies are blended together into the promotional strategy, which, in turn, is blended with product-market, distribution, and pricing strategies into an overall marketing strategy.

Thus, in blending the various forms of promotion into a promotional mix and strategy, management's task is to determine the forms most effective for achieving the promotional objectives and optimize the expenditure on each.[7] There is no ideal promotional mix that fits all marketing situations. Various factors influence the promotional inputs that should be incorporated in a particular promotional mix and strategy, but the most critical are the other components of overall marketing strategy (product-market, distribution, and pricing strategies) and the relative costs of different forms of promotion.

[7] For a good discussion of the various stages in promotional planning and strategy, see J. F. Engel, H. G. Wales, and M. R. Warshaw, *Promotional Strategy* (Homewood, Ill.: Richard D. Irwin, Inc., 1975), pp. 35–38.

product–market factors   NATURE OF THE PRODUCT   Different products require different promotional mixes. Staple branded
convenience items, such as many grocery and drug products, are best promoted primarily through mass consumer advertising, combined with good
display at the retail level. The needed display space is obtained by using
personal selling to persuade dealers and providing them with display materials of proven effectiveness. By contrast, impulse convenience items, such as
gift boxes of candy, are most effectively promoted through heavy emphasis
on personal selling aimed to persuade dealers to display the product where
shoppers will see and buy it. Specialty goods require major emphasis on
advertising (to persuade final buyers to shop or look for the product)
blended with personal selling (to persuade dealers to stock and push the
product). Many industrial products—particularly those of high unit value,
such as machine tools—require an entirely different promotional mix, composed almost entirely of personal selling with perhaps some advertising or
direct mail or display at industrial expositions to locate customers or pave
the way for the salesperson. [8]

PRODUCT COMPLEXITY   Products of a complex and technical nature are
more dependent upon personal selling than are simple, standardized products. A manufacturer of road graders sends highly trained sales representatives to confer with road contractors and governmental buyers, explaining
the machine's unique advantages and how it pays for itself in increased
productivity. They must prove the machine's capabilities to each buyer's
satisfaction. For such products, an actual demonstration is an integral part
of the sales presentation. By contrast, a razor blade manufacturer relies far
less on personal selling, concentrating instead on advertising to consumers to
develop brand recognition and/or preference. The razor blade manufacturer
supports this advertising effort with point-of-purchase displays to remind the
consumer to buy, but relies upon personal selling to persuade dealers to
stock the product.

BRAND DIFFERENTIATION   The degree to which a marketer's brand is differentiated from competitors' brands affects the promotional mix. Individual
brands of bread and sugar have little to differentiate them, and their promotion emphasizes personal selling to get the product stocked in as many retail
outlets as possible and to secure maximum shelf space display. With clearly
differentiable products, such as cosmetics and sporting goods, advertising
aimed at preselling consumers is a major element in the promotional mix.

PURCHASE FREQUENCY   How often final buyers buy the product is an important factor influencing the promotional mix. When final buyers buy a

---

[8] Theodore Levitt argues persuasively that it pays an industrial products marketer to be
favorably well known (through advertising and direct mail) when the salesperson attempts to
make the sale. See his "Communications and Industrial Selling," *Journal of Marketing*, April
1967, p. 21.

product frequently, as consumers buy soap or as industrial buyers purchase typing paper, the marketer is justified in investing a considerable sum in advertising to develop brand recognition or preference and a generally favorable predisposition toward the product. But, when final buyers buy a product only infrequently, as consumers do in buying garden tools, it is difficult to justify the expense of preselling through advertising or direct mail to final buyers. Instead, the emphasis in the promotional strategy for such products is on using personal selling to persuade the proper outlets to stock the product and to push it over competitive brands.

NATURE OF MARKET   Different markets require different promotional mixes and strategies. Most marked, of course, is the contrast between industrial and consumer markets. Advertising plays more of an informative and less of a persuasive role for industrial buyers than for consumer buyers, while, by contrast, personal selling reverses the emphasis on these two roles in cultivating the two types of markets. Thus, advertising's and personal selling's places in the promotional mix depend on the market to which each is directed. Other differences among final buyers in consumer markets—such as those of sex, income, age, education, religion, and place of residence—also influence the promotional mix most appropriate for selling a particular product. Similarly, other differences among final buyers in industrial markets—such as relative size, bargaining power, and buying responsibility—influence the type of promotional mix most appropriate for selling given industrial products.

STAGE IN THE PRODUCT LIFE CYCLE   The promotional mix varies with the stage in the product's life cycle.[9] Promotional mixes vary during the different life-cycle stages, because different kinds of people buy the product during each stage. During a new product's market pioneering stage, the first buyers (i.e., the innovators) differ considerably in their needs for information from those who first buy the product during its market maturity stage. Generally, innovators want to learn more about the product and its features because they must make fairly independent judgments. Thus, they require more personal selling than members of the early and late majorities (who buy at various times during the product's market growth and market maturity life cycle stages), who are for the most part merely following the crowd. Early adopters, who buy a new product later than the innovators, are more skeptical and also rather more demanding in their requirements for product information than even the innovators; generally, they seek this information both from the marketer's advertising and the dealer's personal selling.

The promotion for a mature product generally is directed toward reminding existing customers of its nature and value, while the promotion for a radically different new product usually aims at providing the early buyers with the information they need to make buying decisions. Different promotional mixes vary in their effectiveness in attaining these two quite different promotional objectives.

[9] The product life cycle is discussed in detail in Chapter 8.

MARKET PENETRATION   The relative degree of the product's market penetration influences the promotional mix and strategy. When a brand has significant *market penetration*—that is, when it is already well known to final buyers and middlemen and has a substantial market share—a **sustaining promotional** strategy is appropriate (i.e., one aimed at sustaining this market position). Such a brand already benefits from the special treatment of retailers and other middlemen who are anxious to stock and push easily marketed best sellers. Consequently, the promotional mix for a brand with significant market penetration contains a large proportion of advertising.

When a brand has insignificant market penetration—that is, when it is still struggling for recognition from final buyers and middlemen and has a small market share—a **developmental promotional strategy** is appropriate (i.e., one aimed at improving the brand's market position). Many middlemen are reluctant to stock or push the less popular or new brand because they assume that the risk of not reselling it at a profit is high. Similarly, final buyers, having never heard of or knowing little about the brand, hesitate to buy it even when they find an outlet stocking it. Thus, the promotional mix for a brand with insignificant market penetration requires emphasis on both personal selling, or **push strategy** (to get dealers to stock and push the brand) and advertising, or a **pull strategy** (to get final buyers to ask their dealers to handle the brand or to convince them to go out and buy). [10]

However, even the marketer of a product that has significant market penetration often must use a developmental promotional strategy in cultivating certain markets. Many, perhaps even most, established, successful products have uneven patterns of market penetration in different areas. In those where the brand has deep penetration, sustaining promotion is appropriate; in those where there is shallow penetration, developmental promotion is required.

MARKET SIZE AND LOCATION   Variations in the size of the product's market influence the promotional mix and strategy. For example, a narrow market (in terms of numbers of potential buyers), such as that for shoe manufacturing machinery, is reached effectively through direct mail, whereas a broad market, such as that for cigarettes, is reached effectively through mass advertising. Location of the market is important—different promotional mixes and strategies, for instance, are required for markets concentrated in urban areas and for those widely dispersed in rural areas.

CHARACTERISTICS OF PROSPECTIVE BUYERS   Strongly influencing the promotional mix and strategy are the characteristics of prospective buyers. Experienced professional buyers, such as industrial purchasing agents, are most receptive to promotional messages individually tailored to their specific needs, such as those delivered through salespeople. By contrast, many an

[10] R. G. Hamermesh, M. J. Anderson, Jr., and J. E. Harris, "Strategies for Low Market Share Businesses," *Harvard Business Review,* May-June 1978, p. 98.

inexperienced young housewife is most receptive to impersonal appeals delivered through advertising media which cause her to feel she is following the leads of older, more experienced women. Other characteristics of prospective buyers—such as the relative importance the buyer attaches to the purchase, the amount of time the buyer has available for shopping or searching for the product, and the influence of friends, relatives, and associates—all similarly affect the promotional mix and strategy.

distribution strategy The product's relative degree of market penetration, as noted earlier, has important implications for the promotional mix and strategy. Companies fighting to gain market position for their brands need to invest heavily in both personal selling and advertising to get middlemen to stock and push the product and in many situations to get final buyers to pull the product through the marketing channel.

Those companies with already established market positions for their brands have little need to invest in promotion to keep their current distribution intensity, as dealers are quite willing to continue stocking brands that sell themselves. But, still, such dealers must be reminded to buy by the marketer's sales representatives. Otherwise, they carry insufficient stocks and may be out of stock when consumers come in to buy the product.

The product's marketing channels influence its promotional mix and strategy. If the product is sold directly to the user or consumer, major reliance is placed on personal selling, and advertising is cast in a supporting role. For products sold through longer channels (i.e., those including one or more levels of middlemen), the marketer places less reliance on personal selling by its own sales force and more reliance on its advertising to final buyers and on distributors' and/or dealers' selling efforts. For consumer products sold through channels containing self-service retail outlets, advertising to final buyers is important, effective promotional packaging essential, and effective display critical.

pricing strategy Pricing strategy influences the promotional mix and strategy, both with respect to the brand's price compared to those of competitive brands and the markups allowed middlemen. If the brand is priced higher than the competition, considerable personal selling is needed to get middlemen to stock and push the brand; likewise, heavy advertising to final buyers is required to help the middlemen sell the brand and to get final buyers to buy it. If the brand is mainly sold on the basis of low price, then little promotion is used, except perhaps for some personal selling (to keep dealers handling the brand) and for a little advertising (to publicize the brand's low price and remind final buyers to keep on buying it). Similarly, if the marketer allows middlemen markups on the brand higher than those they obtain on competitive brands, it can often get them to push the brand and may need little consumer or trade advertising. By contrast, if markups on the brand are lower than on competitive brands, the marketer must use heavy advertising to final buyers in order "to force" the middlemen to handle its brand and must use considerable personal selling to retain its present dealers and secure new ones.

relative costs of different forms of promotion   Different forms of promotion vary widely in the cost per message delivered. To make efficient use of limited promotional funds, the advertiser must analyze these cost differences. More important than the cost per message delivered per se is the cost per message delivered to *real prospects*. For example, if certain advertising media, such as television or magazines, provide a low cost per message delivered to their total audiences; but if the proportion of their audiences made up of prospective buyers is very small, they are actually expensive forms of promotion. Direct mail, with a higher cost per message than advertising, may actually be less expensive, because, if the mailing list is a good one, each message is delivered to a real prospect.

Ideally, the marketer should optimize the combination of cost per message received and the productivity of the form of promotion. For example, it may cost $50 to $75 for each sales call made on prospects, while it may cost only a few cents per message for an advertisement to reach the same prospects. However, the ad alone may result in few if any sales, while the sales calls result in some sales. A combination of these two methods of promotion with the low-productive but low-cost advertising message preceding the highly productive but high-cost sales call will further increase the potential productivity of each sales call while also reducing the total cost of making each sale.

THE PROMOTIONAL APPROPRIATION

The amount of the total appropriation for promotion depends directly upon the marketer's promotional objectives. The costs of reaching promotional objectives, in turn, depend upon the marketer's choice of particular forms of promotion and the costs of using each form in the required intensities. The marketer should work out the appropriations for personal selling, advertising, and other forms of promotion in conjunction with each other. If the marketer has arrived at an optimum promotional mix and strategy, it should be easy to determine the amounts of the appropriations for the different forms of promotion in the mix.

To clarify this, consider the steps the marketer has to go through—first, in arriving at an optimum promotional mix, management sets the objectives it expects each form of promotion to achieve; the next step is to determine what activities have to be performed (and in what volume) in order to attain the objectives set for each form of promotion; then management estimates how much it will cost to perform the required volume of activities, thus determining the amount of the appropriation for each form of promotion. Note the really important point here—the marketer can determine the optimum promotional appropriation only if it has found the optimum promotional mix, which, of course, requires considerable planning.

PROMOTION AND DEMAND STIMULATION

Often, one hears the criticism that because promotion creates or stimulates demand, it makes people do what they might not otherwise do or what they do not really want to do. The implication is that promotion has some coercive control over people. While some marketers may wish they had such control, none of them actually do. When people buy items that are needlessly extravagant or frivolous, it is convenient to find a scapegoat—the marketer—to explain away such behavior, since it does not fit into stereotypes of "economic man."

Promotion cannot and does not make people do what they do not want to do, but it does stimulate demand by relating products to prospective buyers' latent needs and wants. Demand is stimulated through promotion aimed at achieving any or all of three rather general **promotional objectives:** (1) to **inform** prospective buyers about the existence of a product and its need- and want-satisfying capabilities, (2) to **remind** present and former users of the product's continuing existence and its various roles in consumption, and (3) to **persuade** prospective buyers that the product's need- and want-satisfying capabilities make it worth buying. Clearly, persuading prospects to buy is the most ambitious of the three objectives, and generally the most difficult and expensive to achieve.

SUMMARY

If you understand the material in this chapter, you have gained numerous important insights on promotion as a key element in overall marketing strategy. You should know how promotion, as a communications process, plays various roles in overall marketing strategy. You should know and understand the nature and distinctive characteristics of the various forms of promotion—personal selling, advertising, point-of-purchase display, packaging, direct mail, and other forms—that comprise the communications media through which the marketer seeks to achieve promotional objectives. (The two generally most important forms of promotion—personal selling and advertising—only briefly discussed in this chapter are covered in detail in the next two chapters.) You should know the significance of the several factors that influence the marketer in choosing and blending the different forms of promotion into promotional mixes and strategies, including those factors involved in other components of overall marketing strategy (product-market, distribution, and pricing strategies) and the relative costs of different forms of promotion. You should also know why the marketer should develop appropriations for each of the forms of promotion more or less simultaneously, and why executives can determine the optimum promotional appropriation only if they have found the optimum promotional mix. If you have gained these insights and understand the reasoning that lies behind them, you have a good understanding of the various roles that promotion can play in overall marketing strategy. You are ready to proceed to Chapters 17 (Personal Selling) and 18 (Advertising) to gain additional insights on planning and managing these two important forms of promotion.

1 Promotion is described as a process of communication between seller and buyer. In what ways significant to marketing does this process differ for personal selling and advertising?

2 Evaluate the various promotion methods with respect to the importance of feedback and the ease or difficulty of achieving it.

3 Does the concept of "noise" have particular relevance in the application of communications theory to promotional strategy?

4 Differentiate between a "push" strategy and a "pull" strategy. When is each appropriate? Use examples.

5 What is the difference between a sustaining promotional strategy and a developmental promotional strategy? When is each appropriate? Give examples.

6 Name and describe three important objectives of promotion, with respect to demand stimulation.

7 Evaluate this statement: "The larger the promotional budget is, the greater the economic waste is to society."

8 Describe the type of promotional campaign that would probably be most appropriate and effective for each of the following: dandruff shampoo, dehumidifiers, white dinner wine, a new indoor tennis facility, automobile wax.

9 Describe the relationship among promotional mix, promotional strategy, overall marketing strategy.

10 How do a marketer's promotional objectives influence the promotional appropriation?

11 "The money spent on promotion would be better spent on developing a better product." Agree or disagree? Why?

12 Why is it that promotional activities are the most criticized marketing activities? Explain.

13 Explain how a golf club manufacturer might adjust its promotional mix to each of the four stages in the product life cycle. How about a cookware manufacturer? A furniture maker?

14 Explain the importance of source effect.

15 Why is it that most marketers use a combination of promotional forms and methods?

16 How does the nature of the product (and its complexity) affect the promotional mix?

CASE PROBLEM

Lockwood Enterprises had built a reputation for turning out fine-quality marine equipment and supplies. Until recently, the company's Marinecraft line had included various sizes of small open boats, up to 18 feet in length, designed as fishing and runabout craft, and five sizes of outboard motors (from 5 to 25 horsepower). The outboard motors were fast becoming market leaders, largely on the basis of their reputation for high-quality and dependable service. Capitalizing on its reputation, Lockwood expanded its offerings two years ago and began making power lawn mowers under a new brand name—Powercraft. Backed by considerable advertising, the lawn mowers received favorable publicity in newspaper lawn and garden sections and were an immediate success. Inspired by the market's acceptance of the lawn mowers and continued good Marinecraft sales, John Lockwood, company president, believed the time was ripe to add a deluxe line of sport fishing boats with built-in motors.

The initial investment in planning and engineering the sport fishing line was large, but the actual time (nine months) required was comparatively short because of Lockwood Enterprises' expertise. The boats ranged in size from 18 to 35 feet and carried the Marinecraft name. Lockwood believed that the new boat line would gain approval within the first year from serious boating enthusiasts and fishermen. Most such people knew about Marinecraft's superior performance record. Lockwood felt that the marketing effort's major challenge would be to reach the select group of boatmen who were regarded as the best potential customers.

The existing line of small outboard motor boats was advertised in a broad range of sporting and boating publications, in addition to numerous general magazines. However, this advertising had not, in Lockwood's opinion, generated enough additional sales in the past to justify the large investment. Yet, he was reluctant to decrease the advertising. He was convinced that a highly trained sales force and favorable word-of-mouth publicity among boatmen, in addition to superior displays at boating shows, were the major factors in the market growth for the established Marinecraft line.

For the more expensive and specialized inboard line, however, Lockwood believed that a good dealer sales training program would be of key importance. Marinecraft, he believed, should not forego advertising for the new line, but he wanted to focus it more sharply on potential buyers. After all, the new line was not meant for everybody.

Lockwood felt more coverage per advertising dollar would result from putting most of the budget into dealer cooperative advertising. The company had not used cooperative advertising previously and management had no idea about dealers' attitudes toward it. Lockwood was also mulling over the possibility of a consumer contest with a first prize of the top sport-fishing boat of the new line. If successful, the contest would induce potential customers to visit dealers' showrooms during the first six weeks after the product launching. Once in a showroom, a potential customer could examine the fine quality of the Marinecraft line, consult with a salesperson, and pick up an informative brochure. So many things could be done that Lockwood wanted to make sure the new line's promotion was not merely a carbon copy of what had been done in the past.

With the heavy investment in the new product line, Lockwood Enterprises needed an effective promotional strategy. The key to the best promotional program, Lockwood believed, was getting the right promotional mix focused as accurately as possible on the most promising potential customers. Despite previous successes, Lockwood was groping for ideas that would enable the company to achieve its high expectations for the new Marinecraft sport-fishing-boat line. He was uncertain about the types of promotion to use and the amount of emphasis to place upon them. With formal introduction of the new line at the season's first boat show not far away, answers were needed soon.

questions:

1. What alternatives are available for Lockwood Enterprises?
2. What course of action do you recommend?
3. What constitutes an "effective" promotional mix?

When you have mastered the contents of this chapter, you should be able to:

1   Give examples of qualitative and quantitative personal selling objectives.
2   Explain the nature and purpose of sales policies and their relationship to personal selling objectives and personal selling strategies.
3   Identify and compare the four basic styles of selling.
4   Describe how management should decide the size of the sales force.
5   Discuss the several problems involved in determining and allocating the personal selling appropriation.
6   Explain how the sales manager implements personal selling strategy through managing the sales force.
7   Contrast the three basic methods for compensating salespersons.
8   Discuss the use of job descriptions and quotas in appraising salespersons' performances.

17

personal
selling

Salespeople are in many respects the "unsung heroes" of marketing. Success in marketing for many, perhaps most, companies depends importantly upon sales representatives' skills in matching company products with customers' needs and, of course, in making sales. Thus, formulating personal selling strategy and managing the salespersons who implement it are not only critical but challenging tasks. Discussion in this chapter relates to (1) planning the personal selling operation, including the setting of objectives, determination of policies, and formulation of strategies; and (2) management of the sales force.

Figure 17-1   A model of personal selling

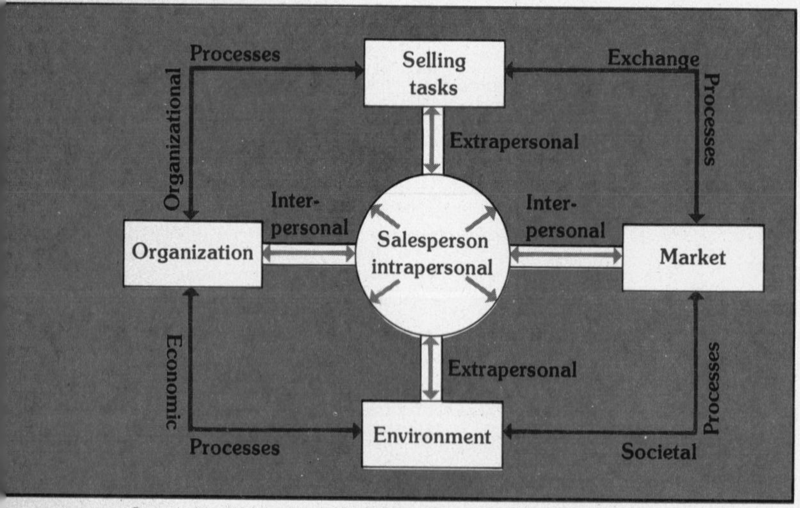

Source: Ben M. Enis, Personal Selling (Santa Monica, California: Goodyear Publishing Company, Inc., 1979), p. 19.

Personal selling is a highly distinctive form of promotion. Like other forms, it is basically communication; but, unlike others, it is two-way rather than one-way communication. Thus, personal selling involves social behavior, both the seller and the prospect (by what they say and do) influencing each other. The outcome of each sales situation depends upon the success both parties have in communicating with each other and in reaching a common understanding of needs and goals.

The social character of personal selling makes it an activity particularly difficult to manage. Generally, management must leave each sales representative free to interact with individual customers in the manner this individual feels is the most effective. Yet, at the same time, management must direct and control the sales force in order to achieve marketing and personal selling objectives.

PLANNING THE PERSONAL SELLING OPERATION

Figure 17-2 shows how personal selling fits into the promotional program. Management's first task, of course, is to decide just what role, if any, personal selling should play in the promotional mix. Some companies shift the entire personal selling activity to middlemen (such as to a selling agent), but this is by no means common. Most producers, especially those who are manufacturers, must set personal selling objectives, determine sales policies, formulate sales strategies, determine the personal selling appropriation, and manage the sales force. As Figure 17-2 indicates, these interrelated tasks collectively make up the personal selling portion of the promotional program.

personal selling objectives

Personal selling has both long-term and short-term objectives. The long-term objectives are broad and general, changing little over time, and concern the contributions management expects personal selling to make to the achievement of overall company objectives. The short-term objectives are specific and relate to the role(s) management assigns to personal selling as a part of both the promotional program and the overall marketing strategy. In certain instances, personal selling's role is minimal, perhaps that of simply having salespeople take orders from the customers. But in most instances personal selling plays considerably more important roles.

Depending upon the overall marketing strategy and the nature of the promotional mix, the objectives of personal selling may be:

1. To do the entire selling job (as when there are no other elements in the promotional mix).
2. To "service" existing accounts (i.e., to maintain communications with present customers, take orders, etc.).
3. To search out and obtain new customers.
4. To secure and maintain customers' cooperation in stocking and promoting the product line.
5. To keep customers informed on changes in the product line and other aspects of marketing strategy.

Figure 17-2 Personal selling as part of the
promotional program

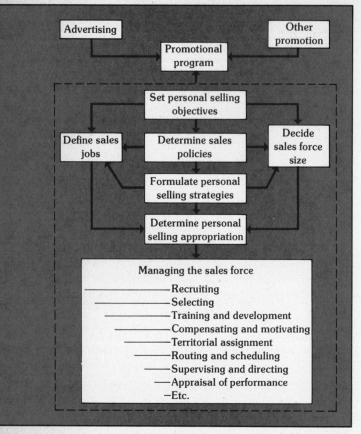

6. To assist customers in selling the product line (as through "missionary selling").

7. To provide technical advice and assistance to customers (as with complicated products and custom-designed products).

8. To assist with (or handle) the training of middlemen.

9. To provide advice and assistance to middlemen on various management problems.

10. To collect and report market information of interest and use to company management.

This list, as you should recognize, is only illustrative of the many objectives that might be assigned to personal selling. Besides these mainly qualitative objectives, certain quantitative objectives are generally assigned to personal selling, such as:

1. To obtain a specified sales volume.
2. To obtain sales volume in ways that contribute to profit objectives (e.g., by selling the proper mix of products).
3. To keep personal selling expenses within specified limits.
4. To secure and retain a specified share of the market.

sales policies   Sales policies are the general rules management sets up to guide itself in making decisions on the personal selling effort. Specifically, sales policies guide management in formulating sales strategies, defining the sales job, and deciding sales force size. Sales policies should derive directly from, and be wholly consistent with, the personal selling objectives. If, for example, one of the personal selling objectives states that "this company expects its sales representatives to provide first-class engineering assistance to both new and old customers," then a sales policy (or policies) is needed to describe how, in general, this objective is to be attained.

formulating personal selling strategy   A company seeks to achieve its personal selling objectives through both its sales policies and its personal selling strategy. Whereas sales policies provide the general guidelines for making decisions on the personal selling effort, personal selling strategies are adaptations of sales policies—personal selling decisions individually tailored to fit particular marketing situations. Formulating personal selling strategy requires management to (1) define the nature of the sales job, and (2) decide the size of the sales force—the two main determinants of the personal selling appropriation.

DEFINING THE SALES JOB   Both personal selling objectives and sales policies influence the nature of the sales job and the kind of people who should make up the sales force. The nature of sales positions varies from company to company because, although salespeople in different companies may have similar duties and responsibilities, differences in personal selling objectives and sales policies cause them to vary their emphasis on specific tasks. Personal selling objectives and sales policies differ, of course, because no two companies use exactly the same overall marketing strategies.

In some situations salespeople must aggressively seek orders, and in others they need only take orders that come to them. But, the degree of emphasis on order taking and order getting varies with different selling jobs. The driver sales representative for a soft drink bottling company is primarily an order taker, since the product is strongly presold to consumers, and retailers reorder automatically for stock. The salesperson calling on householders to sell encyclopedias is much more of an order getter, since he or she has the primary responsibility for creating demand.

The complexity of the product or product line is a second important factor influencing personal selling objectives, sales policies, and the nature of the sales job. When the product is highly technical, the selling job is considerably different than when the product is simple. The computer sales representative and the office stationery sales representative have very different jobs.

A third important factor, the type of customer, affects not only personal selling objectives and sales policies but also the nature of the sales job. The industrial user buying for its own operations needs to be dealt with differently than the middleman buying for resale. Differences in sellers' roles and tasks call for differences in sales job descriptions.

It is possible to group sales jobs into a limited number of categories, at least to draw certain generalizations. Specifically, it is possible to identify four basic styles of selling that cut, to a large degree, across industry boundaries: trade selling, missionary selling, technical selling, and new-business selling. [1]

The trade seller develops long-term relations with a relatively stable group of customers. For the most part, this style of selling is "low key" with little or no pressure, and the job tends to be on the dull and routine side. This style of selling, which predominates in marketing food and apparel and in wholesaling, applies primarily to products that have well-established markets. In such cases, advertising and other forms of promotion are more important than personal selling. One of the trade seller's important responsibilities is to help the customers build up their volume by providing promotional help. For example, the sales representative for a line of breakfast cereals devotes much time to promotional work with retailers and wholesalers—taking stock, refilling shelves, suggesting reorders, setting up displays, and the like.

The missionary seller is responsible for increasing the company's sales volume by assisting customers with their selling efforts. The missionary is only incidentally concerned with order taking and order getting, since any orders obtained are by-products of the missionary's public relations and promotional efforts with customers of customers (the company's indirect customers). The missionary's job is to persuade indirect customers to buy from the company's direct customers. For example, the sales representative for a pharmaceutical manufacturer calls on retail druggists to acquaint them with a new product and to urge them to stock it, hopefully persuading them to order from drug wholesalers (the company's direct customers). Some missionary sellers also call on individuals and institutions who do not buy the product themselves, but who influence its purchase by others—for example, the "medical detail person" calling on doctors and hospitals to acquaint them with new drugs. Missionary selling, like trade selling, is low key and does not require high-level technical training or ability.

The technical seller deals primarily with the company's established accounts and aims to increase their purchases through providing technical advice and assistance. Frequently, though not always, this representative needs a technical background and formal education in engineering or sci-

[1] D. A. Newton, "Get the Most Out of Your Sales Force," *Harvard Business Review,* September–October 1969, pp. 131–141.

ence. The technical seller performs advisory functions similar to those of the missionary but, in addition, makes sales direct to industrial users and other buyers. Technical sellers devote most of their time to acquainting industrial users with technical characteristics of products and with new product applications, and to helping them design installations or processes that incorporate their company's products. In this style of selling the ability to identify, analyze, and solve customers' problems is important. Technical sellers often specialize, either by products or by markets, in selling heavy made-to-order installations, such as steam turbines and electric generators, different technical sellers working with different items in the product line. Other technical sellers specialize in servicing either industrial accounts or governmental procurement agencies.

The new-business seller is responsible for securing new customers—converting prospects into customers. Some experts argue that many companies that now have a single sales force should divide and specialize their sales force into two separate groups—one to concentrate on retaining existing customers and one to specialize in converting prospects into customers. [2] The argument is that different sets of talents are required—retaining existing customers involves performance of rather routine duties, while converting prospects into customers requires creativity, ingenuity, and resourcefulness (all rather scarce talents). Salespeople specializing in new business are a difficult group to manage; turnover among them tends to be high because only a few can continue indefinitely without becoming discouraged by failures to convert prospects into customers.

DECIDING SALES FORCE SIZE One important consideration in deciding sales force size is the rate of sales force turnover. If a company has 100 salespeople, needs all 100 for the coming year's operations, and has a 10 percent annual turnover, 10 new sellers must be recruited during the year to maintain the 100 minimum. The sales force turnover rate is defined as the number of salespeople separated, resigned, fired, and so on per 100 on the sales force. Every sales force should have some turnover. When there is no turnover, the sales force may be growing stale, inefficient salespeople staying on because management has failed to replace them. Management should optimize turnover so as to eliminate "dead wood" and keep costs of turnover as low as possible.

Management's decision on the size of the sales force boils down to estimating the total number of sales representatives needed to achieve the company's personal selling objectives. Consider, for example, the objective with respect to sales volume: if the sales job has been defined accurately and completely, it should be possible to estimate the number of sales dollars that each salesperson should produce; dividing this amount into forecasted sales and making an allowance for the rate of sales force turnover should indicate the number of salespeople needed. Management should make similar esti-

[2] Peter W. Pasold, "The Effectiveness of Various Modes of Sales Behavior in Different Markets," *Journal of Marketing Research*, May 1975, pp. 171-176.

mates for each of the personal selling objectives, the purpose in each case being that of determining the total number of people required to achieve the objectives. Difficulties in making these estimates vary both with the objective and the nature of the seller's activities related to its achievement. It is less difficult, for instance, to estimate the number of people required to reach a quantitative objective (such as total sales volume for the company) than to estimate those required to attain a qualitative objective (such as "securing and maintaining customers' cooperation" or "building good will among the customers of customers"). But, out of the composite of such estimates, management determines the size of the sales force it needs to implement the personal selling strategy.

determining the personal selling appropriation

The logical starting points for determining the amount of the personal selling appropriation are the specific personal selling objectives set by top management for the period just ahead. The personal selling strategy, formulated with a view toward achieving these objectives, must ultimately be translated into the types and amounts of personal selling effort required (as in the definition of the sales job and the decision on sales force size). Sooner or later, management must also deal with the problem of converting these types and amounts of personal selling effort into dollar estimates of the costs involved. Thus, an increase in the sales volume objective may call for the hiring of a certain number of new sales representatives, their training, providing them with expense allowances, securing and assigning additional supervisors, and the like. Therefore, in building the personal selling appropriation, management must (1) estimate the volume of performance for each required activity, and (2) convert these performance volumes into dollar cost estimates. [3]

Although the kind and size of sales force are the main determinants of the total size of the personal selling appropriation, management must make further decisions concerning how it is to be spent. In deciding among alternative uses, management must answer such questions as: Should we hire five additional sales representatives at a total cost of $150,000 or should we invest the same amount in refresher training for present salespeople? Should we add sales supervisors or use the same number of dollars for conducting sales contests? If such questions were resolved rationally, there would be an equating of the marginal productivities of alternative ways of spending the personal selling appropriation. In practice, such allocations are largely made intuitively. Management experiments constantly and is always striving for an improved allocation pattern. Since there is no known way for measuring or predicting the relative effectiveness of expenditures on the different activities, such allocations continue to be made on the basis of management's best judgment.

[3] Rom Markin and Charles Lillis, "Sales Managers Get What They Expect," *Business Horizons,* June 1975, pp. 51-58.

MANAGING THE SALES FORCE

The sales manager's job is to ensure that the sales force plays its assigned roles in implementing the personal selling strategy. This executive's major responsibilities for sales force management include recruiting and selecting, training and development, compensating and motivating, making territorial assignments, routing and scheduling, supervising and directing, and appraising salespeople's performance.

In every company the **job description,** outlining the duties and responsibilities of the salesperson, lies at the heart of sales force management. Effectiveness in sales force management, to put it another way, depends importantly on the completeness and accuracy of the sales job description. Through analysis of the duties and responsibilities making up the job, management derives the set of **qualifications** that salespeople should possess. This furnishes guidance in searching out the best source of recruits and in selecting those with the best qualifications. Comparison of the desired set of qualifications with the qualifications of newly hired sales personnel indicates the needed breadth and depth of initial sales training. Similarly, comparing the job description with the qualifications possessed by the veteran salesperson is a basic technique of seller evaluation and assists in determining the content of refresher sales training. Furthermore, the job description provides guidance for management in designing the sales compensation plan, planning programs for motivating salespeople, and arriving at the best methods for supervising them.

recruiting and selecting sales personnel

Recruiting involves identifying the sources of recruits and choosing recruiting methods. Each source used previously should be analyzed according to the number of recruits obtained and their success or failure as company salespeople. Although internal sources, such as other departments and nonselling sections of the sales department, provide some promising recruits, most companies must look to external sources for an adequate supply of recruits. Among the external sources are educational institutions—universities, colleges, and, of greatly increasing importance, junior colleges. Other external sources include the experienced sales representatives of competitors and other companies, job seekers registered with employment agencies, and "walk-in volunteers." Recruiting methods vary with the source: personal recruiting by executives is used to reach inexperienced candidates from inside the company and from schools, while indirect recruiting methods (e.g., placing classified advertisements in newspapers or trade journals) are used for attracting experienced salespeople.

Systems used for **selecting salespeople** range from simple one-step procedures, consisting merely of an informal personal interview, to complete multistep systems using numerous and varied devices and techniques for gathering information on prospective salespersons. A selection system should be a set of successive "screens," at any one of which job candidates may be dropped from further consideration. The number and relative sophistication of the screens, of course, depend upon the resources manage-

357

ment is willing to invest in its selection process. Among the commonly used selection screens or steps are the interview application, the interview(s), the formal application form, references and recommendations, physical examination, credit reports, and psychological tests (aptitude, intelligence, personality, and others).

training and development of salespeople

The modern sales executive, while considering on-the-job experience as the best sales training, believes strongly that formal sales training contributes significantly to selling effectiveness. Most companies conduct training programs both for newly hired personnel and for their veteran salespeople. Building an effective training program of any kind requires clear definition of objectives, decisions on program content, selection of training methods, and execution of the actual training—professional sales trainers call these steps the A-C-M-E procedure—*a*im, *c*ontent, *m*ethod, and *e*xecution.

For new sales representatives the sales training program generally includes product data, sales techniques, markets, and company information, while for more experienced representatives the content is more specialized, to meet particular needs. Training methods include both individualized techniques, such as on-the-job training, and group techniques, including lectures, group discussion, role playing, and simulations. Executing the training program requires decisions on training duration, the training site, training the trainers, and training materials and aids.

compensating and motivating sales representatives

The duties and responsibilities inherent in each sales job determine the amount of compensation that must be paid to attract and develop people of the desired caliber.[4] Because salespeople enjoy high job mobility, ordinarily they must be paid approximately what competitors' salespeople are paid. Generally, too, because of the strong pull exerted by other firms employing salespeople of similar quality, sales representatives are paid more than either production or office workers.

COMPENSATION METHODS   Each method for compensating salespeople is a combination of all or some of four elements: (1) a fixed portion (salary), (2) a variable portion (commission, bonus, or a share in profits), (3) either reimbursement of expenses or an expense allowance, and (4) such "fringe benefits" as paid vacations, pensions, and insurance. Because "expense" provisions and fringe benefits are never used alone, the three basic compensation methods are (1) straight salary, (2) straight commission, and (3) a combination of salary and one or more variable features.

Each basic method presents a different balance of two underlying purposes of compensation: providing management with power to direct sellers' activities and furnishing them with the incentive to work productively. At the two extremes are the straight salary and straight commission. The

[4]James E. Carey, "Cost and Value in Salesmen's Pay," *Compensation Review*, First Quarter 1975, pp. 30-38.

straight-salary method, in theory, provides management with the maximum power to direct salespersons' efforts along the potentially most productive lines. The company guarantees a total fixed income to the salesperson and has the right to ask them to engage in activities not directly productive of sales. Under the straight-commission method, where the salespeople's earnings are closely related to their selling efforts, they generally resent demands on their time not directly productive of sales. The justification for the straight-commission method is that it provides salespeople with the maximum of direct financial incentive to strive toward high selling efficiency. Neither straight salary nor the straight commission, however, is as widely used as the combination method. By including both a fixed element and one or more variable elements in their plans for paying sales representatives, companies using combination methods seek both to secure needed control and to furnish these employees with necessary motivation.[5]

OTHER INCENTIVES   While the basic compensation plan is the most important motivator of salespeople, most companies also use other forms of incentives to good advantage. Sales meetings provide opportunities for motivating individual salespeople, and for strengthening feelings of group identification. Sales contests offer a mechanism through which salespeople are motivated not only to increase profitable sales volume but to achieve other specific objectives. The judicious use of both sales meetings and sales contests builds both individual and sales force morale and assists in the accomplishment of personal selling objectives.

assigning salespeople to territories   Assigning a salesperson to a territory focuses his or her efforts on a given geographical area containing a grouping of customers and prospects. Each territory represents some potential volume of sales to the company. Whenever a salesperson is assigned to a territory, management has, in effect, matched a specific level of selling skill with the amount of sales opportunity that it believes to be present in that territory.

Therefore, both the relative abilities of salespeople and the relative sales potentials of territories should be considered in assigning salespeople to territories. Too often, however, management treats problems of appraising salespeople's efficiency and evaluating territorial sales potentials independently. Because salespeople differ in efficiency, and because territories differ in sales potential, a rational assignment would put the best salesperson in the most fertile territory, the second-best in the second-most-fertile territory, and so on. Only if the assignment is made in this way is it possible to maximize the total sales in the entire market.[6]

[5] Leon Winer, "A Sales Compensation Plan for Maximum Motivation," *Industrial Marketing Management,* March 1976, pp. 29–36.

[6] Michael S. Heschel, "Effective Sales Territory Development," *Journal of Marketing,* April 1977, pp. 39–43.

routing and scheduling sales calls   Companies fielding trade or missionary salespeople often **route and schedule** their salespeople's calls for them. Besides increasing the chances that salespersons will be on the job when they are supposed to be, formal route and call schedules make it easier to contact them to provide needed and helpful information or last-minute instructions. Planning a salesperson's route can eliminate much backtracking, travel time, and waiting time. Providing a seller with a call schedule makes it possible to adjust more precisely the frequency of call to fit customers' needs, thus securing improved territorial coverage.

Companies fielding technical or new-business salespeople do not generally use formal route and call schedules. Most believe that each salesperson is the best judge of how time should be spent. In addition, in numerous situations, management finds it difficult to predict the amount of time each call will require—as, for example, when salespeople sell products designed to the customer's specifications or when they sell such products as encyclopedias on a house-to-house basis.

supervising and directing sales representatives   Most salespeople—even star performers—need **supervision and direction** to channel their efforts along lines consistent with achievement of the company's personal selling objectives. Supervision and direction involves observing, evaluating, and reporting on salespeople's field performances; correcting their deficiencies in job performance; clarifying their job responsibilities and duties; providing them with on-the-spot motivation; keeping them informed on changes in company policy; helping them solve business and personal problems; and continuing their sales training in the field. Thus, the overall purpose of sales supervision and direction is to improve the sales representatives' job performances.

appraising sales representatives' performances   Successful implementation of the personal selling strategy depends directly on the performance of the salespeople, individually and as a group; consequently, management needs ways of **appraising performance**. Management uses appraisal data in making and predicting the outcomes of decisions on such matters as which salespersons to train further, which to reward, and which to discharge. To distinguish good from poor performance, in other words, management needs standards or norms of comparison.

THE JOB DESCRIPTION   Comparison of what the salesperson does against what the job description says he or she should be doing provides insight into the individual's total performance. However, one problem in using the job description for this purpose is that many of the salesperson's job responsibilities do not lend themselves to quantitative measurement. How, for example, can one gauge how much good will a salesperson builds? Or what quantitative measures are there for determining the salesperson's mental alertness in dealing with customers?

360

The most the job description can do is to define, as clearly as possible, the performance expected in connection with each duty and responsibility. Such performance definitions may include some quantitative standards (e.g., the call frequencies for different classes of accounts). Most (because of their elusive nature) have to be phrased as qualitative statements of what management expects.

QUOTAS The most common yardsticks used for measuring salespeople's performances are called quotas, defined as "quantitatively expressed goals assigned to specific marketing units, such as to individual salespeople or territories." For instance, on the basis of past performance, a salesperson might be expected to produce a predetermined volume of sales; or, on the basis of measured market and sales potentials, a territory might be expected to yield a predetermined volume of sales. Quotas are set in terms of dollar or unit sales volume, gross margin, net profit, expenses, calls, number of new accounts, amount of dealer display space obtained, or other measurable quantities.

The dollar sales volume quota presents a major difficulty. Salespeople's efforts do not always produce sales in the period for which performance is being evaluated, and the results of current selling efforts may materialize only over many future periods. In addition, each salesperson has different working conditions, many influencing the relative ease of making sales. Territory by territory, variations exist in competition, required travel time, and sales potential. Thus, it is rare to find a company that is justified in assigning identical sales volume quotas to all salespeople. Because of competitive, physical, and sales fertility differences among territories, the sales volume quota for each sales representative should be set individually. Another important reason for individually set quotas is that salespeople vary in selling efficiency because of differences in training, experience, and native abilities.

Distinguishing sales results produced by the salesperson from those due to other causes is another major difficulty. Advertising, for instance, is an influence in making many sales, but it is the salesperson who writes the actual order. At other times, the salesperson's supervisor or branch manager may have been the major influence in the customer's buying decision. In such cases, it is next to impossible to determine the salesperson's contribution precisely.

The sales forecast should be the main basis for setting sales volume quotas since carefully prepared forecasts, when intelligently broken down, result in reasonable and attainable quotas. By breaking the forecast down into manageable parts—that is, into sales volume quotas for individual salespeople—management defines the results it expects from the efforts of each. However, it should be recognized that a sales volume quota can be no better than the sales forecast on which it is based. If the forecast is little more than a wild guess, the quota derived from it will be no better. Improvements in sales forecasts and sales volume quotas go hand in hand.

Another important basis for setting sales quotas is input from the salesperson himself. In some markets the salesperson is a better judge of the prospects for future sales than anyone at the home office. For example, a seller of machine tools is likely to know more about the construction of new machine shops and expansion and replacement in existing ones than the sales manager. Furthermore, if the salesperson participates in the preparation of the forecast, he or she is likely to accept it as an attainable goal and to work toward achieving it.[7]

SUMMARY   If you have mastered the material in this chapter, you have gained important insights on planning the personal selling operation and managing the sales force. You should have learned: how, in setting personal selling objectives, management defines the general and specific roles it expects personal selling to play; how, in determining sales policies, it provides itself with guidelines for making decisions in this area; how, in formulating personal selling strategies, management tailors sales policies to fit particular marketing situations and in the process defines sales jobs and decides the size of the sales force; how the kind and size of sales force largely determine the amount of the personal selling appropriation; and how the sales manager implements personal selling strategy through the various tasks this executive performs in managing the sales force. If you understand all these things, you understand the part personal selling plays both in the promotional program and in overall marketing strategy.

[7]Thomas R. Wotruba and Michael L. Thurlow, "Sales Force Participation in Quota Setting and Sales Forecasting," *Journal of Marketing,* April 1976, pp. 11–16.

REVIEW AND DISCUSSION QUESTIONS

1   How do you explain the fact that manufacturers are more inclined to shift the advertising activity to agencies than they are to shift the personal selling activity to middlemen?

2   In what ways do the objectives of personal selling depend upon overall marketing strategy and the nature of the promotional mix?

3   Distinguish between sales policies and personal selling strategy.

4   In each of the following situations, what would you regard as the salesperson's main task? His or her other tasks?
   a. A salesperson selling aluminum drains and gutters to homeowners on a house-to-house basis.
   b. An automobile dealer's salesperson charged with making fleet sales to business and local government agencies.
   c. A salesperson of automatic packaging machinery used by brewers, soft-drink bottlers, and food processors.
   d. A salesperson for a hardware wholesaler calling on retail hardware and variety stores.
   e. A manufacturer's salesperson selling furniture to department stores and discount houses.

5   Do you favor or oppose the proposal that salespeople should specialize either in sales maintenance activities (retaining existing customers) or in sales development (converting prospects into customers)? Why? If you worked for a company that specialized its sales force in this way, would you rather be assigned to sales maintenance or sales development. Why?

6   What factors influence the determination of the personal selling appropriation?

7   What is a sales job description? Suggest some ways a company might go about obtaining job descriptions for its sales personnel. Discuss the relationship of the sales job description to recruiting, selecting, training, supervising, and controlling salespersons.

8   What information does management need to make rational assignments of salespersons to territories? What methods might be used in obtaining this information?

9   Why must management have measures of the performance of sales personnel? How useful is the job description in making performance appraisals? What problems are encountered in using quotas as yardsticks of sales performance?

10   Discuss the relationship between sales forecasting and the setting of sales volume quotas. Should salespeople participate in sales forecasting? In setting sales quotas? Why or why not?

11   Compare and contrast the different types of selling jobs.

12   How would you respond to the criticism that personal selling is often overly aggressive and the main thrust is to sell a product rather than sell a solution to someone's problem?

13   Why is it necessary to clearly define sales jobs?

14   Describe the importance of sales quotas.

15   What do you consider to be the most important characteristics of a sales manager? What sort of background should the person bring to the position?

CASE PROBLEM

The Neary Manufacturing Company of Topeka, Kansas, manufactured and distributed a line of heavy-duty drills. The company very successfully sold its products exclusively to the construction industry. For several months, however, Raymond Neary, company president, had been researching the feasibility of expanding the distribution of the drills. The evidence uncovered numerous alternatives for expanded distribution and it was decided that the mining industry offered the best possibilities in terms of sales potential. While there was agreement on selling the drills to the mining industry, Neary and his sales manager were at odds regarding the organization of the sales force under the new distribution plan.

Neary contended that a separate sales force should be established to call on mining companies. He reasoned that division of marketing line authority on a customer basis would result in a more efficient sales effort. He argued that the construction industry and the mining industry were substantially different and that two sales forces would be required.

Leo LeClaire, sales manager, took the position that a separate sales force was unnecessary and undesirable since the identical products would be sold by each sales force. He also felt that having separate sales forces would double the administrative problems. Finally, LeClaire argued that the Neary sales force was highly competent and could easily take on new customers.

question:

1. What should Neary Manufacturing do regarding its sales force?

When you have mastered the contents of this chapter, you should be able to:

1 Give examples of several types of advertising objectives.
2 Explain the nature and purpose of advertising policies and their relationship to advertising objectives and advertising strategies.
3 Discuss the two key policy decisions relating to advertising organization.
4 Analyze the factors management should consider in deciding to use an advertising agency.
5 Explain how management should formulate advertising strategy.
6 Differentiate demand expansibility and price elasticity of demand.
7 Contrast the several approaches to determining the advertising appropriation.
8 Describe the chief problems in managing the advertising effort.
9 Discuss the problems involved in measuring advertising effectiveness.

18

advertising

Advertising's contribution to marketing success is more indirect than personal selling's, but generally advertising effectiveness and marketing effectiveness go hand in hand. Achieving advertising effectiveness through skilled planning and management of the advertising effort is a key responsibility of marketing management. Discussion in this chapter focuses on (1) planning the advertising effort, including the setting of objectives, determining policies, and formulating strategies; and (2) managing the advertising effort.

Advertising, in sharp contrast with personal selling, seeks to convey the marketer's messages to masses (i.e., large groups) of potential buyers. It takes, in other words, a "shotgun" approach, while personal selling "zeros in" on individuals with a "rifle-like" approach. While the emphasis in this chapter is on planning and managing advertising from the marketer's standpoint, you should also keep in mind advertising's role as a source of information for members of the target audience. Under the marketing concept, a communications medium can serve the marketer's purposes only if it also serves the target audience's needs for information.[1]

PLANNING THE ADVERTISING EFFORT

Figure 18-1 shows how advertising fits into the promotional mix. Management must first decide what role advertising should play in the promotional mix. In some situations, particularly in industrial marketing, management decides that advertising's role should be minimal or even nonexistent. But in most situations—both in consumer and industrial marketing—producers, especially manufacturers, must set advertising objectives, decide on advertising organization, determine advertising policies, formulate advertising strat-

[1] William R. Swinyard and Michael L. Ray, "Advertising-Selling Interactions: An Attribution Theory Experiment," *Journal of Marketing Research,* November 1977, pp. 509-516.

Figure 18-1 Advertising as part of the promotional mix

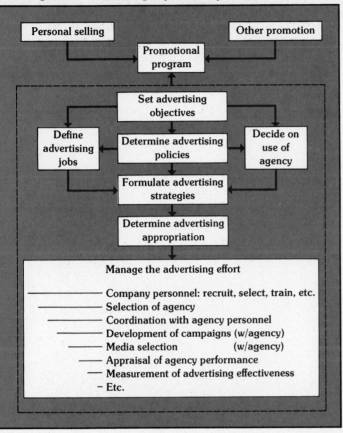

egies, determine the advertising appropriation, and manage the advertising effort. As this figure indicates, these interrelated activities collectively make up the advertising portion of the promotional mix.

ADVERTISING OBJECTIVES   The long-term objectives of advertising, like those of personal selling, are broad and general, and concern the contributions advertising should make to the achievement of overall company objectives. Most companies regard advertising's main objective as that of providing support to personal selling and other forms of promotion. But advertising is a highly versatile communications tool and, depending upon the marketing situation, companies use it to achieve numerous other long- and short-term objectives.[2] Among these objectives are the following:

[2] Norman Strauss, "Advertising: A Multi-faceted Stimulus," *Admap,* April 1977, pp. 188-192.

1. To do the entire selling job (as in mail-order marketing).
2. To introduce a new product (by building brand awareness among potential buyers).
3. To force middlemen to handle the product (pull strategy).
4. To build brand preference (by making it more difficult for middlemen to sell substitutes).
5. To remind users to buy the product (retentive strategy).
6. To publicize some change in marketing strategy (e. g., a price change, a new model, or an improvement in the product).
7. To provide rationalizations for buying (i.e., "socially acceptable" excuses).
8. To combat or neutralize competitors' advertising (competitive advertising, perhaps comparative advertising).
9. To improve the morale of dealers and/or salespeople (by showing that the company is doing its share of promotion).
10. To acquaint buyers and prospects with new uses of the product (to extend the product's life cycle).

This list is not all-inclusive, only illustrative of the wide range of objectives that may be assigned to the advertising effort.

ADVERTISING POLICIES

Advertising policies are the general guidelines management establishes to provide direction in making advertising decisions. Such policies derive directly from the advertising objectives and assist management in formulating advertising strategies. The most basic advertising policy decision, of course, relates to whether the company should advertise at all; if management decides on a "no advertising" policy, as the Hershey Company had for many years, then there is no need for other advertising policies. Most companies, however, have policies outlining the conditions under which they will or will not advertise. Among the most common advertising policy areas are those treated in the following discussion.

general scope of advertising effort

Top management sets relatively specific limits for its advertising effort. Sometimes the policy is to permit only product-related advertising, but more frequently management also permits a limited amount of institutional (i.e., company image-building) advertising. Less frequently, a few companies, such as the Warner and Swasey Company (a diversified marketer of machine tools and other industrial goods), permit some advertising aimed to mold general public opinion. Oil companies and public utilities, in response to negative public attitudes concerning their role in the energy shortage (not to mention the large profits in times of rising prices), have been known to change the scope of their advertising effort toward changing the general public's opinion of their products, services, and policies.

advertising and the competition Commonly, management spells out the general relationship that company advertising should bear to the competitors and/or their advertising. Many companies have policies prohibiting any advertising mention of competitors whatsoever, although, in recent years, more advertisers have been using **comparative advertising**, in which the advertiser's product is compared directly with those of competition, which are clearly identified by brand name. Some, as a policy matter, insist on matching or exceeding the advertising efforts of their competitors. In a number of industries, it is common for individual companies to participate, under certain conditions, in industry-wide advertising efforts (called **horizontal cooperative advertising**). Whether or not a given company should participate in industry advertising depends on such factors as the significance of competition from products of other industries, comparative effectiveness of its own advertising, and its normal share of the market.

advertising and the middlemen Another common policy relates to the use or nonuse of **vertical cooperative advertising**, that is, advertising whose costs are shared by the company and its retailers.[3] Quite often cooperative advertising stimulates middlemen to extra effort because they are sharing its cost. Manufacturers also use vertical cooperative advertising to expand the quantity of advertising a dollar buys (by getting dealers to pay part of the costs), to get dealers to stock the product by using the offer of cooperative advertising as bait, to secure local advertising media rates (which are usually lower than those charged national advertisers), to encourage retailers to advertise in order to identify themselves as local outlets where consumers can find the product, and to provide local advertising support for national advertising campaigns.

advertising and the audience A growing number of advertisers have policies concerning the general approach advertising should take relative to the target audience. Some, for instance, frown upon the use of humor. Others insist upon positive appeals, strictly forbidding negative or scare appeals. One area offering the greatest opportunity for variety in approach concerns advertising to multinational markets. Some advertisers believe that appeals should be adjusted to local cultural variations in each foreign market; others treat all foreign markets identically (as does Coca-Cola).[4]

ADVERTISING ORGANIZATION

Two key policy decisions relate to advertising organization: (1) the nature of advertising jobs inside the company, and (2) the use or nonuse of an advertising agency. The availability of professional outside help from advertising agencies provides an organi-

[3] Edward H. Zimmerman, "Make Your Co-op Advertising Pay Off," *Product Marketing,* February 1977, pp. 17–21.
[4] Thomas E. Barry and Roger L. Tremblay, "Comparative Advertising Perspectives and Issues," *Journal of Advertising,* No. 4, 1975, pp. 15–20.

zational alternative whereby the advertiser may shift all or part of the planning, producing, and placement of advertising to an agency. If the company decides to advertise at all, management must decide who will do what part of the actual work. Who should participate in formulating advertising strategy? (Sometimes agencies have major voices in strategy formulation.) Who should plan the advertising program and prepare the campaigns? Who should write the copy, develop the appeals and themes, do the illustrations, and select the type styles? Who should determine the size and position of advertising space, arrange for the use of various media, write and produce the radio and TV commercials, choose the programs to sponsor, and draft the master advertising schedule? These are some of the many tasks involved in the actual work of advertising. Management must decide either to have company personnel do this work, or to secure the services of an advertising agency, or to use a combination.

defining advertising jobs inside the company

In a company organized under the marketing concept, the top advertising executive serves in a staff capacity and reports directly either to the chief marketing executive or to a director of marketing communications or promotion. How large the advertising executive's staff is, and the nature of its duties and responsibilities, depend upon how much, if any, of the advertising work is "farmed out" to an agency.

Determination of advertising policy and formulation of advertising strategy, because of their close relationships to overall marketing strategy, are generally not, and should not be, delegated to an agency. Furthermore, when an advertising agency is used, the advertising executive, at the very minimum, should actively be involved in the agency's planning of advertising campaigns, thus ensuring that they fit in with overall marketing strategy. Top management holds the advertising manager responsible for success or failure of advertising, and this holds true whether the firm's own advertising department discharges the entire task of advertising or whether all or parts of it are handled by an agency.

deciding on use of an advertising agency

Whether a company should have its own pool of talent or tap the skills of an agency depends on who can do the job best and most effectively. Important factors to consider in making this decision are the functions and cost of an agency, advertiser–agency relationships, and required advertising skills.

NATURE OF AN ADVERTISING AGENCY   An advertising agency is a group of experts on various phases of advertising and related marketing areas.[5] In its operations, it resembles other organizations that provide expert assistance on specialized business problems—the management consulting firm, the marketing research firm, and the firm specializing in design and administra-

[5] For a good discussion of the advertising agency as a force in the advertising business, see "The Advertising Agency—What It Is and What It Does for Advertising," *Advertising Age*, November 21, 1973, pp. 34ff.

tion of incentive campaigns for salespeople and dealers. But in the way it normally receives its compensation, the advertising agency is distinct from other consulting organizations.

COMPENSATION OF AGENCIES   The **commission system** is the traditional and most widely used method of compensating advertising agencies. Agencies pay media for space and time used on behalf of advertisers at the *card rate* less a certain discount, usually 15 percent, and bill clients at the card rate. Thus, agencies receive their basic compensation in the form of the discount from advertising media rather than from advertisers, and this has been the source of considerable controversy.

Advertisers, especially large ones, maintain that agencies may overspend for media because their compensation comes from media commissions. Advertising agencies, as might be expected, have been the main defenders of the commission system, but some have been losing their liking for it. Part of the growing disenchantment traces to the consent decree (resulting from an antitrust suit brought by the U.S. Department of Justice), which, in effect, made it possible for media to grant commissions to other than recognized agencies and in general made the commission system more difficult to enforce and more open to attack.

Even more of the agencies' disaffection for the commission system results from the increasing cost of providing a wide range of services to advertisers: services that include, among others, advertising pretesting, test marketing, research on advertising effectiveness, and marketing counsel and aid in marketing research. At one time agencies performed these services free, but now they bill advertisers for such extras on a **cost-plus** or **fee** basis. Fees or charges amount to roughly one-third of the gross incomes of advertising agencies. Some agencies have replaced the commission system entirely with a fee arrangement under which media commissions received are credited toward payment of the agreed fee.

ADVERTISER-AGENCY RELATIONSHIPS   Through long-standing practice, certain relationships between advertisers and their agencies have become standardized. The five most important are: (1) the agency refrains from having two accounts whose products are in direct competition, (2) the advertiser refrains from using two agencies to handle the advertising for the same product, (3) the agency obtains advance approval before it commits the advertiser to expenditures, (4) the advertiser pays the agency for media and other invoices promptly and within the cash discount period, and (5) the agency passes on to the advertiser the exact dollar amounts of all cash discounts granted by media.

REQUIRED ADVERTISING SKILLS   The decision to use an agency often hinges upon the skills required to carry out the advertising effort. Few manufacturers can afford to have in their employ all the different talents employed by advertising agencies to develop and produce large-scale advertising programs. Characteristically, too, agencies allow much greater latitude

TABLE 18-1   WORLD'S TEN LARGEST ADVERTISING AGENCIES IN 1977

	1977 Gross Income (millions)	1977 Billings (millions)
1. Dentsu, Inc.	$212.6	$1,415.
2. J. Walter Thompson	189.	1,262.
3. Young & Rubicam	164.7	1,105.9
4. McCann-Erickson	162.6	1,083.5
5. Ogilvy & Mather International	127.9	866.3
6. BBDO International	118.6	781.1
7. Leo Burnett	116.0	786.5
8. SSC & B, Inc.	100.5	656.0
9. Ted Bates & Co.	98.8	730.9
10. Grey Advertising	97.2	641.7

Source: Reprinted with permission from the April 17, 1978, issue of Advertising Age. *Copyright 1977 by Crain Communication, Inc.*

for creative activity than does a manufacturer-controlled advertising operation. Creative people in agencies may give freer rein to their imagination because they do not work directly for the advertiser. It is usually the agency team which sees the need and the way to break with the advertiser's traditional approach and produce advertisements and campaigns that are fresh and original. When the advertising effort requires considerable and varied skills, an outside agency is more likely to have them than a manufacturer-controlled advertising operation. Table 18-1 shows the 10 leading advertising agencies in U.S. billings for 1977.

ADVERTISING STRATEGY

Advertising strategies are individually tailored to fit particular marketing situations. An **advertising strategy** is aimed at achieving advertising objectives and should be consistent with existing advertising policies (if it is not, management should then either reshape the strategy or alter the policies). Advertising strategy formulation requires management to "size up" the extent of the advertising opportunity through analysis of different aspects of the particular marketing situation (product-market, distribution, promotion, and pricing).

product–market aspects   DEMAND EXPANSIBILITY   If demand can be stimulated through advertising alone, it is said to be **expansible**. A product has an expansible demand if (with no change in price) advertising results in greater sales. To stimulate **primary demand** (i.e., demand for a *type* of product, such as cassette recorders in general) on a profitable basis, then, demand must be expansible.

372

An expansible demand is not a necessary condition for the profitable stimulation of **selective demand** (i.e., demand for a specific brand, such as for Wollensak cassette recorders), inasmuch as selective demand advertising may succeed in winning away customers from competing brands. Nevertheless, existence of an expansible demand adds to the chances of success for selective, as well as primary, demand advertising. Moreover, advertising aimed at stimulating selective demand may win nonusers of the product type to the manufacturer's brand, may win some users of competing brands, and may even increase the brand's consumption among present users.

BRAND DIFFERENTIATION   A particularly critical factor in appraising advertising opportunity is the extent to which the brand differs from competing brands. Brand differences and similarities should be identified, and appraisals made of their relative importance to specific market segments. Differences that a segment of the market considers important furnish the source of selective advertising appeals. If a brand is not very different from competing brands—and consumers know it—the most the manufacturer can hope to accomplish through advertising is brand acceptance. There must be brand differences of substantial importance to consumers if advertising is to succeed in developing brand preference or brand insistence.

For some products buyers can detect some hidden brand differences through use. If the consumer must use the product in a certain way to detect hidden differences, the marketer must provide directions for use (on the package and possibly in the advertising). Thus, a cake mix manufacturer provides careful directions both on the package and in its advertising to ensure that the end result is an acceptable cake. If the hidden difference is not detectable through use (e.g., it may take several weeks of using a facial cream to determine its effect on the complexion), the advertiser may attempt to convince buyers of the integrity of the firm itself or may use endorsements of the brand by respected public figures or experts. Whenever a brand possesses important hidden differences, there is opportunity for advertising to exploit them profitably.

STAGE IN THE PRODUCT LIFE CYCLE   The potential effectiveness of advertising depends importantly upon management's recognition of the stage in the product life cycle that the product is in and upon its skill in adjusting the thrust of the advertising effort accordingly. Advertising has a different job to do in each stage of the product life cycle. The type of advertising necessary is shown by the "advertising spiral" in Figure 18-2. Relative to the product life cycle, stimulation of primary demand precedes stimulation of selective demand—consumers must want the generic product (as marketing people describe a *type* of product) before they can want some brand of it.

Thus, after introducing a new generic product, the innovating company should concentrate on advertising to stimulate primary demand. As the product type gains acceptance (during the market growth and market maturity stages), the innovating company gradually changes its advertising

Figure 18-2 The "advertising spiral" showing the various
advertising stages in the life of a product

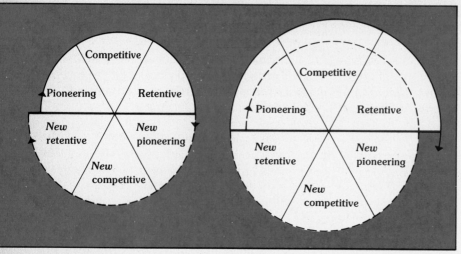

Source: Otto Kleppner, Advertising Procedure (Englewood Cliffs,
New Jersey: Prentice-Hall, Inc., 1979), p. 52.

to stimulate selective demand. For example, when Mercedes first introduced
a diesel automobile into the American market, the major thrust of its advertising was to persuade consumers to buy a diesel instead of a gasoline en-
gine. After Peugeot and then General Motors entered the market, Mercedes
shifted its advertising emphasis to the special advantages of Mercedes over
other diesel cars. An innovating company (for a new type of product), therefore, must be willing to expend considerable money on primary demand
advertising, whereas followers usually must concern themselves only with
selective demand advertising. Some products in the market maturity stage
continue to benefit from advertising aimed at stimulating primary demand,
because they compete directly or indirectly with some different product type.
For example, tea, certainly not a new product, must continually and directly
compete with coffee for primary acceptance. As another example, home
organs and high-fidelity record players compete indirectly, especially since
many prospective buyers cannot afford to buy both. It is not unusual, then,
for mature products to be promoted through primary demand advertising.

For most products in the market maturity stage and for some in the
market decline stage, much advertising effort is directed toward retaining
present customers. Usually, retentive advertising takes the form of reminding
past buyers to buy the brand. Quite often, retentive advertising features
special deals, such as two-for-one offers or reduced prices.

THE PRODUCT AND CONSUMER NEEDS AND WANTS   Marketing professionals have long recognized that if a product will not sell without advertising, it
will not sell with advertising. For a product to sell at all, with or without

advertising, it must appeal to and satisfy some needs and wants of some consumers at least as well as competing items. Advertising, in other words, possesses no magic capable of causing people to buy things they do not need or want; however, it may help them to rationalize purchases of products they want but do not need in a strict economic sense. Who needs custom-made shirts at double the price of factory-made shirts? Only a small percentage of men who require unusual sizes actually need custom-made shirts, but many men want them for prestigious reasons that relate to their concepts of status or their evaluation of quality.[6] Appeals to these other wants help consumers to rationalize uneconomic but satisfying wants.

In appraising a product with regard to advertising opportunity, the important questions to ask are: Do potential buyers have needs or wants that this product or brand is capable of satisfying? How important, or how strong, are these needs or wants? If there are strong needs or wants for the product, the chances are that considerable advertising opportunity exists. If the product is capable of satisfying only comparatively weak and less basic needs or wants, there is not as much advertising opportunity.

distribution aspects   DISTRIBUTION INTENSITY   For advertising to attain maximum effectiveness, people influenced by it must be able to find stores that carry the brand. This is a matter of achieving the proper distribution intensity, considering the time consumers are willing to spend looking for the product. If consumers will spend only a little time looking for the product, its distribution should be widespread. If consumers will spend considerable time searching for the product, its distribution can be more selective. Company strategy on distribution intensity should be closely correlated with the coverage of the proposed advertising.

MIDDLEMEN'S COOPERATION   Even with proper distribution intensity, sales and good will are lost if dealers do not carry sufficient stocks to meet increased demand resulting from advertising. To prevent out-of-stocks from developing, the manufacturer should make certain that dealers know of the anticipated sales increase before the advertising appears. The manufacturer should also see to it that dealers obtain reorders promptly. Securing and maintaining the needed cooperation of the middlemen is, of course, the responsibility of the sales force; therefore, it is important to coordinate the advertising and personal selling efforts.

promotional mix aspects   In sizing up the extent of the advertising opportunity, management must consider the other elements in the promotional mix. Management's task is to select the appropriate elements in the proper amounts to achieve as near an optimum a mix as possible. Thus, in determining advertising's role in the mix, management must simultaneously consider advertising's interactions and interrelations not only with

---

[6] Raymond A. Marquardt and Anthony F. McGann, "Does Advertising Communicate Product Quality to Consumers?" *Journal of Advertising*, No. 4, 1975, pp. 27-31.

personal selling but with such other possible promotional elements as point-of-purchase display and packaging. If, for example, management concludes that a certain amount of advertising will make point-of-purchase displays twice as effective in terms of making sales, then it would probably decide to include that amount of advertising for this purpose.

pricing aspects ADVERTISING, PRICE, AND THE FINAL BUYER   The final buyer should consider the advertised item worth the price asked. This does not mean that the advertised item should be priced identically with its unadvertised or even its advertised competitors. Its price should represent reasonable value in the final buyer's mind. If the final buyer considers it superior to competing brands, its price may be higher; if the final buyer considers it inferior, its price must be lower. Advertising cannot persuade final buyers to pay an unreasonable price. Yet many ultimate consumers feel that advertised brands are worth higher prices than unadvertised brands because they are more confident that they are buying what they want.

Manufacturers of nationally advertised brands aiming to secure and retain consumer confidence must maintain consistent product quality and service. Generally, consumers will pay a small price premium because of their confidence in consistent benefits from their favorite advertised brands. Beyond that small premium, the favorite brand's price can exceed an unadvertised brand's price only by the amount at which its buyers value its additional advantages. Consumers determine this added value by personal observation and product use or by accepting the advertiser's claims when they are unable to observe and evaluate the differences for themselves. If the advertised brand has no important differences, hidden or otherwise, its price can be no higher than those of its competitors.

PRICE ELASTICITY OF DEMAND   In sizing up the advertising opportunity, management should also determine whether the product's demand is **price-elastic**. Demand is price elastic if a price reduction increases total revenue (price × quantity sold), and if a price rise reduces total revenue. Demand is **price-inelastic** if a price reduction decreases total revenue (i.e., the unit volume does not increase enough to compensate for the lower price per unit) and a price rise increases total revenue. Normally, however, and contrary to the economist's usual assumption, the adjustment of revenue to a price change is not immediate. So a practical marketer finds advertising useful in "spreading the word" of a price reduction on a product with an elastic demand, thus speeding up the receipt of increased total revenue.

THE ADVERTISING APPROPRIATION

After management has formulated the advertising strategy, it must determine the advertising appropriation. It should do this, as emphasized in Chapter 16, in conjunction with its determination of the total promotional appropriation. In determining the advertising appropriation, management secures estimates for such cost factors as media usage and advertising research studies. At some point management decides whether the company can afford the estimated expense of the proposed advertising effort—if the answer is "no," it must then rework the advertising strategy to bring the costs into line with what the company can afford. That advertising is a big business is illustrated by the more than $25 billion spent in 1977. Table 18-2 shows the 10 leading advertisers in 1977 by advertising expenditures, as well as their spending as a percentage of sales. Note the sometimes wide variation in advertising as a percent of sales, from industry to industry and from one company to another.

Whether the company can afford the costs involved in implementing a proposed advertising strategy depends partly on the potential ability of the advertising to return enough additional gross margin dollars to pay for itself. But it also depends on the funds the company has available. If there is not enough money to support an adequate advertising effort (i.e., to implement an effective advertising strategy), it is best not to advertise at all and to concentrate instead on other promotional methods.

Whether the sales resulting from the advertising are immediate or deferred is also significant. If advertising results in quick sales, the advertising costs are met largely as they are incurred from the great number of gross margin dollars available. If the advertising investment pays off only over or after a considerable period, financing the advertising requires a larger outlay. Companies short of working capital can advertise under the first condition but not under the second; this, in turn, causes them to use advertising strategies aimed to result in quick rather than deferred sales. Better-financed companies may choose advertising strategies aimed to produce either quick or deferred sales or both, depending on the relative attractiveness of the different payoffs.

TABLE 18-2   TOP TEN U.S. ADVERTISERS, 1977

Rank	Advertiser	1977 Expenditure	
		Millions	% of Sales
1	Procter & Gamble	$460	5.7
2	General Motors	312	0.5
3	General Foods	300	5.6
4	Sears Roebuck	290	1.7
5	K-Mart	210	2.1
6	Bristol Myers	203	9.3
7	Warner-Lambert	201	7.9
8	Ford Motor Co.	184	0.4
9	Phillip Morris, Inc.	184	3.5
10	American Home Products	171	8.7

Source: Reprinted with permission from the August 28, 1978, issue of Advertising Age. Copyright 1978 by Crain Communication, Inc.

There is a difference between the way advertisers should determine their appropriations, and the way most of them actually do. The majority, because of difficulties encountered in isolating the effectiveness of advertising, rely on such traditional methods as the percentage-of-sales approach. The method advertisers should use is called the incremental approach, but it can only be applied when the advertising strategy is directed solely to the achievement of profit-related objectives.

incremental approach   The incremental approach is derived from the analytical tool economists call **marginal analysis**. It puts the problem of determining the appropriation (when the advertising strategy is totally profit-related) into an appropriate conceptual framework since, logically, the advertiser should set the appropriation at the amount that maximizes advertising's net profit contribution. It is necessary, in other words, to analyze the relationship of advertising as a cause and sales as the effect.

Figure 18-3 depicts the relationship of advertising to unit sales volume. Some sales would be made even without any advertising, and this is indicated at point X_1. As advertising is begun and as increments of expenditure are added, unit sales volume first expands rather slowly, then more rapidly, and, finally, additional expenditure has less and less effect. This indicates that there is a minimum size appropriation beneath which advertising expenditures are unduly costly in terms of the resulting sales. It also indicates that, beyond a certain point, increases in advertising expenditures are accompanied by diminishing returns in terms of unit sales volume. In fact, some experts hypothesize that if people have viewed a commercial

Figure 18-3   Relationship of advertising to unit sales volume

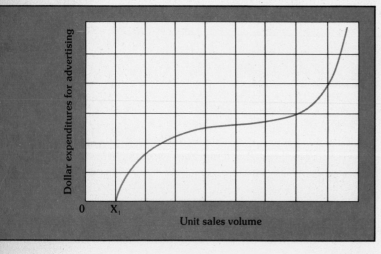

Figure 18-4 Determining the optimum advertising
appropriation

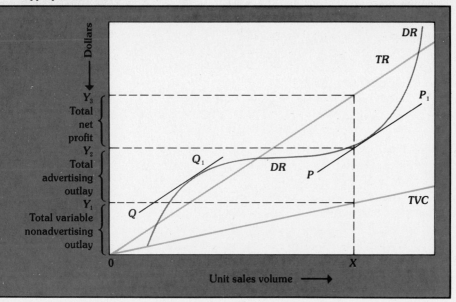

three times they have learned what the product is, the benefits offered, and finally, by the third commercial, whether the product fulfills their individual needs. It is pointless to advertise too little; at the same time, it may be counterproductive to advertise too much.[7]

Figure 18-4 shows how to obtain the optimum appropriation if the marketer knows the nature of the advertising-to-sales relationship and makes two assumptions. One assumption is that price remains constant, which means that total sales revenue *(TR)* varies at a constant rate with changes in sales volume. The second assumption is that total variable non-advertising costs *(TVC)* vary at a constant rate. In order to determine the advertising appropriation that maximizes net profit, one must find the point on the advertising-sales curve *(DR)*, where a tangent can be drawn parallel to the total sales revenue curve *(TR)*. One such line is QQ_1, but the point of tangency on this line is one where total costs exceed total revenues. The tangent line the decision maker seeks is PP_1, for here the point of tangency is also the profit-maximizing point. On the vertical axis, the optimum advertising appropriation is represented by the distance Y_1Y_2, total variable nonadvertising outlay by OY_1, and total net profit by Y_2Y_3.

[7] Howard Kamin, "Advertising Reach and Frequency," *Journal of Advertising Research,* February 1978, pp. 21-28.

percentage-of-sales approach　　This is a widely used traditional method of determining the advertising appropriation. In this method, management applies some arbitrary percentage to past sales figures, forecasted sales, or some combination of the two and, supposedly, up comes the amount of the appropriation. This simplicity, in fact, is about the only good thing about this approach because it is difficult to defend on logical grounds, especially if advertising objectives are at all profit-related. It assumes, for one thing, that the advertising cost per unit of product remains constant regardless of the sales volume; this is not a valid assumption because, as shown in Figures 18-3 and 18-4, sales do not have a straight-line relationship with advertising. More important, it implicitly assumes that advertising follows sales and not the other way around. Further, the percentage figure in most cases can come only from past sales records and past advertising expenditures—there is little assurance that past percentage relationships will hold in the future.

objective-and-task approach　　There are three steps in this method: (1) define objectives in terms of desired sales volumes, net profits, and the like; (2) estimate the amount of advertising space and time needed to achieve these objectives; and (3) express this amount of advertising in dollars to arrive at the amount of the appropriation. This method is logical in that it treats advertising as a cause of sales rather than as an effect. If used to maximize the net profit contribution of advertising, this method is equivalent to the incremental approach; however, unfortunately, most users appear to concentrate more on the effect of advertising on sales than on net profit. Without a profit-maximization emphasis, this method may produce an appropriation that increases costs rather than profits.

other approaches　　Three other common approaches to determining the advertising appropriation should be mentioned. The first is the *arbitrary method,* in which the appropriation is decided either "by pure guess" or "by allotting all the advertiser can afford." The second is called *matching competitors' expenditures;* the advertiser, in effect, permits its competitors to set its appropriation. The third is the *tax per unit of product,* in which a fixed sum is put into the "advertising pot" for each unit of the product sold or expected to be sold. As should be clear, none of these approaches is defensible on logical grounds.

MANAGING THE ADVERTISING
EFFORT

company advertising personnel　　Implementing the advertising strategy is one of the advertising manager's most important responsibilities. The people who do the actual advertising work may be company employees (those in the advertising department), agency personnel, or a combination. As advertising department head, the advertising manager recruits, selects, trains, motivates, supervises, directs, and appraises that department's staff.

Managing an advertising department can be a challenging assignment, especially when (as is often true) people having the needed talents prefer the more free-wheeling environment of, and greater glamor associated with, advertising agencies. Difficulties in recruiting and retaining people with scarce creative talents largely explain why so many advertising departments are small, often consisting only of an advertising manager, perhaps one or two assistants, and a few clerical workers and secretaries. These firms delegate almost all advertising creation and production to their advertising agencies.

selection of the advertising agency

There are no standardized procedures for selecting advertising agencies. Advertisers decide to use agencies because they require unique or additional talent to help them carry out their advertising efforts. The problem of agency selection, then, involves evaluating the qualifications of competing agencies and requires comparisons of their pools of talent. Therefore, an advertiser should, for each agency, investigate the backgrounds and professional qualifications of the key personnel who may be assigned to the account. It is advisable, too, to analyze each agency's record in serving other accounts, especially those having similar marketing and advertising problems. In most companies, several executives, including the advertising manager, participate in evaluating the agencies competing for the account, but the final selection is usually made by an individual—most often the president, and next most often the advertising manager.

coordination with agency personnel

When an advertising agency is used, the advertising manager, working along with the agency account executive or account supervisor, is responsible for coordinating its activities with related company activities. At the minimum, the advertising manager should be involved in the agency's planning and conduct of advertising campaigns, thus ensuring that they are consistent with company advertising and overall marketing strategy. Beyond that, the advertising manager must be concerned with such matters as checking out the agency's proposed campaigns with company legal personnel, making certain that advance approval is given before the agency commits the company to various expenditures, and coordinating research studies conducted by the agency and company.

developing advertising campaigns

DEFINING CAMPAIGN OBJECTIVES   The first step in developing an advertising campaign is the clear definition of its objectives. [8] **Campaign objectives** should be consistent with the objectives the company sets for its overall advertising effort, and they should

---

[8] An excellent discussion of the various stages and elements of a complete advertising campaign may be found in Otto Kleppner, *Advertising Procedure,* 7th ed. (Englewood Cliffs, N.J.: Prentice-Hall, Inc., 1979), pp. 488-513.

be specific. Some campaign objectives can be expressed quantitatively—for example, "to introduce a new product in a particular market area and obtain a 10 percent market share within the first year." Whenever possible, campaign objectives should be stated quantitatively, as that greatly simplifies later appraisals of their achievement. Sometimes, however, certain campaign objectives are qualitative, such as "building dealer loyalty" or "improving the morale of sales personnel." Such objectives are important and appropriate; however, it is difficult to measure the extent of their achievement.

DETERMINING THE CAMPAIGN BUDGET   Determining the **campaign budget** involves estimating how much it will cost to achieve the campaign's objectives. If the campaign objectives are profit-related and stated quantitatively, then the amount of the campaign budget is determined by estimating the proposed campaign's effectiveness in attaining them. If campaign objectives are not directly related to profit (i.e., if the objective is to build a particular type of company image), then there is little basis for predicting either the campaign's effectiveness or determining the budget required.

CREATION OF THE ADVERTISEMENTS   The actual preparation of the advertisements for a campaign involves creativity of a high order. It is difficult and probably impossible to evaluate such creativity quantitatively. The actual advertisements are produced by the advertising field's creative people—the copy writers and artists—but the overall qualitative evaluation and approval of their outputs are the responsibilities of agency executives and the advertiser's marketing and advertising executives.

An early step in producing an advertising campaign is to develop a campaign theme—a keynote idea or concept that will provide continuity over time and result in significant impact upon the target market segments. Some advertisers change themes annually or even seasonally. For example, Schlitz beer introduces a new theme every year or two. Others continue with a single theme almost indefinitely, until it loses most of its appeal. Maidenform's "I dreamt I . . ." theme was continued for more than a dozen years because it lost little of its power to draw readers', viewers', and listeners' attention to the product.

Language or visual messages projecting the central theme must be created. Most advertisements use both language and visual messages. An effective message generally meets three criteria: (1) it attracts the audience's attention, (2) it is understandable, and (3) it is believable. In a society where most people are exposed daily to hundreds of advertising messages, creating an ad capable of attracting attention is difficult and requires unusual talent—it is not only possible to come up with an ad that fails to attract much attention but also possible to succeed too well, so that other elements in the ad divert attention from the product (which is a potential pitfall for ads featuring humor). Likewise, constructing a message that conveys that desired impression without confusion or misunderstanding is not easy. Clarity in communications is an art, and it is difficult to tell in advance whether or not an audience will understand a particular message in the way intended. Similarly, special care is needed to ensure that the audience will believe the message conveyed. If, for example, an ad states that the advertiser's product is more effective than any competitive product, generally the audience must be provided with sufficient proof. Otherwise, much of the audience may reject the entire message as a wild and unsubstantiated claim that should not be believed. If the audience does not believe Mrs. Olsen's claim that Folger's coffee is better because it is mountain grown, they will probably refuse to buy it.

MEDIA SELECTION Most of the campaign budget is used for purchasing space and time in different media. Advertising media include (among others) newspapers, magazines, television, radio, outdoor posters, and transportation cards. Even though the agency usually handles the actual media selection, the advertiser should evaluate its choices.

What factors influence media selection? The most fundamental, of course, are the nature of the target market segment and the type of product. The distinctive characteristics of various media are important—for instance, because newspapers are issued daily, some advertisers use them and others avoid them. The campaign budget is important—small budgets require a concentration of expenditures in a few media for best results, whereas large budgets must be spread over many media to avoid a premature onset of diminishing returns. Ideally, but rarely attainable, media circulation (general exposure) should cover only those geographical areas where the advertiser's product is available (otherwise there is "waste circulation").

Conceptually, media selection is a problem in determining optimum allocation of the campaign budget. It involves dividing the budget among different media—newspapers, magazines, television, outdoor posters, and so on—so as to equate the marginal returns from each. Practically speaking, this is difficult to accomplish; consequently, most companies, relying largely on data on past media expenditures and past results, use a "try, try again" approach—starting with some feasible allocation, testing it to find possible improvements, and making those changes that seemingly would raise total effectiveness. Computer models for media selection have been developed in an attempt to simplify the task; but their one great limitation lies in the difficulties in quantifying certain factors used in comparing media—for example, the value of a particular medium's prestige with its audience.

Relative cost, or *cost comparison,* is used as a selection factor when making choices among media in the same classification—for example, between two magazines. Because each medium has a different size of circulation and a different advertising rate, the comparison technique is to convert circulation and rate figures to a common basis. Magazines, for instance, are compared according to the cost of reaching 1,000 readers with a given amount of advertising space; thus, the cost of using a full page of magazine space is calculated as follows:

$$\text{Cost per } 1{,}000 = \frac{\text{Page Rate} \times 1{,}000}{\text{Circulation of Magazine}}$$

Cost comparisons of other media follow similar patterns.

For newspapers, the technique varies slightly—newspapers quote their rates by the **agate line**, of which there are 14 in a space one column wide and 1 inch deep; thus, the cost-comparison yardstick for newspapers is called the **milline rate**—the cost of reaching 1 million readers with one agate line of advertising—which is calculated as follows:

$$\text{Milline Rate} = \frac{\text{Agate Line Rate} \times 1{,}000{,}000}{\text{Circulation of Newspaper}}$$

appraisal of agency performance

Because the agency plays a critical role in the advertising effort, the advertiser should continually appraise the agency's services and effectiveness. The key criteria for evaluating agency performance are (1) its effectiveness in meeting specific campaign objectives, and (2) its contribution to the reaching of the advertiser's advertising and overall marketing objectives. Formal reviews of the agency's performance should occur at least once a year. News of an advertiser's dissatisfaction with its present agency's performance travels fast, and other agencies are generally anxious to provide a substitute. Consequently, there is considerable agency switching by advertisers, and this serves as a partial brake on the inclination of some agencies to perform sloppily or to overspend their clients' funds.

measuring advertising effectiveness

Advertising effectiveness should be measured in terms of criteria derived from campaign objectives and the advertiser's overall advertising and marketing objectives. Unfortunately, however, most measures of advertising effectiveness in current use are rather superficial; they include size of audience, program ratings, readership scores, and numbers of inquiries received (all of which pertain almost exclusively to campaign objectives alone).

If advertising objectives are directly sales-related (i.e., if they are aimed to increase sales, to improve market share, etc.), then it is possible, of course, to determine (usually through special research studies) whether or not the advertising has been effective in reaching them. However, as should now be clear, advertising is only one of the causes of sales, market share, and the like. Other aspects of the overall marketing strategy (product-market; distribution; other forms of promotion, including personal selling; and pricing) all contribute to the making of sales, and it is difficult to isolate the sales effect of any one of these aspects.

Some advertisers seek to pretest advertising effectiveness before the advertising is run, rather than relying only on predictions of effectiveness by advertising professionals. Pretesting may take such forms as "consumer opinion panels," actual sales in "test markets," or "attitude studies" made among consumers to determine the likely impact of prototype advertising appeals and approaches. Motivation research studies are also used in attempts to determine in advance the relative effectiveness of different advertising appeals and media.

SUMMARY   If you have mastered the material in this chapter, you have gained important insights on planning and managing the advertising effort. You should have learned how, in setting advertising objectives, management defines both the broad and specific roles it expects advertising to play in the promotional mix and in the overall marketing strategy; how, in determining advertising policies, it sets up the general rules to guide itself in making advertising decisions; how, in approaching the question of advertising organization, it defines advertising jobs within the company and decides on the use of an advertising agency; how, in formulating advertising strategies, management fits the advertising effort to particular product–market, distribution, promotion, and pricing aspects that make up the total marketing situation; how, in determining the advertising appropriation, management simultaneously determines the total promotional appropriation and balances the proposed advertising strategy with what the company can afford; how, in managing the advertising effort, management concerns itself with administering company advertising personnel, selecting an advertising agency, developing advertising campaigns, appraising agency performance, and measuring advertising effectiveness. If you understand all these things, you understand the part that advertising plays both in the promotional mix and in overall marketing strategy.

REVIEW
AND
DISCUSSION
QUESTIONS

1   Analyze the relationships that the different short-term advertising objectives should bear to marketing management's long-term goals.

2   What relationship is there between effective advertising strategy and the product life cycle?

3   How are advertising decisions affected by each of the following?
    a. Company policy on distribution intensity
    b. Marketing channels for the product
    c. Competitors' advertising practices
    d. Price of the product

4   Is it essential to use an advertising agency? Why or why not? How would you characterize the "ideal" relationship between a company and its advertising agency?

5   Under what circumstances would you advise a manufacturer to switch advertising agencies? Under what circumstances might an advertising agency voluntarily "resign" a manufacturer's account?

6 | Compare and contrast the following approaches to determining the size of the advertising appropriation:
a. Incremental.
b. Percentage-of-sales.
c. Objective-and-task.
d. Arbitrary.
e. Matching competitors' expenditures.

7 | To what extent should the sales forecast be considered in determining the size of the advertising appropriation?

8 | What are the social responsibilities of advertising? Do you feel advertising successfully carries out these responsibilities?

9 | In the following situations, on which form of promotion, advertising or personal selling, would you place major emphasis? Give reasons in each case.
a. Persuading retailers to stock a new low-calorie soft drink.
b. Convincing people of the benefits of a physical fitness program.
c. Selling a landscaping and grounds maintenance program for industrial plants.
d. Selling extension telephones to homeowners.
e. Selling the services of a marketing consulting organization.

10 | For each of the 10 advertising objectives mentioned in the text, cite two examples that illustrate each objective in action.

11 | Explain the role of and importance of advertising from the following vantage points:
a. The manufacturer.
b. The middleman (wholesaler and retailer).
c. The consumer.
d. The media.
e. The advertising agency.

12 | Explain the rationale behind vertical cooperative advertising. Do the same thing for horizontal cooperative advertising.

13 | What are the advantages of comparative advertising? The potential dangers? On balance, is it a good idea for a manufacturer to use comparative advertising?

14 | Distinguish between primary demand advertising and selective demand advertising. Use examples.

15 | How would you go about choosing an advertising agency? What criteria would you use in the selection process?

CASE PROBLEM

Allstate Electronics is a medium-sized manufacturer of radios, televisions, and a wide range of electronic components and systems. Allstate products are distributed nationally by a field sales force of 88 people. The company does only a limited amount of advertising, relying instead on the personal selling effort, point-of-purchase displays, and an occasional sales promotion such as a consumer contest or a premium program. Most company advertising is to the trade in industry publications directed at radio and TV dealers.

It has long been Allstate policy to rely on dealer support for promoting the product line. Management is convinced that an aggressive and enthusiastic dealer does more to sell the customer than does advertising. Industry research shows that this is especially true when a large number of potential buyers without strong brand preferences enter the retail stores.

Until two years ago, Allstate gave its retail dealers a special 8 percent discount (over and above the normal trade discount) on every Allstate product unit they sold. This was Allstate's way of providing dealers with an incentive to push the brand when customers were in the store. After a change in management, the 8 percent "rebate" policy was discontinued, with the statement that all parties concerned would gain more if Allstate consumer advertising was increased. However, only a minimal increase in the consumer advertising (and a 30 percent increase in trade advertising) occurred. Dealers did not appear upset with the new policy at the time it was initiated. In fact, the dealers' only comments were that the promised increase in consumer advertising pleased them. When the increased advertising did not materialize, there was considerable unhappiness among dealers and Allstate sales declined. Although the decline was moderate, dealers' increasing concern and the prospect that the sales slip might continue caused management to reconsider emphasizing consumer advertising.

Results of a research study by a trade association showed that the Allstate brand in terms of consumer recognition was not even close to the leaders. This bothered management considerably. Management knew that the company made quality products.

After a lengthy discussion between Allstate marketing people and the advertising agency, it was decided to embark on an intensive consumer advertising campaign. The campaign objective was to increase consumer recognition of Allstate products. It was also agreed that the radio and television lines would receive the major initial attention. The sales slump had been most pronounced in these lines.

A major stumbling block arose when the agency's account supervisor recommended a comparison advertising campaign as the quickest and best way to gain brand recognition. Allstate management, however, wanted no part of any advertising mentioning competitors' names. Richard Hangen, the account supervisor at Franklin-Sharon Advertising, Inc., argued that comparison advertising would guarantee that people would remember the Allstate name and—at the same time—it would show the Allstate brand to advantage over the competition. Hangen was not sure exactly what comparisons would be made among Allstate and the others, nor was he sure which competitors the Allstate advertising should go head to head against. He was, however, convinced that comparison advertising would increase the Allstate recognition factor.

Doris Cole, marketing services director for Allstate, disagreed with Hangen, saying that the comparison advertising would only confuse consumers. She was reluctant, too, to give competitors "free" advertising by naming them in Allstate ads. Besides, she argued, the risk was great that something said in the advertising could haul the company into court, as had happened in similar campaigns. Cole contended that Allstate had many points to stress and that advertising space was too valuable to waste on mentioning competitors' names, brands, and claims. Finally, she was not convinced that it was ethical to compare any Allstate product with competitive versions; it was inevitable, she said, that the advertising would imply that the competitive brands were less than satisfactory and would be presented in an unfavorable light.

While there was agreement that stepped-up consumer advertising was in order for Allstate, something had to be worked out regarding whether or not to use comparison advertising.

questions:

1. Do you agree with Hangen or with Cole?
2. What are the advantages of comparison advertising? The disadvantages?

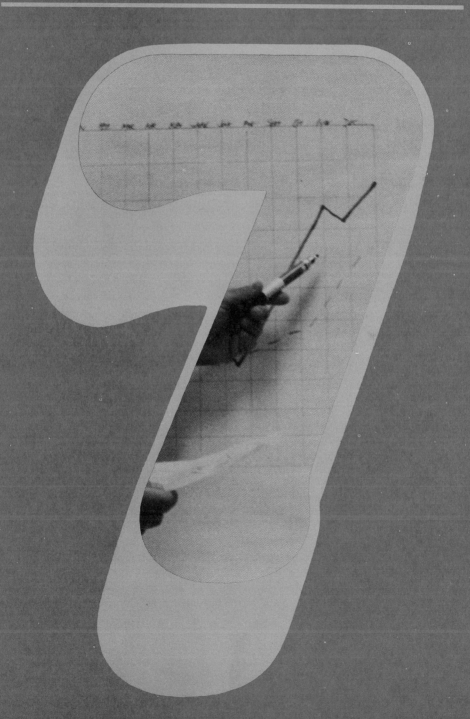

PART SEVEN
MARKETING
STRATEGY

When you have mastered the contents of this chapter, you should be able to:

1   Explain why answering the question, "Does marketing cost too much?" requires consideration of values added by marketing activities.

2   Contrast the conditions under which increases in marketing costs result in (a) lower total costs, and (b) higher total costs.

3   Identify the possible offsetting benefits of nonprice competition that increases the prices consumers pay.

4   Give examples of the ways in which marketing costs have been reduced in the past.

5   Evaluate the criticism that marketing induces "frivolous" and excessive buying.

6   Evaluate the criticism that marketing contributes to environmental pollution.

7   Explain how society influences marketing through public opinion and political pressure.

8   Analyze the implications for marketing strategy formulation of legal restraints on decisions involving competitive action, products, price, marketing channels, and promotion.

19

marketing
and society

Marketing is a social institution; it operates within a social milieu. Modern marketers must recognize the significance of interactions between marketing and society. Whereas businessmen and society once viewed marketing's role as simply that of providing the mechanism through which production and purchasing power are converted into consumption, both have broadened that view considerably. Both recognize that marketers through their manipulation of the controllables—products, distribution, promotion, and price—exert influences on, and help to mold, not only consumption patterns but public attitudes and general economic and social well-being. Both recognize that society not only through its buying behavior but through public opinion, political pressure, and legislative action exerts influences on how marketers can and should manipulate the controllables. Modern marketers, in other words, in formulating and implementing overall marketing strategies, are keenly aware that they are influencing *and* being influenced by society.

HOW MARKETING INFLUENCES SOCIETY—THE ECONOMIC ASPECTS

Marketing, in performing its traditional economic role—that is, in serving as the mechanism through which production and purchasing power are converted into consumption—incurs substantial costs that society ultimately must pay. Since marketing costs can account for more than half of the total price paid by the final buyer, important questions arise: Does marketing cost too much? What is the effect of marketing costs on total costs? Are there any offsetting benefits? What, if anything, can be done to reduce marketing costs?

does marketing cost too much?

The costs of marketing bulk large in the prices that buyers pay—no recent studies have been made on marketing costs, but most experts say that out of each dollar the ultimate consumer spends, roughly 50 cents goes for the costs of performing marketing activities.[1] For some products, of course, marketing costs are a much lower proportion of the price the consumer pays—automobiles and appliances, for example, cost considerably more to make than to market. For other products, marketing costs are a much higher proportion of the price the consumer pays—perfume and cosmetics, for example, cost little to make but a great deal to market. But, out of all the dollars the consumer spends for goods and services, about half go to pay for the costs of marketing.

Table 19-1 is a breakdown of the costs of growing wheat, converting it into flour, and marketing the finished flour to the consumer. In this table, the different costs are listed generally in the order that they are incurred (all except for railroad and truck charges, which are incurred at several stages). Notice that all but two of the costs—farmer's growing cost and the miller's grinding costs—are marketing costs, accounting for 52 percent of the $1.00 the consumer pays for the flour.

Does marketing cost too much? To answer this question we must compare the costs and the benefits. Consider the wheat and flour example again and ask yourself, "Are the marketing activities performed here worth what they cost the consumer?" Generally, wheat is grown in different areas than those in which flour is consumed; therefore, it is certainly necessary to move the product (both as wheat and as flour) from production areas to consumption areas; the farmer's wheat marketing expenses (2 percent of the total) are

---

[1] For a concise discussion of several studies on marketing costs, see P. D. Converse, H. W. Huegy, and R. V. Mitchell, *Elements of Marketing*, 7th ed. (Englewood Cliffs, N.J.: Prentice-Hall, Inc., 1965), pp. 662-625.

TABLE 19-1 BREAKDOWN OF THE COSTS
REPRESENTED IN THE AMOUNT OF FLOUR SOLD AT
RETAIL FOR $1.00*

	Cents
Farmer for growing the wheat	36.0
Farmer for marketing the wheat (mostly for transportation)	2.0
Country elevator (mostly for storage)	3.0
Terminal elevator (mostly for storage)	2.5
Flour miller for buying wheat	5.0
Flour miller for grinding wheat	12.0
Flour miller for marketing flour (including storage)	7.0
Wholesaler's costs (including storage)	3.5
Retailer's costs (including storage)	16.0
Railroad and truck charges (for transportation)	13.0
Consumer pays	$1.00

*Figures adapted from P. D. Converse, H. W. Huegy, and R. V. Mitchell, *Elements of Marketing*, 6th ed. (Englewood Cliffs, N.J.: Prentice-Hall, Inc., 1958), p. 8, to reflect current conditions.

mainly those of getting it to the country elevator, and other enterprises (country elevator, terminal elevator, the miller, wholesaler, and retailer) pay out another 13 percent of the total for railroad and truck charges—thus, a total of about 15 percent of the consumer's dollar goes for adding **place utility** to the product (i.e., moving it from production areas to consumption areas). Is 15 cents out of the $1.00 price too much for the consumer to pay for this added place utility?

Then, too, wheat is grown at one time and flour is consumed at a later time. The country elevator's marketing charges (3 percent of the total) are mostly for storing wheat until it accumulates enough to ship to the terminal elevator (with charges of 2.5 percent of the total), which, in turn, stores the wheat until the flour miller buys it. After finishing grinding the wheat into flour, the miller performs storage activities until it is bought by wholesalers, who store the flour until it is bought by retailers, who in turn store the flour until the consumer finally buys. Considering all these storage operations, perhaps as much as 20 percent of the consumer's dollar goes for adding **time utility** to the product. The time utility makes a product that is harvested over a period of two or three months in late summer available for purchase and consumption 12 months a year. Is 20 cents out of the $1.00 price too much for the consumer to pay for this added time utility?

Well, 15 cents for place utility and 20 cents for time utility adds up to only 35 cents—what does the consumer get for the other 17 cents of the 52 cents in total marketing costs? In the movement of wheat to the miller, its ownership is transferred three times—farmer to country elevator, country elevator to terminal elevator, and terminal elevator to miller. In movement of flour to the consumer, ownership is again transferred three times—miller to wholesaler, wholesaler to retailer, retailer to consumer. Thus, a total of six ownership transfers occur from the time the farmer sells the wheat until the consumer finally buys the flour. Clearly, most of the remaining 17 cents goes for the costs of effecting ownership transfers (i.e., for adding **possession utility** to the product). These costs go for performing marketing activities such as grading (all wheat is not the same quality), buying and assembling, selling (including personal selling, advertising, display, and packaging), extending credit to buyers (i.e., marketing financing), and risk bearing (e.g., the risks of the wheat or flour spoiling, being destroyed, stolen, etc.). Of course, each seller also expects its operation to return a profit over and above the costs it incurs. Is 17 cents of the $1.00 price too much for the consumer to pay for the added possession utility?

Generally speaking, then, marketing activities add value to a product by changing its ownership and its time and place of consumption. Kansas wheat at harvest time is of less value to the farmer than (after being converted into flour) it is six months later (change of time) after it has been shipped and received in Boston (change of place) and when it is finally bought by a housewife (change of ownership). Converting the wheat into flour, of course, also adds value to the product (through adding **form utility**), but value in this case is added by manufacturing, not marketing, operations.

*effect of marketing costs on
total costs*
Sometimes a company can reduce its total costs by increasing its marketing costs (thus benefiting consumers by making it possible for them to pay a lower price). For example, a company through increasing its advertising and personal selling expenditures may so increase a product's sales that the unit costs of manufacturing the product decrease more than the marketing costs have increased. Thus, the total costs are reduced. From the standpoint of society, as long as production costs fall faster than marketing costs rise, consumers benefit through lower prices—and this is the typical pattern of development for products going through the market growth stage of their life cycles. Extensive marketing, which made possible greater production efficiency reduced the price of the average color television set from over $1,000 to under $300 and that of hand-held electronic calculators from $100 to less than $10.

However, increased marketing costs sometimes result in greater, not lower, total costs. As a product moves into the market maturity stage of its life cycle, for instance, competitors must fight harder to retain their shares of a total market that is first growing at a declining rate and then shrinking at an increasing rate. While there is some tendency for price competition to develop, most marketers try to avoid it (largely because of fears of setting off a price war) and rely on increased marketing expenditures (e.g., for additional advertising, or for improved packaging) to help them hold their market shares. This increases total costs throughout the industry (unit production costs are generally already as low as they will get), and marketers seek to pass on the increased costs in the form of higher prices to consumers. Is paying the cost of this type of marketing activity worth it to consumers? Or does nonprice competition in this sort of competitive setting simply represent an economic loss to society? Your answer to these questions depends upon your economic philosophy and the value, if any, you attach to the possible offsetting benefits, such as greater product and brand choice available to the consumer.

*possible offsetting benefits of
nonprice competition that
increases prices consumers pay*
Most Americans agree that strong competition is a necessary feature of capitalism. So they accept, although not enthusiastically, as one of the "costs of capitalism," additions to marketing costs that make for higher prices. They hope, of course, that the higher costs will be more than offset by other benefits of capitalism—a wider variety of competing brands from which to choose, having more ready and convenient access to sources of supply, and the like. Most Americans also realize that intense price (rather than nonprice) competition often drives many competitors out of the market, reducing the total number to a handful of large companies (i.e., an oligopoly), a situation that discourages newcomers from entering the market. You will also recall (from Chapter 14) that oligopolistic competition generally evolves to the point where prices among competitors stabilize, not

necessarily at the lowest possible level, so oligopolistic competition may not reduce the price consumers pay.

reducing marketing costs Not until rather recently has marketing been the target of formal cost-cutting efforts. With the development of large-scale business organizations early in the twentieth century, "scientific management experts" devoted most of their efforts to improving manufacturing efficiency and cutting production costs. However, certain marketing costs have also been reduced through the years as enterprising business managers detected profitable opportunities to engage in lower-cost marketing operations—the mail-order house, department store, chain-store system, supermarket, and discount house all are institutions that at the time they appeared made possible lower marketing costs than those of the institutions previously existing. At the producers' and wholesalers' distribution levels, other cost-reducing developments have been taking place—for example, new and better designed warehousing facilities making possible economical usage of materials-handling equipment and mechanized order-processing systems. A growing number of manufacturers have set up automatic reordering systems whereby middlemen's inventory requirements are handled almost entirely by computer—thus reducing the middlemen's buying costs and the manufacturer's personal selling costs. Furthermore, more and more marketers are using marketing research: for reducing the number of product failures (incurring costs to society as well as to the marketer); for studying final buyers' needs and wants in order to provide more efficient (and lower cost) distribution; and for improving the efficiency of other aspects of marketing activities. However, many opportunities still exist for increasing marketing efficiency (and reducing marketing costs) and for passing some portion of the savings along to consumers in the form of lower prices.

HOW MARKETING INFLUENCES SOCIETY— BUYER BEHAVIOR
Marketers manipulate the controllables—products, distribution, promotion, and price—in order to influence buyer behavior. Many marketing activities provide information to prospective buyers in the hope of persuading them to buy. Critics of marketing, especially those who object to certain advertising and personal selling activities, express strong doubts about the social value of marketing's role in persuasion. Their argument is that many people are hoodwinked into wasting their money on frivolous items that contribute little or nothing either to the buyer or to society. Since many more consumers have discretionary income (to spend as they please) today than a generation ago, this criticism takes on added force. However, criticisms of this type are often related to individual value judgments, such as those based on the belief that society would be better off if more people went to symphony concerts rather than to sports events or movies. But even

the critic with this belief must admit that marketers have been instrumental in making it possible for more Americans, as well as a higher proportion of the total population, to enjoy symphonic music regularly today than was true 50 years ago—for example, marketers of records, tapes, and cassettes have brought symphony music to millions while other marketers, by paying the costs of radio and television time as part of their advertising efforts, have provided millions more with the opportunity to enjoy symphony concerts in their homes.

The criticism that marketing induces frivolous and excessive buying, however, is valid, particularly when it relates to buying by low-income and ghetto consumers. Studies of marketing in ghetto areas show that numerous low-income people are easily persuaded to buy more than they can afford. [2] Ghetto residents appear to be particularly gullible in accepting false and misleading claims about products at face value, and they are often lured into making purchases—through "easy credit terms," for example—that are beyond their means.

Language difficulties, which characterize many low-income people, make them less sophisticated in their buying than they otherwise would be. For the segment of the U.S. population made up of people whose native language is Spanish, English is for many only a partially understood second language. For much of the black population, word usage is sufficiently different to create communication problems, presenting marketers with the danger of unintentionally misrepresenting their products.

Whether the net influence of marketing on buyer and social behavior is favorable or unfavorable, critics and noncritics agree that there is influence. Because of the strong marketing emphasis placed upon such items, most Americans buy deodorants, detergents, automobiles, sporting equipment, and work-saving appliances, to name only a few. Marketing professionals, defending the system, argue that increased consumption makes for more business profits and jobs and, hence, rising incomes and higher standards of living. Marketing critics, attacking the system, argue that higher incomes are of no value if they are wasted on unnecessary purchases and that material things are of no value if the buyer has little time or energy left over after working hours to enjoy them. [3]

The arguments of the critics have been strengthened by the growing realization that the supply of natural resources is not inexhaustible. Industrial nations faced the first real peace-time material shortage with the development of the world-wide energy crisis in the mid-1970s. With this crisis came recognition that ever-increasing consumption is not necessarily the

---

[2] For more information on this topic, see D. Caplovitz, *The Poor Pay More* (New York: The Free Press, 1963); and F. D. Sturdivant, *The Ghetto Marketplace* (New York: The Free Press, 1969).

[3] For an excellent discussion of marketing as a social system, as well as the various interactions that occur between marketing and society, see Sidney J. Levy and Gerald Zaltman, *Marketing, Society, and Conflict* (Englewood Cliffs, N.J.: Prentice-Hall, Inc., 1975).

road to ever-increasing standards of living, but that, instead, it might lead to economic disaster. The emphasis of society began to shift from mass consumption to conservation.

HOW MARKETING
INFLUENCES SOCIETY—THE
ENVIRONMENT

Society is increasingly concerned with ecology and the need for preserving the environment from further human pollution. Business and industry are leading contributors to environmental pollution, but there are others—for example, inadequate municipal sewage disposal facilities, lack of controls over population growth, and unwisely located airports. Marketers, in particular, must accept responsibility for certain aspects of environmental pollution.

Packaging, a prominent feature of modern marketing, is a serious pollutant. Until the early 1900s, numerous products—among them butter, rice, crackers, coffee, and soap—were sold from bulk stock in unpackaged form. In attempting to differentiate their brands and develop buyer preferences, marketers of these products joined the *packaging revolution*. Other marketers, who previously sold their products in reusable containers (such as milk, soft drinks, and beer), in increasing numbers have switched to disposable or "throwaway" packages. The packaging industry annually turns out more than 650 pounds of packaging material per person in the United States. A city of the size of Dallas, Texas, must dispose of 430,000 tons of waste packaging, and the New York City metropolitan area more than 4,100,000 tons. Complicating the problem are the disposal methods—one, incineration, is itself an atmospheric pollutant; some types of packaging—plastic, for instance—appear almost impossible to recycle or disintegrate.

Marketing also adds to environmental pollution through its development and promotion of disposable products. For example, as paper napkins replace cloth napkins, the volume of trash requiring disposal increases. The same thing happens with disposable diapers, drinking cups, bottles, beverage cans, and so forth. Society seems to prefer the added convenience of disposability but, increasingly, voices objections to the added pollution involved. Unfortunately, too, disposability often makes it possible to reduce the prices consumers pay—the soft drink industry, for example, estimates that it costs 30 cents to collect six returnable bottles, considerably more than the cost of six aluminum cans or throwaway bottles.

Critics contend that marketing contributes to environmental pollution in still other ways. Some say that marketers adversely affect the appearance of the landscape through roadside advertising and obscure natural beauty with outdoor billboards. Others object to "pollution of the airwaves" through excessive numbers of commercials on radio and television programs, as well as through sponsorship of programs with little or no cultural importance.

The modern marketer recognizes the need for an efficient system of information feedback to measure success in evaluating and servicing the target market's needs and wants. Unfortunately, most marketers' marketing information systems have a narrow scope, focusing mainly on the short term and on that portion of society the marketer considers as a target market. The manufacturer of snowmobiles, for example, can rely upon its marketing information system to provide insights about prospective buyers' reactions to its product's performance characteristics, the dealers who sell it, and its price. But this marketing information system is not of much help in providing feedback from nonusers of snowmobiles. Thus, unless the snowmobile manufacturer makes special investigations, it may not learn that nonusers find its product's noise level highly offensive, or that ecologists are worried about damage to wilderness areas from indiscriminate snowmobile usage, until it meets strong pressures from society to control—perhaps even to outlaw—its product.

Since marketers have not often bothered to investigate society's reactions to their marketing practices, society has often taken the initiative in communicating its displeasure through various forms of social pressure against offenders. The mildest form of social pressure is public opinion aimed at causing the offending marketers to change their ways. When public opinion does not accomplish the desired result, stronger action takes the form of political pressure, with an implied threat of ultimate legal action to force the offender to abide by society's wishes. And the strongest form of social pressure is restrictive legislation outlawing the unpopular product or marketing activities.

public opinion Consumers' and the general public's dissatisfaction with marketing (and the business system in general) finds expression through the **consumerism movement**. One writer defines consumerism as "the actions of individuals and organizations (consumer, government, and business) in response to consumers' dissatisfactions arising in exchange relationships.[4] In other words, consumerism may be viewed as a protest against business injustices and the efforts to correct those injustices.

Consumerism is not new. The consumer movement started in the early 1900s, fueled by rising prices and Upton Sinclair's writing. Sinclair's *The Jungle,* focusing on the meat packing industry, made the public aware of the need for consumer protection and contributed strongly to the passage of the Meat Inspection Act (1906), the Pure Food and Drug Act (1906), and the Federal Trade Commission Act (1914). A second wave of consumerism appeared in the late 1920s. Two books, *100,000,000 Guinea Pigs* and *Your*

[4]W. J. Stanton, *Fundamentals of Marketing,* 5th ed. (New York: McGraw-Hill Book Company, 1978), p. 556.

Money's Worth, both published in the early 1930s, were widely read and quoted, and through their impact on public opinion forced several manufacturers to modify or abandon worthless or dangerous products.[5] Consumer organizations, such as Consumers Union (a nonprofit organization set up in 1936), test and rate products and provide their members with more complete and accurate buying information. Consumers Union publishes a monthly magazine, *Consumer Reports,* and an annual *Buying Guide,* both providing comparisons and ratings of competing brands of different products with hidden characteristics that are difficult to evaluate.

The consumer-oriented publications have their greatest impact on members of upper-middle- and upper-income groups. The vast majority of middle- and low-income consumers, who would have much to gain from more complete and accurate product information, are not effectively reached by these media. Consequently, the leaders of the consumerism movement have turned increasingly to the news media. If these leaders identify a particular product defect or uncover some other marketing abuse, they are quick to prove its newsworthiness and the resulting publicity rapidly spreads through newspapers, television, and radio. During the late 1960s and early 1970s, for instance, Ralph Nader, a leading crusader for consumer protection, achieved nationwide news coverage in publicizing product deficiencies and abuses. Leading groups of environmentalists and ecologists have also been successful in securing news coverage to publicize "companies responsible for polluting and destroying the environment."

Not much research has been reported on the success of these efforts to influence business activities. But there is no doubt that some business managers have yielded to the force of public opinion before political and legal pressures were applied. One study conducted during 1970 in Austin, Texas, illustrates the power of public opinion.[6] Local press media had carried strong criticisms of the effects of phosphate-based detergents on pollution, and the researchers arranged with several "experimental" stores for the display of information about the phosphate content of each detergent brand on sale. During a three-month period, large numbers of shoppers in the experimental stores switched to brands of lower phosphate content, and the "leading brand" (which had a high phosphate content) lost 30 percent of its market share. Yet during the same period in the "control" stores (where phosphate content information was not displayed), practically no shift in the buying of different brands occurred. Thus, this study provided evidence of the potential power that public opinion has in shifting patronage from one brand to another. The results also have a strong implication for marketers— it is not only wise but profitable to keep track of public opinion!

[5] See A. Kallet and F. J. Schlink, *100,000,000 Guinea Pigs* (New York: Vanguard Press, Inc., 1933); and S. Chase and F. J. Schlink, *Your Money's Worth* (New York: The Macmillan Company, 1934).

[6] Karl E. Henion, "The Effect of Ecologically Relevant Information on Detergent Sales," *Journal of Marketing Research,* February 1972, pp. 10-14.

political pressure   When the weight of public opinion fails to bring about results desired by society, the next step often involves applying political pressure on the offending marketer. When local business executives, for instance, ignore numerous complaints, some of which have been publicized, that their companies are using misleading advertising or polluting the environment, then a demand to "cease the offense" made by the mayor or other local official may bring about the desired correction. Officials at all governmental levels—local, state, and federal—are in positions to apply political pressure to bring about results desired by society.

Two striking examples of the application of political pressure are provided by the actions taken by recent presidents concerning price changes in basic industries. Early in the administration of President John F. Kennedy, the United States Steel Corporation announced a price increase only a few days after Kennedy administration officials had persuaded the United Steel Workers Union to accept minimal pay increases in order to keep inflation from getting worse. President Kennedy effectively used the prestige of his office in bringing pressure to bear on U.S. Steel and other industry members to "roll back" steel prices. During his administration, President Lyndon B. Johnson succeeded in bringing about similar rollbacks of copper and aluminum prices—President Johnson used the term *jawboning* to describe the use of political pressure and leverage to bring about a desired action.

HOW SOCIETY INFLUENCES MARKETING—LEGISLATIVE ACTION

When the force of public opinion or political pressure or both proves ineffective in bringing about the actions it desires, society sometimes resorts to legislative action. From the standpoint of the marketing decision maker, the law limits the power of decision; but the relationship of the law to marketing decision making is often vague, since law is a complex of limitations coming from different sources. There are not only both federal and state law-making bodies but courts at both levels which, in handing down judicial interpretations, set precedents for decisions in later cases. Furthermore, some governmental agencies (e.g., the Federal Trade Commission and the Food and Drug Administration) are charged with administering various pieces of legislation, while others (e.g., the Antitrust Division of the U.S. Department of Justice) carry out the enforcement provisions of other pieces of legislation. Small wonder, then, that lawyers are reluctant or unable to state what the law is in every possible situation.

Thus, by and large, the law provides no clear-cut guides for marketing decision making. But it is convenient to think of the body of law as "the rules of the game," even though the rules are subject to differences in judicial and administrative interpretation and are almost continually changing. It is not surprising, then, that the legal implications of specific marketing decisions are sometimes difficult to predict.

The following discussion is organized around the five main decision areas in marketing which are most affected by legal restraints: competitive action, product, price, marketing channels, and promotion. The intent is to convey an appreciation of the legal boundaries, however vague and even ill defined they may sometimes be, within which the marketer must make certain decisions.

competitive action   Many marketing decisions have, purposely or not, considerable impact on competitors. In fact, nearly every marketing decision has at least some effect on competition. This is certainly inherent in most decisions on those marketing areas discussed later in this section—decisions on products, prices, marketing channels, and promotion. Our concern at this point is with those decisions that may directly affect competition and possibly expose the marketer to antitrust prosecution.

DECISIONS INVOLVING EXPANSION   Decisions involving expansion, particularly if the company is already large, should be made only after considering possible antitrust prosecution—the legal danger is that the company may be charged with unlawfully monopolizing or attempting to monopolize a market. There are only two avenues of corporate growth—one through gradual natural expansion, the other through merger with or acquisition of other firms. Either may lead to antitrust prosecution.

Legal restraints on growth have gradually become more restrictive. The first piece of federal antitrust legislation, the Sherman Antitrust Act of 1890, declared monopolization or attempts to monopolize illegal. The Clayton Antitrust Act, enacted in 1914, prohibits a corporation from acquiring stock in a competing corporation in the same industry or line of commerce, and prohibits a holding company from acquiring the stock of two or more competing corporations when acquisition would substantially lessen competition, or restrain commerce, or tend to create a monopoly. Generally, the courts have defined **monopoly power** as the power to control prices or the power to exclude competition—with strong emphasis on the word "power." Frequently, the extent of power has been measured in terms of relative market share.

The merger or acquisition route to expansion is fraught with legal complications, but companies that choose to take the natural growth route also have their problems. Once a company becomes large, and as it gains an increasing market share, management begins to fear adverse action by the government. In such a company management tends to suppress its competitive skills.

DECISIONS REQUIRING COOPERATIVE RELATIONS WITH COMPETITORS   Marketing decisions requiring any sort of cooperative relationship with competitors should be made only after considering possible violations of antitrust laws. Particularly vulnerable to antitrust prosecution are price agreements with competitors, for they are illegal per se. This means, in effect, that the courts will declare them illegal without considering any mitigating circumstances. The courts have held that it is illegal for competitors even to exchange information about prices.

It is illegal not only for competitors to fix prices among themselves, but also for them to agree upon uniform terms of sale. Use by competitors of the same basing point for pricing and collusion among bidders is also illegal.[7] Marketers "skate on thin legal ice" when they permit themselves to be drawn into any sort of pricing arrangement with their competitors.

DECISIONS ON COMPETITIVE TACTICS   The law limits the tactics a marketer can use in fighting a competitor. It is illegal, for example, for a marketer to misrepresent or disparage a competitor's products, its methods of doing business, or its financial standing and reliability. It is also illegal for a marketer to cut off a competitor's source of supply, whether by individual effort or through collusion with others.

decisions on products

There are several reasons why legal restraints have been imposed on product decisions. Some resulted from legislative efforts to preserve and maintain competition. Others trace to the legal protection afforded individual companies against having their products duplicated by competitors. Still others stem from the desire of lawmakers and governmental agencies to protect consumers' interests.

NEW PRODUCT ADDITIONS   Decisions on new products may be equivalent to those on expansion discussed earlier. If a new product decision is tied to one on a merger with or an acquisition of another firm, it is illegal if it tends to "substantially lessen competition or tend to create a monopoly." Similarly, if a new product decision involves buying certain assets from another firm, antitrust prosecution may result on the grounds that competition may be affected adversely. From a legal standpoint, the safest way for a company to secure new products is through its own research and development efforts.

PRODUCT DESIGN   Patent law imposes certain restraints on product design decisions. Holders of *design patents* are protected against others using their designs during the term the patent is in force—which may be for three and one-half, seven, or fourteen years. During the time a design patent is in force, its holder has what, in effect, is a monopoly over its use. The holder may, if it wishes, license others to use the patent, but, except in rare instances, the law does not compel it to do so. Thus, the law prohibits a marketer from selling a product that is too similar to one patented and made by a competitor. (The courts declare a product as being "too similar" if consumers regard its design or outward appearance as identical to that of a competitor's product.)

[7] A basing point is a geographical location from which F.O.B. prices are quoted.

There is a trend toward national legislation regulating other aspects of product design. The Child Protection and Toy Safety Act of 1969, for instance, empowers the U.S. Secretary of Health, Education, and Welfare to order dangerous toys to be taken off the market. Another example is that of the U.S. Department of Transportation, which has the power to develop and enforce motor vehicle safety standards. With the growing concern of society about environmental pollution, the federal government set up the Environmental Protection Agency, which has the power to establish and enforce environmental protection standards. The costs of added consumer protection are often high. Safety regulation (e.g., mandatory seat belts) and environmental regulations (e.g., emission controls) have increased the costs, and hence the retail prices, of the average automobile by several hundred dollars during the 1970s. Despite the costs incurred, even more comprehensive legal restrictions on product design are likely to be imposed in the future. Marketers must keep in mind the existence of such restraints in making decisions on product design. Failure to do so is costly. In 1978 in announcing the recall of the Pinto to replace a dangerous gas tank, Ford Motor Company executives estimated that the replacements would cost the company $75,000,000. The general trend of court decisions and government agency actions with respect to product liability is to throw even more responsibility upon the marketer to protect the consumer from dangerous products.

PRODUCT QUALITY   In some product areas, the law limits the marketer's discretion in making decisions on product quality. The Food, Drug, and Cosmetics Act—enacted by Congress in 1938—authorizes the establishment of mandatory minimum quality standards for food products. It also gave the Food and Drug Administration the power to fix standard grades for specific kinds of food products on a permissive basis (packers may accept the standards or not at their own option). This act also prohibits the adulteration and sale of any food, drug, therapeutic device, or cosmetic that may endanger public health. There are also numerous state and local laws relating to the quality of individual products, such as milk, cheese, and cream.

PRODUCT PACKAGING AND LABELING   The Fair Packaging and Labeling Act (1966) provides that the package label must disclose product identity, name and location of manufacturer, packer or distributor, net quantity of contents (weight, measure, numerical count, and net quantity of a serving or application when represented). The net quantity statement must appear on the main display panel in adequate type size and near the main printing of the trade name.[8]

Special laws, applicable to some industries, further regulate the type and content of the information that the product label must carry. Among these are laws requiring different marketers to include label information on fabric flammability, fiber content, type of fur, nature and percentages of

[8] "Federal Trade Commission Proposed Regulations Under the Fair Packaging and Labeling Act," CCH 50, 173, July 1967, *CCH Newsletter 313* (extra edition), June 28, 1967.

wool and other components, identification of synthetic fabrics by generic names, and prescribed warnings on products adjudged in some way to be dangerous. State and local laws also regulate the labeling of specific products.

In all industries not covered by special laws, the Federal Trade Commission maintains a constant watch for instances of misbranding (which generally means some form of misrepresentation on a label as to the composition, properties, or origin of the product). To comply with the law, a label must be accurate and complete in all essential details.

price decisions No class of marketing decisions is more hedged in by legal restraints than price decisions. Federal antitrust laws (the Clayton Act and Robinson-Patman Act) have implications for pricing, inasmuch as the "power to control prices" is one of the tests courts apply in determining the existence of monopoly power. Among state laws affecting pricing decisions are those forbidding sales below cost.

PRICE DISCRIMINATION The Clayton Act, as amended by the Robinson-Patman Act, prohibits any direct or indirect price discrimination by a seller among different purchasers of commodities of like grade and quality, where the effect is to injure competition. The law prohibits price discrimination, but it does permit certain differentials in price; the seller must be prepared to justify any price differences it grants if it is charged with price discrimination. Proving that price differentials are justified (in terms of differences in cost in serving different customers) is difficult.

Price discrimination resulting from the attempts of sellers to meet competitors' prices were apparently legalized under the Robinson-Patman Act, although court decisions in cases of this sort have been inconsistent.

The marketer, if it grants quantity discounts, must make them equally available to all its customers. Thus, a noncumulative quantity discount (i.e., one based on the size of a single order and shipment) is easy to justify legally. Cumulative quantity discounts (i.e., those based on how much a customer buys over an extended period) are difficult to justify legally, as there is no way a marketer can make such a discount equally available to all its customers.

A functional discount is a type of price differential that is evidently legal. A functional discount, by definition, is one based on difference in function—for instance, one given to a wholesaler but not to a retailer. Consider, for example, the paper products manufacturer who sells part of its output through wholesalers and the rest directly to retailers—ordinarily, the manufacturer must sell to the wholesalers at a lower price than it uses in selling to retailers. Under the law, if a wholesaler and a retailer do not compete directly with each other, a marketer can legally charge the wholesaler a lower price.

RESTRICTIONS ON MINIMUM PRICES Many states have legislation regulating minimum resale prices. More than half have unfair trade practices acts which forbid sales below cost. These are laws that apply to all goods sold by wholesalers and retailers, and they do not require that the goods be branded or that formal price-fixing agreements be signed. The laws of the various states differ with respect to what "cost" means, with cost being interpreted to mean all the way from invoice cost to invoice cost plus freight and handling charges plus a fixed markup percentage. In addition, over 20 states have laws outlawing below-cost sales of specific products, such as liquor, beer, and cigarettes.

At the federal level, one restraint on below-cost sales exists. The Federal Trade Commission prosecutes marketers who sell their products below cost with the intention of driving competitors out of the market. Such below-cost pricing is regarded as an unfair competitive practice.

marketing channel decisions

With comparatively few exceptions (e.g., the liquor industry in certain states), the law does not interfere with the marketer's freedom to determine its own marketing channels, or to "pick and choose" from among the available middlemen. But once the marketer establishes buying-selling relationships with its middlemen, the law is concerned with the nature of these relationships.

EXCLUSIVE DEALING   **Exclusive dealing** is an arrangement by which a marketer agrees to permit dealers to handle its product only if they agree to buy all their requirements for this type of product from the manufacturer and none whatever from competing suppliers. Generally speaking, any contract with buyers requiring them to buy all their needs from one supplier is illegal. But a necessary condition for illegality is that competition be impaired or threatened. This condition is practically always present and easy to prove.

TYING CONTRACT   The Clayton Act outlaws the **tying contract**, a device closely related to exclusive dealing. A tying contract involves the sale or lease of products on condition that the buyer or lessee buy or use certain other items that the seller or lessor offers to supply. For a marketer to make effective use of either exclusive dealing or tying contracts, it must possess powerful leverage with respect to at least some of the products offered for sale—for instance, when a manufacturer markets a brand so strongly preferred by consumers that dealers do not dare refuse to stock it.

AUTOMOBILE DEALERS FRANCHISE ACT   This act relates specifically to certain aspects of manufacturer-dealer relations in the automobile industry. Its stated purpose is "to balance the powers now heavily weighted in favor of automobile manufacturers, by enabling franchised automobile dealers to bring suits in the district courts of the United States to recover damages sustained by reason of the failure of automobile manufacturers to act in good faith in complying with terms of franchises or in terminating or not renewing franchises with their dealers." **Good faith** is defined as the duty to act in a fair and equitable manner to guarantee freedom from coercion, intimidation, or threats of coercion or intimidation. Although this act applies only to the automobile industry, it may be a forerunner of legal controls over manufacturer-dealer relations in other industries.

promotion decisions   Of all the promotion decisions, those on advertising are most affected by legal restraints. Advertising has received more attention from lawmaking bodies and enforcement agencies than has personal selling, probably because advertising exposes itself to large audiences, whereas personal selling generally does not. (See Fig. 19-1) Furthermore, advertising, whether printed or spoken, is recorded in publications and the logs of television and radio stations, where it may be inspected later by public authorities.

FALSE ADVERTISING   The Wheeler-Lea Act, a 1938 amendment to the Federal Trade Commission Act of 1914, expanded the earlier law's prohibition against "unfair methods of competition" to prohibit "unfair or deceptive

Figure 19-1   A self-regulating mechanism for advertising

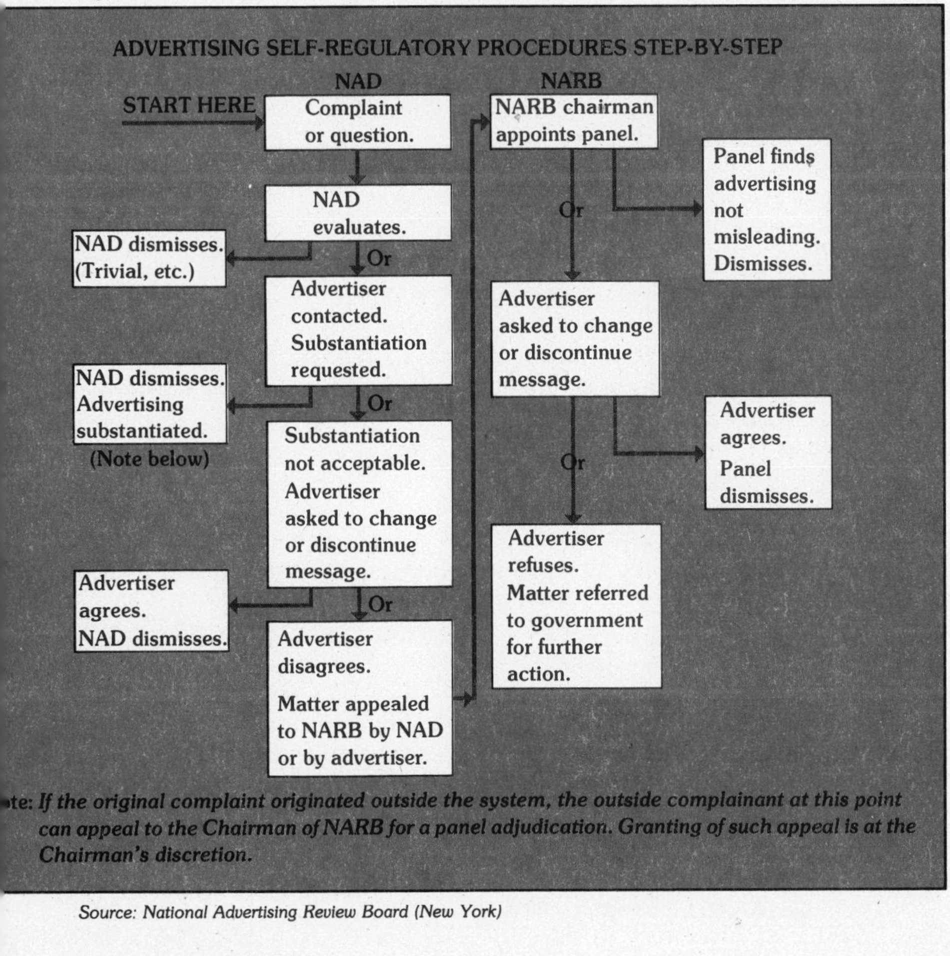

ADVERTISING SELF-REGULATORY PROCEDURES STEP-BY-STEP

Note: *If the original complaint originated outside the system, the outside complainant at this point can appeal to the Chairman of NARB for a panel adjudication. Granting of such appeal is at the Chairman's discretion.*

Source: National Advertising Review Board (New York)

acts or practices." Under both pieces of legislation, the FTC is responsible for preventing false and deceptive advertising. For example, Slenderella bread advertising claiming less calories per slice (because the slices were thinner) was held to be deceptive and, hence, illegal. The Wheeler-Lea Act specifically outlaws the dissemination of any false advertisement to induce the purchase of foods, drugs, devices, or cosmetics. This act also strengthened the FTC's enforcement procedures. As a result, in recent years the FTC has gone as far as to require **corrective advertising** to overcome the effects of deceptive advertising. For example Anacin was required to spend $24 million saying its product does *not* relieve tension (the sum it had previously spent making such a claim).

BAIT ADVERTISING   Bait advertising, simply defined, is advertising under false pretenses. The FTC considers bait advertising "an alluring but insincere offer to sell a product or service which the advertiser in truth does not intend or want to sell." Its purpose is to attract consumers interested in buying the advertised product in order to sell them a substitute product, usually at a higher price or on terms more advantageous to the advertiser. Thus, the chief aim of a bait advertisement is to obtain leads on persons interested in buying merchandise of the general type advertised. The FTC prosecutes bait advertisers as engaged in "deceptive acts."

DECEPTIVE PRICE ADVERTISING   The FTC has been especially active in seeking to prevent the advertising of deceptive prices. While the commission has prosecuted dishonest price advertisers at an ever-increasing rate, it has provided marketers with enough of the basic ground rules to encourage widespread voluntary avoidance of deceptive price advertising. According to the FTC, the law is violated whenever the term "list price" means anything but the usual price at which the product is sold at retail. The same applies to other terms, such as "manufacturer's suggested retail price," "catalog price," and "nationally advertised price."

ADVERTISING TO CHILDREN   An increasing interest has been developing, both upon the part of society and government in advertising to children. The evolving opinion is that children's lack of buying experience and gullibility makes them unfair prey of aggressive advertisers. Pressures have been brought by the FTC to control such advertising.

PROMOTIONAL ALLOWANCES AND SERVICES   The Robinson-Patman Act provides that if a customer is offered an allowance, a discount, or some other form of compensation for displaying, handling, advertising, or otherwise promoting a product, that same payment or consideration must be made available on proportionally equal terms to all other customers competing in the product's distribution. Thus, if a manufacturer offers to share the cost of newspaper advertising with a particular retailer on a 50-50 basis to comply with the law, it must find some way to make the same offer available on proportionally equal terms to all other customers who compete with that particular retailer.

SUMMARY   You should now understand why modern marketers, in formulating and implementing marketing strategies, must recognize that they are both influencing and being influenced by society. Marketers must keep their responsibilities to society in mind as they plan the manipulation of the controllables, since marketing activities have important influences not only on buyer behavior but on general economic well-being and the quality of the environment. Society, in general, expects marketers to serve its members' consumption needs efficiently, honestly, and responsibly. The reactions of society to marketing activities are expressed not only daily at the nation's checkout counters and cash registers but also over the long run through public opinion, political pressure, and legislative action. The marketing strategist, therefore, not only must know what society expects but must anticipate its reaction to marketing moves. If you have gained this understanding of the important interactions of marketing and society, you are ready to move on to Chapter 20, which focuses more specifically on the formulation and implementation of overall marketing strategy.

REVIEW AND DISCUSSION QUESTIONS

1   What are marketing's social responsibilities? Does marketing fulfill its social responsibilities? Explain.

2   Does marketing cost too much? Justify your position.

3   In what ways does marketing "add value" to a product?

4   Identify as many criticisms of marketing as you can and provide solutions as to how marketing might correct these shortcomings.

5   "Marketing induces frivolous and excessive buying and it makes people materialistic." Agree or disagree? Explain.

6   "Advertising is deceptive, it makes people want things they really don't need, and advertising is wasteful." Evaluate this statement.

7   Legal restraints appear to affect advertising decisions more than they do personal selling decisions. Why?

8   To what extent do the different types of legal restraints on marketing strengthen or weaken the position of consumers as participants in the economic process? Explain.

9   Do you believe that corrective advertising is an effective deterrent to deceptive or fraudulent advertising? Why or why not? Elaborate.

10   When the weight of public opinion fails to bring about results desired by society, the next step often involves applying political pressure on the offending marketer. Discuss.

11   "Competition serves as a sort of natural protector of the public interest." If this is so, why have legal restraints on marketing decisions been imposed? What is the value of "voluntary" regulation (vs. government imposed regulation)?

12   What implications for marketing strategy formulation are there in the various legal restraints placed upon marketing? Explain.

13   "The law prohibits price discrimination, but it does permit certain differentials in price." Explain.

14   Analyze the extent to which the law imposes restraints upon a manufacturer's choice of marketing channels and the conduct of its relationships with intermediaries.

CASE PROBLEM

Richard Metzger, marketing manager of the Petersen–McGee Toy Company, a national manufacturer of a wide variety of well-known toys and other children's products, had just delivered a speech before a regional convention of a large consumer organization. Metzger's speech, before a group of nearly 200 people, was on "The Bright Side of the Market Place," and dealt with the things marketers were currently doing to provide a better standard of living for the American population.

During the question-and-answer session that followed the 45-minute talk, one gentleman impatiently called out for the mobile microphone. He commended Metzger for the job Petersen–McGee was doing and for the interesting speech. "However," he said, "you have not been objective in your presentation because never once did you call upon marketers to do something about the deception and fraudulence we see literally every day in the marketplace." As the man spoke, a number of affirmative nods indicated to Metzger that the speaker was saying something the others believed. The gentleman continued.

"You marketers, and I'm calling you one of them, Metzger, only because it's every marketer's responsibility and not because I'm accusing you personally, but you marketers are all alike. Your main goal is to sell your product and make money. It doesn't really matter how you do it as long as the bottom line is acceptable, because that's how you measure success.

"For so many years we've been taken to the cleaners. We've been told, not asked, what products are good for us. And we've been told when we need something and when we don't, and we've been told why doing it your way is the best way. Frankly, I'm tired of it. Consumers are being manipulated as though they were pawns. The advertising, the selling, the inferior products, the lousy service, the broken promises, you name it, marketers and marketing are selling us a bill of goods. They're happy as long as they separate us from our cash. That's the important thing. Not whether it's the right thing for someone, just whether they can get our money.

"You marketers manipulate us by creating false needs and making us feel unworthy or making us feel totally inept if we don't buy Product X. And you do it by these slick ads and soft sells that get you in the real subtle ways. We just can't get our money's worth in all of this. Like I said, I'm sick and tired of it. When are you going to think of us first and yourselves second, which is the way it should be? When are you going to give us what we want in product quality, service, warranties, truthful advertising, more reasonable prices, less puffery in advertising, and more value? Now you force on us what you think is best. Well, how about making available for us what we really want? And, you know, you just might come out a lot better for it.

"I might be getting carried away, but let me just cite advertising to kids, something you surely know a lot about. Now, myself, I've got three kids. Do you realize what I go through just because you marketers are trying to hard-sell my kids by bombarding them with ad after ad after ad and making them feel deprived and underprivileged if they don't have one of your 'Slam Bang Super-Duper Motorized Top Scoop Back Hoe Front End Loader Sizzle Sozzle Construction Outfits'? You know, the one that'll make them the 'leader of the gang'? Sure you do. You make it look like the kid will be considered unacceptable unless he does what you want him to do and if he does buy your product he'll be more accepted by his peers. For shame!

410

"Well, I've got to put up with it for breakfast foods, snacks, candies, oh, candies, do I ever, and fast-food restaurants, as well as toys like you make. Children have great imaginations and marketers continually exploit the child's difficulty in distinguishing between what is real and what is fantasy. Ads have a habit of being misleading, especially to children.

"Marketers entice the kids by playing on their inability to recognize differences between editorial and program content and advertising content. You know, the old 'Hey, kids, use the vitamin that good ol' Yogi Bear likes best so you, too, can grow big and strong like me' trick.

"Or, how about all those ads that beg the kids to ask their parents to buy something for them. The implication is that if the parents don't buy the product for the child, they are preventing his peer group acceptance or inhibiting his growth or development of muscles, or whatever. It's absurd.

"Ah, well, I could go on and on. I've only hit a tiny speck of the problems with marketing. It affects youngsters and older people alike. Marketing blatantly forces on people a style of life that they have little say about and at a price they really can't afford, either socially or economically. Marketing is coercive because it forces things on us. Marketing, especially advertising, is misleading and it manipulates people. In short, Mr. Metzger, marketing is nothing short of morally bankrupt. It doesn't do any good to complain or to make known your wishes, because no one hears you. Consumerism is just what the marketing establishment wants it to be and it's sure not for the good of the people. Marketing is socially irresponsible, Mr. Metzger. I know it and so do you if you're honest with yourself. So, how can you, for nearly one hour, stand up there, and talk like marketing is the greatest thing since ice cream. The bright side of the marketplace. Bosh! C'mon, Mr. Metzger, let's get with it. My question to you is 'When is marketing going to recognize that it has a social responsibility and then do something about it by giving the consumer what he or she wants—and that's satisfaction?' And, besides, marketing costs too much compared with what we get out of it."

Metzger, completely silent during the five-minute oration by the gentleman, sensed he was on the spot and he knew he had to come up with a solid answer to the critic's attack on marketing.

questions:

1. Do you agree with the critic's appraisal of marketing? Why or why not?
2. What are marketing's social responsibilities? How well do you feel that marketing fulfills those responsibilities?
3. How can there be assurance that marketing will act in a socially, ethically, and legally responsible manner?
4. What should Metzger say in his rebuttal to the critic's charges?
5. Does marketing cost too much? Why or why not?

When you have mastered the contents of this chapter, you should be able to:

1   Contrast the relative importance of, and need for, formalized overall marketing strategies under conditions of (a) no direct competition, (b) pure competition, (c) monopolistic competition, and (d) oligopolistic competition.

2   Analyze how a marketer in an industry characterized by monopolistic or oligopolistic competition should go about making decisions on products, distribution, promotion, price, and the timing of marketing actions.

3   Explain the three main factors involved in selecting inputs to overall marketing strategy.

4   Explain how a marketer should go about achieving an optimum combination of inputs to its overall marketing strategy.

5   Outline the several problems that confront marketers in implementing and timing their marketing strategies.

6   Explain the nature and purpose of a marketing audit.

20

overall
marketing strategy

Basically, a company's overall marketing strategy is its competitive posture in the marketplace. Management shapes various aspects of this posture as it formulates strategies for each controllable (product, distribution, promotion, and pricing). Management's mission is to manipulate the controllables in terms of the uncontrollables in ways that both meet the target market's needs and wants and facilitate achievement of the company's overall goals. To accomplish this, management unifies the company's product-market, distribution, promotion, and pricing strategies into an appropriate overall marketing strategy (i.e., into a deliberately planned competitive posture). Discussion and analysis in this chapter are aimed to help you integrate your previous knowledge of marketing and to gain added insights on (1) overall marketing strategies and decisions in different competitive settings, (2) the formulation of overall marketing strategy, (3) the implementation of marketing strategy and timing, (4) positioning, and (5) the evaluation of overall marketing strategy.

Throughout this book the emphasis has been on a systems approach to managing marketing operations. In managing marketing, many decisions are made—each seemingly independent, all in fact interrelated. (See Fig. 20-1) Thus, if a marketer changes its product's price by a substantial amount, it must also reevaluate other parts of the company's overall marketing strategy. If the price change is small, the need for reevaluation is not so great, although the marketers should still consider possible changes in the other controllables. Significant change in any of the controllables influences the effectiveness of the other controllables. The ultimate success of changes in a controllable in meeting desired objectives depends on the marketer's skill (and luck) in maintaining an optimum combination of strategies—that is, in keeping the company's overall marketing strategy in balance.

Management, in formulating and implementing overall marketing strategy, concerns itself primarily with identifying opportunities to serve target markets profitably and serving them so effectively that it is difficult for

Figure 20-1 Various stages in decision making—planning, action, and control phases

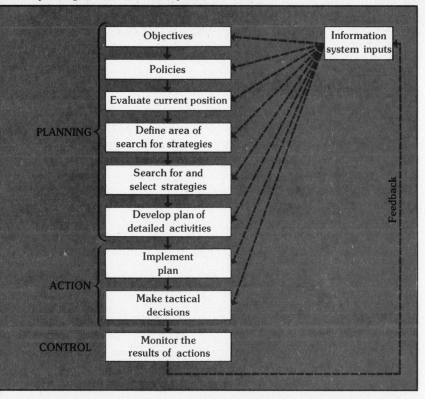

Source: David J. Luck and O. C. Ferrell, Marketing Strategy and Plans (Englewood Cliffs, New Jersey: Prentice-Hall, Inc., 1979), p. 9.

competitors to take business away on a profitable basis. But competitive postures are either aggressive or defensive. When a marketer's products are already established in the market, there is strong temptation to adopt a defensive posture—that is, to maintain a holding action. But the danger in defending the status quo is in yielding the initiative to competitors. If these competitors develop successful product innovations, they may break established customer loyalties and buying patterns in the process.

Seven-Up, for instance, first broke into the soft drink market not by introducing another cola, root beer, or other standard flavor, but by developing and marketing an entirely new flavor—lemon-lime. As Seven-Up succeeded in carving out a market segment for itself, certain other bottlers, such as Coca-Cola and Pepsi-Cola, dropped their predominantly defensive overall marketing strategies, introduced new flavors of their own, and took the offensive. Had Coca-Cola, for example, continued its defensive strategy, it would merely have tried to retain or increase its share of the market for cola drinks. With Seven-Up's introduction of the lemon-lime flavor, the total market for soft drinks expanded, and the competitor restricting itself to the traditional flavors found itself with a shrinking share of the total market.

COMPETITIVE SETTINGS   The importance of (and need for) formalized overall marketing strategies (i.e., deliberately planned competitive postures) varies with the competitive setting. There are four basic kinds of competitive setting: (1) no direct competition, (2) pure competition, (3) monopolistic competition, and (4) oligopolistic competition.

no direct competition   There are **no direct competitors** for either the monopolists or the marketer of a radically new and different product in its market pioneering life-cycle stage. But both need formalized overall marketing strategies: the monopolist because it has indirect competitors (such as the deBeers Consolidated diamond monopoly has) contending for the same prospects' interest and buying decisions; the innovating marketer because it has only a limited period free from direct competition. Both the monopolist and the innovating marketer must initiate and stimulate primary demand—that is, demand for the product category—through promotional strategies designed to influence final buyers and middlemen. Both need distribution strategies providing for marketing channels, middlemen's cooperation, and systems for the product's physical distribution. Both require a pricing strategy: the monopolist (at least in theory) being free to maximize profits through "charging what the traffic will bear"; the innovating marketer generally choosing either a price-skimming or a penetration-pricing strategy, depending upon how soon it expects direct competitors to enter the market. Most important, both the monopolist and the innovating marketer need to integrate individual product-market, distribution, promotion, and pricing strategies into overall marketing strategies consistent with the long-term goals of each. Such consistency is obtained when all the elements of the strategy are in balance. Therefore, the marketer of a product that has no close substitutes must take care in choosing a target market, in distributing, in promoting, in pricing, and in integrating all of these into an overall marketing strategy suitable for achieving the organization's long-term goals.

pure competition   Economists define **pure competition** as a market situation with many buyers and sellers, none of whom is powerful enough to control or to influence the prevailing market price. The economist assumes, among other things, that (1) no single buyer or seller is so large that he can appreciably affect the product's total demand or supply; (2) all sellers' products are homogeneous, so buyers are indifferent as to which sellers they buy from; (3) no artificial restraints on prices of any kind exist (i.e., no governmental price fixing, nor any administering of prices by individual companies, trade associations, labor unions, or others); and (4) all buyers are fully informed of all sellers' prices.

If these assumptions held true, no marketer would ever have to formulate overall marketing strategy. Each seller would be too small to gain business through price cutting at the expense of its competitors and, if it did cut the price, competitors would immediately match it. No marketer could compete by offering a better product, because product differentiation is ruled out. It would be futile for a marketer to advertise or otherwise promote its product, inasmuch as all potential buyers are already fully informed and buy solely on the basis of price. Because the economist also implicitly assumes that sellers and buyers are in direct contact, no marketer would need to worry about marketing channels or physical distribution. Under pure competition there are no marketing controllables, and there is no need for marketing strategies.

Probably the nearest thing to pure competition is found in the distribution of certain agricultural commodities, such as the crops of truck farms. For the sellers of such commodities, the critical marketing decisions (besides that of deciding which crop to grow) relate to physical distribution: moving the commodities in time and space. A New Jersey truck farmer, for instance, has the choice of shipping each day's pick of the string bean crop to wholesale produce markets in Philadelphia or New York, or to delay sending them to market for a day or two hoping for a rise in price. But if a truck farmer is shipping a highly perishable commodity, such as strawberries or mushrooms, there may not even be the option of storing the output a short time.

monopolistic competition

Most modern marketers operate under conditions that approximate monopolistic competition, which means that some or all of the assumptions of pure competition do not hold. Specifically, monopolistic competition exists when there are many sellers of a generic kind of product but each seller's brand is in some way differentiated from every other seller's brand. The number of sellers is sufficiently large that the actions of any one have no perceptible effect upon others, and their actions have no perceptible effect upon that seller. Furthermore, under monopolistic competition, it is comparatively easy for additional competitors to enter the market. This competitive setting describes that of many products during late phases of their market growth and during much of their market maturity life-cycle stages.

Nearly every seller's brand of product, whether it be peanut butter or lipstick, can be differentiated (at least in final buyers' minds) from competing brands. Most ultimate consumers appear convinced that different brands of even such "identical" products as aspirin, coffee, and vinegar are not exactly alike, providing individual marketers with opportunities to build brand preferences among buyers and, hence, to control some share of the market.

Of even greater significance is the fact that most ultimate consumers (and many industrial buyers) are not fully informed—often not even adequately informed—about offerings of competing sellers. Thus, for instance, it is common to find two competing (and even neighboring) supermarkets selling identical, branded items at different prices. Ultimate consumers, in fact, in making many buying decisions, particularly for low-priced items, are often overwhelmed by the sheer variety of products and brands from which to choose, and make no attempt to find the best bargains.

Competitive settings characterized by monopolistic competition not only provide marketing opportunities for the marketer but also demand marketing skill. If a seller (producer or middleman) can differentiate its product, it has a market message to relate through its promotional strategy, which provides it with some control over its product's distribution and price. Such a seller needs skill both in formulating an appropriate overall marketing strategy and in implementing it in the competitive struggle for survival and success.

oligopolistic competition   Many modern marketers operate under conditions approximating oligopolistic competition. This competitive setting exists when the number of competitors is small enough that they are individually identified and known to each other and it is difficult for new competitors to enter the market. Each competitor is of sufficient importance (i.e., it is a large enough organization and has a large enough market share) that changes in its overall marketing strategy have direct repercussions on the others. Each marketer in an oligopolistic industry must weigh the possible reactions of each of its competitors in formulating and implementing its own overall marketing strategy. Oligopolistic competition develops in the marketing of many products either during a late phase of their market growth or an early phase of their marketing maturity.

In the United States, there are oligopolies in such industries as automobiles, appliances, soap and detergents, and shoes in the consumer goods field and in steel, aluminum, textile machinery, and machine tools in the industrial goods field. A strong trend exists for the more successful firms to continue growing, and for the less successful to fail or disappear (through merger). The soap and auto industries provide dramatic examples, both having been reduced from numerous competitors to a small group.

Indications are that there will be more, not fewer, oligopolistic industries in the future. Governmental agencies and congressional committees try continually to discourage the merger movement as a threat to "free competition." Proposed mergers are denied and complete mergers are declared illegal when they are proved in conflict with the antimonopoly laws. However, the drift toward oligopoly is continuing but through the slower process of expansion by the successful and failure by the others.

Oligopoly produces the most aggressive competition. When a few large producers dominate an industry, the competitive moves of any one can have a significant effect on the entire market: when one of the large soap companies introduces a new liquid detergent or low-phosphate detergent, its competitors risk a rapid loss of market share if they do not respond appropriately and immediately. For this reason, competitors' actions are watched closely, and marketing changes by one firm are almost certain to be matched or countered in some way by its competitors. Changes in one competitor's product, in its distribution, in its promotion—if they hold promise of increasing its market share—are imitated, improved upon, or otherwise countered by its competitors as rapidly as they can launch their counteroffensives. Price changes by individual industry members are matched by others almost immediately. Industry-wide price adjustments often take place so quickly that they appear to result from collusion when, in fact, there has been none.

However, when collusive action is attempted in oligopolies, the small number of competitors makes it particularly easy. As a case in point, in the 1960s five large makers of power switch gear assemblies were found guilty of having conspired to fix prices on bids for government contracts. Collusive arrangements are common among small companies participating in local oligopolistic situations (e.g., local bakeries and dairies), but they are unusual (perhaps because they are not easy to hide from federal law enforcement agencies) among large national competitors.

MARKETING DECISIONS IN A COMPETITIVE SETTING

In any industry characterized by monopolistic or oligopolistic competition, an individual marketer skilled in planning and applying the marketing controllables has an opportunity to win the buying preferences of certain market segments on a more-or-less permanent basis. Under monopolistic competition, the number of competitors is large enough that the actions of any one have no perceptible effect upon the others and their actions have no perceptible effect upon that competitor; but this does not mean that any one marketer can afford wholly to ignore its competitors' marketing activities. Skill (and/or luck) in such matters as product innovation, distribution, and promotion makes some companies major contenders in their industries, while others with little marketing skill (and/or luck) fall by the wayside. In other words, the potential for monopolistic competition to evolve into oligopolistic competition is almost always present. Thus, nearly every marketer needs to consider both its competitors' marketing moves and their possible reactions to its own marketing decisions. Every marketing decision is influenced to some extent by competitors' actions and likely reactions.

the product

Whether a marketer is an innovator or a follower, its product decisions (if they are to prove successful) must take into account the probable timing of competitors' actions. For example, much of the research and testing that goes into developing a new product may be wasted if a competitor introduces a similar new product to the market first. The competitor gets not only credit for the innovation but also first "crack" at the market. In attempting to prevent such occurrences, manufacturers sometimes feel compelled to market new products that are not fully perfected. Furthermore, when one marketer introduces a new or greatly improved product, its competitors must be prepared to introduce competitive substitutes as soon as they can determine that the innovation is a marketing success; this, too, causes some to sacrifice extensive testing for earlier market introduction.

Business history is full of examples of companies that slipped from positions of industry leadership (or even that disappeared entirely) following their competitors' introduction of new products that these companies were unwilling or unable to imitate, or were too long in matching. Consider what happened in the washing machine industry after the mass introduction of fully automatic washers. The total number of washing machine manufacturers shrank greatly, as manufacturers who failed to introduce automatic washers or who were too long in doing so withdrew from the industry. The Maytag Company, which had been the industry's sales leader for nearly 30 years, dropped way back, while the Whirlpool Corporation took over first position. Several trade magazines attributed this status change to Whirlpool's fairly early introduction of an automatic washer and Maytag's failure to do so. However, the introduction of automatics did not guarantee success, since many companies that later left the industry had tried to market automatics. Nevertheless, the decision not to introduce an automatic evidently did guarantee failure for many others.

distribution MARKETING CHANNELS Decisions on marketing channels are comparable to the military commander's choice of battlefield. Products, if they are to compete successfully, must be on sale in places where target buyers expect to buy them. If most ultimate consumers, for instance, expect to find photographic film in drugstores and at drive-up film processing booths (in shopping centers) and customarily buy their film in such places, it is difficult for a film producer to sell its product through hardware stores or service stations. Some film, to be sure, is sold through unconventional outlets but, assuming other marketing circumstances to be equal, it is easier to sell a product through outlets where target customers expect to find it. Ultimate consumers, seeing film in a hardware store, might buy it on impulse when they remember that they need film, but when they start out with the primary purpose of buying film, they usually go to stores that always carry film. Similar generalizations hold for other levels of distribution. Retailers seeking to buy a supply of some particular product ordinarily contact suppliers who they know handle such products.

However, sometimes a marketer finds that it cannot use the customary channel. Retail druggists, for example, may already stock two makes of film and, hence, may refuse to stock a third brand which, from their standpoint, might result in larger inventories with no increase in sales volume and therefore lower rates of stockturn. Thus, the marketer of a new film may find that its most feasible alternative is to persuade other types of retailers, such as grocers, to stock its brand, trying to overcome the unconventional outlet handicap through offering a better product, a lower price, a more effective promotional program, or some combination of these or other factors.

PHYSICAL DISTRIBUTION   Decisions on physical distribution are similar to those the military commander makes on logistics. Both the marketer and the military strategist want to have the right resource at the right place at the right time; but, while the military strategist looks upon cost as a minor consideration, the marketer regards obtaining physical distribution at a reasonable cost as highly important. In managing physical distribution, the marketer seeks to maximize the economic value of its products by getting and having them where they are wanted and at the time wanted, at reasonable cost. [1]

Competitors' actions and operations influence physical distribution decisions. If, for example, a Chicago luggage manufacturer has no competitors with plants or warehouses in the Pacific Northwest, it may serve that area directly from its Chicago factory by ordinary truck or rail shipments. However, if a competitor opens a new plant in Seattle, the Chicago manufacturer then may either have to use a faster transportation method, such as air freight, or change its storage method, perhaps by opening its own warehouse in Seattle, or both. The manufacturer's decision should depend upon which alternative will provide the necessary level of service demanded by customers at a reasonable total expenditure on shipping, on storage, and on investment in inventories. If it continues with its previous physical distribution arrangement unchanged, the Seattle-based competitor may gain a strong competitive edge through its ability to provide faster delivery service to customers in that area—so they can reduce their own inventory investments. However, the Chicago manufacturer also has other alternatives: it can improve its product, make it more attractive pricewise (to dealers, consumers, or both), or support it with heavier and/or more effective promotion—or it can put together some combination of these and other factors. Normally, any move at all requires that overall marketing strategy be revised.

promotion   The promotional strategies chosen by a marketer— that is, the methods it chooses to use to stimulate market demand—are related to its sales expectations. If, for example, a marketer believes that a 5 percent sales increase is possible during the coming year, it may plan an advertising program and/or increase the strength and effectiveness of its sales force to the extent it thinks necessary to achieve the higher sales volume. However, in changing promotional strategy, the marketer should not assume that its competitors will continue their present promotional efforts. If a leading firm in an industry increases its annual advertising budget from $10 million to $15 million, its main competitors may decide they have to either make similar increases or lose market share.

---

[1] Donald J. Bowersox, *Logistical Management,* 2nd ed. (New York: Macmillan Publishing Co., Inc., 1978), p. 4.

If market demand for the product is expansible, all or most firms in the industry may benefit from the increased advertising—that is, industry sales would increase enough to more than cover the increased advertising costs. If, however, market demand is not expansible, total industry sales will not increase and the added advertising reduces most firms' gross margins and net profits. As with other components of overall marketing strategy, a competitor's increased promotional efforts can be countered in more ways than by simply matching or exceeding the increased promotion. For example, a marketer might decide to launch a new or improved product, strengthen its distribution system (perhaps by offering special incentives to dealers to get them to push the product more), or make its price more attractive.

Promotional effort provides a major means whereby a marketer can gain a competitive edge. Both the number of dollars invested in promotion and the effectiveness with which they are used are important. Two competitors may match each other's promotional expenditures dollar for dollar, but one gets back many more sales dollars in return than the other. Two advertising campaigns cost the same number of dollars, but one, because it uses more powerful selling appeals, reaches a larger or more receptive audience, or for some other reason produces considerably more sales volume. Two otherwise identical advertising campaigns differ in effectiveness because one fits in more appropriately with its sponsor's overall marketing strategy than the other. Similar generalizations hold for the productivity of the sales forces. The company with the more effective sales force management gets back more sales dollars per dollar spent on its sales force than one with less effective management.

price   The price a marketer places on its brand must generally be "in the same ballpark" as those on competing items. Although some brands of superior quality or prestige may be marketed successfully at higher-than-average prices, it is poor strategy to allow a price to get too far out of line with prices on directly competitive items. When competitive prices drop, the marketer of the quality brand should seriously consider cutting its price as well. When competitive prices go up, the marketer of the quality brand may consider raising its price.

Most marketers pursuing aggressive marketing strategies prefer not to rely on price as the main competitive weapon. They seek differential advantages over their competitors by stressing other elements in their marketing strategies—for example, products, distribution methods and systems, or promotion. Therefore, when prices in an industry are more or less uniform, this often indicates not only industry members' keen awareness of each other's prices but also their common desire to avoid using price as a main basis for competition.

Despite the general reluctance of marketers to use pricing as a competitive weapon, there are times when price competition provides the most appropriate course of action. Retailers opening new stores offer sweeping price reductions for a short time to overcome consumers' established shopping patterns and to attract them into the store. The same is true when a

marketer uses penetration pricing in introducing a new product or in entering a new market. Furthermore, if a competitor introduces a new product,
comes up with an effective new promotional gimmick, or the like, a price
reduction may be a necessary competitive move to hold market share or to
minimize its loss. Then, too, at all distribution levels, price reductions are
regularly used for clearing out last year's models and seasonal merchandise.

Some marketers use price as the main competitive weapon. To do so
successfully, they must combine high efficiency (resulting in large sales volumes and low dollar unit costs) with willingness to accept low profits per
sales dollar. Many discount department stores, such as K-Mart and Zayre,
consistently strive to sell at prices under those of competitors. However, even
in these cases, price is only one element in overall marketing strategy. Customarily, the discount department store also emphasizes "known" brands or
equivalent brands of its own, shopping convenience, ease of parking, and
heavy promotion.

timing marketing actions

A marketer's decisions on whether to lead or follow
its competitors are critical. Not every marketer
should (or can) be an innovator. While the innovator may gain an important
competitive edge because it is first with something new, it must also assume
substantial risks. If its competitors are prepared to follow quickly, the innovators may gain very little and, in fact, may be worse off from having been
first.

Consider the risks that a marketer accepts when it decides to lead in
introducing a radically new product—that is, a true product innovation. One
is that the first marketer of a new product stands more chance of failing than
those who follow—for example, the first marketer of ballpoint pens met
eventual failure, whereas those entering the market later scored great successes. A second risk is that the innovation may flop—Procter & Gamble,
for example, once tried to market a liquid dentifrice, Teel, nationally; consumers would not accept it and Procter & Gamble had to withdraw it from
the market. Then there are risks in just trying to get to the market first; a
marketer may invest heavily in R & D, find what it thinks is an innovation,
decide to test-market it, learn that the innovation has little chance for success, and drop it at this point—General Foods had this type of experience
with both frozen baby foods and "instant frozen ice cream sodas."

But the marketer that leaves the innovations to its competitors also
takes risks. The greatest hazards are those of being caught by surprise by
competitors' marketing moves and of losing a substantial market share before it can launch an effective countermove. The marketer that lets its competitors do the innovating must be prepared to counter their successful innovations (products or otherwise) quickly and effectively.

positioning in the market

As important as timing in a company's strategy is
positioning in the marketplace. The term positioning
is defined as the collective perceptions consumers or users have of a company and/or its product in relationship to other companies and products. In

the minds of consumers or users each product has some perceptual relationship to other products.

Positioning is involved in a number of dimensions of marketing strategy. It is involved in the perception of product type. Thus, when General
Foods introduced freeze-dried coffee, it made a strong effort to position the
product in the minds of consumers as being completely different from instant coffee, since the appearance and use of the two products were similar.
GF attempted to persuade consumers that here was a unique product that
tasted like ground coffee and was as convenient as instant coffee.

Some products are positioned on the basis of quality. When General
Motors introduced its compact Cadillac, the Seville, it took great pains to
build a strong image of quality and comfort. The price was set high, and the
emphasis in promotion was on the car's unique quality features, so that
customers would not equate small with less.

Many products are positioned on the basis of price. J. C. Penney, for
example, positions most of its merchandise slightly below medium price.
Yet, at the same time it emphasizes the quality of its merchandise, so that
customers perceive Penney products as being a good buy for the money.

Positioning is significant to consumers in that it provides a basis for
comparing alternative choices in the marketplace. The marketer can guide
the consumer by furnishing clues to help position its product in relationship
to others. But, if the marketer is unaware of the consumer's need and provides no positioning clues, consumers position the product themselves. This
positioning may not be what the marketer wanted.

FORMULATING OVERALL MARKETING STRATEGY

Formulating overall marketing strategy requires integration of all dimensions of the marketing effort.
Ideally, the marketer should have some foolproof sys-
tem for determining whether or not the combination of inputs going into the
overall marketing strategy is optimal and, therefore, whether or not the
resulting profit (and other desired outputs, in terms of the company's goals)
is also optimal. Unfortunately, no such foolproof system has yet been devised, but some experimental work has been done in the building of mathematical models for determining marketing strategies. However, few companies rely at all on mathematical models for strategy determination. Until
such models become more sophisticated, the best that can be done is to
apply a systematic approach to strategy formulation.

What is a systematic approach to strategy formulation? It is an approach that involves evaluation of the possible inputs to the overall marketing strategy in terms of the likely outputs. Each aspect of each major input
(i.e., product-market, distribution, promotion, and pricing strategies) is analyzed and evaluated for its probable impact on the desired output (i.e.,
achievement of the marketer's objectives). Then selections are made from
the various inputs in such a way that the combination (i.e., the overall
marketing strategy) is the best for achieving the desired outputs.

COMPETITORS' COUNTERMOVES The relative effectiveness of possible **countermoves** by competitors varies with different marketing inputs, and the marketer must take this into account in selecting inputs. Most competitors easily and quickly match or otherwise adjust to price changes; however, they find it difficult (and sometimes impossible) to follow or retaliate against product innovations. This explains why many marketers seek to gain differential advantage over their competitors by varying product characteristics or by altering promotion rather than prices. Retail price wars often develop because some retailers fail to evaluate alternative strategies intelligently. Anxious or even desperate to increase volume, an individual retailer unobtrusively lowers prices, hoping that competitors will not notice this action or will not copy it. Of course they do, and the result is a price war. If, instead, the retailer emphasizes superior customer service as its chief competitive weapon, it may not be copied, and the retailer will gain a competitive advantage. A marketer desiring to improve the "hitting power" of its overall marketing strategy should give first consideration to those moves involving inputs that are least subject to effective retaliatory actions by competitors.

SYNERGISTIC POTENTIAL Some marketing inputs have **synergistic potential** (i.e., are capable of being mutually reinforcing), and the marketer should consider this in working toward an optimum overall marketing strategy. For example, an investment in point-of-purchase displays designed to tie in with a national advertising campaign often increases the total impact of a promotional effort far more than equal investment in additional advertising. Displays and advertisements can be made mutually reinforcing, since the display repeats the advertising message at a time when the consumer is in an outlet where the product is on sale.

Similarly, product inputs and marketing channel inputs are mutually reinforcing or not, depending on the effectiveness with which they are integrated. For instance, when a marketer distributes its product through self-service retailers, potential buyers should be able to identify the product from its package and to obtain from it information that clerks would otherwise have to provide. When bed sheets are sold in full-service retail stores, they are frequently not packaged. Salesclerks inform the customers as to brand name, thread count, and shrink resistance. But when sheets are sold in self-service stores, where the help of salesclerks is not available, individual packaging provides a way of communicating product information to the consumer.

SUBSTITUTABILITY The selection of marketing inputs is affected by their degree of substitutability. It is important to know the extent to which one input can substitute for another, inasmuch as profit goals or resource limitations may prevent a decision maker from making unlimited use of all inputs. Marketing strategists must ask themselves such questions as these: Will product quality higher than in competitive brands substitute for a promotional budget smaller than those of competitors? Will a larger promotional budget substitute for shortcomings in dealer cooperation? Will a price lower than competitors substitute for sparse distribution? Consideration of substitutables helps in determining which input(s) to include and which to emphasize in the overall marketing strategy.

OPTIMUM COMBINATION OF MARKETING INPUTS

PRODUCTIVITY In formulating overall marketing strategy, the marketer should recognize that not all inputs have equal **productivity**. Some inputs require a minimum level of use before they begin to have measurable effects—for example, an advertising message must be repeated several times before consumers become aware of it. A single spot television commercial may have almost no effect on viewers, but after it has been repeated several times, viewers begin to hear, see, and remember it. If the marketer cannot afford a sufficient number of TV spots to succeed in passing the threshold of consumers' awareness, it is better off concentrating on some other advertising input, where the cost of crossing the threshold of awareness is lower. The lower cost per consumer contact of radio, magazines, and billboards often makes it possible, with a limited budget, to provide a much stronger impact on consumers than with TV.

ECONOMIES OF SCALE The choice of a combination of marketing inputs is also affected by **economies of scale**—that is, by efficiencies resulting from operating above a minimum level of activity. For instance, a direct-to-retailer marketing channel may offer a producer strong advantages in terms of communications and promotional effort and, in areas where its retail outlets are geographically concentrated, the cost per sales call may be low enough for direct-to-retailer distribution to be economical. Yet in other areas, where the retail outlets handling its product are widely scattered, the costs of using the direct channel may be out of line with the costs of alternative channels. In this instance, economies of scale dictate different marketing channels in the two areas. Similar economies of scale apply in many marketing inputs, such as those involving advertising media, adding new items to the product line, servicing products directly or through middlemen, and so on. When possible economies of scale are involved, inputs already at an economical volume usually represent the most productive investment of resources.

INPUT ELASTICITY Different marketing inputs vary in their effects on demand, and the marketer needs to consider this in selecting the best combination. A marketer may have to make several pricing decisions for a single product, and the choice of the best combination depends partly on an analysis of price **elasticity** of demand. For example, when distributors and dealers follow suggested prices, the marketer, in effect, establishes selling prices at all three distribution levels. An understanding of variations in price elasticity at each level helps the marketer determine whether increasing wholesalers' and retailers' margins is likely to be more or less effective than decreasing the prices consumers are asked to pay. If the consumer demand for a product is price-inelastic, a 5 percent increase in dealer and/or wholesaler margins may be more effective, because of the resulting increase in promotional efforts by these middlemen, than a 5 percent decrease in prices to consumers. Actually, such decisions are much more complex than this example implies, since not only must price elasticities be taken into account, but simultaneous comparisons need to be made of promotional and product elasticities. Although estimating price, promotional, and product elasticities is not easy, it should be tried, for even crude results are better than pure intuition.

IMPLEMENTATION OF MARKETING STRATEGY

Marketing inputs require different amounts of time to implement; therefore, they must be prepared and introduced in some planned sequence aimed toward making the chosen overall marketing strategy effective at a given target date. Thus, a marketer who decides to increase the size of its sales force substantially must allow from several months to a year or more to recruit and train new recruits to the point where they become productive sales personnel. If a marketer wants to open a new marketing channel, it may find even more time is needed to effect the change. Likewise, in implementing advertising strategy, the marketer finds that TV advertising schedules are generally booked a year in advance. Also, it is often necessary to repeat advertising messages over weeks or even months before they begin to impact on sales. The marketer must skillfully coordinate all such inputs if it is to succeed in putting its overall marketing strategy into effect.

In addition, all inputs to the overall marketing strategy do not retain their previously achieved levels of effectiveness for the same lengths of time. A marketer's new product or package will probably continue to attract buyers up to the time some competitor introduces a better product or more attractive package; such competitive innovations can occur at almost any time. One advertising theme may lose its effectiveness after a single season of use, while another may continue to attract new buyers for years. Consequently, in planning the inputs to overall marketing strategy, the marketer must consider each input's relative rate of decay in effectiveness.

Figure 20-2 shows how one marketer developed a sequence for the introduction and continued application of each input in its overall marketing strategy. Working back (in time) from the target date for introducing the product to final buyers, the marketer scheduled each input with sufficient lead time to be fully effective at the target date. Since the target introduction date at retail was May 1, wholesalers had to solicit dealers' orders 30 to 60 days before that, and sales personnel had to get wholesalers' orders still earlier. The marketer planned the advertising program and scheduled it for release in media on and following May 1. Previous experience had taught a valuable lesson: If advertisements reach prospective final buyers before dealers have the advertised item in stock, much of the advertising expenditure is

Figure 20-2 Time schedule for introduction of
a new product

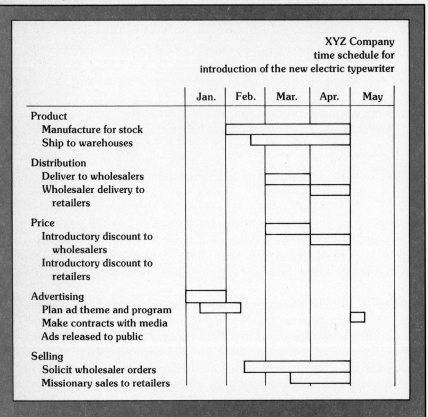

XYZ Company
time schedule for
introduction of the new electric typewriter

	Jan.	Feb.	Mar.	Apr.	May
Product					
Manufacture for stock					
Ship to warehouses					
Distribution					
Deliver to wholesalers					
Wholesaler delivery to retailers					
Price					
Introductory discount to wholesalers					
Introductory discount to retailers					
Advertising					
Plan ad theme and program					
Make contracts with media					
Ads released to public					
Selling					
Solicit wholesaler orders					
Missionary sales to retailers					

wasted, and if dealers stock the new item much before appearance of the advertising, they have initial difficulty in selling it, lose interest in it, and fail to give it their best efforts when the advertising does appear. Thus, in this case, the marketer believed it highly important to have the dates of product availability and appearance of promotion close together in order to obtain the desired results in terms of advertising effectiveness and dealer effort. Timing is an important factor in putting an overall marketing strategy into effect.

EVALUATING OVERALL MARKETING STRATEGY

Overall marketing strategy is a composite—built up, or put together, by blending various inputs (products, marketing channels and physical distribution systems, advertising, personal selling, other promotion, and prices) in different combinations to achieve desired outputs (i.e., objectives), such as some targeted return on investment, market share, and brand image). Overall marketing strategy is also dynamic; its nature, both its specific inputs and the desired outputs, must change with changes in the company, its competitive situation, its markets, and the economic climate. The marketer must monitor the overall marketing strategy continually, as the tendency is always present for the mix of inputs to get out of balance, thus reducing their effectiveness in achieving the desired outputs, which also change from time to time. Therefore, the marketer needs some systematic basis for evaluating overall marketing strategy.

the marketing audit

Marketing experts recommend marketing audits for evaluating overall marketing strategy. A marketing audit is a systematic, critical, and unbiased appraisal of the basic marketing objectives and policies and of the organization, methods, procedures, and personnel employed to achieve those objectives and implement those policies.

Proponents of the marketing audit stress the importance of focusing on the overall marketing strategy and the methods used in implementing it. Thus, not every evaluation of marketing personnel, organization, or individual inputs of marketing strategy is a marketing audit—most such evaluations are only parts of an audit. A true marketing audit, then, is a systematic and comprehensive appraisal of a company's total marketing operation.[2]

There are no standardized formats for making marketing audits. Each firm should design the type of marketing audit most appropriate to fit its own needs. However, as the definition suggests, each audit should cover at least six main aspects of marketing operations:

1. *Objectives.* Each marketing input should have clearly stated objectives (in terms of specific desired outputs).
2. *Policies.* Both explicit and implicit policies should be appraised from the standpoint of their consistency in achieving the marketing objectives.
3. *Organization.* Does the organization possess the necessary capabilities to achieve the marketing objectives? Are planning and control systems appropriate for the organization?
4. *Methods.* Are the individual strategies used for carrying out the stated policies appropriate? What opportunities are there for improvement?
5. *Procedures.* Are the specific steps (who does what and how) in implementing individual strategies logical? Are they well designed? Are those chosen best fitted to the situation?
6. *Personnel.* All executives playing key roles in planning marketing operations and strategy, as well as those responsible for implementation of marketing programs, should be evaluated in terms of their effectiveness relative to stated objectives, policies, and other aspects of marketing operations.

[2] E. J. Kelley, *Marketing Planning and Competitive Strategy* (Englewood Cliffs, N.J.: Prentice-Hall, Inc., 1972), p. 121.

Figure 20-3   Elements of a systematic marketing audit

Part I. The Marketing Environment Review

A. *Markets*

1. What are the organization's major markets and publics?
2. What are the major market segments in each market?
3. What are the present and expected future size and characteristics of each market or market segment?

B. *Customers*

4. How do the customers and publics see and feel toward the organization?
5. How do customers make their purchase or adoption decisions?
6. What is the present and expected future state of customer needs and satisfaction?

C. *Competitors*

7. Who are the organization's major competitors?
8. What trends can be foreseen in competition?

D. *Macroenvironment*

9. What are the main relevant developments with respect to demography, economy, technology, government, and culture that will affect the organization's situation?

Part II. The Marketing System Review

A. *Objectives*

10. What are the organization's long-run and short-run overall objectives and marketing objectives?
11. Are the objectives stated in a clear hierarchical order and in a form that permits planning and measurement of achievement?
12. Are the marketing objectives reasonable for the organization, given its competitive position, resources, and opportunities?

B. *Program*

13. What is the organization's core strategy for achieving its objectives and is it likely to succeed?
14. Is the organization allocating enough resources (or too much resources) to accomplish the marketing tasks?
15. Are the marketing resources allocated optimally to the various markets, territories, and products of the organization?
16. Are the marketing resources allocated optimally to the major elements of the marketing mix, i.e., product quality, personal contact, promotion, and distribution?

C. *Implementation*

17. Does the organization develop an annual marketing plan? Is the planning procedure effective?
18. Does the organization implement control procedures (monthly, quarterly, etc.) to ensure that its annual plan objectives are being achieved?
19. Does the organization carry out periodic studies to determine the contribution and effectiveness of various marketing activities?
20. Does the organization have an adequate marketing information system to service the needs of managers for planning and controlling operations in various markets?

Source: Philip Kotler, Marketing Management (Englewood Cliffs,
New Jersey: Prentice-Hall, Inc., 1976), pp. 450–451.

Figure 20-3 (continued)

D. *Organization*

21. Does the organization have a high-level marketing officer to analyze, plan, and implement the marketing work of the organization?
22. Are the other persons directly involved in marketing activity able people? Is there a need for more training, incentives, supervision, or evaluation?
23. Are the marketing responsibilities optimally structured to serve the needs of different marketing activities, products, markets, and territories?
24. Do the organization's personnel understand and practice the marketing concept?

Part III. *Detailed Marketing Activity Review*

A. *Products*

25. What are the main products of the organization? What are the generic products?
26. Should any products in the line be phased out?
27. Should any products be added to the line?
28. What is the general state of health of each product and the product mix as a whole?

B. *Prices*

29. To what extent are prices set on cost, demand, and/or competitive criteria?
30. What would the likely response of demand be to higher or lower prices?
31. How do customers psychologically interpret the price level?
32. Does the organization use temporary price promotions and, if so, how effective are they?

C. *Distribution*

33. Are there alternative methods of distributing the product that would result in more service or less cost?
34. Does the organization render adequate service, along with the product, to its customers?

D. *Personal Selling*

35. Is the sales force large enough to accomplish the organization's objectives?
36. Is the sales force organized along the best lines of specialization (territory, market, product)?
37. Does the sales force show high morale, ability, and effectiveness? Are they sufficiently trained and incentivized?
38. Are the procedures adequate for setting quotas and evaluating performance?

E. *Advertising*

39. Does the organization adequately state its advertising objectives?
40. Does the organization spend the right amount on advertising?
41. Are the themes and copy effective?
42. Are the media well chosen?

F. *Publicity*

43. Does the organization have a carefully formulated program of publicity?

G. *Sales Promotion*

44. Are sales promotions used by the organization and, if so, are they well conceived?

In making a marketing audit, too, it is important for a company to examine both its market and its products. Fundamentally, in examining the market, the auditors should try to answer four key questions:

1. Who is buying what, and how?
2. Who is selling what, and how?
3. How is the competition doing?
4. How are we doing?

In appraising the product line, there are two big questions:

1. Does the product line meet the demands of the market?
2. Does the product line have the proper breadth and length?

The main purpose of a marketing audit, therefore, is to uncover opportunities to improve the effectiveness of the total marketing operation. The marketing audit should be "in addition" to the normal procedure for controlling the progress of the annual marketing plan; it is designed to reveal something about the long-run optimality of the company's total marketing program.[3] In carrying out a marketing audit, management should seek to identify strengths as well as weaknesses—areas of marketing strength which may have potentials for further exploitation, areas of marketing weakness requiring correction and improvement. In addition, even though the word "audit" implies an after-the-fact evaluation (a carryover from financial jargon), a true marketing audit should help not only in evaluating past performance but in formulating overall marketing strategy for the future.

SUMMARY   You should now have a good "picture" of the entire field of marketing. From your study of this chapter, which reviewed much of the content of the first 19 chapters, you should have found yourself fitting together most of what you had learned previously about the many aspects of the subject into an integrated and comprehensive understanding of marketing. You should also have gained important additional insights on overall marketing strategy: you should understand why and how the nature and composition of overall marketing strategies vary with, and are influenced by, different competitive settings. You should understand why and how in formulating overall marketing strategy the marketer seeks a combination of inputs that is optimal in terms of the desired outputs. You should understand why and how in implementing overall marketing strategy the marketer coordinates the various inputs, paying particular attention to the timing aspects of their application. And you should understand why in evaluating overall marketing strategy the marketer

[3] Philip Kotler and Richard S. Lopata, "The Marketing Audit," in *Marketing Manager's Handbook,* Steuart H. Britt, ed. (Chicago: The Dartnell Corp., 1973), p. 1074.

should systematically and comprehensively appraise the total marketing operation with an eye toward future improvements. If you have this feeling and know these "whys and hows," you know basically what marketing is all about.

REVIEW AND DISCUSSION QUESTIONS	
1	Identify and describe the four basic kinds of competitive settings a marketer might face.
2	Do you feel that viewing marketing as a system of interrelated parts and activities has resulted in more efficient and effective total marketing programs? Explain. Describe a "systematic" approach to marketing strategy formulation.
3	Do you believe that the marketing concept is a myth and given only superficial attention, or do you feel that it is a reality in that marketing management makes a conscious, determined effort to put the marketing concept into practice? Do marketing policies, strategies, and total programs reflect adherence to the marketing concept?
4	"After all is said and done, it makes little difference how you 'mix the ingredients' of your total marketing programs as long as you do what your competitors do because competition literally dictates what you can and cannot do." Agree or disagree? Justify your position.
5	What is meant by "synergistic potential"? Explain. Use examples.
6	Explain the concept of positioning. What is its significance from the viewpoint of the marketer? The consumer? Give examples.
7	Marketers should recognize that not all inputs to marketing programs have equal productivity. Explain.
8	In what way is the selection of marketing inputs affected by their degree of "substitutability"?
9	How important is timing in the development of marketing strategy? Explain. Give some examples of good timing. Poor timing.
10	What is a marketing audit? What should be the scope of an audit? Is a marketing audit necessary to have a successful marketing program? Explain.
11	"Basically, a company's overall marketing strategy is its competitive posture in the marketplace." Explain.
12	In your opinion, what determines "marketing effectiveness"?

CASE PROBLEMS

(Case A): **Walpole Tool Company was a small manufacturer of a limited line of power tools for home use. The company had been started only a few years ago by a man who had been employed by a leading home power tool producer and who decided to establish his own business with capital he had accumulated over a long period.**

Todd Upshaw, owner and president of Walpole Tool Company, took a very active part in the technical development of his tools, using the experience he had gained over many years dealing with power tools. Upshaw had developed a complicated set of attachments that would allow a standard drill to be converted into a jigsaw or a mini-circular saw. Many competitive drill kits were on the market—drills that could be used not only for drilling, but also for sanding, buffing, mixing paint, and as power screwdrivers. To

Upshaw's knowledge, there was no drill attachment that could convert the basic unit into a jigsaw or a circular saw. He did know, however, that one industry leader was in the process of developing a jigsaw attachment.

While the new attachments were rather complicated, Upshaw felt that there was a need for this type of product and that the new product was technically sound, reliable, and safe to use. He recognized that an elaborate set of instructions would have to accompany the product, since it was not a simple matter to convert the drill into either a jigsaw or a circular saw.

Walpole Tool Company had always operated "close to the vest," in that it did not have enough capital to venture into new areas. Consequently, Walpole had been a follower to industry leaders, waiting until a product idea had proven successful before it got into the market. Walpole was content to follow this policy and it was not surprising that its market share was quite small.

Upshaw was considering whether or not to abandon his policy of being a follower and, with his new product, become a leader in the industry.

questions:

1. Should Walpole Tool Company introduce the new product?
2. What are the risks that must be accepted when introducing a new product?

(Case B): Charlestown Enterprises, Inc., was a small manufacturer of sporting goods equipment whose products were distributed to consumers primarily through department stores, discount houses, and hardware stores. Three years ago, Charlestown Enterprises had been one of the first companies to crack the "street hockey" market. Currently, street hockey equipment (sticks, pucks, and nets) accounts for 16 percent of Charlestown's sales.

Street hockey is a game essentially similar to ice hockey, except that it is played on the street or any paved or smooth surface, with a few modifications of the standard ice hockey rules. The game had been played for years in both Canada and the United States, but its popularity had really boomed during the past three years. Street hockey was played during all 12 months of the year and was enjoyed by children and adults alike.

Because of the necessity to have special equipment for street hockey, several companies recognized the need and developed products to fit that need. Competition had become quite intense, but Charlestown Enterprises had managed to gain and hold a solid share of the market. However, its market position was being jeopardized by a new competitor who had just introduced an unbreakable street hockey stick. Replacement of hockey sticks represented the consumer's largest expenditure.

The stick looked like a regular hockey stick, except that it was of a synthetic composition. The unbreakable synthetic stick served to eliminate a nagging problem of the standard wooden hockey sticks, which were vulnerable to breakage.

Charlestown Enterprises had no competitive product and its management acknowledged that it was very likely that the innovation would catch on with street hockey enthusiasts, although there would always be a market comprised of those who wanted to play with the "real thing." Charlestown's management was undecided as to whether it should go to work in developing a competitive substitute for the new hockey stick or stay with the standard wooden stick.

question:

1. What should Charlestown Enterprises do?

(Case C): Pellegrino's, Inc., was a regional marketer of a wide line of Italian meats and other foods. Pellegrino products were distributed intensively in a three-state area in the northeastern part of the United States. Pellegrino brand products could be found in a variety of stores, including supermarkets, delicatessens, sandwich and pizza shops, and restaurants. Consumer demand for Pellegrino products had steadily climbed to the point where it was the most asked-for brand of Italian food in each of the three states in which it was distributed. Pellegrino had recently introduced its own pizza mix and it, too, met with immediate success. The company was progressive and continually made an effort to supply consumers and users with the best product possible at reasonable prices.

Josephine Pellegrino, president of the company and granddaughter of its founder, was instrumental to the great success of the company. She had displayed a keen sense of management, and the result was easily seen in the outstanding reputation enjoyed by the company. Her overall marketing strategy was obviously succeeding.

Pellegrino was discussing a company matter with Ed Primavera, assistant marketing manager, when the subject of a marketing audit came up. Primavera felt that, despite the marketing success of the company, a marketing audit should be undertaken in light of the fact that Pellegrino's had never had any kind of systematic evaluation of its overall marketing strategy. Pellegrino felt strongly that there was no need for any evaluation, since things had been going along so well for so long and, further, with its hold on the market it was most unlikely that Pellegrino's, Inc., could be doing anything wrong. Besides, Pellegrino reasoned, doing a marketing audit would consume a great deal of her time—time that could be better spent managing the shop.

questions:

1. Should Pellegrino's, Inc., have a marketing audit?
2. What are the purposes of a marketing audit?
3. Does an obviously successful overall marketing strategy preclude the necessity for a marketing audit?

(Case D): Madden's Sports Center, a small independent retail sporting goods store located in a Boston suburb of 25,000 population, sold a wide line of sporting goods. For years the Sports Center was known as a quality sporting goods outlet, carrying brand names such as Wilson, Spalding,

McGregor, Rawlings, and many other top brands of baseball, football, hockey, basketball, golf, tennis, bowling, and skiing equipment and supplies.

Dick Madden, proprietor, had built an excellent reputation for the store over the 20 years of its existence. In addition to serving retail customers, Madden's Sports Center supplied equipment and uniforms for all the town's public school athletic teams and most of its youth teams in the community, such as Little League baseball, Pee Wee hockey, Bantam basketball, and Pop Warner football.

Recently, however, Madden had become quite concerned over the increasing competition from discount houses and department stores, especially those in nearby shopping centers. The vigorous competition resulted primarily from the lower prices charged by the bigger stores. He was not overly concerned about his "wholesale" or school and league business, because his relationship with the administrators was solid and he had always provided them with the best products and the best service. He was, though, concerned about the possibility of losing some of his retail patronage to the price competition of the bigger stores. Madden felt that his assortment of sporting goods was competitive with those of the discount houses and department stores, but he knew he could not compete with them on the basis of price. He prided himself on the personal service that he and his employees gave customers, but he did not think that would continue to offset his higher prices.

questions:

1. How can Dick Madden's Sports Center meet the strong competitive threat of the bigger retail sporting outlets?
2. Must he compete on a price basis in order to survive, or are there other, or nonprice, ways for him to compete?

GLOSSARY

ADMINISTERED PRICES   prices set by management and held stable over time.   [p. 293]

ADVERTISING   an impersonal, paid form of communication to prospective customers with the goal of achieving sales—it involves standard messages, to large numbers of receivers.   [p. 366]

ADVERTISING AGENCY   a group of experts on various phases of advertising and related marketing areas which provides assistance on advertising to client advertisers.   [p. 370]

AGENT MIDDLEMAN   negotiates sales or purchases or both but does not take title to the goods in which it deals.   [p. 225]

ASSEMBLING   involves bringing together either (1) different quantities of a wide variety of items for sale by a single establishment (retailer) or (2) a large quantity of similar items for resale in a particular region (central wholesalers).   [p. 50]

AUDIT (MARKETING)   a systematic, critical, and unbiased appraisal of the basic marketing objectives and policies and of the methods employed to achieve these objectives.   [p. 429]

AUTOMATIC SELLING   the sale of goods to consumers through coin-operated machines.   [p. 254]

BAIT ADVERTISING   advertising under false pretenses to attract consumers interest in the advertised product in order to sell a substitute product.   [p. 408]

BRAND DIFFERENTIATION   the degree to which a brand is differentiated from similar brands in the view of prospective buyers.   [p. 181]

BRAND IMAGE   a stereotype resulting from all the impressions consumers receive about a particular brand.   [p. 146]

437

BRANDING   is the physical means of achieving product differentiation by providing identification—it bridges the gap between management's promotional program and the consummation of sales to final buyers. [p. 181]

BREAK-EVEN POINT   the total number of units of a product which must be sold to cover total fixed costs. [p. 290]

BROKER   an agent who represents either buyer or seller in negotiating purchases or sales without having physical control over the goods involved. [p. 225]

CHAIN-STORE SYSTEM   a group of retail stores of essentially the same type, centrally owned and with some degree of centralized control of operation. [p. 246]

COGNITIVE DISSONANCE   when a person makes an important decision, dissonance or discomfort will almost always occur. After the decision the person tends to expose his or herself to information perceived as likely to support the choice. [p. 147]

COMMISSION HOUSE   an agent who customarily exercises physical control over and negotiates the sale (without consulting the principal) of goods belonging to principals. [p. 226]

COMPARATIVE ADVERTISING   the advertiser's product is compared directly with those of competition, which are clearly identified by brand name. [p. 369]

CONSUMER COOPERATIVE   a retail business owned and operated by ultimate consumers to purchase and distribute goods and services primarily to its members. [p. 251]

CONSUMER GOODS   goods destined for final consumption by individuals (ultimate consumers) and households. [p. 157]

CONSUMERISM   the actions of individuals and organizations (consumer, government, and business) in response to consumers' dissatisfactions arising in exchange relationships. [p. 399]

CONTAINERIZATION   the development of methods by which a large number of units of a product are combined into a single compact unit for storage and transportation. [p. 207]

CONTRIBUTION PRICING   pricing that does not cover total allocated costs of a product but covers something more than direct (or variable) costs. [p. 297]

CONVENIENCE GOODS   items the consumer buys frequently, immediately, and with minimum shopping effort. [p. 158]

COST-PLUS PRICING   involves making a cost estimate and adding a margin to cover marketing expenses and profit. [p. 320]

COUPONING   a form of promotion that offers the prospect a reduction in price to persuade the individual to try the product. [p. 338]

CUSTOMER OR MARKET DIVISION OF AUTHORITY   line authority is divided by type of customer or market. [p. 32]

CUSTOMER SERVICE   provides assistance and advice on such things as product installation, operation, maintenance, and repair. [p. 52]

DATA BANK   provides an orderly basis for storing the myriad bits of information that flow into a marketing information system.   [p. 66]

DELIVERED PRICING   the seller pays all freight costs, building them into its price quotation.   [p. 300]

DEMAND EXPANSIBILITY   expansible demand can be stimulated by advertising alone (with no change in price).   [p. 372]

DEMOGRAPHIC BASES FOR SEGMENTATION   include: income, age, education, stage in the life cycle, social class, sex, occupation, religion and race.   [p. 115]

DEPARTMENT STORE   a large retailing unit handling a wide variety of shopping and specialty goods and organized into separate departments for purposes of merchandising, promotion, and control.   [p. 244]

DIFFERENTIAL ADVANTAGE   the advantage one firm gains over competitors by building customer loyalty.   [p. 131]

DIFFUSION   the social process of spreading information about new products or services to persuade potential users to accept them.   [p. 137]

DIRECT MAIL   a form of promotion that pin points the target audience by sending the message direct to the prospect by mail.   [p. 337]

DISCOUNT HOUSE   a retailing business that features a large selection of general merchandise, competes on a low price basis, and operates on a low markup with minimum customer service.   [p. 252]

DISCRETIONARY INCOME   what people have left after paying taxes and buying essential food, clothing, shelter, transportation, and other items a household regards as necessities.   [p. 134]

DISPOSABLE PERSONAL INCOME   what people have left after paying taxes.   [p. 133]

DISTRIBUTION   is concerned with the activities involved in transferring goods from producers to final buyers and users; it includes physical activities and the legal, promotional and financial activities performed in the course of transferring ownership.   [p. 198]

DISTRIBUTION SYSTEM RESPONSIVENESS   the ability of a system to communicate needs back to the supplying plant and get needed inventory into the field.   [p. 203]

DROP SHIPMENT WHOLESALER   does not physically handle the goods it sells. When goods are ordered the manufacturer ships them directly to the retailer, but bills the drop shipper at factory prices.   [p. 224]

EXCEPTION REPORTS FROM M.I.S.   provides executives certain kinds of information only when a given situation shifts outside a range of acceptable normalcy.   [p. 67]

EXCLUSIVE DISTRIBUTION   involves using a single middleman—a retailer, for example—in each market area.   [p. 277]

FAMILY BRAND   the use of a single identifying name to cover several products marketed by the same firm.   [p. 182]

FAMILY LIFE CYCLE   a basis for market segmentation that describes families in terms such as; young married with no children, married with children under 12, etc.   [p. 117]

F.O.B. PRICING the marketer quotes his price at the factory (or other point of sale) and the buyer must pay all freight from that point. [p. 299]

FRANCHISE permission given to a retailer to market the franchise company's products or services under a common brand and method of operation. [p. 255]

FRINGE MARKET the buyers who find a source of supply acceptable but not preferred. [p. 132]

GEOGRAPHIC DIVISION OF LINE AUTHORITY line authority is divided on a geographical basis, e.g. Southern sales manager, Eastern sales manager, etc. [p. 31]

GENERAL LINE WHOLESALER carries a broad assortment of goods within a single merchandise line but may also carry limited stocks in closely related lines. [p. 221]

GENERAL STORE a small business, not departmentalized, usually located in a rural or isolated community and primarily engaged in selling a general assortment of merchandise—the most important of which is food.

GRADING is the act of separating or inspecting nonmanufactured goods according to established specifications. [p. 49]

GUARANTEES express or implied, are promises made by a seller to buyers assuring them that they will receive certain services or satisfactions. [p. 178]

HARD CORE MARKET a firm's hard core market is that segment composed of brand loyal buyers. [p. 132]

HEDGING a way of transferring the risk of a price decline on products traded on commodity markets. [p. 55]

HETEROGENEITY OF MARKETS the reason for segmentation based on the realization that not all buyers are alike, that they differ in many ways. [p. 130]

HORIZONTAL COOPERATIVE ADVERTISING the individual companies in an industry participate in industry-wide advertising effort to increase primary demand for the product. [p. 369]

HORIZONTAL INTEGRATION growth of a marketing institution (e.g., retailer) by operation of multiple stores. [p. 246]

IMAGES buyers see themselves and the products they buy in terms of images—formalized impressions, residing consciously or unconsciously, in the minds of individuals with regard to particular subjects. [p. 145]

INDUSTRIAL GOODS goods destined for use in the commercial production of other goods or in connection with carrying on some business or institutional activity. [p. 157]

INDUSTRIAL USERS buy to further the operation of businesses or other institutions. [p. 112]

INFLUENTIAL a person who serves as an opinion leader of a group. [p. 136]

INNOVATIONS products that are perceived by potential users as new and different from previously existing products. [p. 166]

INTEGRATED RETAILING reduces marketing costs by eliminating, simplifying, or consolidating various activities involved in the marketing process—e.g., bypassing the wholesaler. [p. 243]

LIFE STYLE a distinctive mode of living in a dynamic society—measures activities, interests, opinions, and demographics. [p. 147]

MANUFACTURERS' AGENT an agent who represents manufacturers of non-competing but related lines of goods with limited authority on price and terms of sale. He has an exclusive territory, and the contractual relationship is a long term one. [p. 227]

MARGINAL PROPENSITY TO CONSUME the proportion of an increase in consumer income that will be spent rather than saved.

MARKDOWN the difference between what a product is originally marked to sell for and what it actually sells for. [p. 73]

MARKET the aggregate demand of the potential buyers for a product—an aggregate demand is a composite of the individual demands of all potential buyers. [p. 110]

MARKET MEASUREMENT STUDIES (MARKET POTENTIAL) obtain quantitative data on potential demand—how much of a particular *product* can be sold to individual market segments over some future period. (This is an industry figure). [p. 91]

MARKET PENETRATION the share of the market possessed by a particular brand. [p. 342]

MARKET SEGMENT a group of buyers or buying units who share qualities that make the group distinct and make it of significance to marketing. [p. 111]

MARKETING the managerial process by which products are matched with markets and through which the consumer is enabled to use or enjoy the product. [p. 6]

MARKETING CHANNEL a path traced in the direct or indirect transfer of ownership to a product, as it moves from producer to ultimate consumers or industrial users. [p. 202]

MARKETING CONCEPT has three main goals: (1) Most important, a customer orientation. (2) Subordination of departmental aspiration to overall company goals. (3) Unification of company operations. [p. 17]

MARKETING CONTROLLABLES areas over which marketing management has decision-making responsibility. [p. 6]

MARKETING INFORMATION SYSTEM an organized set of procedures, information-handling routines, and reporting techniques designed to provide the information required for making marketing decisions. [p. 65]

MARKETING INTELLIGENCE an organized procedure to collect regularly from diverse outside sources information of potential usefulness for the making of marketing decisions. [p. 78]

MARKETING MIX   the total of marketing inputs—price, product, promotion, distribution—that make up a marketing strategy.   [p. 7]

MARKETING RESEARCH   information from outside sources (other than intelligence and forecasting) gathered on both routine and non-routine bases. The systematic gathering, recording, and analyzing of data about marketing problems to facilitate decision making.   [p. 88]

MARKETING UNCONTROLLABLES   areas that affect marketing decisions and strategy but over which marketing management has no control. (e.g., competition, legal environment, science and technology). [p. 7]

MARKUP   the amount by which an item's intended selling price exceeds its cost to the seller.   [p. 72]

MASS COMMUNICATIONS MEDIA   ways of reaching large audiences, e.g., newspapers, magazines, AM & FM radio, television.   [p. 16]

MASS DISTRIBUTION   provides maximum sales exposure for a product by distributing it in every outlet that might carry such an item.   [p. 277]

MEDIA   advertising media are the alternative means of reaching prospects with advertising messages—they include (among others) newspapers, magazines, television, radio, and outdoor signs.   [p. 383]

MERCANTILE CREDIT   credit granted by manufacturers and wholesalers to middlemen.   [p. 55]

MERCHANDISING   knowing what the customer wants and making it available at the right time or place for him or her to buy.   [p. 35]

MERCHANT MIDDLEMAN   takes title to (that is, buys) and resells merchandise.   [p. 199]

MIDDLEMEN   situated in the marketing channel between producers and final buyers, they specialize in performing activities directly related to the purchase and sale of goods in their flow to the final user.   [p. 198]

MISSIONARY SELLING   the missionary seller is responsible for increasing the company's sales volume by assisting middleman customers with their selling efforts.   [p. 354]

MODEL BANK   designed to provide management with suggested courses of action or answers to problems from the MIS.   [p. 67]

MOTIVATION   the most important factor in governing the activities of the individual.   [p. 142]

MOTIVATION RESEARCH   research which probes psychological and sociological variables affecting buyers' behavior.   [p. 93]

NEED SATISFACTION   psychological studies indicate that human activity, including buying behavior, is directed toward satisfying certain needs.   [p. 144]

NONPRICE COMPETITION   refusing to use price as a competitive input—maintaining price exactly equivalent to competitors' prices.   [p. 422]

NONPROBABILITY SAMPLE   results from a process in which judgment (and, therefore, bias) enters into the selection of the members of a sample.   [p. 99]

NONSAMPLING ERRORS the accidental (or deliberate) mistakes or errors that can happen during any of the stages of data collection, recording, and enumeration. [p. 100]

OBSERVATIONAL METHOD information is obtained by observing and recording consumers' actions in a market situation. [p. 97]

OLIGOPOLISTIC PRICING in an oligopoly, prices are very sticky; competitors are reluctant to change them. [p. 318]

ONE-PRICE POLICY selling a product to all like customers for exactly the same price, as opposed to negotiated prices. [p. 298]

OPERATING DATA marketing information from the company's own financial, accounting, sales and production records. [p. 69]

OPERATING RATIOS operating data expressed as a percent of net sales to allow comparison with other periods or other firms. [p. 70]

PACKAGING in addition to providing product protection, it is designed to attract customers' attention, furnish needed product information, and propel them into buying. [p. 178]

PENETRATION PRICING uses a low introductory price for a new product to speed up the product's wide acceptance before competitors enter the market. [p. 314]

PERSONAL SELLING person-to-person contacts between potential buyers and sellers with the goal of achieving sales—it provides personalized sales messages for individual customers. [p. 351]

PHYSICAL DISTRIBUTION is concerned with the actual movement and storage of products after their production and before their consumption. [p. 200]

PLACE UTILITY value added to a product by removing it from the point of production to the point of consumption. [p. 394]

POINT-OF-PURCHASE DISPLAY the display of merchandise at the point of sale to directly move customers to buying action. [p. 336]

POOLING the practice by cooperatives of mixing the outputs of members and paying each the average price received during the season. [p. 217]

POSITIONING the collective perceptions consumers or users have of a company and/or its product in relationship to other companies and products. [p. 427]

PRICE ELASTICITY demand is price elastic if a price reduction increases total revenue. [p. 376]

PRICE SKIMMING uses a high introductory price for a new product to skim the "cream" of demand before competitors enter the market. [p. 314]

PRIMARY DEMAND demand for a *type* of product (not any specific brand). [p. 372]

PRIMARY GROUPS groups of people engaged in intimate face-to-face contact and cooperation, who are fundamental in determining the social nature of the individual. [p. 135]

PRIVATE BRANDS those brands owned by middlemen (wholesalers or retailers) rather than by manufacturers. [p. 183]

PROBABILITY SAMPLE results from a process of random selection whereby each member of a universe has a known chance of being selected for the sample. [p. 99]

PRODUCERS' COOPERATIVE an association representing the collective of small producers who desire to gain more control over the distribution of their output in the hope of exerting favorable influences on demand. [p. 217]

PRODUCT an all inclusive term that includes services as well as physical goods—a bundle of utilities consisting of various product features and accompanying services. [p. 156]

PRODUCT DESIGN SIMPLIFICATION does not improve the product from the user's viewpoint, but makes it simpler and cheaper to make. [p. 175]

PRODUCT DIFFERENTIATION convincing customers of a difference between a product and its competitors that makes them reluctant to accept substitutes. [p. 56]

PRODUCT DIVISION OF LINE AUTHORITY line authority is divided by product or group of products. e.g., sales manager for Product A, sales manager for Product B, etc. [p. 32]

PRODUCT LIFE CYCLES products have a certain length of life during which they pass through certain identifiable stages: market introduction, growth, maturity, decline, and discontinuance. [p. 162]

PRODUCT MANAGER serves as a deputy marketing director for a particular product or product group. His role is essentially a staff one. [p. 33]

PRODUCT MIX the total line of products offered by a company. [p. 189]

PRODUCT OBSOLESCENCE the incorporation of product changes that accelerate the rate of obsolescence of products in consumers' possession, making them discard existing products for new ones. [p. 186]

PRODUCT PLANNING serving buyers' changing product preferences through continuing adaptation of products or services offered. [p. 48]

PROMOTION concerns the marketers activities in *communicating* both with members of the target market and the middlemen to increase the chance that planned sales take place. [p. 330]

PROMOTIONAL MIX the combination, types, and amounts of different forms of promotion used by a particular marketer. [p. 338]

PSYCHOGRAPHIC BASES FOR SEGMENTATION based upon how people act rather than where they are or what they are, e.g., personality. [p. 118]

PULL STRATEGY to force middlemen to handle the product by advertising heavily to the ultimate consumer. [p. 342]

QUOTAS quantitatively expressed goals assigned to specific marketing units, such as individual sales people or territories—the most common yard stick for measuring sales people performance. [p. 361]

RACK JOBBERS   display their own merchandise in retail stores, and retailers pay only for goods sold and retain a portion of the profit.   [p. 223]

RATIONALIZATION   the mental process of finding reasons to justify an act or opinion that is actually based on other motives or grounds than those stated, although this may not be apparent to the rationalizer. [p. 143]

REFERENCE GROUP   the people with whom an individual regularly associates.   [p. 135]

REMERCHANDISING   aims to improve the product's market and profitability by increasing sales to present markets—it leaves basic features of the physical product unchanged but makes changes in the accompanying services.   [p. 177]

RESALE PRICE MAINTENANCE   actions by a manufacturer to prevent the resale of his products by middlemen below some established price.   [p. 301]

RESIDENT BUYER   differs from other agents in that it represents buyer only—usually retailers who are located far from the market.   [p. 229]

RETAILER-OWNED   COOPERATIVE   a   wholesale   establishment owned and operated by its independent retailer customers.   [p. 250]

RETAILERS   a merchant, or occasionally an agent whose *main* business is selling directly to ultimate consumers.   [p. 199]

RETAILING   consists of the activities involved in selling directly to the ultimate consumer.   [p. 199]

RETENTIVE ADVERTISING   for products in the marketing maturity stage—reminds past buyers to buy the brand.   [p. 374]

SALES ANALYSIS   periodic examination of sales records to provide information for marketing decisions.   [p. 76]

SALES FORCE TURNOVER RATE   the number of sales people separated, resigned, or fired per 100 on the sales force over a fixed period of time.   [p. 355]

SALES FORECAST   an estimate of sales tied to a particular marketing program and assuming a particular set of economic and other forces outside the forecasting unit.   [p. 78]

SALES POTENTIAL   the maximum possible sales opportunities open to a specified *company* selling a good or service during a stated period for particular market segments.   [p. 91]

SAMPLING ERRORS   errors tracing to the sample itself, causing it not to be completely representative of the universe from which it is drawn. [p. 100]

SECONDARY INFORMATION   published material from government and trade sources not gathered for the specific research purpose in mind, but that may be useful.   [p. 96]

SELECTIVE DEMAND   demand for a specific brand of a product.   [p. 373]

SELECTIVE DISTRIBUTION   manufacturer restricts the number of outlets at each distribution level.   [p. 277]

SELF-IMAGE the picture a person has of himself—the kind of person he considers himself to be and that he imagines others consider him to be. [p. 146]

SELLING AGENT operates on an extended contractual basis with principal, negotiates *all* sales of a specified line of merchandise or the entire output of its principal and has full authority with regard to price and terms of sale. [p. 228]

SERVICE BUSINESS a business that markets services rather than products. [p. 38]

SHARE-OF-THE-MARKET the percent of the total market for a particular product held by a particular company. [p. 92]

SHOPPING CENTER a group of stores and other commercial establishments planned, developed, and managed as a unit, with off-street parking and related to the trading area served. [p. 257]

SHOPPING GOODS items the consumer selects and buys after making comparisons on such bases as suitability, quality, price, and style. [p. 158]

SIMULATION a simulated market environment is set up in a laboratory under the assumption that the actions and reactions of buyers will predict what will happen in real market conditions. [p. 98]

SITUATION ANALYSIS preliminary exploration of data sources which will help the researcher identify the nature of the problem to be studied. [p. 95]

SOCIAL ROLE the way a person sees his position in the social groups in which he holds membership. [p. 136]

SOCIOLOGICAL INFLUENCES the influences of group pressures on consumer behavior. [p. 135]

SORTING THEORY regards the entire economic process as starting with conglomerations, going through various types of sorting, and ending with assortments. [p. 130]

SOURCE EFFECT in marketing communication it is important to recognize the effect of the message source's reputation upon the way a message is received. [p. 333]

SPECIALTY GOODS items for which significant numbers of consumers are habitually willing to make a special purchasing effort. [p. 159]

SPECIALTY WHOLESALER carries only part of a merchandise line, but within its restricted range it has a very complete assortment. [p. 222]

STANDARDIZING insuring that basic qualities of a product are designated consistent with established characteristics and that products are produced and offered in conformance with these standards. [p. 49]

STATISTICAL BANK a set of instructions that automatically analyzes all incoming data to provide standardized reports from the MIS to managers who need them. [p. 66]

STATUS SYMBOLS people express their personalities more in symbols than in words (e.g., mannerisms, dress, ornaments, possessions), and most people are increasingly concerned about their status; different products vary in their status symbol value. [p. 138]

STOCKTURN RATE   indicates the speed at which the inventory "turns over"—the number of times the average inventory is sold during an operating period.   [p. 74]

SUPERMARKET   a large retailing business unit selling mainly food and grocery items upon the basis of low-margin appeal, high turnover, wide variety and assortment, self service, and heavy emphasis on merchandise appeal.   [p. 251]

SUPPORTING ACTIVITIES   do not relate directly to ownership transfers but support or contribute to other marketing activities—include: marketing financing, marketing risk bearing, and marketing information.   [p. 54]

SURVEY METHOD   information is obtained directly from individual respondents, either through personal interviews, mail questionnaires, consumer panels, or telephone interviews.   [p. 96]

TEST MARKETING   a proposed new strategy is tested under real market conditions in one or more selected markets.   [p. 98]

TIME UTILITY   value added to a product by storing it from the time it is produced until the time it is consumed.   [p. 394]

TRADE CREDIT   credit offered by suppliers to their customers.   [p. 54]

TRADE DISCOUNT   a price differential according to type of customer, e.g., retailer or consumer.   [p. 299]

TRADE SELLING   the trade seller develops long-term relations with a relatively stable group of customers.   [p. 354]

TRADING DOWN   adding a lower-priced version of a product with the hope that it will carry some of the prestige of the original higher-priced product.   [p. 188]

TRADING UP   adding a higher-priced, more prestigious product version with the main goal of increasing sales of a present lower-priced version.   [p. 188]

TRUCK WHOLESALER   combining selling, delivery and collection in one operation—range of stock is limited, but delivery is immediate.   [p. 223]

TYING CONTRACTS   the sale or lease of products on condition that the buyer or lessee buy or use certain other items that the seller or lessor offers to supply.   [p. 406]

UNFAIR PRACTICES ACTS   state laws prohibiting the sales of goods below cost.   [p. 406]

ULTIMATE CONSUMER   (frequently called consumers) buy goods or services either for their own or for their families' personal consumption.   [p. 112]

VERTICAL COOPERATIVE ADVERTISING   advertising whose costs are shared by the manufacturer and its retailers.   [p. 369]

VERTICAL INTEGRATION   growth of a retailing institution (e.g. chain stores) by combining retailing and wholesaling (and even production) activities.   [p. 248]

VOLUNTARY CHAIN   a group of retailers banded together to achieve some of the advantages of a chain store system.   [p. 250]

WHEEL OF RETAILING HYPOTHESIS   McNair's hypothesis that new retailing institutions start on a price appeal basis and evolve as high cost, high service operations vulnerable to new types.   [p. 260]

WHOLESALERS   buy and resell merchandise to retailers and other wholesalers and to industrial users, but do not sell in significant amounts to ultimate consumers.   [p. 199]

WHOLESALING   involves the activities resulting in selling to buyers other than ultimate consumers.   [p. 199]

NAME INDEX

Alderson, Wroe, 130*n*, 132*n*, 156*n*
Anderson, M. J., Jr., 342*n*
Assmus, Gert, 169*n*
Axel, Helen, 12*n*

Bailey, E. L., 102*n*
Baltera, Lorraine, 148*n*
Barry, Thomas E., 371*n*
Barville, G. R., 185*n*
Becker, Boris W., 257*n*
Becker, Helmut, 257*n*
Bellenger, D. N., 102*n*
Berelson, B., 143*n*
Bowersox, Donald J., 421*n*
Britt, Steuart H., 142*n*, 436*n*
Brooks, Douglas G., 289*n*
Brown, Kevin V., 188*n*
Buell, Victor P., 33*n*, 34*n*

Caplovitz, D., 399*n*
Carey, James E., 358*n*
Catry, Bernard, 163*n*
Cayley, M. A., 113*n*
Chase, S., 400*n*
Chevalier, Michel, 163*n*
Clarke, C. J., 176*n*
Claycamp, Henry J., 168*n*
Converse, P. D., 393*n*
Copeland, Melvin T., 157
Corey, E. Raymond, 183*n*
Crane, E., 331*n*

Cravens, David W., 123*n*
Cunningham, M. T., 176*n*

Deakin, Michael, 294*n*
Dean, Joel, 312
Doppeit, N., 68*n*
Duncan, D. J., 132*n*

El Ansary, Adel I., 279*n*
Engel, J. F., 113*n*, 339*n*
Enis, Ben M., 350*n*
Erickson, L. G., 46*n*

Ferrell, O. C., 415*n*
Festinger, L., 147*n*
Fiorillo, H. F., 113*n*
Forman, W., 102*n*
Fornell, Claes, 333*n*
Frank, Ronald E., 120*n*
Frankel, Lester R., 100*n*
Frankel, Martin R., 100*n*
Freud, Sigmund, 143, 144
Freund, John E., 101*n*

Gardner, David M., 296*n*
Gibson, Lawrence D., 66*n*
Golden, Harry, 238*n*
Goldman, Arieh, 261*n*
Green, P. E., 101*n*
Greenberg, B. A., 102*n*

Hamelman, Paul W., 185*n*
Hamermesh, R. G., 342*n*
Hardin, David K., 93*n*
Harris, J. E., 342*n*
Henion, Karl E., 400*n*
Henry, Walter A., 139*n*
Heschel, Michael S., 360*n*
Hills, Gerald E., 123*n*
Hise, Richard T., 184*n*
Hollander, S. C., 261*n*
Hovland, C. I., 333*n*
Huegy, H. W., 393*n*
Hunt, Shelby D., 257*n*

Jain, Arun K., 138*n*
Janis, L., 333*n*
Johnson, Lyndon B., 401
Jones, D. Frank, 291*n*
Joy, O. Maurice, 79*n*

Kallet, A., 400*n*
Kamin, Howard, 379*n*
Katz, E., 137*n*
Kelley, Eugene J., 17*n*, 332*n*, 429*n*
Kendall, C. L., 178*n*
Kennedy, John F., 401
Kleppner, Otto, 374*n*, 381*n*
Kotler, Philip, 5*n*, 38*n*, 40*n*, 430*n*, 432*n*
Kratchman, Stanley H., 184*n*

Lambert, Zarrell V., 296n
Levitt, Theodore, 9n, 340n
Levy, Sidney J., 40n, 397n
Lewis, R. J., 46n
Lillis, Charles, 356n
Lopata, Richard S., 432n
Luck, David J., 89n, 415n
Lunt, P. S., 138n
Lynn, R. A., 294n

Magee, J. F., 203n
Markin, Rom, 356n
Marquardt, Raymond A., 375n
Maslow, A. H., 144, 145n
Mason, J. Barry, 237n
Massy, William F., 120n
Mayer, Morris L., 237n
Mayes, Charles G., 66n
Mayes, Mel S., 271n
Mazze, Edward M., 185n
McGann, Anthony F., 375n
McGuire, William J., 145n
McNair, M. P., 260, 261n
Michman, Ronald D., 139n
Mitchell, R. V., 393n
Monroe, Kent B., 296n
Mowrer, O., 142n
Myers, James H., 167n

Nader, Ralph, 400
Newman, J. W., 144
Newton, D. A., 354n
Nichols, Donald, 79n
Nugent, Christopher, 66n

Pan, Judy, 79n
Pasold, Peter W., 355n
Perles, B. M., 101n
Peterson, R. T., 336n
Pletcher, B., 185n
Plummer, Joseph T., 113n, 119n, 147n, 148n
Prasad, V. Kanti, 334n

Rathmell, John M., 5n
Ray, Michael L., 366n
Richard, Elizabeth A., 119n
Ring, L. Winston, 334n
Robertson, Thomas S., 139n
Robicheaux, Robert A., 279n
Rogers, E. M., 138n
Rosenbloom, Bert, 260n
Russ, Frederick A., 178n

Schlink, F. J., 400n
Schomer, Arthur J., 207n
Schoner, B., 100n
Shapiro, Benson P., 296n
Sinclair, Upton, 399
Smallwood, John E., 163n
Smith, A. B., 261n
Smith, Wendell R., 111n
Snyder, G. H., 251n
Spencer, Hollester, 30n
Sporleder, T. L., 46n
Stanton, W. J., 399n
Staudt, Thomas A., 174n
Steiner, G., 143n
Stephenson, P. R., 208n
Strauss, Norman, 367n
Sturdivant, F. D., 141n, 397n

Sturman, Stephen, 119n
Swinyard, William R., 366n

Tauber, Edward M., 167n
Taylor, Donald A., 89n
Thurlow, Michael L., 362n
Tremblay, Roger L., 369n
Tull, D. S., 101n
Twedt, Dik W., 88n

Udell, J. C., 288n
Uhl, K. P., 100n
Ulrich, Thomas, 184n

Varble, Dale L., 190n
Villani, Kathryn E. A., 147n
Vollman, Thomas, 66n

Wales, Hugh G., 89n, 339n
Walters, C. Glenn, 118n, 129n
Warner, W. Lloyd, 138
Warshaw, M. R., 339n
Webster, Frederick A., 186n
Webster, Frederick E., Jr., 5n, 148n, 149n
Whitmore, Neil M., 271n
Willet, R. P., 208n
Wind, Yoram, 120n, 148n, 149n, 168n
Winer, Leon, 359n
Woodruff, Robert B., 123n
Wotruba, Thomas R., 362n

Zaltman, Gerald, 397n
Zimmerman, Edward H., 369n

SUBJECT INDEX

Acquisitions, corporate, 402, 403
Administered prices, 312, 320
  defined, 293
Adopter groups, in diffusion
  process, 137-138
Advertisers, top ten U.S., 377
Advertising. *See also* Promotion
  bait, 408
  to children, 408
  comparative, 369
  competitors as factor in, 369,
    421-422
  corrective, 408
  costs of, 335-336, 344, 376-380,
    383-384
  deceptive price, 408
  demand stimulated by, 51-52,
    372-375
  displays tied in with, 51-52, 425
  and distribution intensity, 278
  effectiveness of, 51-52, 384-385
  false, 408
  as form of promotion, 334-336,
    367-368, 375-376
  horizontal cooperative, 369
  information value of, 28
  larger role of, 16
  legislation affecting, 407-408
  management of, 380-385
  in marketing concept, 28
  and middlemen, 311, 369
  objectives of, 367-368

Advertising. *See also* Promotion
(cont.)
  organization for, 369-372
  planning in, 366-367
  policies of, 368-369
  production costs lowered by,
    395
  productivity of, 426
  as pull strategy, 342
  to reduce cognitive dissonance,
    147
  retentive, 374
  and sales, 377-380, 384
  strategy for, 370, 372-376
  supportive to selling, 28
  timing of, 427-428
  vertical cooperative, 369
  and women's role, 140
Advertising Age, 92
Advertising agencies
  in ad campaigns, 381-384
  deciding on use of, 370-372
  defined, 370
  division of responsibilities in, 38
  performance appraisal of, 384
  selection of, 381
  world's ten largest, 372
Advertising campaigns, 381-384
Advertising media
  selection of, 383-384
  spending for, 371
Advertising Procedure, 374n, 381n

"Advertising spiral," 373, 374
Advisory group, in MIS
  operation, 66
Agate line, advertising rates by,
  384
Age, market segmentation by,
  115-116, 120
Agent
  defined, 199
  in distribution process, 201
Agent middlemen
  in marketing channels, 268-270
  types of, 225-230
  as wholesaling establishment,
    219
Aggregate demand, defined, 110
Agricultural marketing
  through auction companies, 229
  through commission houses,
    226-227
  competitive setting of, 417
  costs of, 393-394
  grading in, 49, 50
  need for middlemen in, 57,
    269-270
  power of enterprises in, 216-218
Agriculture
  cooperatives in, 217-218
  demand for products of, 216,
    217
  pricing in, 319-320
Air freight transportation, 206

451

Analysis of variance (ANOVA), 101, 102
Antitrust legislation, 402-403, 405, 418
Appropriation. *See also* Costs
  advertising, 376-380
  personal selling, 356-357
  promotional, 344
Assembling, defined, 50
Assets, consumers' liquid, 134
Auctions, for commodities, 229, 319
Audit
  marketing, 429-432
  store, 97-98
Automatic selling, 254-255
Automobile Dealers Franchise Act, 406-407

"Back-to-the-city movement," 141
Bait advertising, defined, 408
Banks
  as credit source, 54
  marketing by, 39
Basing point, defined, 403n
Bayesian analysis, 102
Behavior, buyer. *See* Buyer behavior
Below-cost sales, restrictions on, 406
Benefit structure analysis, 167
Bidding, competitive, 320
Branches, effectiveness of, 76
Brand differentiation
  and advertising, 375
  under monopolistic competition, 417, 418
  packaging for, 179
  product differentiation through, 181, 182-183
  and promotional mix, 340
Branding, defined, 181
Brands
  of agricultural products, 217
  consistency of quality of, 177
  of convenience goods, 158
  and distribution intensity, 278
  dual distribution of, 272-273
  family vs. individual, 182-183
  identification of, 179-182
  image of, 146-147
  loyalty to, 132
  multiple, 183
  personality of, 146
  pricing of advertised, 378
  private, 183
  of shopping goods, 159
  sold in discount houses, 252, 253
  of specialty goods, 159

Break-even analysis, in pricing, 290-291, 322-323
Brokers, 225-226
  defined, 225
Budget, household, 117
Buildings, marketing of, 161
Business
  marketing, 35-38
  segmentation by kind of, 121-122
  service, 38-40, 214, 215, 216
Business espionage, 78
Business forecasting, 56
Business philosophy, shifts in, 28-29
Business Statistics, 101n
Business Week, 92
Buyer behavior
  defined, 128
  effect of, on channel usage, 272, 274-275
  effect of, on pricing, 292-293
  external influences on, 129-141
  habitual, 158
  of industrial users, 148, 149, 160
  influence of marketing on, 396-398
  motivation research into, 93
  psychological factors in, 141-147
  role of life-styles in, 147-148
Buyers. *See also* Consumers
  bargaining power of, 292-293, 298
  behavior of. *See* Buyer behavior
  resident, 229
  segmentation of, 111-123
Buying
  defined, 50
  as marketing activity, 47, 50-51
Buying groups, department store, 245

Canonical analysis, 102
Case problems
  advertising policies, 386-389
  buyer behavior, 151
  competition from shopping mall, 263-264
  marketing organization, 42-43
  marketing research, 104-106
  market segments in banking, 124-125
  need for middlemen, 59
  overall marketing strategy, 437-440
  pricing management, 303-304
  pricing strategy, 325-326
  product development, 170-171
  product-market strategy, 192-193

Case problems *(cont.)*
  promotional strategy, 346-347
  relations with middlemen, 283-284
  role of advertising, 21-22
  sales force management, 363-364
  sales forecasts, 83-84
  size of orders, 210-211
  social role of marketing, 410-411
  use of manufacturers' agent, 231-233
Cash-and-carry wholesalers, 224
Cash discounts, 299
Catalog of Mailing Lists, 337n
Census results, error in, 100
Central city shopping districts, 258-260
Centralization, of staff activities, 35
Central tendency, measures of, 101
Chain-store systems, 241, 242, 246-249
  defined, 246
Change, company's attitude toward, 27
"Channel captain," 215
Chief marketing executive, 31
Child Protection and Toy Safety Act, 404
Chi-square test, 101
Cities
  marketing in central, 141, 397
  segmentation by size of, 115
Clayton Antitrust Act
  and corporate growth, 402
  and pricing, 293, 298, 405
  and typing contract, 406
"Clearance sales," 297
Clubs, "of-the-month," 244
Cluster analysis, 102
Cognitive dissonance, on buyers' part, 147
Collusion, on price changes, 419
Commercial Atlas and Marketing Guide, 1978, 12n
Commercial banks, marketing by, 39
Commission houses, 226-227
  defined, 226
Commissions
  to advertising agencies, 371
  to salespeople, 359
Commodities, pricing of, 319-320
Commodity exchanges, 55, 319
Common Market, 114
Communication(s)
  feedback in, 332-333, 335
  growth of mass media of, 16

Communication(s) *(cont.)*
  with middlemen, 280-281
  one-step vs. two-step, 333
  one-way vs. two-way, 332
  organizational problems in, 10
  personal selling as, 351
  in promotion, 330-334
Community shopping centers, 258
Company goals
  in marketing concept, 18, 20
  and marketing organization,
    26-27
Company operations, unification
    of, 18, 20
Comparative advertising, 369
Compensation
  for advertising agencies, 371
  for salespeople, 358-359
Competition
  advertising and, 369
  company's attitude toward, 27
  countermoves in, 425
  and differential advantage, 131
  and distribution intensity, 278
  in fringe markets, 132
  growth in, 11
  legislation affecting, 402-403,
    405, 406
  and marketing concept, 27, 29
  market research on, 92
  monopolistic, 318-320, 417-419
  no direct, 416
  nonprice, 395, 422
  oligopolistic, 319, 320, 395-396,
    418-419
  postures toward, 415, 416
  price, 56, 395-396
  pricing strategy and, 291-292,
    295-296, 300, 310-314,
    316-321
  during product life cycle, 164,
    165
  pure, 416-417
  as uncontrollable, 8
Competitive bidding, 320
*Competitive Distribution in a Free,
  High-Level Economy . . . ,*
    261n
Competitive settings
  marketing decisions in, 419-424
  types of, 416-419
Computers
  in media selection, 383
  in MIS operation, 66, 76, 80
  and physical distribution, 16
  simulation with, 80, 205
Conditioning, in learning, 142
Confidence interval, 101, 102
Conservation vs. consumption, 29
Consumer Behavior, 118n, 129n,
    139n

Consumer cooperative, defined,
    251
Consumer durables, on
    installment plan, 54
Consumer goods
  classification of, 157-160
  defined, 157
  promotion of, 341
  wholesalers of, 219, 220,
    221-222, 226
Consumerism
  defined, 399
  development of, 399-400
Consumer market, segmentation
    of, 112, 114-120, 121
Consumer protection, costs of,
    404
Consumers. *See also* Buyers;
    Marketing channels
  of convenience goods, 158
  decision making by, 128-129
  loyalty of, 132
  as marketing "targets," 7
  motivation of. *See* Buyer
    behavior
  needs of, in product planning,
    167
  readiness of, to buy, 119
  of shopping goods, 158-159
  of specialty goods, 159-160
  survey of buying power of, 79
  ultimate. *See* Ultimate
    consumers
  as users vs. nonusers, 119
Consumers Union, 400
Consumption
  vs. conservation, 29
  effect of package size on,
    179-180
  frivolous, 396-398
  segmentation by patterns of.
    See Market segmentation
Containerized shipping, 16, 206,
    207
Contract, tying, 406
Contribution pricing, 297
Controllables. *See also* Marketing
    strategy
  influence of, on price, 308-311
  price as, 288, 310, 312, 320
  in product-market relation, 6, 7
  studies of influences of, 91-92
Controlling, in marketing
    business, 37
Convenience goods
  defined, 158
  promotion of, 340
  retailing of, 249
Convenience stores, 15
Cooperative marketing
  associations, 217-218

Cooperatives
  consumer, 251
  retailer-owned, 250, 252
Core market, 132
Corrective advertising, 408
Correlation and association,
    101-102
Cost of goods sold, 69-70, 72, 75
  defined, 69
Cost-plus pricing, 320-321
Costs. *See also specific topics*
  and buying decisions, 47
  as departmental goals, 10
  effect of, on prices, 289-291,
    296-297
  fixed, 289, 290, 291, 297
  in marketing channel choice,
    275-276
  in mass retailing, 243, 245-248
  profitability through reduced,
    174, 175-177, 184
  and profit goal, 26
  variable, 289-291, 296, 297
Countermoves, competitors', 425
County and City Data Book, 92
Couponing, promotion through,
    338
Credit
  as influence on spending, 14-15,
    134
  installment, 54-55, 134, 135
  management of, 37
  mercantile, 55
  through selling agents, 228
  and size of income, 134
  trade, 54
Crops, grading of, 49, 50
Cultural factors
  as influence on buyer behavior,
    139-141
  as influence on marketing, 9
Customer orientation. *See*
    Marketing orientation
Customers. *See also* Buyers;
    Consumers
  analysis of sales by, 78
  division of authority by, 32-33
  loyalty of, 56
  service to, 27, 52, 203
Customization of products, 186,
    187

Data analysis, methods of,
    101-102
Data bank, 66
Dealers. *See* Middlemen;
    Retailers; Wholesalers
Debt. *See* Credit
Deceptive price advertising, 408
Decision making
  in competitive settings, 419-424

Decision making *(cont.)*
  by consumers, 128-129. *See also*
    Buyer behavior
  information-based, 65, 67
  intuition-based, 64-65
  in market segmentation, 123
  in physical distribution, 202-208
  process of, 64, 88-90, 419
Delivered pricing, 300
Delivery time, 207
Delphi technique, 99
Demand
  aggregate, 110
  in economic theory, 130
  estimating, 323
  expansibility of, 372-373, 422
  in extractive industries, 216,
    217
  heterogeneous segments of, 130
  as marketing goal, 46
  measurement of potential, 91
  price elasticity of, 310-311,
    314-315, 318, 376, 426-427
  primary, 372-374, 416
  in product life cycle, 164
  selective, 373, 374
  stimulated by promotion, 51-52,
    345, 372-375
Demographic market
    segmentation, 115-118, 120
Departmental goals
  conflicts among, 10-11
  in marketing concept, 18, 20
Department stores, 244-246
  competitors of, 241, 242, 261
  discount houses as, 252
  organization in, 35-37
Depth interviewing, 143, 144
Design patents, 403
Design simplification, product,
    175-176
Development, product. *See*
    Product development
Developmental promotional
    strategy, 342
Differential advantage, of a seller,
    131
Differentials, price, 297, 298-300,
    405
Differentiation
  of brands. *See* Brand
    differentiation
  of products, 56, 215, 310, 312
  of services, 215
Diffusion
  defined, 137
  process of, 137-138
Diffusion of Innovations, The, 138n
Direct mail, promotion through,
    334, 337-338
Direct sale, efficiency of, 57-58

Discontinuance of products, 184,
    185
Discount houses, 252-254
  defined, 252
  early history of, 274-275
  pricing by, 423
  and product service, 178
Discounts
  functional, 405
  in pricing, 298-299, 405
  quantity, 298-299, 405
  seasonal, 299
Discretionary income
  and buyer behavior, 134-135,
    140
  increases in, 13-14
Discriminant analysis, 102
Discrimination, price, 293, 405
Dispersion, measures of, 101, 102
Display, point-of-purchase
  advertising used with, 51-52,
    425
  as form of promotion, 336-337
Disposable personal income
  and buyer behavior, 133
  growth in, 12-13
Disposable products, as
    pollutants, 398
Distinctiveness of products,
    312-320
Distribution. *See also* Marketing
    channels; Middlemen;
    Retailers; Retailing;
    Wholesalers
  of agricultural products, 417
  by brokers, 226
  in competitive settings, 420-421
  costs of, 203, 206, 208-209, 224
  defined, 198
  definitions in, 198-200
  dual, 272-273
  elements of, 200-202
  exclusive, 277, 278, 311
  in extractive industries, 214-218
  house-to-house, 239-240
  intensity of, 276-278, 375
  in marketing concept, 28
  market research on, 91
  mass, 277, 278, 311
  physical. *See* Physical
    distribution
  role of producers in, 214-218
  role of wholesalers in, 218-230
  selective, 277, 278, 311
  strategy of, 200, 201, 311, 343
  total system of, 208-209
Diversification, product-mix,
    189-190
Dollar profit, targeted, 294
Double search, of buyers and
    sellers, 130-131

Drop shipment wholesalers, 224
Dual distribution, 272-273
  defined, 272
Dun's Review, 92
Durable goods
  and income fluctuations, 135
  life cycle for, 165, 166
  replacement of, 164, 165
  service for, 178
  sold in discount houses, 253,
    254
  wholesalers of, 220, 221, 226

Early adopters, in diffusion
    process, 138, 341
Early majority, in diffusion
    process, 138, 341
Econometric model building, 79
Economic forecasting, 56
Economic man, model of, 130
Economics, and buyer behavior,
    129-135
Economies of scale, 428
Economy
  effect of, on marketing, 9
  effect of, on pricing, 293
Education, market segmentation
    by, 117
Efficiency
  in distribution system, 206, 209
  marketing, 46, 57-58
  operating, 75, 76
  in production, 112
  in retail sales, 74
  of selling activities, 51
80-20 principle, 76
Elasticity of demand, price,
    310-311, 314-315, 318, 376,
    426-427
Elements of Marketing, 393n
Environment
  effect of, on marketing, 7-9,
    11-17
  effect of marketing on, 498
Environmental Protection Agency,
    404
Espionage, business, 78
Ethnic groups, and buyer
    behavior, 139
European Economic Community,
    114
Evaluation matrix for products,
    167, 168
Exception reports, 67
Exclusive dealing, defined, 406
Exclusive distribution, 277, 278,
    311
Executive opinion, jury of, 79
Executives
  chief marketing, 31

Executives *(cont.)*
line, 31
staff, 33
Expansibility of demand, 372–373, 422
Expansion, corporate, 402
Expense ratio, 71
Expenses, defined, 69
Experimental method, in marketing research, 98
Extractive industries. *See also* Agricultural marketing; Agriculture
assemblers of products of, 219
distribution in, 214–218

Fabricating parts, 161–162
defined, 161
Factor analysis, 102
Factories, location of, 53–54
"Factors," 228
Factual survey, in marketing research, 97
Fair Packaging and Labeling Act, 404
False advertising, 408
Family
life cycle of, 117–118
as primary group, 135
spending and saving by, 133
Fashion, and buyer behavior, 140
Federal Reserve Bulletin, 92
Federal Trade Commission, 401, 405, 406, 408
Federal Trade Commission Act, 399, 408
Feedback
in communication, 332–333, 335
to marketers, from society, 399
Field sales, 35
Financing, marketing, 54–55
Fixed costs, in pricing decisions, 289–291, 297
F.O.B. pricing, 299, 300
Focus group, in marketing research, 97
Food, Drug, and Cosmetics Act, 404
Food and Drug Administration, 401, 404
Forbes, 92
Forecasting, sales, 55–56, 78–79, 203, 362
Forgotten Pioneers, 238n
Form utility, added to products, 394
Franchise, defined, 255, 271
Franchising, 255–257, 271
Free association, in motivation research, 144

Freight absorption pricing policy, 300
Fringe market, 132
Full-cost pricing, 296–297
Functional discounts 405
Fundamentals of Marketing, 399n
Futures market, 55n

General line wholesalers, 221–222, 223
General merchandise chains, 15
General merchandise wholesalers, 220–221, 223
Geographic deployment of inventory, 204, 205
Geographic division of authority, 31–32, 33
Geographic market segmentation, 184
consumer, 114–115
industrial, 122
Geographic price differentials, 299–300
Ghetto areas, marketing in, 141, 397
Ghetto Marketplace, The, 141n, 397n
Goals
company, 18, 20, 26–27
departmental, 10–11
of marketing, 46, 57
in marketing research, 95
Good faith, defined, 409
Government intervention, in pricing, 293, 298–299
Grading of products, 49–50, 217
defined, 49
Gross margin, defined, 70
Gross margin ratio, 70–71
Guarantees
against price declines, 301
product, 178
Guide to Consumer Markets, 1977–78, A, 12n, 13n

Halo effect, 182, 188
Hard-core market, 132, 319, 320
Hedging, defined, 55n
Heterogeneity of markets, 130–132
Holding costs, 203
Horizontal cooperative advertising, 371
Horizontal integration
of chain stores, 246–247, 248
of department stores, 244–245
Households
budget life cycle of, 117
gross income of, 133
growing number of, 12
House-to-house selling, 237–240

Human Behavior: An Inventory of Scientific Findings, 143n

Income
and credit, 134
discretionary, 13–14, 134–135, 140
disposable personal, 12–13, 133
distribution of, 14, 115, 116
expectations of, 134
family, 133
household gross, 133
market segmentation by, 115, 120
real, 12–13
supernumerary, 13–14
Incremental approach to advertising appropriations, 378–379
Independent stores, 240–242, 250
defined, 240
Indirect interviews, 97
Industrial goods
categories of, 160–162
defined, 157
marketing of, 269, 270, 271
product identification in, 181
promotion of, 341
service for, 177–178
wholesalers of, 219–222, 224–226
Industrial market, segmentation of, 112, 120–122
Industry
advertising by, 369
desired place in, 27
standardization in, 50
Industry product life cycle, 162, 163, 165, 166
Inflation, spending during, 133
Influential
defined, 136
role of, in marketing, 137
Information. *See also* Communication(s)
from advertising, 28
marketing, 56, 64–80, 88–90, 96–98
from packaging, 335, 425
value and cost of, 103
Information-based decision making, 65, 67
Information retrieval, in MIS design, 76
Innovation, product. *See also* Market pioneering stage
advertising during, 373–374
and competition, 419–420, 423, 425
and product line policy, 166–169

Innovator
  company as, 163–164
  in diffusion process, 138
  promotion aimed at, 341
Inputs, marketing
  optimum combination of,
    426–427
  selection of, 425–426
Installations, defined, 160
Installment credit
  equivalent to personal debt, 134
  essential to marketing, 54–55
  and income fluctuations, 135
Insurance companies
  marketing by, 39–40
  risks covered by, 55
Integrated retailers, large-scale,
  242–249
Integration
  horizontal, of stores, 244–248
  of marketing activities, 30–31
  in product making/marketing,
    175, 176–177
  retail growth through, 243
  vertical, of chain stores, 248
Interpretive survey, 97
Interviewing
  depth, 143, 144
  indirect, 97
Intuition-based decision making,
  64–65
Inventory
  of chain stores, 247
  costs of, 176, 203, 206, 209
  location of, 204–205
  management of, 53, 54, 208–209
  size of, 202–203, 204
  "turnover" in, 74–76, 292
  valuation of, 75
Inventory risk, 55
Investment, target return on
  (ROI), 294, 295
Invoices, sales, 77

Jawboning, 402
Jet air freight, 16
Job description, in sales, 357, 361
Jungle, The, 399
Jury of executive opinion, 79

Labeling, regulation of, 404–405
Laggards, in diffusion process, 138
Lasting distinctiveness of
  products, 312, 313
Late majority, in diffusion process,
  138, 341
Leadership, price, 300
Learning, factors influencing,
  142–143

Learning Theory and the Symbolic
    Processes, 142n
Legislation
  as influence on marketing, 8,
    401–409, 418
  on pricing, 293, 298–299
Leisure time, and buyer behavior,
  140
Life cycle
  family, 117–118
  product. See Product life cycle
Life Study of Consumer
    Expenditures, The, 133n
Life-style
  in buyer behavior, 147–148
  defined, 147
  and discretionary income, 135
  and market segmentation, 119
Limited-function wholesalers,
  223–225
Liquid assets, consumers', 134
Logistical Management, 421n
Low-income groups, marketing to,
  141, 397
Loyalty, customer, 56
Luxuries
  markets for, 14, 115
  specialty goods as, 159

Magazines, advertising in,
  383–384
Mail-order houses, 243–244, 261
Mail-order wholesalers, 225
Malls, shopping, 258, 260
Management
  advertising, 380–385
  inventory, 53, 54, 208–209
  pricing, 288–324
  sales force, 31–35, 357–362
Management consultants, 38
Management materials, marketing
  of, 162
Managerial Economics, 312n
Manufacturers. See also
    Marketing channels
  buying by, 47
  credit extended by, 54, 55
  in distribution process, 200,
    214–216
  effect of shopping centers on,
    260
  operating statements of, 69–70
  sales by, to discount houses, 254
  wholesalers owned by, 219
Manufacturers' agents, 227
Manufacturing firm, marketing
  by, 31–35
Marginal analysis, and advertising
  costs, 378
Markdown, defined, 73

Markdown ratio, 74
Market(s)
  changes in, 11–15
  core, 132
  defined, 110
  in economic theory, 130
  effect of, on channel usage,
    272
  finding new, 183–184
  fringe, 132
  futures, 55n
  hard-core, 132, 319, 320
  heterogeneity of, 130–132
  share of the, 92
Market decline stage, 165
  advertising during, 376
  pricing during, 310, 313, 319,
    320
Market growth stage, 164
  competition during, 417, 418
  costs during, 395
  pricing in, 309–310, 312,
    316–318, 320
  promotion during, 341, 373–374
Marketing
  activities in, 46–58
  agricultural. See Agricultural
    marketing
  assessing opportunities in, 17
  of convenience goods, 158
  costs of, 392–396
  decision making in, 415,
    419–424
  defined, 6, 46
  efficiency in, 46, 57–58
  emerging role of, 4–21
  environment affecting, 7–9,
    11–17
  financing in, 54–55
  function of, 4–5
  in ghetto areas, 141, 399
  goals of, 46, 57
  as influence on society, 392–398
  integration of activities in,
    30–31
  misdirected effort in, 76–77
  by nonprofit organizations, 5,
    29–31, 38, 40–41
  risk bearing in, 55–56
  of shopping goods, 159
  and social responsibility, 29
  society's influence on, 399–409
  of specialty goods, 159–160
  test, 98
  timing of actions in, 423
Marketing, Society, and Conflict,
  397n
Marketing audit, 429–432
  defined, 429
Marketing Behavior and Executive
    Action, 130n, 156n

Marketing channels. *See also*
  Distribution
  changes in, 15-16
  in competitive settings, 420-421
  control of, 214-216, 217
  defined, 202, 268, 281
  determination of, 274-278
  vs. direct sale, 58
  division of authority by, 32-33
  factors in use of, 272-274,
    278-281
  legislation affecting, 406-407
  in marketing concept, 28
  product inputs and, 425
  and promotional mix, 343
  types of, 268-271
Marketing Communications, 331n
Marketing concept
  features of, 17-18
  implementing, 19-20
  organization under, 34-35
  planning and operating under,
    18, 19
  product objectives under, 167
  product planning under, 167
  transition to, 27-31
Marketing Decision Making, 123n
Marketing Definitions, 6n, 110n,
  198n
*Marketing Education and the Real
  World,* 257n
*Marketing for Nonprofit
  Organizations,* 5n, 38n
Marketing information, 56, 64-65
Marketing information system
  (MIS)
  components of, 66-67
  defined, 65
  inputs into, 68-80
  marketing research and, 88-
    90
  outputs of, 67-68
Marketing inputs
  implementation of, 427-428
  optimum combination of,
    426-427
  selection of, 425-426
Marketing intelligence, 78, 92
Marketing in the Service Sector, 5n
Marketing Management, 430n
Marketing Manager's Handbook,
  432n
Marketing mix
  defined, 7
  marketing research in, 88
Marketing organization
  company goals and, 26-27
  in manufacturing firm, 31-35
  in marketing business, 35-38
  in nonprofit organization, 40-41
  in service business, 38-40

Marketing organization *(cont.)*
  and transition to marketing
    concept, 27-31
Marketing orientation
  adoption of, 11-17
  conditions preceding, 9-11
  in marketing concept, 18, 19
*Marketing Planning and
  Competitive Strategy,* 332n,
  433n
Marketing policy
  formulation of, 30
  and middlemen's cooperation,
    280
Marketing research, 6, 19, 79-80.
  See also Research and
    development
  costs of, 102-103
  defined, 88
  designs in, 98-99
  errors in, 99, 100-101
  information through, 56
  lower costs through, 398
  and marketing information
    system, 88-90
  procedure of, 93-102
  in product planning, 169
  risk reduction by, 55
  scope of, 91-93
  top 20 organizations in,
    94
Marketing Research, 89n
*Marketing Research: A
  Management Information
  Approach,* 102n
*Marketing Research: Information
  Systems, and Decision
  Making,* 100n
Marketing research firms, 38
Marketing strategy
  defined, 7
  evaluating, 428-432
  implementation of, 427-
    428
  overall, 414-432
  pricing strategy in, 309
  promotional strategy in,
    330-331, 339
Marketing Strategy and Plans,
  415n
Market maturity stage, 164-165
  advertising in, 373-374
  competition in, 417, 418
  costs in, 395
  pricing in, 310, 312-313,
    317-320
  product-market strategy in, 183,
    186, 188
  promotion in, 341
Market measurement studies, 91
Market news, 56

Market penetration
  through individual branding,
    182-183
  and promotional mix, 342
Market pioneering stage, 164. *See
  also* Innovation, product
  marketing strategy during, 416
  pricing in, 309, 312, 314-316,
    321
  promotion during, 341
Market potential
  defined, 91
  in marketing channel choice,
    275
Market segment, defined, 111
Market segmentation
  based on market heterogeneity,
    130
  concept of, 113
  consumer, 112, 114-120, 121
  decision process in, 123
  defined, 122
  industrial, 112, 120-122
  need for, 111-112
  role of self-image in, 146
Market Segmentation, 113n, 120n
Market share
  as pricing objective, 314, 317,
    318-319
  as product objective, 167, 168
  target, 295
Markup
  in decision making, 72-73
  defined, 72
  and inventory turnover, 292
  in middlemen's pricing,
    321-322, 343-344
Mass communications media, 16
Mass distribution, 277, 278, 311
Mass production vs. market
  segmentation, 111, 112
Mass retailers, 242-249
Materials handling, 206-207, 208
Measurement studies, market, 91
Measures of central tendency and
  dispersion, 101, 102
Meat Inspection Act, 399
Media
  advertising, 371, 383-384
  growth of mass, 16
Mercantile credit, 55
Merchandising
  activities in, 48-52
  defined, 35, 48
  re-, 177-183
  responsibility for, 35-37
  scrambled, 251
Merchant. *See also* Middlemen
  defined, 199
Merchant wholesalers, 219-225,
  270, 271

457

Mergers, legislation concerning,
    402, 403, 418
Middle class, growth of, 14
Middlemen. *See also* Marketing
    channels; Retailers;
    Wholesalers
  advertising costs shared by, 369
  agent, 219, 225-230, 268-270
  analytical ratios used by, 72-76
  assembling by, 50
  buying by, 50
  classifications of, 199
  cooperation of, 279-281, 296,
    377
  credit extended by, 54
  defined, 198
  development of, 16
  in distribution process, 200-202,
    208-209
  effect of, on channel usage, 274
  gross margins expected by, 311
  in industrial goods marketing,
    161, 162
  legislation affecting, 406-407
  markup pricing by, 321-322,
    343-344
  operating statements of, 69, 70
  and pricing policies, 300, 301
  private branding by, 183
  and product development, 49
  and product sizes, 176
Milline rate, in advertising, 384
Mining, demand for products of,
    216
Missionary selling, 354, 360
Model bank, 67
Model building, econometric,
    79
Models, new, of products, 184,
    185-186
Modern Retailing, 237n
Monopolistic competition
  defined, 417
  marketing strategy under,
    417-418, 419
  pricing under, 318-319, 320
Monopoly
  legislation preventing, 402, 403,
    405, 418
  marketing strategy under, 416
  pricing under, 312, 313-314,
    320
Monopoly power, defined, 402
Motivation
  of consumers. *See* Buyer
    behavior
  in learning, 142
  psychological explanations of,
    143-144
  research into, 93
Motivation and Personality, 145n

*Motivation Research and
    Marketing Management,*
    144n
Multidimensional scaling, 102
Multiple brands, 183
Multiple purchasing influence, 160
Multivariate analysis, 102

Nation's Business, 92
Needs
  and buyer behavior, 144-145
  consumer, in product planning,
    167
  hierarchy of, 144-145
  as influence on marketing, 9
Neighborhood shopping centers,
    257-258
Net loss, 69
Net profit, 69, 70
Net profit ratio, 71-72
New-business selling, 355
Newspapers, advertising in, 384
Nielsen Retail Index, 92n
Noise, in communication, 332
Nondurable goods, wholesalers of,
    220, 221
Nonprobability samples, 99-100
Nonprofit organizations
  lack of marketing input in,
    40-41
  marketing as element of, 5, 38
  and marketing concept, 29-30,
    31

Observational method, in
    marketing research, 97-98
Obsolescence of products, 15, 48
  planned, 184, 186
Occupation, market segmentation
    by, 118
Oil companies, advertising by, 370
Oligopolistic competition, 319, 320
  defined, 418
  marketing strategy under,
    418-419
  price stabilization under,
    395-396
Oligopolistic pricing, 318, 320
Oligopoly, defined, 318
100,000,000 Guinea Pigs, 399,
    400n
One-price policy, 298
Operating data, as information
    source, 69-76
Operating ratios, 70-72
Operating statement, 69-71, 73-75
Opinion survey, in marketing
    research, 97
Orders
  processing of, 207
  size of, 207

Order takers vs. order getters,
    353
Organization. *See also*
    Management
  advertising, 369-372
  defined, 26
  marketing. *See* Marketing
    organization
  under marketing concept, 34-35
  model of buying, 149
  nonprofit, 5, 29-30, 31, 38,
    40-41
  as system, 29-30
Organizational Buying Behavior,
    148n, 149n
Outlets, effectiveness of, 76
Ownership groups, department
    store, 245, 246
Ownership transfers, 7. *See also*
    Marketing channels

Packaging, 178-181
  as form of promotion, 334, 337
  information from, 337, 425
  as marketing activity, 52
  as pollutant, 398
  regulation of, 404-405
Palletization, 16
Party plan selling, 239
Patents, design, 403
Peer groups, and buyer behavior,
    135-136
Penetration-pricing strategy,
    314-317, 427
Perception, buyers', 145-147
Performance appraisal
  of advertising agency, 384
  of salespeople, 360-362
Perishable distinctiveness of
    products, 312-313,
    315-317, 320
Personal consumption spending,
    133-134
Personal debt, and consumer
    spending, 134
Personality, and market
    segmentation, 118-119
Personality and Persuasibility, 333n
Personal selling. *See also* Sales
  costs of, 51, 335, 344, 356-357
  early emphasis on, 28
  management of, 34, 35
  in market growth stage, 164
  model of, 350
  objectives of, 351-353, 355-356
  planning operation of, 351-357
  production costs lowered by,
    395
  in promotional program,
    334-335, 351, 352
  as push strategy, 342

Personal selling. *See also* Sales
(cont.)
   strategy for, 353-356
   to reduce cognitive dissonance,
     147
Personal Selling, 350n
Personnel. *See* Organization; Sales
   force
Physical distribution
   in agriculture, 417
   changes in, 16
   in competitive settings, 421
   costs of, 203, 206, 208-209, 224
   defined, 200
   elements of, 52-54, 202-208
Physical plant
   management of, 37, 38
   as marketing activity, 48
Piggyback service, 16, 206
Place utility, added to products,
   394
Planned obsolescence, 184, 186
Planning
   in advertising, 366-367
   under marketing concept, 18, 19
   in marketing research, 95-102
   product, 47-49, 167, 169
Point-of-purchase display
   advertising used with, 51-52,
     425
   as form of promotion, 336-337
Political pressure, as influence on
   marketing, 8, 403
Pooling, defined, 217
Population, and marketing, 11-12,
   115, 141
Positioning in the market
   defined, 425
   and marketing strategy, 424
Possession utility, added to
   products, 394
Predictive models, in MIS, 67
Preliminary exploration, in
   marketing research, 94-95
Premium-pricing strategy, 317
Premiums, as form of promotion,
   338
Prestige builder, in product line,
   301
Pretests, of advertising, 385
Price(s)
   administered, 293, 312, 320
   competition in, 56, 426-427
   as consumer motivation, 130
   as controllables, 310, 312, 320
   and distribution strategy, 201
   effect of controllables on,
     308-311
   guarantees against declines in,
     301
   market research on, 91

Price(s) *(cont.)*
   physical distribution costs in,
     209
   policies concerning, 295-302
   procedures for setting, 319-323
   under pure competition,
     416-417
   stabilization of, 294-295
   suggested resale, 301
   as uncontrollables, 312, 319
   uniformity of, 297-298
Price differentials, 297-299, 405
   geographical, 299-300
Price discrimination, 293, 405
Price elasticity
   defined, 310
   of demand, 310-311, 314-315,
     318, 376, 426-427
Price fixing, 419
*Price Policies and Marketing
   Management,* 294n
Price-skimming strategy, 314-316,
   317
Price space, in product line,
   300-301
Price wars, 319, 425
Pricing
   advertising and, 376
   in competitive settings, 422-423
   contribution, 297
   cost-plus, 320-321
   delivered, 300
   factors influencing, 288-293
   F.O.B., 299, 300
   full-cost, 296-297
   leadership in, 300
   legislation affecting, 402-403,
     405-406, 419
   management of, 288-324
   markups in. *See* Markup
   and middlemen's cooperation,
     280
   under monopolistic competition,
     318-319, 320
   under monopoly, 312, 313-314,
     320
   objectives of, 293-295
   oligopolistic, 318, 320, 419
   penetration, 314-317, 423
   as promotional device, 301-302
   responsibility for, 30
   transportation costs in, 299-300
Pricing strategy
   and competitive situation,
     312-313
   defined, 308
   and marketing strategy, 309
   during product life cycle,
     314-319
   for products of lasting
     distinctiveness, 313-314

Pricing strategy *(cont.)*
   and promotional mix, 343
   role of controllables in, 308-311
Primary demand, 373, 374, 416
   defined, 372
Primary groups, and buyer
   behavior, 135-136
Private branding, 183
Probability samples, 99, 100-101
*Proceedings of the Conference of
   Marketing Teachers from
   Far Western States,* 132n
Producers
   brokers used by, 226
   defined, 200
   and marketing channels,
     214-218, 273-281
Producers' cooperative marketing
   associations, 217-218
Product development
   in competitive setting, 419-420,
     423, 425
   costs of, 314, 316
   as merchandising activity, 48-49
Product evaluation matrix, 167,
   168
Product innovation. *See*
   Innovation, product
Production
   costs of, 289, 395
   efficiency in, 112
   facilities and equipment for,
     160-161
   management's emphasis on, 28
   marketing of materials for,
     161-162
   mass, 111, 112
Productivity, of marketing inputs,
   430
Product life cycle, 162-166
   advertising during, 373-374
   costs during, 395
   marketing strategy during, 416,
     417, 418
   pricing during, 309-310,
     312-321
   promotion during, 341
   shortened by R&D, 15
Product line
   and branding, 182
   diversification into related,
     189
   extension of, 189
   as influence on selling, 354
   pricing policy for, 300-301
   simplification of, 184, 185
Product manager, 33-34, 35
Product-market factors
   in advertising strategy, 372-375
   in pricing, 309-311
   in promotional mix, 340-343

Product-market interrelationship, 6-7
Product-market strategies, 174-191, 330
Product-mix diversification, 189-190
Product planning
  as marketing activity, 47-49
  phases of, 167, 169
Products
  analysis of sales by, 78
  and channel usage, 272, 274
  classification of, 157-162
  competitors' reactions to, 419-420, 423, 425
  customization of, 186, 187
  defined, 156
  differentiation of, 56, 215, 310, 312
  distinctiveness of, 312-320
  division of authority by, 32
  evaluation of new, 91
  form utility added to, 394
  grading of, 48, 49-50
  guarantees of, 178
  integration in making/marketing of, 175, 176-177
  legislation affecting, 403-405
  in marketing definition, 6
  need for policies on, 167
  new models of, 184, 185-186
  objectives concerning, 166-167
  obsolescence of, 15, 48, 184, 186
  orientation toward, 9-10
  patents on design of, 403
  perceptions of, 145-147, 424
  place utility added to, 394
  possession utility added to, 394
  quality of, 177, 404
  replacement strategy for, 188
  service for, 177-178
  simplification of design of, 175-176
  standardizing of, 48, 49-50
  time utility added to, 394
Profit
  advertising's contribution to, 378-380, 382
  as company goal, 26-27
  net, 69, 70, 71-72
  from new products, 166
  as pricing objective, 293-294
  as product objective, 167, 168
  targeted dollar, 294
Profitability, product-market strategies for, 174-191
Profit-and-loss statement, 69-70
Projection, and buyer behavior, 144
Projection of past sales, 79

Project planning, for marketing research, 95-102
Promotion. See also Advertising; Personal selling
  communications in, 330-334
  in competitive settings, 421-422
  costs of, 335-336, 344
  demand stimulation by, 51-52, 345, 374-377
  discounts as, 299
  and distribution strategy, 201
  forms of, 334-338
  legislation affecting, 407-409
  market research on, 91
  objectives of, 345
  and pricing, 301-302, 311
  strategy for, 330-331, 338-344
Promotional guarantee, 178
Promotional mix, 338-344
  advertising in, 367-368, 375-376
  defined, 51
Promotional Strategy, 339n
Protective guarantee, 178
Psychographic market segmentation, 118-119
Psychology, and buyer behavior, 141-147
Public image, pricing and, 308-309
Public opinion, as influence on marketing, 8, 399-400
Public utilities, advertising by, 368
Pull strategy, 342
Purchasing
  by cooperative marketers, 218
  frequency of, 340-341
  by industrial users, 112, 122
Purchasing influence, multiple, 160
Purchasing power, growth in, 12-13
Pure competition
  defined, 416
  marketing strategy under, 417
Pure Food and Drug Act, 399
Push strategy, 342

Quantity discounts, 298-299, 405
Questionnaires, in marketing research, 96-97
Quotas, sales, 361-362
  defined, 361
"Quota" sample, 99-100

Race, and market segmentation, 118
Rack jobbers, 223
Rail freight transportation, 206
Rationalization, and buyer behavior, 143-144

Raw materials
  cost of, 161
  defined, 161
  as factor in location, 54
  product differentiation in, 181
  quality of, 177
Readiness to buy, consumers', 119
Real income, growth in, 12-13
Recruiting, of sales personnel, 357-358
Reference groups, and buyer behavior, 135-137
Regional shopping centers, 258, 259, 260
Regression analysis, 79, 101, 102
Religion
  and buyer behavior, 139-140
  market segmentation by, 118
Remerchandising, 177-183
Reorder time, 207
Replacement, of products, 188
Replacement sales, of durables, 164, 165
Resale prices, suggested, 301
Research, marketing. See Marketing research
Research and development. See also Marketing research
  increased spending for, 15
  in marketing concept, 28
  vs. marketing research, 102
  in market orientation, 19
Research for Marketing Decisions, 101n
Resident buyers, 229
Retail chain, organization in, 37
Retailer-owned cooperatives, 250, 252
Retailers. See also Marketing channels; Middlemen
  analytical ratios used by, 72-76
  assembling by, 50
  defined, 199
  in distribution process, 201-202
  mass, 242-249
  operating statements of, 69, 70
  organizational structures of, 35-37, 38
  product planning by, 49
  and resident buyers, 229
  ten largest U.S., 239
Retailing
  defined, 199
  forms of, 237-261
  markup in, 292. See also Pricing
  new institutions in, 15-16
  self-service, 52
  size of, 236-237, 238
  trends in, 260-261
Retentive advertising, 374

Return on investment (ROI),
  target, 294, 295
Reverse integration, in product
  making/marketing, 176,
  177
Risk bearing, marketing, 55-56
Risk reduction, 55-56
Risk transfer, 55
Robinson-Patman Act, 293, 405,
  408
*Role and Organization of
  Marketing Research, The,*
  102*n*
Run-out strategy, 319

Salary, of salespeople, 358, 359
Sales. *See also* Selling
  advertising as cause of,
    377-380, 384
  analysis of records of, 76-78
  below-cost, 406
  in break-even analysis, 322, 323
  "clearance," 297
  direct, 57-58
  80-20 principle in, 76
  field, 35
  fixing terms of, 403
  forecasting, 78-79
  in insurance, 39-40
  management's emphasis on, 28
  in operating statements, 69-71,
    73-75
  policies concerning, 353
  projection of past, 79
  and promotional strategy,
    421-422
  replacement, 164, 165
  target return on, 294
Sales and Marketing Management,
  92
Sales force
  defining jobs of, 353-355
  management of, 31-35, 357-362
  methods for compensating,
    358-359
  opinion poll of, 79
  size of, 355-356
  turnover rate of, 355, 356
Sales forecast
  defined, 78-79
  and inventory size, 203
  quotas based on, 362
  risk reduction by, 55-56
*Sales Management's Survey of
  Buying Power,* 96
Sales potential
  defined, 91
  in marketing channel choice,
    275
Sales return and allowances ratio,
  71

Sales volume
  advertising and, 378-379, 382
  in break-even computations,
    290, 291
  as departmental goal, 10
  increased profitability through,
    174, 177-190
  as product objective, 167, 168
  quotas for, 361, 362
  in target ROI, 294
  of wholesalers, 218, 219
Sampling
  as form of promotion, 338
  in marketing research, 99-101
Saturation, market, 164, 165,
  186
Saving, patterns of, 133-134
Scale, economies of, 426
Science, as marketing
  uncontrollable, 8
Scrambled merchandising, 251
Seasonal discounts, 299
Seasonal factor in marketing, 53,
  54
Segmentation, market. *See* Market
  segmentation
Selective demand, 374
  defined, 373
Selective distribution, 277, 278,
  311
Self-image, and market
  segmentation, 146
Self-service retailing, 52
Selling
  activities involved in, 51-52
  automatic, 254-255
  house-to-house, 237-240
  as marketing activity, 47
  party plan, 239
  personal. *See* Personal selling
Selling agents, 228-229
Semimanufactured goods, defined,
  161
Service businesses
  in distribution process, 214, 215,
    216
  marketing by, 38-40
Services
  differentiation of, 215
  distribution of, 5
  for products, 156-157, 177-178
Service wholesalers, 222-223
Sex, market segmentation by, 118
Share-of-the-market information,
  92
Sherman Antitrust Act, 402
Shipping
  containerized, 16, 206, 207
  costs of, 208, 209
Shopping centers, 257-260
  defined, 257

Shopping districts, central city,
  258-260
Shopping goods, 158-159, 160
  customization of, 187
  defined, 158
  retailing of, 245, 249
Shopping malls, 258, 260
Shortages, costs of, 203
Short-term financing, 54
S.I.C. system, 121-122
Significance, tests of, 101, 102
Simplication
  of product design, 175-176
  of product line, 184, 185
Simulation
  in inventory storage, 205
  of marketing decisions, 80
  in marketing research, 98
Situation analysis, in marketing
  research, 95
Size, product, 175-176
Size of user, segmentation by, 122
Social Aspects of Marketing, 5*n*
Social classes
  hierarchy of, 138
  segmentation by, 118
Social Indicators, 133*n*
Social philosophy, company's,
  27
Social role, in groups, 136
Society
  as influence on marketing,
    399-409
  marketing's influence on,
    392-398
Sociological factors
  and buyer behavior, 135-139
  and marketing, 9
Sophisticated methods of
  forecasting, 79
Sorting theory, and buyer
  behavior, 130-131
Source effect, in communications,
  333-334
Specialists, proliferation of, 10
Specialty goods, 159-160
  defined, 159
  promotion of, 340
  retailing of, 245
Specialty stores, 242
Specialty wholesalers, 222, 223
Spending, personal consumption,
  133-134
Split-run test, 98
Stabilization, price, 294-295
Staff authority, marketing, 31,
  33-35
Standard Industrial Classification
  System, 121-122
Standardizing of products, 49-50,
  176, 177

Statistical bank, 67
  defined, 66
Statistical methods of data
    analysis, 101-102
Status symbols, 138-139
*Status System of a Modern
    Community, The,* 138n
Stockturn
  and product sizes, 176
  rate of, 74-76
Storage
  costs of, 206, 208, 224
  as marketing activity, 47, 52, 53
  in warehouses, 204, 205
Store audit, 97-98
Stores. *See also* Retailers
  chain, 241, 242, 246-249
  convenience, 15
  department, 241, 242, 244-246,
    249, 252, 261
  independent, 240-242, 250
  quality, 242
  specialty, 242
*Study of Consumer Expenditures,
    Incomes, and Savings,* 133n
Suburbia, as market segment, 115,
    141
Supermarkets, 251-252, 254, 261
  defined, 251
Supernumerary income, 13-14
Supply, in economic theory, 130
Supporting activities in marketing,
    48, 54-56
Survey method, in marketing
    research, 96-97
Survey of Current Business, 92
Survey of Marketing Research, A,
    88n
Sustaining promotional strategy,
    342
Synergistic effect, in company
    operations, 20
Synergistic potential, of marketing
    inputs, 425

Targeted dollar profit, 294
Target market share, as pricing
    objective, 295
Target return on investment
    (ROI), 294, 295
Target return on sales, 294
Technical selling, 355

Technology, as marketing
    influence, 8, 15
Territories, sales, 78, 359-360, 361
Test marketing, 98
Tests of significance, 101, 102
Theory of Cognitive Dissonance, A,
    147n
Time series analysis, 102
Time utility, added to products,
    396
Timing, in marketing strategy,
    427-428
Trade credit, 54
Trade discounts, 299
Trade-off analysis, in channel
    choice, 275-276
Trade selling, 354, 360
Trading down, 187, 188
Trading stamps, 338
Trading up, 187, 188
Traffic builder, in product line,
    301
Train, shipping by, 206
Transportation. *See also* Physical
    distribution
  costs of, 208, 209, 224, 299-300
  as marketing activity, 52, 53-54
  modes of, 206
Transport time, 206
Truck, transportation by, 206
Truck wholesalers, 223
t-test, 101
Turnover
  inventory, 74-76, 292
  sales force, 355, 356
Tying contract, defined, 406

Ultimate consumers
  defined, 112
  as problem solvers, 130
  sales to. *See* Marketing
    channels; Retailers;
    Retailing
Uncontrollables, 7-9
  in buyer behavior, 133-134
  price as, 312, 319
  studies of influences of, 92-93
Unfair Trade Practices Acts, 293,
    406
Unit contribution to fixed costs,
    290
"Unitized" trains, 16, 206

Unsophisticated methods of
    forecasting, 79
Urbanization, segmentation by,
    114-115
U.S. Department of Commerce,
    92
U.S. Department of
    Transportation, 404
U.S. Office of Business
    Economics, 92

Variable costs, in pricing
    decisions, 289-291, 296,
    297
Variable pricing, 298
Vending, automatic, 254-255
Vertical cooperative advertising,
    369
Vertical integration, of chain
    stores, 248

Wall Street Journal, 92
Warehouses, 204-207
  costs of, 208, 209
  owned by chain stores, 248
Wheeler-Lea Act, 408
Wheel of retailing hypothesis,
    260-261
Wholesalers. *See also* Marketing
    channels; Middlemen
  analytical ratios used by, 72-76
  assembling by, 50
  credit extended by, 55
  defined, 199
  in distribution process, 200-201,
    218-230
  merchant, 219-225, 270, 271
  operating statements of, 69, 70
  organizational structures of, 35,
    37, 38
  price discounts to, 405
  product planning by, 49
  types of, 219-230
Wholesaler-sponsored groups of
    retailers, 250, 252
Wholesaling, defined, 199
Women, role of, 140
Word-association tests, 144

Your Money's Worth, 399-400